The sky begins to light up a few days before the **CHINESE NEW YEAR** (left) and reaches a fiery crescendo by midnight, when Beijing's residents launch fireworks from every patch of outdoor space in the city. Find a high floor or a roof for a prime view of the world's biggest fireworks show. The cacophony is not to everyone's liking, and it can be dangerous, but the display is stunning in its breadth and length. The Chinese continue to fire rockets for 15 days.

My favorite way of getting around Beijing is **ON BICYCLE** (above). On two wheels, I pass cars and buses stuck in traffic, coast through the narrow *hutongs*, and pause for any particularly appealing streetside snacks. Bicycle rentals are cheap and easy. I suffered from bike rage until I realized the rules of the Beijing road: 1) Might Is Right— yield to any vehicle bigger than you; and 2) keep your eyes trained on what's ahead of you.

Frommer's® Beijing

My Beijing
by Jen Lin-Liu

BEIJING, A CAPITAL AS HUGE AND SPRAWLING AS LOS ANGELES, doesn't blow you away with its beauty. Hazy smog hovers over the city, and in spring it is engulfed by sandstorms from the Gobi Desert. I lived here for a year and then left, dismayed by the traffic, pollution, and weather. But a few years later I returned, and I've called Beijing home ever since. What brought me back? The chance to witness the world's next superpower in the making. I've watched clusters of skyscrapers spring up before my eyes. Fusion restaurants open by the week. If I ignore the bar scene for a month, I'm clueless about the new hot spots.

Beijing is also a study in contrasts. Tian'anmen Square and the Forbidden City have a grandness that few other attractions possess. But I find solace in the *hutongs,* the old alleys of single-level courtyard dwellings in which I live. The human-scale *hutongs* are rapidly being bulldozed; the ones that remain often feel like a quaint village lane, where vendors sell everything from toilet paper to beer from wagons pulled behind their bicycles.

That Beijing has managed to keep me as a longtime resident is a testimony to the city's energy, quirks, and, yes, beauty. Read on and discover a few of my favorite things.

The **DRUM TOWER (left)**, originally built in the 13th century, provides an unobstructed view of the crowded, old labyrinth of alleys in central Beijing. Drumming performances such as this one echo down Beijing's wide avenues and start every other hour. My friends and I sometimes take over the square behind the tower for an impromptu game of ultimate frisbee; it's also a great place to launch a kite. At night, the tower is stunning and lights up like a beacon.

Beijing sits on a patch of desert, which makes the man-made wonder of **HOUHAI LAKE (above)** all the more spectacular. A sunset ramble on the pedestrian path always clears my mind after a long day of writing. In the dead of winter, middle-aged and elderly Beijingers strip down to their Speedos and plunge into icy pools cut out of the frozen lake. In the warmer months, locals and tourists alike gather en masse, riding kayaks, gondolas, and boats shaped like swans.

Starting around eight o'clock on weekend mornings, Tibetans in bright robes, elderly men in Mao suits, long-haired urban artists, and other vendors set up stands at the **PANJIAYUAN OUTDOOR MARKET (left)**. Among the items for sale are 1960s-era posters of Mao Utopian scenes, black-and-white photographs of now-destroyed Beijing neighborhoods, and replicas of antique Chinese furniture. (Be prepared to bargain down to half-price.) Even when I'm not actively shopping, I enjoy visiting the market to absorb the carnival-like atmosphere.

The practitioners of **WATER CALLIGRAPHY (below)** are elderly men who hang out at Beihai Park and the Temple of Heaven. They wield 4-foot-long calligraphy brushes that look more like mops than writing instruments. The characters they scrawl disappear within minutes into the dry Beijing air, but practitioners appear unfazed by the ephemeral nature of their hobby. They sometimes let me hold their brushes to practice my own strokes—so don't be shy to ask if you'd like to try.

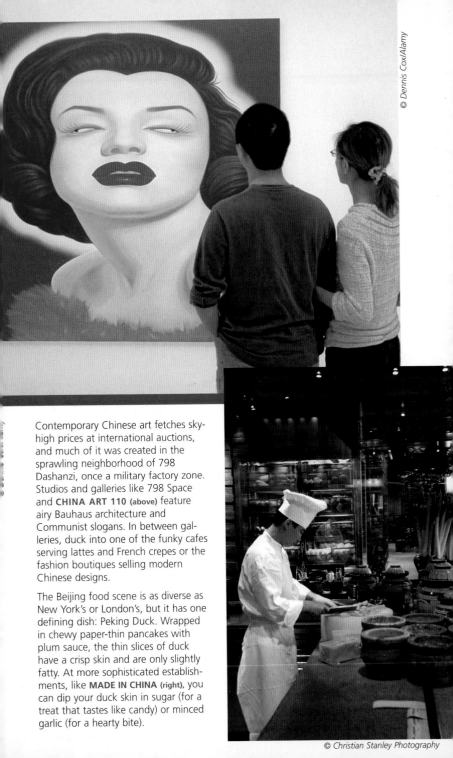

Contemporary Chinese art fetches sky-high prices at international auctions, and much of it was created in the sprawling neighborhood of 798 Dashanzi, once a military factory zone. Studios and galleries like 798 Space and **CHINA ART 110 (above)** feature airy Bauhaus architecture and Communist slogans. In between galleries, duck into one of the funky cafes serving lattes and French crepes or the fashion boutiques selling modern Chinese designs.

The Beijing food scene is as diverse as New York's or London's, but it has one defining dish: Peking Duck. Wrapped in chewy paper-thin pancakes with plum sauce, the thin slices of duck have a crisp skin and are only slightly fatty. At more sophisticated establishments, like **MADE IN CHINA (right)**, you can dip your duck skin in sugar (for a treat that tastes like candy) or minced garlic (for a hearty bite).

The **GREAT WALL OF CHINA** (below) stretches from the eastern coast to the far desert interior, and some of its most dramatic sections meander along mountain passes just north of Beijing. If you're a hiker like me, hire a private vehicle to take you to more remote sections like Jiankou and Jinshanling, where you can hike and even camp on unrestored, several-hundred-years-old parts of the Wall.
© *Chu Yong/AGE Fotostock*

Frommer's®

Beijing
5th Edition

by Jen Lin-Liu & Sherisse Pham

Here's what the critics say about Frommer's:

"Amazingly easy to use. Very portable, very complete."
—*Booklist*

"Detailed, accurate, and easy-to-read information for all price ranges."
—*Glamour Magazine*

"Hotel information is close to encyclopedic."
—*Des Moines Sunday Register*

"Frommer's Guides have a way of giving you a real feel for a place."
—*Knight Ridder Newspapers*

WILEY
Wiley Publishing, Inc.

About the Authors

Jen Lin-Liu is a Beijing-based food and travel writer. She first came to China in 2000 as a Fulbright Scholar, and has written for *Time Out Beijing, Newsweek, The Wall Street Journal*, the Associated Press, and other publications. She is author of the forthcoming book *Serve the People: A Stir-Fried Journey Through China* (Harcourt, June 2008).

Sherisse Pham graduated from the University of British Columbia and then quickly took off to Asia to set up camp. After a year in Taiwan, she sailed across the straights and took up residence on the mainland. She has lived in China for three years and is currently a Beijing-based freelancer.

Published by:

Wiley Publishing, Inc.

111 River St.
Hoboken, NJ 07030-5774

ISBN: 978-0-470-17593-4

Editor: Jamie Ehrlich
Production Editor: Eric T. Schroeder
Cartographer: Tim Lohnes
Photo Editor: Richard Fox
Production by Wiley Indianapolis Composition Services

Front cover photo: Group of youth walk past a Beijing opera sculpture in downtown Beijing
Back cover photo: Peking Opera House

For information on our other products and services or to obtain technical support, please contact our Customer Care Department within the U.S. at 800/762-2974, outside the U.S. at 317/572-3993 or fax 317/572-4002.

Wiley also publishes its books in a variety of electronic formats. Some content that appears in print may not be available in electronic formats.

Manufactured in the United States of America

5 4 3 2 1

Contents

List of Maps

Acknowledgments

Jen thanks Sherisse Pham, Karen Xiaolin Wang, and Jamie Ehrlich for their dedication to this project. She'd also like to thank Caroline and Dave Simons, her soon-to-be parents-in-law, for their help in doing the walking tours, and her fiancé Craig Simons for his companionship in exploring China's capital, a city they now call home.

Sherisse thanks Karen Xiaolin Wang for her excellent fact-checking work and help with occasional translations. A hearty thank you also goes out to Jen Lin-Liu, my wonderful coauthor. And finally, I'd like to thank our editor Jamie Ehrlich for adding that final polish and piecing it all together.

An Invitation to the Reader

In researching this book, we discovered many wonderful places—hotels, restaurants, shops, and more. We're sure you'll find others. Please tell us about them, so we can share the information with your fellow travelers in upcoming editions. If you were disappointed with a recommendation, we'd love to know that, too. Please write to:

Frommer's Beijing, 5th Edition
Wiley Publishing, Inc. • 111 River St. • Hoboken, NJ 07030-5774

An Additional Note

Please be advised that travel information is subject to change at any time—and this is especially true of prices. We therefore suggest that you write or call ahead for confirmation when making your travel plans. The authors, editors, and publisher cannot be held responsible for the experiences of readers while traveling. Your safety is important to us, however, so we encourage you to stay alert and be aware of your surroundings. Keep a close eye on cameras, purses, and wallets, all favorite targets of thieves and pickpockets.

Frommer's Star Ratings, Icons & Abbreviations

Every hotel, restaurant, and attraction listing in this guide has been ranked for quality, value, service, amenities, and special features using a **star-rating system.** In country, state, and regional guides, we also rate towns and regions to help you narrow down your choices and budget your time accordingly. Hotels and restaurants are rated on a scale of zero (recommended) to three stars (exceptional). Attractions, shopping, nightlife, towns, and regions are rated according to the following scale: zero stars (recommended), one star (highly recommended), two stars (very highly recommended), and three stars (must-see).

In addition to the star-rating system, we also use **seven feature icons** that point you to the great deals, in-the-know advice, and unique experiences that separate travelers from tourists. Throughout the book, look for:

Finds	Special finds—those places only insiders know about
Fun Fact	Fun facts—details that make travelers more informed and their trips more fun
Kids	Best bets for kids and advice for the whole family
Moments	Special moments—those experiences that memories are made of
Overrated	Places or experiences not worth your time or money
Tips	Insider tips—great ways to save time and money
Value	Great values—where to get the best deals

The following **abbreviations** are used for credit cards:

AE	American Express	DISC	Discover	V	Visa
DC	Diners Club	MC	MasterCard		

Frommers.com

Now that you have this guidebook to help you plan a great trip, visit our website at **www.frommers.com** for additional travel information on more than 3,600 destinations. We update features regularly to give you instant access to the most current trip-planning information available. At Frommers.com, you'll find scoops on the best airfares, lodging rates, and car rental bargains. You can even book your travel online through our reliable travel booking partners. Other popular features include:

- Online updates of our most popular guidebooks
- Vacation sweepstakes and contest giveaways
- Newsletters highlighting the hottest travel trends
- Online travel message boards with featured travel discussions

What's New in Beijing

A better question might be, what isn't new in Beijing? From new subway lines and sparkling shopping malls and highways to sparkling shopping malls and restaurants, the bulldozers and jack-hammers are working overtime as the capital prepares to host the Olympics. Visit sooner rather than later if you'd like to absorb more of the rapidly disappearing character of old Beijing.

GETTING TO KNOW BEIJING Traffic, which has been horrendous for years, has gotten even worse, with jams coming at all hours of the day and on the weekends too. The city has begun to sporadically ban private cars with odd or even license plates on certain days, and such days see congestion lighten dramatically. But with a thousand new cars hitting the streets every day, gridlock is the norm.

The capital's previously sparse subway system was given a boost in the fall of 2007 with the opening of **Line 5,** which runs past the east gate of the Temple of Heaven, up to Dong Dan, Dong Si, Lama Temple and further north to the east side of Yayun Cun (Asian Games Village). The subway system will be further improved by the summer of 2008, just in time for the Olympics, with the opening of **Lines L1, 8,** and **10. Line L1** should be particularly handy for travelers, as it connects the airport with Dong Zhi Men, an extensive bus and subway interchange point in central Beijing, and **Line 8** is particularly important for Olympic goers, as it will connect passengers to Olympic Park and the Olympic Sports Center. It juts off of **Line 10,** which runs along the east and north side of third-ring road, with stops at China World (Guomao) and Gongti Beilu, near the Sanlitun Bar Street.

A new bus and subway terminal at Dong Zhi Men will be open by summer 2008, and an interchange was recently completed at Xi Zhi Men. The Da Zhalan area is undergoing an intensive renovation that will result in the bulldozing of many old alleys and the installation of a pedestrian street, new shops, and a trolley.

In the *hutong* (the traditional alley neighborhoods of Beijing) not far from Hou Hai Lake, the alley of Nan Luogu Xiang has blossomed into a gentrified neighborhood of cafes, bars, restaurants, and shops. It's an ideal place to see old Beijingers rubbing elbows with the hip, urban youth of China.

Finally, a much anticipated project at the former American embassy near Tian'an Men Square and its environs known as **The Legation** opens in early 2008, with restaurants including an outpost of Daniel, the well-known French restaurant in New York.

WHERE TO STAY The old central neighborhoods of Beijing offer some wonderful new accommodations that provide comfort and character. At the top of the list are **Hotel Côté Cour S.L.,** an elegant boutique hotel that is set in a traditional Chinese courtyard and **Hotel Kapok,** a trendy, Chinese-managed four-star boutique property set just steps away from the Forbidden City. **Gu Xiang 20,** on the boutique shops-and-cafe crammed alley of

Nan Luogu Xiang, offers pleasant views of the *hutong* from its third-floor rooms. For those seeking a flavor of old Beijing on a tighter budget, **Qomolangma Hotel, Peking Downtown Backpackers Accommodation,** and **Hutonger** are good bets. Though not in the central alley neighborhoods of Beijing, **Days Inn Joiest** near the Temple of Heaven, is also a good budget option.

For those looking to splurge, Beijing is no longer short of luxurious accommodations, with close to a dozen five-star hotels having opened in the two years running up to the Olympics. One of our top picks is the **Raffles Beijing,** which is steps away from Tian'an Men Square and the Forbidden City and brings a colonial, old-world charm to the burly capital. Not far from the Raffles is **The Regent,** an elegant property with touches of sandalwood and Chinese antiques throughout, and next door is its four-star sister hotel **The Park Plaza,** which offers a great location and value. In the nascent just-booming financial district (Jinrong Jie) in the west of town, the **Ritz Carlton, Financial Street** and **The Westin Beijing, Financial Street** offer deluxe accommodations and a retreat from the chaotic streets of Beijing. In the far north of town, the stylish **Beijing Marco Polo Parkside** offers views of the Olympic Stadium and Park.

The growth of five-star hotels has spurred existing ones to renovate, including the **Shangri-La Beijing,** which features the luxurious new Valley Wing of executive rooms and the **Hilton Beijing,** which now bills itself as a boutique property. The **St. Regis Beijing,** known for its top-notch service, will be reopening the spring of 2008 after remodeling its rooms.

As of press time, several other five-star hotels in the central business district were planning to open in time for the Olympics, including the **Mandarin** Oriental, **JW Marriott,** a second **Ritz Carlton,** and the much-anticipated **Park Hyatt Beijing,** which we predict will be the city's swankiest hotel when it opens in early 2008. See chapter 5.

WHERE TO DINE   Turn to our list of specialty dishes in appendix A, and point to the Chinese characters for the dish. It's as easy as that.

Northern Chinese cuisine, with its emphasis on noodles, dumplings, garlic, and chiles, is not the most refined of cuisines, but it's hearty, fulfilling, and nothing like the Chinese food in your home country. For a choice of 60 varieties of dumplings and home-style dishes, visit the perennially packed and inexpensive **Xian'r Lao Man.** In a pleasant park with rooftop alfresco dining, **Xiao Wang Fu** offers terrific Peking duck and home-style favorites. If you'd like to sample inventive Chinese cuisine and don't mind splurging, the **Whampoa Club Beijing** serves Hong Kong-born chef Jereme Leung's interpretation of northern food.

A slew of stylish Chinese restaurants have opened in the last couple of years, including the very-hyped **Lan.** A Philippe Starck–designed emporium of kitsch, Lan is the flagship of a popular chain of Sichuan restaurants and offers decent spicy fare. Less assuming and more effective in its design is **People 8,** a Taiwanese-owned fusion restaurant with a dimmed, subterranean setting. Equally dark in its setting is the Buddhist-inspired vegetarian haven of **Pure Lotus.**

Set menus, which take the stress out of ordering, seem to be the new trend in Beijing, with restaurants ditching paper menus and leaving you to the whims of their chefs. The classy **Source,** set in a Chinese courtyard, offers a set menu of Sichuan dishes. Hidden in the *hutong* is **Dali Courtyard,** another gem that offers set courses of southwestern Chinese cuisine. In a more modern setting nearby is

Paper, which features a series of small platters of Cantonese cuisine.

European and continental cuisines continue to improve in the capital. Set in an alley in a courtyard is **Vineyard,** which offers a hearty English breakfast, pastas, and terrific thin-crust pizza. Several popular European restaurants are scattered near the embassy district, including the Brazilian-inspired continental cuisine of **Alameda,** the elegant and homey Spanish tapas of **Mare,** and the traditional Italian fare of **Assaggi.**

Five-star hotels in Beijing have broken the mold of offering boring hotel food. The Shangri-La Beijing's **Blu Lobster** brings a touch of London-style molecular gastronomy with a menu featuring foams, foie gras, and lobster, of course. **Cepe,** in the Ritz Carlton Financial Street, offers some of the city's best Italian cuisine in an elegant setting. The Raffles Beijing's **Jaan** serves delicious French cuisine and offers decently priced lunch options.

Finally, in a testimony to Beijing's cosmopolitan dining scene, the Persian **Rumi** offers delicious grilled kebabs, stews, and hummus in a pristine white setting. **Haiku by Hatsune** offers a trendy atmosphere of models chowing down on sushi rolls and sake. See chapter 6.

EXPLORING BEIJING By the time you arrive, the Forbidden City should be finished with an extensive renovation, which saw the removal of a controversial Starbucks. The nearby **National Museum** plans to reopen its doors in 2009, after a three-year renovation project. Also in the area, the **Legation,** a high-end luxury project featuring restaurants, bars, and galleries, aims to open by early 2008.

Fahai Si, a temple in the far west of Beijing with Buddhist murals, has recently undergone a renovation and should be open by the time you arrive.

Several new museums have opened in Beijing, including the well-curated **Beijing Planning and Exhibition Hall** and the **Capital Museum,** both of which give a look at Beijing's past and present. For film buffs, the **China National Film Museum** is a must-see. While not exactly a museum, **Happy Valley** is the capital's answer to Disneyland. The theme park features intense roller coasters and themed lands including the Tibetan Shangri-La, a Greek village, and a Mayan temple. See chapter 7.

SHOPPING The general trend in Beijing is towards temperature-controlled Western-style shopping malls. The best of the bunch are **The Place** and **Shin Kong Place,** both located in the central business district. For books, try the **Foreign Language Bookstore,** which offers a significantly larger selection of books than before, and **Timezone 8 Art Books** in the 798 art district. For Beijing-inspired design, **Things of the Jing,** not far from the 798 art district, and **Bannerman Tang's Toys and Crafts,** are places for unique souvenirs. See chapter 9.

BEIJING AFTER DARK The capital's renowned music scene continues to get bigger with the opening of a number of venues, including **MAO Livehouse, D-22,** and **The Star Live.** The very popular venue **Yu Gong Yi Shan** has moved to snazzier digs near the *hutong.* Two popular bars that offer live music regularly are **Salud,** on the gentrified street of Nan Luogu Xiang, and **Stone Boat Bar,** a cozy spot in a Beijing park.

If it's DJs you're looking for, **Alfa, China Doll, Mix,** and **Vic's,** all located at or near Worker's Stadium, offer dancing until the early morning hours. In the university district, **Lush** and **Propaganda** have sweaty dance floors and debauchery for the younger set.

For those looking for a slightly more elegant setting, **Face Bar** offers wine and cocktails in a southeast-Asian inspired setting, and **Q Bar** has become well-known for its bartending team. And for those seeking a non-alcoholic yet hedonistic treat, the gelato cafe **Gustamenta** offers dessert even at late-night hours. See chapter 10.

AROUND BEIJING The Great Wall finally boasts respectable lodgings, allowing you to appreciate its ancient ramparts at sunset and sunrise. If expense is no object, treat yourself to **The Commune,** a set of avant-garde architectural homes converted into a boutique hotel, set near **Juyong Guan.** New to this edition is a side-trip to **Jiankou.** It's a challenging, rarely-traversed part of the wall, where you can take a pristine 5-hour hike with gorgeous scenery. Afterwards, tuck into a country meal (Chinese-style) at the **Mountain Bar Lodge,** which also offers bungalow-style accommodations. See chapter 11.

1

The Best of Beijing

The best of Beijing is a study in contrasts—from the ritzy elegance of restaurants located in the snazziest of hotels to the humble yet lively fare available in local dining rooms. We give you a healthy dose of traditional Beijing life, which is rapidly disappearing as the city is bulldozed away to make room for tall skyscrapers. We recommend that you take in a local punk band to get a glimpse of the capital's vibrant youth culture, but also visit an antiquated Peking opera hall, and fraternize with seniors at the city's numerous gardens and parks. For all its big-city development, Beijing's lakes and parks provide solace—a place where you can go to ponder the contradictions that make up this fascinating capital.

1 The Most Unforgettable Beijing Experiences

- **Strolling around the Back Lakes:** You'll find everything around these man-made lakes, from historic courtyard homes, to tranquil spots, to amusing entertainment. Speedo-clad elders dive into the lake year-round—including the chilly winter months—and ducks congregate on a small man-made island on the western end of the lake. Visit around sunset for a particularly romantic experience, and stroll to the nearby restaurants and bars for dinner and drinks. See p. 158.

- **Sinking Your Teeth into Crisp, Juicy Peking Duck at Made in China:** A hotel restaurant it is, but this is the best place to enjoy the capital's most famous dish, and the dining room—set in the middle of an open kitchen—is the best place to see chefs perform their magic. See p. 87.

- **Investigating the Northeast Corner of the Forbidden City:** Away from the main north–south axis on which the former palace's grander halls stand, there's a more human scale similar to that of the rapidly disappearing *hutong* beyond the palace's walls, although with much greater luxury. Venturing far from the main arteries is well worth the effort—you'll find treasures like the ornate theater building where the Empress Dowager Cixi watched her favorite operas on demand and the well in which she ended the life of her nephew's favorite concubine. See p. 126.

- **Praying for a Smog-Free Day with the Monks at Beijing Temples:** Many of the capital's temples have once again become genuine places of worship, as well as tourist attractions. The **Yonghe Gong** (p. 137) has an active and approachable community of Tibetan monks (although under careful scrutiny by the authorities), while the leafy **Fayuan Si** (p. 134) houses amicable Chinese Buddhist monks in Beijing's most venerable temple. **Baiyun Guan** (p. 133) is the Daoist alternative, where blue-frocked monks wear their hair in the rarely seen traditional manner—long and tied in a bun at the top of the head.

- **Bargaining for Fakes:** At **Panjiayuan Jiuhuo Shichang,** the first asking prices for foreigners are at least 10 to 15 times those asked of Chinese, but don't let that deter you from visiting. This weekend market has the city's best selection of bric-a-brac, including row upon crowded row of calligraphy, jewelry, ceramics, teapots, ethnic clothing, Buddha statues, paper lanterns, Cultural Revolution memorabilia, army belts, little wooden boxes, Ming- and Qing-style furniture, old pipes, opium scales, painted human skulls, and more conventional souvenirs. A whole other genre of fakes can be found at the Ritan Office Building, where samples of Marc Jacobs jackets and Diane von Furstenberg dresses cram the racks. See p. 171 and p. 177 for both markets.

- **Haggling for Tea at Malian Dao:** If you're serious about tea, this is the only place to go. Malian Dao may not have all the tea in China, but it does have over a mile of shops hawking tea leaves and their paraphernalia. Most shops are run by the extended families of tea growers from Fujian and Zhejiang provinces, and you might rate this friendly street as the highlight of your visit. See p. 183.

- **Attending Beijing Opera at the Zhengyici Xilou:** The Zhengyici, last of a handful of theaters that supported Beijing Opera from its beginnings, only occasionally hosts performances and is under constant threat of permanent closure. But the scarcity of performances only makes the experience of watching the colorful operas in this intimate, traditionally decorated space all the more precious. *Tip:* Ask your hotel staff to call and ask about performance schedules and tickets. See p. 187.

- **Unwinding at a Traditional Teahouse:** Several quiet teahouses offer you the chance to remove yourself temporarily from the tourist rush. The teahouse in the **Sanwei Bookstore** (p. 190) offers live traditional music with its bottomless cups of jasmine. For a little extra, **The Teahouse of Family Fu** (p. 196) in the Back Lakes area brews your oolong *(wulong)* in the Chinese version of the tea ceremony. Both teahouses are furnished with replica Ming dynasty tables and chairs and make ideal spots for reading, writing, or doing absolutely nothing.

- **Seeing a Band at Yugong Yishan:** The owners of the now defunct Loup Chante have created what Beijing lacked for years: an atmospheric venue showcasing an eclectic range of musical styles, from Mongolian mouth music to acid jazz. It's stuffy, smoky, difficult to find, and run by serious and talented musicians. See appendix A for more about Beijing music.

- **Hiking along the Great Wall at Jiankou:** Our favorite part of the wall is so untouristed that there isn't even a ticket booth—or a tacky postcard tout—in sight. The 5-hour hike meanders along a vertigo-inducing stretch of wall that isn't for the faint of heart—but it's an unforgettable experience. See p. 205.

- **Bicycling through the Hutong Neighborhoods:** We can't get enough of the *hutong*. After taking a stroll, hop on a bike for a completely different experience in the capital's old neighborhoods. See p. 147.

2 The Best Splurge Hotels

- **The Peninsula Beijing** (Jinyu Hutong 8; ℂ **866/382-8388** or 010/8516-2888): Despite the huge boom in five-star hotels in the capital, The Peninsula still manages to stay on top with its constant upgrades and its impeccable English-speaking staff. There's an understated elegance to the entire complex, complete with a luxury shopping arcade and afternoon tea in the lobby. Wireless Internet and marble bathtubs with television screens anchored in front of them are standout amenities in nearly all rooms. See p. 65.
- **Raffles Beijing** (Dong Chang'an Jie 1; ℂ **800/768-9009** [toll-free from U.S.] or 010/6526-3388):

Located in a historic European building just steps away from Forbidden City, the distinguished Raffles has an old-world charm that few hotels in the capital can match. See p. 65.
- **Hotel Côté Cour S.L.** (Yanyue Hutong 70; ℂ **010/6512-8020**): A glut of new courtyard hotels has opened in the capital's old neighborhoods, but none matches the elegance and style of Hotel Côté Cour S.L., with rooms decorated in Chinese antiques and green and wood tones. The public spaces, like an elegant lounge and a spacious center patio, are perfect for unwinding after a hectic day touring the city. See p. 68.

3 The Best Moderately Priced Hotels

- **Gu Xiang 20** (Nanluogu Xiang 20; ℂ **010/6400-5566**): This lovely three-star hotel is smack in the middle of one of old Beijing's gentrifying neighborhoods. The stylish rooms are decorated with Chinese antiques and flat-screen TVs, and third-floor rooms have picturesque views of the *hutong*. See p. 69.
- **Far East Youth Hostel** (Tieshu Xie Jie 113; ℂ **010/5195-8561,** ext. 3118): The best budget option in Beijing is located at the center of one of the city's most interesting *hutong*

neighborhoods, only a 10-minute walk from both the Heping Men and Qian Men metro stops. It has clean, nicely renovated three-star rooms at unbeatable rates—you can get down to ¥200 ($27/£13) with a little bargaining). See p. 76.
- **Feiying Binguan** (Xuanwu Men Xi Dajie 10; ℂ **010/6317-1116**): This is the most "hotel-like" branch of Youth Hostelling International in Beijing. Dorms have in-room bathroom and brand-new floors, and beds are only ¥60 ($8/£4). See p. 76.

4 The Most Unforgettable Dining Experiences

- **Made in China** (Dong Chang'an Jie 1 [inside Grand Hyatt]; ℂ **010/8518-1234**): It's not just the Peking duck that's fantastic—it's nearly everything on the menu, from spicy Sichuan-style string beans to the passion fruit and pear champagne sorbet. We visit this lively restaurant regularly, sharing the experience with

out-of-town guests or simply enjoying it selfishly on our own. See p. 87.
- **Chuan Jing Ban Canting** (Gongyuan Tou Tiao 5; ℂ **010/6512-2277**): Sichuan food has conquered the capital, and this ubiquitous cuisine, loved by Beijingers and Sichuanese alike, is best enjoyed in this chaotic, crowded restaurant

owned by the Sichuan Provincial Government. It will also be one of the cheapest meals you can have in Beijing, with the price of an entire meal averaging no more than ¥40 ($5.35/£2.65) per person. See p. 90.

• **Cepe** (Jincheengfang Dong Jie 1 [inside Ritz Carlton, Financial Street] ⓒ **010/6601-6666**): Unexpectedly, there is flawless northern Italian cuisine in the Middle Kingdom. This lovely restaurant, in the Ritz Carlton, Financial Street, has its own mushroom humidor for its imported Italian fungi and makes its pasta fresh daily. See p. 103.

• **Whampoa Club Beijing** (Jin Rong Jie Jia 23; **010/8808-8828**): Ambitious Hong Kong–born chef Jereme Leung brings his inventive cuisine to the capital after opening a successful first branch of the restaurant in Shanghai. Leung has tamed Northern cuisine to a level of refinement never tasted before.

5 The Best Things to Do for Free (or Almost)

• **Go Bohemian at Factory 798:** We left Factory 798 out of the previous edition, reasoning that an ad hoc gathering of performance artists, painters, and sculptors in a former military complex wasn't something the regime would tolerate. We were wrong. Market rents are now charged, so don't expect to pick up a bargain, but there's no need to make a purchase: The Dashanzi art district makes for a thoroughly enjoyable afternoon of gallery and cafe hopping. See p. 144.

• **Pay Your Respects to the Chairman:** While Jung Chang's *Mao: The Untold Story* subjects the Great Helmsman to a Cultural Revolution–style denunciation, you'll find no trace of such disrespect inside **Chairman Mao's Mausoleum,** set to the south side of Tian'an Men Square. While there are souvenir vendors, this is far from the kitsch experience you may expect. See p. 121.

• **Exercise with Elders:** At the break of dawn each day, retired Beijingers flock to numerous local parks. Aside from *taijiquan* and ballroom dancing, you may spy master calligraphers practicing their art with oversize sponge-tipped brushes, or amateur troupes performing Beijing Opera or revolutionary airs from the 1950s. See section 6 of chapter 7, "Parks & Gardens."

2

Planning Your Trip to Beijing

Visiting China isn't as hard as you might think it is. If you can manage Paris by yourself without speaking French, you can manage Beijing without Mandarin. Tens of thousands of visitors travel in China independently each year, making arrangements as they go and without more than a guidebook and phrase book to help them. You can certainly arrange various levels of assistance, either on arrival or from home, but you can also travel just as freely as you would elsewhere, perhaps using agents to get your tickets and picking up the odd day tour.

But whether you plan to travel at random, with a pre-booked route, or with a fully escorted tour, it's *vital* that you read this chapter carefully in order to understand how the way you travel, even in many other developing nations, doesn't apply here. Much supposed wisdom on China travel is far from wise, and what's good advice in the rest of the world is often the worst advice in China. Without absorbing what's below, some of the rest of this guide may seem inscrutable.

So put down your preconceptions, and read on . . .

1 Visitor Information

NATIONAL TOURIST OFFICES

The China mainland travel industry is, in general, a quagmire of deception that provides no truly reliable information either within China or via its overseas operations. The branches of the China National Tourism Administration in foreign countries are called **China National Tourist Offices.** Nominally nonprofit, they used to be little more than agents for the state-owned China International Travel Service (CITS), but they now offer links to a variety of operators. Don't expect them to be accurate about even the most basic visa or Customs regulations, and don't expect them to update their websites, which sometimes give conflicting information and can't even get the names of tour operators right.

Tourist offices are in the following locations:

- In the **United States:** 350 Fifth Ave., Suite 6413, Empire State Building, New York, NY 10118 (© **212/760-8218/8807;** fax 212/760-8809; ny@cnta.gov.cn); 600 W. Broadway, Suite 320, Glendale, CA 91204 (© **818/545-7505;** fax 828/545-7506; la@cnta.gov.cn).
- In **Canada:** 480 University Ave., Suite 806, Toronto, ON M5G 1V2 (© **866/599-6636;** fax 416/599-6382; www.tourismchina-ca.com).
- In the **U.K.:** 71 Warwick Rd., London SW5 9HB (© **020-7373-0888;** fax 020-7370-9989; london@cnta.gov.cn).
- In **Australia:** Level 19, 44 Market St., Sydney, NSW 2000 (© **02/9299-4057;** fax 02/9290-1958; sydney@cnta.gov.cn).

BEIJING ONLINE

Be cautious of official sources of information and unofficial Chinese-run sources alike, especially if they also offer travel services. Canadian-owned but Beijing-based *Xianzai* (www.xianzai.com) offers a weekly e-mail newsletter with hotel, restaurant, and airfare advertising (often including special offers only publicized locally), and a diary of events. The site also offers an assortment of other newsletters with information on travel in China.

Expat magazines, such as *that's Beijing* (www.thatsbj.com) and *Time Out,* have a certain amount of Beijing news, information about what's on, and new restaurant reviews online, along with modest features on Beijing life.

For an ad- and spam-free general discussion of any Beijing (or other China) travel issues not covered in this book, subscribe to the e-mail discussion list *The Oriental-List.* To subscribe, send a blank e-mail to subscribe-oriental-list@ datasinica.com.

2 Entry Requirements & Customs

ENTRY REQUIREMENTS

PASSPORT   Visitors must have a valid **passport** with at least 6 months' validity from time of entry into the country, and two blank pages remaining (you *may* get away with just one blank page).

VISAS   All visitors to **mainland China** (as opposed to Special Administrative Regions of Hong Kong and Macau) must acquire a visa in advance. Visa applications typically take 3 to 5 working days to process, although this can be shortened to as little as 1 day if you apply in person and pay extra fees. "L" (tourist) visas are valid for between 1 and 3 months. Usually 1 month is granted unless you request more, which you may or may not get according to events in China at the time. Double-entry tourist visas are also available. It varies, but typically your visit must *begin* within 90 days of the date of issue.

You should apply for a visa in person at your nearest **consulate,** although it's possible to obtain Chinese visas in other countries while you're on an extended trip. To apply for a visa, you must complete an **application form,** which can be downloaded from many consular websites or acquired by mail. Visas are valid for the whole country, although some small areas require an extra permit from the local police. Temporary restrictions,

sometimes for years at a time, may be placed on areas where there is unrest, and a further permit may be required to enter them. In general, do not mention Tibet or Xinjiang on your visa application, or it may be turned down flat.

Some consulates request that you show them an airline ticket, itinerary, or proof of sufficient funds, or they claim to issue visas only to those traveling in groups (while happily carrying on business with individuals who have none of the supporting documentation). Such guidelines provide consulates with a face-saving excuse for refusing a visa should there be unrest or political difficulties, or should Tibet or Xinjiang appear on the application.

One **passport photograph** is required per adult, as well as for any child traveling on a parent's passport.

A complete list of all Chinese embassies and consulates, including addresses and contact information, can be found at the Chinese foreign ministry's website: www. fmprc.gov.cn/eng (or various mirror sites around the world). Click on "Missions Overseas." Many consulates (including all those in the U.S. and Canada) will only accept applications in person; applications by post or courier must go through an agent, who will charge additional fees. Contacting some embassies can be very

China

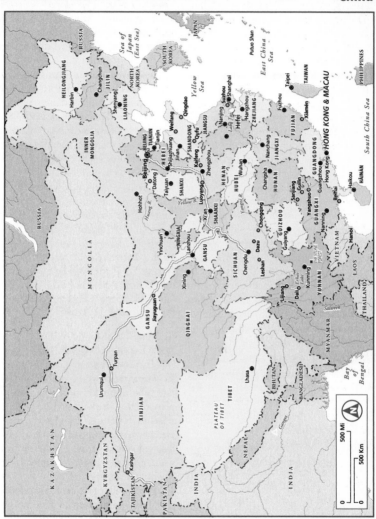

difficult: Many telephone systems are automated, and reaching a human can be next to impossible; faxes and e-mails usually don't receive a reply; and websites are often out of date.

What follows are visa fees and requirements for some countries:

- **United States:** Single-, double- and multiple-entry visas are US$100. Visit www.china-embassy.org, which has links to all U.S. consular sites and a downloadable application form. Applications must be delivered and collected by hand, or sent via a visa agency.

- **Canada:** Single-entry visas are C$50; double-entry C$75. Visit www.china embassycanada.org for an application form. Applications must be delivered and collected by hand, or sent via a visa agency.
- **United Kingdom:** Single-entry visas are £30; double-entry £45. There's a supplementary charge of £20 for each package dealt with by mail. Visit www.chinese-embassy.org.uk for an application.
- **Australia:** Single-entry visas are A$30; double-entry A$45. Add A$10 per package dealt with by mail or courier, and a pre-paid return envelope. Visit http://au.china-embassy.org/eng for an application.
- **New Zealand:** Single-entry visas are NZ$60; double-entry NZ$90. Add NZ$15 per package dealt with by mail or courier, and a pre-paid return envelope. Visit www.chinaembassy.org.nz or www.chinaconsulate.org.nz for an application.

Note: The visa **fees** quoted above for each country are the current rates for *nationals of that country,* and can change at any time. In addition to the visa fees quoted, there may be supplementary fees for postage. Payment must always be in cash or by money order.

VISA EXTENSIONS   Single-entry tourist visas may be extended twice for a maximum of 30 days each time at the PSB Exit/Entry Division offices in most cities. The office in Beijing (© 010/8402-0101) is on the south side of the eastern North Second Ring Road, just east of the Lama Temple metro stop (Mon–Sat 8:30am–4:30pm). Applications take 5 working days to process. Bring your passport and two passport photos (these can be taken at the office for ¥30/$4/£2). Extension fees vary by nationality: U.S. citizens pay ¥760 ($101/£51), U.K. citizens ¥469 ($63/£31), Canadians and Australians ¥160 ($21/£11).

GETTING A VISA IN HONG KONG
Nationals of most developed nations do not require a visa to enter Hong Kong, and visas for mainland China are more easily obtainable there than anywhere else.

The cheapest tourist visas are available at the **Visa Office of the PRC,** 7th floor, Lower Block, China Resources Building, 26 Harbour Rd., Wanchai (© 852/3413-2424; www.fmcoprc.gov.hk; Mon–Fri 9am–noon and 2–5pm). Here a single-entry tourist visa costs HK$780 ($100) for U.S. citizens, HK$450 ($58) for citizens of the U.K., and HK$150 (US$19) for Canadians and Australians. Same-day service costs an extra HK$250 (US$32). For urgent departures, or 6-month "F" *(fangwen)* visas, go to **Grand Profit International Travel Agency,** 705AA, 7th Floor, New East Ocean Centre, 9 Science Museum Rd., Tsimshatsui (about a 15-min. walk east of Nathan Rd.; © 852/2723-3288).

CUSTOMS
WHAT YOU CAN BRING INTO CHINA
In general terms, you can bring anything into China for personal use that you plan to take back with you, with the usual exceptions of arms and drugs, or plant materials, animals, and foods from diseased areas. There are no problems with cameras or video recorders, GPS equipment, laptops, or any other standard electronic equipment. Two unusual prohibitions are "old/used garments" and "printed matter, magnetic media, films, or photographs which are deemed to be detrimental to the political, economic, cultural and moral interests of China," as the regulations put it. Large quantities of religious literature, overtly political materials, or books on Tibet might cause you difficulties but, in general, small amounts of personal reading matter in non-Chinese languages do not present problems.

Customs officers are for the most part easygoing, and foreign visitors are rarely searched. Customs declaration forms have now vanished from all major points of entry, but if you are importing more than US$5,000 in cash, you should declare it, or theoretically you could face difficulties at the time of departure—although, again, this is highly unlikely.

WHAT YOU CAN TAKE HOME FROM CHINA

An official seal must be attached to any item created between 1795 and 1949 that is taken out of China; older items cannot be exported. But, in fact, you are highly unlikely to find any genuine antiques, so this is moot (however, a genuine antiques dealer would know how to obtain the seal).

3 Money

CURRENCY

While for most destinations it's usually a good idea to exchange at least some money before you leave home so you can avoid the less-favorable rates at airport currency-exchange desks, mainland China is different. RMB yuan are not easily obtainable overseas, and rates are worse when they can be found.

There is no legal private money-changing in mainland China. Nationwide outlets offer the same rates on a daily basis. You can exchange currency at the airport when you arrive, at larger branches of the Bank of China, at a bank desk in your hotel, or at major department stores. Shops that offer to exchange money at other than formal Bank of China exchange counters do so illegally, and are known for rate shenanigans and passing fake bills, which are fairly common. *Do not deal with black market money-changers.*

Keep receipts when you exchange money, and you can **reconvert** excess RMB yuan into hard currency when you leave China, although sometimes not more than half the total sum for which you can produce receipts, and sometimes these receipts must be not more than 3 months old.

Hotel exchange desks will only change money for their guests but are open very long hours, 7 days a week. **Banking hours** vary from branch to branch but are limited on Saturday, and banks are closed on Sunday. For more information, see "Banks, Currency Exchanges & ATMs"

in the "Fast Facts: Beijing" section of chapter 4.

YUAN NOTES There are notes for ¥100, ¥50, ¥20, ¥10, ¥5, ¥2, and ¥1, which also appears as a coin. The word *yuan* is rarely spoken, and sums are referred to as *kuai qian,* "pieces of money," usually shortened to just *kuai. San kuai* is ¥3. Notes carry Arabic numerals as well as numbers in Chinese characters, so there's no fear of confusion. The next unit down, the *jiao* (¥0.10), is spoken of as the *mao.* There are notes of a smaller size for ¥0.50, ¥0.20, and ¥0.10, as well as coins for these values. The smallest and almost worthless unit is the *fen* (both written and spoken), or cent. Unbelievably, when you change money you may be given tiny notes or lightweight coins for ¥0.05, ¥0.02, and ¥0.01, but this is the only time you'll see them except in the bowls of beggars or donation boxes in temples. The most useful note is the ¥10 ($1.35/65p), so keep a good stock. Street stalls, convenience stores, and taxis are often unhappy to receive ¥100 ($13/£6.65) notes.

ATMs

There are many ATMs in China, but with few exceptions, only a selection of Bank of China machines accept foreign cards. Check the back of your ATM card for the logos of the **Cirrus** (www.mastercard.com), **PLUS** (www.visa.com), and **Aeon** (www.americanexpress.com) systems, and then contact the relevant company for a list of working ATM locations

Exchange Rates: the Yuan, the Dollar, the Pound & the "Crawling Peg"

In a bid to avert a trade war with the U.S., China allowed a 2% appreciation of the yuan in 2005. It is no longer pegged solely to the U.S. dollar, but rather to a basket of currencies, in an arrangement known as a "crawling peg." The U.S. dollar has recently been trading around ¥7.56, the pound sterling at ¥15.50, and the euro at ¥10.45. For this edition, we have taken ¥7.5 to the U.S. dollar and ¥15 to the British pound as an approximate conversion, as major appreciation of the yuan seems unlikely. The latest rates can be found at www.xe.com/ucc.

in Beijing, which is fairly well served. The capital also has four Citibank branches (the most convenient being at Oriental Plaza) and two non-VIP branches of HSBC. Both banks have ATMs that take just about any card ever invented. Bank of China machines have a limit of ¥2,500 ($333/£167) per transaction, while HSBC and Citibank machines have a limit of ¥3,500 ($467/£233). These banks often allow a second transaction the same day. Bank of America members can withdraw from China Construction Bank ATMs without a fee. Call ℂ **95533** within China for locations. *Note:* If you have memorized your PIN as a word, be sure to learn it as a number.

TRAVELER'S CHECKS

Traveler's checks are only accepted at selected branches of the Bank of China, at foreign exchange desks in hotels, and at the exchange desks of some department stores. In bigger bank branches, checks in any hard currency and from any major company are welcome, but at department-store exchange desks, currencies of the larger economies are preferred. You can exchange U.S. dollars in cash at most branches of almost any Chinese bank, so even if you plan to bring checks, having a few U.S. dollars in cash (in good condition) for emergencies is a good idea. Checks attract a marginally better

exchange rate than cash, but the commission (generally 1%) to cash checks makes the result slightly worse (worse still if you paid the general 1% to 4% commission when buying them).

CREDIT CARDS

Although Visa and MasterCard signs abound, credit cards are of limited usefulness—in many cases only the Chinese versions of the cards are accepted. You can use foreign cards at most hotels, but they are accepted only at relatively upmarket restaurants outside hotels, and at those souvenir shops where you are paying well over the odds—in fact, if a shop accepts foreign credit cards, you might consider looking elsewhere.

You can also obtain cash advances on your MasterCard, Visa, Diners Club, or Amex cards at major branches of the Bank of China, with a minimum withdrawal of ¥1,200 ($160/£80) and 4% commission, plus whatever your card issuer charges you—this expensive way to withdraw cash only makes sense for emergencies. If you do plan to use your card while in China, it's a good idea to call your issuer in advance to let them know that you'll do so.

EMERGENCY CASH American Express runs an **emergency check cashing system,** which allows you to use one of your own checks or a counter check (more

What Things Cost in Beijing	Yen¥	U.S.$	U.K.£
Taxi from airport to city center (use meter!)	64.00–96.00	8.53–12.80	4.26–6.40
Up to 3km (2½ miles) by taxi	10.00	1.33	0.67
Metro ride	3.00	0.40	0.20
Local telephone call	0.48	0.06	0.03
Hearty bowl of beef noodles at a basic restaurant	4.80	0.64	0.32
Regular coffee at Starbucks	12.00	1.60	0.80
McDonald's set meal for one	18.00	2.40	1.20
Tasty dinner for two at a simple home-style restaurant	30.00	4.00	2.00
Dinner for two in restaurants around foreigner-frequented bar areas	100.00	13.33	6.67
Dinner for two in top hotel restaurants	640.00	85.33	42.67
Bottle of beer at an ordinary restaurant or store	3.00	0.40	0.20
Bottle of beer in a foreigner-frequented bar district	30.00	4.00	2.00
Admission to the Forbidden City	60.00	8.00	4.00
Admission to the Lama Temple	24.00	3.20	1.60

expensively) to draw money in the currency of your choice from selected banks. Consult American Express for a list of participating banks before leaving home.

You can also have money wired from **Western Union** (© **800/325-6000;** www.westernunion.com) to you at many post offices and branches of the Agricultural Bank of China across China, including 49 in Beijing. Western Union charges a $14 service fee for money transfers of up to $1000 to China from the US. You must present valid ID to pick up the cash at the Western Union office.

4 When to Go

The biggest factor in your calculations on when to visit Beijing should be the movement of domestic tourists, who during the longer public holidays take to the road in tens or even hundreds of millions, filling transportation, booking out hotels, and turning even the quieter tourist sights into litter-strewn bedlam.

PEAK TRAVEL SEASONS Chinese New Year (Spring Festival) Like many Chinese festivals, this one operates on the lunar calendar. Solar equivalents for the next few years are February 7, 2008; January 26, 2009; February 14, 2010; and February 3, 2011. The effects of this holiday are felt from 2 weeks before the date until 2 weeks after, when anyone who's away from home attempts to get back, including an estimated 150 million migrant workers. If you are flying from overseas to Beijing, this won't affect you, but a land approach may be difficult, except in the few days immediately surrounding the holiday. Banks, as well as smaller restaurants and businesses, may be shut for a week. But main attractions are mostly open.

Labor Day & National Day In a policy known as "holiday economics," the May 1 and October 1 holidays have now been expanded to 7 days each (including 1 weekend—most people are expected to work through the weekend prior to the holiday in exchange for 2 weekdays, which are added to the official 3 days of holiday). These two holidays now mark the beginning and end of the domestic travel season, and mark the twin peaks of leisure travel, with the remainder of May, early June, and September also busy. The exact dates of each holiday are not announced until around 2 weeks before each takes place.

CLIMATE For the best weather, visit Beijing in September or October when warm, dry, sunny days with clear skies and pleasantly cool evenings are the norm. The second best time is spring, late March to mid-May, when winds blow away the pollution but also sometimes bring clouds of scouring sand for a day or two, turning the sky a livid yellow. Winters can be bitter, but the city is much improved visually under a fresh blanket of snow: The gaudy colors of the Forbidden City's palaces are emphasized, as is the Great Wall's bleakness. Summers are humid and hot, but air-conditioning makes them tolerable. The number of foreign visitors is high during summer, but the Chinese themselves mostly wait until the weather cools before traveling.

Beijing's Average Temperatures & Rainfall

	Jan	Feb	Mar	Apr	May	June	July	Aug	Sept	Oct	Nov	Dec
Temp. (°F)	26	31	43	57	68	76	79	77	69	57	41	30
Temp. (°C)	-3	-1	6	14	20	24	26	25	21	14	5	-1
Days of Rain	2.1	3.1	4.5	5.1	6.4	9.7	14.5	14.1	6.9	5.0	3.6	1.6

HOLIDAYS A few years ago the Chinese were finally granted a 2-day weekend, but while offices close, shops, restaurants, post offices, transportation, and sights all operate the same services 7 days a week. Most sights, shops, and restaurants are open on public holidays, too, but offices and anything government-related close for as much time as possible. Although China switched to the Gregorian calendar in 1911, some public holidays (and many festivals—see the following "Beijing Calendar of Events") are on a lunar cycle, with solar dates varying from year to year. Holidays are **New Year's Day** (Jan 1), **Spring Festival** (Chinese New Year's day and the following 2 days—see "Peak Travel Seasons" above, for exact dates in coming years), **Labor Day** (May 1 plus up to 4 more weekdays and a weekend), **National Day** (Oct 1 plus extra days, as for Labor Day).

BEIJING CALENDAR OF EVENTS

Festivals are more family affairs in Beijing, which doesn't have much of a calendar of public events compared with some other parts of China.

Winter

Spring Festival (Chun Jie), or Chinese New Year, is still the occasion for large lion dances and other celebrations in Chinatowns worldwide, but in mainland China it's mainly a time for everyone to return to his or her ancestral home and feast. Fireworks are now banned in Beijing; however, temple fairs have been revived but are mostly fairly low-key shopping opportunities without much of the color or professional entertainers of old. But in the countryside, there's been a gradual revival of stilt-walking and masked processions. New Year is on the day of the first new moon after January 21, and can be no later than February 20.

Lantern Festival (Deng Jie) perhaps reached its peak in the late Qing dynasty, when temples, stores, and other public places were hung with fantastically shaped and decorated lanterns. Many people paraded through the streets with lightweight lanterns in the shapes of fish, sheep, or other animals, and hung others, often decorated with riddles, outside their houses. There are modest signs of a revival. This festival always falls 15 days after Spring Festival.

Spring

Tomb-Sweeping Festival (Qingming) is frequently observed in Chinese communities overseas, and more often in rural areas of China, as a family outing on a free day near the festival date. It's a day for honoring ancestors by visiting and tidying their gravesites, and making offerings of snacks and alcohol, which often turns into a picnic. April 4.

Autumn

The last remnant of the **Mid-Autumn Festival (Tuanyuan Jie),** except among literary-minded students, is the giving and eating of *yuebing* (moon cakes), circular pies with sweet and extremely fattening fillings. Traditionally it's a time to sit and read poetry under the full moon, but pollution has made the moon largely invisible. Takes place the 15th day of the 8th lunar month (usually Sept).

National Day itself is for avoiding Tian'an Men Square, especially if the government considers the anniversary important enough for one of its military parades, when the square may be blocked to you anyway. October 1.

5 Travel Insurance

Check your existing insurance policies and credit card coverage before you buy travel insurance. You may already be covered for lost luggage, cancelled tickets, or medical expenses. The cost of travel insurance varies widely, depending on the cost and length of your trip, your age, your health, and the type of trip you're taking.

TRIP-CANCELLATION INSURANCE Trip-cancellation insurance helps you get your money back if you have to back out of a trip, if you have to go home early, or if your travel supplier goes bankrupt. Allowable reasons for cancellation can range from sickness to natural disasters to a government department declaring your destination unsafe for travel. Insurers usually won't cover vague fears, though, and in 2003 travelers were not given refunds for SARS-related cancellations.

MEDICAL INSURANCE For China, purchase travel insurance that includes an air ambulance or scheduled airline repatriation. Be clear on the terms and conditions—is repatriation limited to life-threatening illnesses, for instance? While there are advanced facilities staffed by foreign doctors in Beijing, regular Chinese hospitals are to be avoided. They may charge you a substantial bill, which you must pay in cash before you're allowed to leave. If this happens to you, you'll have to wait until you return home to submit your claim, so make sure you have adequate proof of payment.

LOST-LUGGAGE INSURANCE On U.S. domestic flights, checked baggage is covered up to $2,800 per ticketed passenger. On international flights (including U.S. portions of international trips), baggage is limited to approximately $9.07 per pound, up to approximately $635 per checked bag. If you plan to check items more valuable than the standard liability, see if your valuables are covered by your homeowner's policy, or get baggage insurance as part of your comprehensive travel-insurance package. Read the policy carefully—some valuables are effectively uninsurable, and others have such high excess charges that the insurance is not worth buying.

If your luggage is lost, immediately file a lost-luggage claim at the airport. For most airlines, you must report delayed, damaged, or lost baggage within 4 hours of arrival. The airlines are required to deliver luggage, once found, directly to your house or destination free of charge, although don't expect that necessarily to work with domestic Chinese airlines.

6 Health & Safety

STAYING HEALTHY
GREATEST RISKS
The greatest risk to the enjoyment of a holiday in China is one of **stomach upsets** or more serious illnesses arising from low hygiene standards. Keep your hands frequently washed and away from your mouth. Only eat freshly cooked hot food, and fruit you can peel yourself—avoid touching the part to be eaten once it's been peeled. Drink only boiled or bottled water. *Never* drink from the tap. Use bottled water for brushing your teeth.

The second most common cause of discomfort is an **upper respiratory tract infection,** or **common cold,** which is caused by **heavy pollution.** Many standard Western remedies or sources of relief (and occasionally fake versions of these) are available over the counter, but bring a supply of whatever you are used to. If you have sensitive eyes, you may wish to bring an eye bath and solution.

If you regularly take a nonprescription medication, bring a plentiful supply with you and don't rely on finding it in China. Feminine hygiene products such as panty-liners are widely available in Beijing, but tampons are not.

GENERAL AVAILABILITY OF HEALTHCARE
See "Fast Facts: Beijing" in chapter 4 for a list of reliable (and very expensive) clinics with up-to-date equipment and English-speaking foreign-trained doctors.

Should you begin to feel unwell in China, your first contact should be your hotel reception. Many major hotels have doctors on staff who will give a first diagnosis and treatment for minor problems, and who will be aware of the best places to send foreigners for further treatment.

Be very cautious about what is prescribed for you. Doctors are poorly paid, and many earn kickbacks from pharmaceutical companies for prescribing expensive medicines. Antibiotics are handed out like candy; indeed, dangerous and powerful drugs of all kinds can be bought over the counter at pharmacies. In general, the best policy is to stay as far away from Chinese healthcare as possible.

BEFORE YOU LEAVE
Plan well ahead. If you intend merely to visit Beijing, you may not need to bother with some of the inoculations listed below, but take *expert* advice (not website hearsay) on the latest situation. Some inoculations are expensive, some need multiple shots separated by a month or two, and some should not be given at the same time as others. So start work on this 3 or 4 months before your trip.

For the latest information on infectious diseases and travel risks, and particularly on the constantly changing situation with malaria, consult the World Heath Organization (www.who.int) and the Centers for Disease Control in Atlanta (www.cdc.gov). Note that family doctors are rarely up to date on vaccination requirements, so when looking for advice at home, consult a specialist travel clinic.

To begin with, your standard inoculations, typically for **polio, diphtheria,** and **tetanus,** should be up to date. You may also need inoculations against **typhoid fever, meningococcal meningitis, cholera, hepatitis A and B,** and **Japanese B encephalitis.** If you will be arriving in mainland China from a country with **yellow fever,** you may be asked for proof of vaccination, although border health inspections are cursory at best. See also advice on **malaria,** below.

WHILE YOU ARE THERE

Mosquito-borne **malaria** comes in various forms, and you may need to take two different prophylactic drugs, depending upon the time you travel, whether you venture into rural areas, and where you go. You must begin to take these drugs 1 week *before* you enter an affected area and *for 4 weeks after you leave it, sometimes longer.* For a visit to Beijing and other major cities only, prophylaxis is usually unnecessary.

Standard precautions should be taken against exposure to **strong summer sun.** Its brightness may be dimmed by Beijing's pollution, but the sun's power to burn is undiminished.

The Chinese are phenomenally ignorant about **sexually transmitted diseases,** which are rife. As with the respiratory disease SARS, the government denied there was any AIDS problem in China until it grew too large to be contained. Estimates of the spread of infection are still highly conservative. Condoms, including Western brands, which should be your first choice, are widely available in Beijing.

STAYING SAFE

China is one of Asia's safest destinations. As anywhere else, though, you should be cautious of theft in places such as crowded markets, popular tourist sites, bus and railway stations, and airports. Take standard precautions against pickpockets (distribute your valuables around your person and wear a money belt inside your clothes). The main danger of walking the ill-lit streets at night is of falling down an uncovered manhole. There's no need to be concerned about dressing down or not flashing valuables—it's automatically assumed that all foreigners, even the scruffiest backpackers, are astonishingly rich, and the average Chinese cannot tell a Cartier from any other shiny watch.

Visitors should be cautious of various **scams,** especially in areas of high tourist traffic, and of Chinese who approach and say in English, "Hello friend! Welcome to China!" or something similar. Scam artists who want to practice their English and suggest moving to some local haunt may leave you with a bill which has two zeros more than it should, and with trouble should you decline to pay. "Art students" are a pest, approaching you with a story about raising funds for a show overseas, but in fact enticing you into a shop where you will be lied to extravagantly about the authenticity, uniqueness, originality, and true cost of various paintings you will be pressured into buying. The man who is foolish enough to accept an invitation from pretty girls to sing karaoke deserves all the hot water in which he will find himself, up to being forced by large, well-muscled gentlemen to visit an ATM and withdraw large sums to pay for services not actually provided.

If you are a **victim of theft,** make a police report (go to the same addresses given for visa extensions earlier in this chapter; you are most likely to find an English-speaking policeman there). But don't expect sympathy, cooperation, or action. The purpose is to get a theft report to give to your insurers for compensation.

Harassment of **solo female travelers** is very rare, but slightly more likely if the traveler appears to be of Chinese descent.

Traffic is a major hazard for the cautious and incautious alike. In mainland China, driving is on the right, at least occasionally. The rules of the road are routinely ignored for the one overriding rule, "I'm bigger than you so get out of my way," and pedestrians are at the bottom of the pecking order. Cyclists come along the sidewalk, and cars mount it right in front of you and park across your path as if you don't exist. Cyclists go in both directions along the bike lane at the side of the road, which is also invaded by cars looking to mount the sidewalk to park. The edges of the main road also usually have cyclists going in both directions. The vehicle drivers are gladiators, competing for any way to move into space ahead, constantly changing lanes and crossing each other's paths. Pedestrians are like matadors pausing between lanes as cars sweep by to either side of them. Pedestrians often edge out into traffic together, causing cars to swerve away from them, often into the paths of oncoming vehicles, until one lane of traffic parts and flows to either side, and the process is repeated for the next lane.

DEALING WITH DISCRIMINATION

In mainland China, in casual encounters, non-Chinese are treated as something between a cute pet and a bull in a china shop, and sometimes with pitying condescension because they are too stupid to speak Chinese. At sights, Chinese tourists from out of town may ask to have their picture taken with you, which will be fun to show friends in their foreigner-free hometowns. ("Look! Here's me with the Elephant Man!") Unless you are of Chinese descent, your foreignness is constantly thrust in your face with catcalls of *"laowai,"* a not particularly courteous term for foreigner, and a bit like shouting "Chinky" at a Chinese you encounter at home. Mocking, and usually falsetto, calls of "Helloooooo" are not greetings but are similar to saying "Pretty Polly!" to a parrot. Whether acknowledged or not (and all this is best ignored), these calls are usually followed by giggles. But there's little other overt discrimination, other than persistent overcharging wherever it can possibly be arranged. In general, however, once some sort of communication is established, foreigners get better treatment from Chinese, both officials and the general public, than the Chinese give each other. People with darker skin do have a harder time than whites, but those who do not speak Mandarin will probably not notice.

7 Specialized Travel Resources

TRAVELERS WITH DISABILITIES

China is not a good choice for travelers with disabilities. If you do choose to come here, travel with a specialist group (although such tours to China are rare) or with someone fully familiar with your particular needs. The Chinese hide people with disabilities, who are rarely seen unless reduced to begging, when they may even be subjected to taunting (although this won't happen to foreigners).

China is difficult for those with limited mobility. The sidewalks are very uneven, and public buildings, sights, and hotels almost always have stairs with no alternative ramps. In theory, some major hotels in the largest cities have wheelchair accessible rooms, but rarely are they properly executed. Metro stations do not have lifts, and any escalators usually run up only.

GAY & LESBIAN TRAVELERS

Homosexuality was only removed from an official list of mental illnesses in 2001, but the situation (while still grim) has improved in recent years. Beijing has a few gay bars of note, and the expatriate magazine *Time Out* recently broke the longstanding taboo against using the words "gay" and "lesbian." **The International Gay & Lesbian Travel Association (IGLTA) (© 800/448-8550** or 954/776-2626; www.iglta.org) lists three gay-friendly organizations dealing with inbound visitors to China. See p. 189 for a description of the gradually improving scene.

SENIOR TRAVEL

There are no special arrangements or discounts for seniors in China, with the exception that some foreign brand-name hotels may offer senior rates if you book in advance (although you'll usually beat those prices simply by showing up in person, if there are rooms available).

FAMILY TRAVEL

Beijing is not the place to make your first experiment in traveling with small children, although it's a better choice than anywhere else in China. Your biggest challenges will be the lack of services or entertainment aimed at children, the lack of familiar foods outside the bigger hotels and fast-food chains (unless your children have been brought up with Chinese food), and hygiene.

Some children find Chinese strangers a little too hands-on, and may tire of forced encounters (and photo sessions) with Chinese children met on the street. But the Chinese put their children firmly first, and stand up on buses while the young ones sit.

China is grubby at best, and for children who still have a tendency to put their hands in their mouths, constant vigilance will be necessary, or constant toilet visits will result. Older children should be instructed on frequent hand-washing and special caution with food.

Some familiar Western brands of disposable diapers, along with familiar creams and lotions, are available in Beijing.

China accepts children traveling on a parent's **passport,** although the child's photo must be submitted along with the parent's when a visa application is made.

Beijing **hotels** generally don't charge for children 12 and under who share a room with their parents. Almost all hotels will add a bed, turning a double room into a triple, for an extra ¥80 to ¥100 ($11–$13/£5.35–£6.65), which you can often bargain down.

Although **babysitting** services are not uncommon in the best hotels (the Sino-foreign joint-ventures with familiar names, in particular), in most cases the babysitters will speak very little English or none at all, will have no qualifications in child care, and will simply be members of the housekeeping staff.

All **restaurants** welcome children, but outside the Western fast-food outlets, some Chinese copies of those, and major hotels, don't expect high chairs or special equipment except very occasionally. The general Chinese eating method of ordering several dishes to share will at least allow your child to order whatever he or she deems acceptable (although it will not taste the same in any two restaurants), while allowing you to try new dishes at each meal.

Although Chinese food in Beijing is different from (and mostly vastly superior to) Chinese food served in the West, it would still be wise to acclimatize children as much as possible before leaving by making trips to the local Chinese restaurant. In many cases only chopsticks will be available, so consider taking forks and spoons with you to China. You can now find McDonald's (complete with play areas), KFC, and Pizza Hut in Beijing, and almost all hotels of four stars or up have coffee shops which deliver poor attempts at Western standards.

Keep in mind that although Western cooking is available at many excellent Beijing restaurants, authenticity comes at a price. Cheap bakeries, however, often sell buttery cakes and close relatives of the muffin containing raisins and chopped walnuts.

In general, **attractions** for children are few, and exploring temples may quickly pall. Success here will depend upon your ability to provide amusement from nothing, and the sensitivity of your antennae to what captures your child's imagination.

Discounts for children on travel tickets and entrance fees are based on height, not age. There are variations, but typically children below 1.1m (3 ft., 7 in.) enter free and travel free if they do not occupy a seat on trains and buses. Children between 1.1m and 1.4m (4 ft., 7 in.) pay half price. Many ticket offices have marks on the wall at the relevant heights so that staff can quickly determine the appropriate price.

STUDENT TRAVEL

There are no particular benefits or discounts available to foreign students traveling in China unless they are registered at Chinese educational institutions (and then not many).

8 Planning Your Trip Online

SURFING FOR AIRFARES

The "big three" online travel agencies, **Expedia.com, Travelocity.com,** and **Orbitz.com,** sell most of the air tickets bought on the Internet. (Canadian travelers should try Expedia.ca and Travelocity.ca; U.K. residents try Expedia.co.uk and Opodo.co.uk.) Also remember to check **airline websites** for Web-only specials. For the websites of airlines that fly to and from your destination, go to section 10, "Getting There," in this chapter.

Do *not* buy China domestic travel online from English-language sites, as the markups are horrendous.

SURFING FOR HOTELS

Booking hotel rooms online in China is not a good idea, unless money is no object or you absolutely must stay at a specific hotel at a very busy time of the year. There are no online services offering Chinese hotel rooms at discounts lower than you can get for yourself, whatever they may tell you. There is a case to be made for booking the first couple of nights of your stay at a joint-venture hotel, as major international hotel chains have their best *published* rate online, but do not book far in advance.

9 The 21st-Century Traveler

INTERNET ACCESS AWAY FROM HOME

Despite highly publicized clamp-downs on cybercafes, monitoring of traffic, and blocking of websites, China remains one of the easiest countries in the world in which to get online.

WITHOUT YOUR OWN COMPUTER

In central Beijing, government clamp-downs have significantly reduced the number of Internet cafes *(wangba)*. Those still in operation tend to charge from ¥4 to ¥20 (55¢–$2.65/25p–£1.35) per hour.

Online Traveler's Toolbox

- **ATM Locators:** Visa ATM Locator (www.visa.com) gives locations of PLUS ATMs worldwide; MasterCard ATM Locator (www.mastercard.com) provides locations of Cirrus ATMs worldwide.
- **Online Chinese Tools** (www.mandarintools.com) has dictionaries for Mac and Windows users, Chinese calendars for conversions between the solar and lunar calendars (on which most Chinese festivals are based), and more.
- **China Pulse** (www.chinapulse.com/wifi) provides listings of restaurants, cafes, and hotels in Beijing that have wireless Internet access. Choose "Browse Hotspot Listings" and click on the entries to find out what network is available, and whether there's a charge involved.
- **The Oriental-List** is a noncommercial mailing list dedicated solely to the discussion of travel in China. This spam-free list, moderated to stay on-topic, offers swift answers to just about any China travel question not already dealt with in these pages. To subscribe, send a blank e-mail to subscribe-oriental-list@datasinica.com.
- **Travel Warnings** are available at: http://travel.state.gov, www.fco.gov.uk/travel, www.voyage.gc.ca, and www.smartraveller.gov.au.
- **Universal Currency Converter** (www.xe.com/ucc) posts the latest exchange rates of any currency against the ¥RMB.
- **Weatherbase** (www.weatherbase.com) gives month-by-month averages for temperature and rainfall for individual cities in China.
- **Xianzai.com** (www.xianzai.com) provides free entertainment listings for Beijing and other Chinese cities, as well as special offers from China for hotels and air tickets.
- **Zhongwen.com** (www.zhongwen.com), an online dictionary, looks up English and Chinese and provides explanations of Chinese etymology using a system of family trees.

For a list of locations, see "Fast Facts: Beijing" in chapter 4. Also keep your eyes open for the *wangba* characters; see appendix B.

Many media websites, and those with financial information or any data whatsoever on China which disagrees with the Party line, are blocked from mainland China, as are even some search engines.

WITH YOUR OWN COMPUTER

Many cafes and hotels in Beijing offer wireless connectivity in public areas. Most hotels also offer free in-room Wi-Fi connections.

Mainland China uses the standard U.S.-style RJ11 telephone jack also used as the port for laptops worldwide. Cables with RJ11 jacks at both ends can be picked up for around ¥8 ($1.05/55p) in Beijing department stores and electrical shops. Standard electrical voltage across China is 220v, 50Hz, which most laptops can handle, but North American users in particular should check. For power socket information see "Fast Facts: Beijing" in chapter 4.

Those with on-board Ethernet can take advantage of broadband services, which are sometimes free in major hotels.

Ethernet cables are often provided, but it's best to bring your own.

USING A CELLPHONE IN CHINA

All Europeans, most Australians, and many North Americans use GSM (Global System for Mobiles). But while everyone else can take a regular GSM phone to China, North Americans, who operate on a different frequency, need a more expensive tri-band model.

International roaming charges can be horrendously expensive. Buying a pre-paid chip in China with a new number is far cheaper. You may need to call up your cellular operator to "unlock" your phone in order to use it with a local provider.

For Beijing, **buying a phone** is the best option. Last year's now unfashionable model can be bought, with chip and ¥100 ($13/£6.65) of pre-paid airtime, for about ¥800 ($107/£53); you pay less if a Chinese model is chosen. Europeans taking their GSM phones, and North Americans with tri-band phones, can buy chips (quan-qiutong) for about ¥100 ($13/£6.65). Recharge cards (shenzhouxing ka) are available at post offices and mobile-phone shops. Calling rates are low, although those receiving calls pay part of the cost.

10 Getting There

BY PLANE

On direct, nonstop flights, China's own international airlines always offer rates slightly lower than those of foreign carriers. Cabin staff try to be helpful but are never quite sure how. Air China only recently suffered its first and only fatal accident and should not be confused with China Airlines from Taiwan, at quite the other end of the scale. **Departure tax** is now included in the price of your ticket.

FROM NORTH AMERICA Among North American airlines, **Air Canada** (www.aircanada.com), **Continental Airlines** (www.continental.com), **Northwest Airlines** (www.nwa.com) (via Tokyo), and **United Airlines** (www.ual.com) fly to Beijing.

Air China (www.airchina.com.cn) also operates direct flights to Beijing from various cities in North America. **Japan Airlines** (www.jal.co.jp) flies via Tokyo to Beijing, as does **All Nippon Airways** (www.ana.co.jp). **Korean Air** (www.koreanair.com) and **Asiana Airlines** (us.flyasiana.com) fly via Seoul.

FROM THE UNITED KINGDOM **British Airways** (www.britishairways.com) flies to Beijing. Fares with **KLM Royal Dutch Airlines** (www.klm.com) via Amsterdam, **Lufthansa** (www.lufthansa.com) via Frankfurt, or **Finnair** (www.finnair.com) via Helsinki, can often be considerably cheaper. Fares with eastern European airlines such as **Tarom Romanian Air Transport** (www.tarom.ro) via Bucharest, and **Aeroflot** (www.aeroflot.com) via Moscow, or with Asian airlines such as **Pakistan International Airlines** (www.piac.com.pk) via Islamabad or Karachi, **Malaysia Airlines** (www.malaysiaairlines.com.my) via Kuala Lumpur, or **Singapore Airlines** (www.singaporeair.com) via Singapore, can be cheaper still. There are even more creative routes via Ethiopia or the Gulf States.

FROM AUSTRALASIA Sydney is served by **China Eastern, Air China,** and **Qantas** (www.qantas.com.au) to Beijing and Shanghai, and by Air China and **China Southern** to Guangzhou, where you can catch a connecting flight to Beijing. **Air New Zealand** (www.airnewzealand.com) flies to Shanghai, and there are possible indirect routes with **Philippine Airlines** (www.pal.com.ph) via Manila, **Malaysian Airlines** (www.malaysiaairlines.com.my) via Kuala Lumpur, and **Vietnam Airlines** (www.vietnamairlines.com) via Ho Chi Minh City.

Hong Kong's **Cathay Pacific** (www.cathay pacific.com) flies directly from six Australian cities and Auckland.

BY ROAD

Foreign visitors are not permitted to drive their own vehicles into China, unless arrangements are made far in advance with a state-recognized travel agency for a specific itinerary. The agency will provide a guide who will travel in your vehicle, or in a second vehicle with a driver, and make sure you stick to the planned route. You will have to cover all the (marked-up) costs of guide, driver, and extra vehicle if needed, and of Chinese plates for your vehicle. The agency will book and overcharge you for all your hotels and for as many excursions as it can. Forget it.

BY TRAIN

From Hung Hom station in Kowloon (Hong Kong), expresses run directly to Beijing's West Station on alternate days (see www.kcrc.com for schedules and fares). From Moscow there are weekly trains via Ulan Bator in Mongolia to Beijing, and weekly via a more easterly route directly to Harbin in China's northeast and down to the capital. There's also a separate weekly run from Ulan Bator to Beijing. Trains run twice-weekly from Hanoi in Vietnam to Beijing West via Guilin. There's also a service between Beijing and Pyongyang in North Korea, but you'll only be on that if you've joined an organized tour.

BY SHIP

There are ferry connections from Incheon in South Korea (http://english.tour2korea.com) and from Shimonoseki and Kobe in Japan (www.celkobe.co.jp) to Tianjin, a couple of hours from Beijing.

11 Packages for the Independent Traveler

For many destinations around the world, buying an unescorted package tour of pre-booked flights, internal travel, and hotels is a way of tapping into lower prices than you can obtain by buying each individual element yourself. China, as in so many other ways, is different.

Since China re-opened to foreign tourism in the early 1980s, all foreign tour operators have been required to use official state-registered travel companies as ground handlers. All arrangements in China were usually put together by one of three companies, China International Travel Service (CITS), China Travel Service (CTS), or China Youth Travel Service (CYTS). Controls are now loosening, foreign tour companies are now allowed some limited activities in China, and the range of possible Chinese partners has increased, but in effect, CITS and the like are the only companies with nationwide networks of offices, and most foreign tour companies still turn to them.

They work out the schedule at the highest possible prices and send the cost to the foreign package company, which then adds its own administration charges and profit margins, and hands the resulting quote to you. You can get the same price yourself by dealing with CITS (which has many offices overseas) directly. But if things go wrong, you will be unlikely to obtain any compensation whatsoever. If you book through a tour operator in your home country, you can expect to obtain funds and compensation if this becomes necessary.

Other than convenience, there's little benefit and a great deal of unnecessary cost in buying a package. You'll get better prices by organizing things yourself as you go along.

Warning: *Never* book directly over the Web with a China-based travel service or "private" tour guide. Many are not licensed to do business with foreigners, many individuals have not been licensed as guides, and both will hugely overcharge and frequently mislead you (in the most charming way possible).

If money is no object, then start with the list of tour companies in the next section, nearly all of whom will arrange individual package tours (particularly Abercrombie and Kent, and Steppes East). Or you can contact the China National Tourist Offices (see section 1 in this chapter) to find properly registered Chinese agencies who can help you.

12 Escorted General-Interest Tours

Escorted tours are structured group tours with a group leader. The price usually includes everything from airfare to hotels, meals, tours, admission costs, and local transportation, but not usually domestic or international departure taxes. Almost all include a visit to Beijing, but very few tackle Beijing alone, or in any depth. For that you'll need to ask the companies below to organize an independent tour for you (but you'd be better off just to jump on a plane and be completely at liberty once you arrive).

Again, due to the distorted nature of the Chinese industry, escorted tours do not usually represent savings, but rather a significant increase in costs over what you can arrange for yourself. Foreign tour companies are for now required to work with state-owned ground handlers, although some book as much as they can directly or work discreetly with private operators they trust. But even as markets become more open, most arrangements will continue to be made with the official state operators, if only for convenience. Please read the brochures skeptically (one man's "scenic splendor" is another's "heavily polluted"), and carefully read the advice in this section.

As with package tours (see previous section), the arrangements within China itself are managed by a handful of local companies, whose cupidity often induces them to lead both you and your tour company astray. Various costs, which should be in the tour fee, can appear as extras; itineraries are altered to suit the pocket of the local operator; and there are all sorts of shenanigans to separate the hapless tourist from extra cash at every turn, usually at whatever point the tour staff appear to be most helpful. (The driver has bottles of water for sale on the bus each day? You're paying three times the shop price.)

EVALUATING TOURS

When choosing a tour company for China you must, of course, consider cost, what's included, the itinerary, the likely age and interests of other tour group members, physical ability required, and the payment and cancellation policies, as you would for any other destination. But you should also investigate:

Shopping Stops These are the bane of any tour in China, designed to line the pockets of tour guides, drivers, and sometimes the ground handling company itself. A stop at the Great Wall may be limited to only an hour so as to allow an hour at a cloisonné factory. The better foreign tour operators design their own itineraries and have instituted strict contractual controls to keep these stops to a minimum, but they are often unable to do away with them altogether, and tour guides will introduce extra stops whenever they think they can get away with it. Other companies, particularly those companies that do not specialize in China, just take the package from the Chinese ground handler, put it together with flights, and pass it on uncritically. At shopping stops, you should never ask or accept your tour guide's advice on what is the "right price." You are shopping in the wrong place to start with, where prices will often be 10 to 15 times higher than they should be. Your driver gets a tip, and your guide gets 40% of sales. The "discount" card you are given marks you for yet higher initial prices and tells the seller to which guide commission is owed. So ask your tour company how many of these stops are included, and simply sit out those you cannot avoid.

Tipping   There is *no* tipping in mainland China. If your tour company advises you to bring payments for guides and drivers, costs that should be included in your total tour cost are being passed on to you through the back door. Ask what the company's tipping policy is and add that sum to the tour price to make true comparisons. Some tour guides are making as much as *400 times* what an ordinary factory worker or shop assistant makes, mostly through kickbacks from sights, restaurants, and shops, all at your expense, and from misguided tipping. Some tour operators say that if they cut out the shopping stops, then they have to find other ways to cover the tour guides' income or there'll be no tour guide. Shopping-free trips are nearly always accompanied by a higher price or a higher tip recommendation (which is the same thing). The guides are doing so well that now, in many cases, rather than receive a salary from the ground-handling company, they have to *pay* for the privilege of fleecing you. The best tour companies know how China works, make what arrangements they find unavoidable, and leave you out of it. A middle path is to put a small sum from each tour member into a central kitty and disburse tips as needed, but only for truly exceptional service and at a proper local scale which short-time visitors from developed nations are incapable of assessing. Foreign tour leaders can be tipped according to the customs of their country of origin, and most companies issue guidelines for this.

Guides   Mainland guides rarely know what they are talking about, although they won't miss a beat while answering your questions. What they will have on the tip of their tongue is an impressive array of unverifiable statistics, amusing little stories of dubious authenticity, and a detailed knowledge of the official history of a place which may bear only the faintest resemblance to the truth. Their main concerns are to tell foreigners what they want to hear, and to impress them with the greatness of China. So you may be told that the Great Wall can be seen from outer space (silly), that China has 5,000 years of culture (what does this actually mean?), and that one million people worked on building the Forbidden City (it was only 100,000 on last year's trip). Guides are short-changed by China's shoddy and politically distorted education system, and also tend to put the potential profit from the relationship first.

Ask your tour company if it will be sending a guide and/or tour manager from home to accompany the trip and to supplement local guides. This is worth paying more for, as this person's presence ensures a smoother trip and more authoritative information.

TOUR COMPANIES

Between them, the following tour companies (a tiny selection of what's available) serve just about all budgets and interests. The companies are from the United States, Canada, China, the United Kingdom, and Australia, but many have representatives around the globe. Plus you can often just buy the ground portion of the trip and fly in from wherever you like.

- **Abercrombie and Kent** (U.S.): Top-of-the-range small group tours, with the very best accommodations and transport. © **800/554-7016;** fax 630/954-3324; www.abercrombiekent.com (U.S.). © 0845/0700-610; fax 0845/0700-607; www.abercrombiekent.co.uk (U.K.). © 1300/851-800; www.abercrombiekent.com.au (Australia). © 0800/441-638 (New Zealand).

- **Academic Travel Abroad** (U.S.): Tours in China for The Smithsonian (educational, cultural) and National Geographic Expeditions (natural history, soft adventure). © **877/338-8687;** fax 202/633-6088; www. smithsonianjourneys.org.; © 888/ 966-8687; www.nationalgeographic expeditions.com.

- **Adventure Center** (U.S.): Small group tours aimed at those who are usually independent travelers; one tour includes the Eastern Qing Tombs and walking on several stretches of the Great Wall. © **800/ 228-8747** or 800/227-8747; www. adventurecenter.com.

- **China Focus** (U.S.): Larger groups at budget prices, but with additional costs to cover extras. © **800/868-7244** or 415/788-8660; fax 415/788-8665; www.chinafocustravel.com.

- **Elderhostel** (U.S.): Educational tours for seniors. © **800/454-5768** or 877/ 426-8056; www.elderhostel.org.

- **Gecko's Adventures** (Australia): Down-to-earth budget tours for small group tours of 20- to 40-year-olds, using smaller guesthouses, local restaurants, and public transport. © **03/ 9662-2700;** fax 03/9662-2422; www. geckosadventures.com.

- **Intrepid Travel** (Australia): Slightly more adventurous tours with small groups, following itineraries that are a deft mix of popular destinations and the less-visited. One trip includes 4 days of trekking on the Great Wall. © **1300/364-512** (in Australia) 3/9473-2626 (outside Australia); fax 03/9419-4426; www.intrepidtravel. com (Australia).

- **Laurus Travel** (Canada): Small group tours from a Vancouver-based China-only specialist, run by a former CITS guide. © **877/507-1177** or 604/438-7718; fax 694/438-7715; www.laurustravel.com.

- **Monkey Business** (China): Beijing-based outfit specializing in organizing onward travel on the Trans-Siberian express. © **010/6591-6519;** fax 010/ 6591-6517; www.monkeyshrine.com.

- **Pacific Delight** (U.S.): A large variety of mainstream trips for a wide range of different group sizes, with endless permutations for different time scales and budgets. Watch for extra costs. © **800/221-7179;** www. pacificdelighttours.com.

- **Peregrine Adventures** (Australia): Sister company of Gecko's Adventures (see above), Peregrine offers small group trips with good quality centrally located accommodations; trips include visits to private houses and smaller restaurants frequented by local people and, possibly, walks and bike rides. © **03/9662-2700;** fax 03/8601-4344; www.peregrine adventures.com (Australia). © 800/ 227-8747 (U.S.).

- **R. Crusoe & Son** (U.S.): Small group tours include extras such as a visit to areas of the Forbidden City usually closed to the public. © **800/ 585-8555;** fax 312/980-8100; www. rcrusoe.com.

- **Ritz Tours** (U.S.): Groups range in size from 10 to 40 people, and ages range widely; parents often bring children. Ritz is the foremost U.S. tour operator to China in terms of volume. © **800/900-2446;** www.ritz tours.com.

- **Steppes East** (U.K.): Tours organized to very high standards. Its itineraries are merely suggestions that can be adapted to your specifications. © **01285/880980;** fax 01285/ 885888; www.steppeseast.co.uk.

13 Recommended Books

The best single-volume introduction to the people of China and their world is **Jasper Becker**'s *The Chinese* (John Murray, 2000). Longtime resident of Beijing and former Beijing bureau chief for the *South China Morning Post,* Becker delivers an immensely readable account of how the Chinese got to be who they are today; their pre-occupations, thoughts, and fears; and the ludicrous posturings of their leaders.

Old Beijing can now only be found in literature. The origins of many Western fantasies of the capital, then called Khanbalik, lie in the ghost-written work of **Marco Polo,** *The Travels of Marco Polo.* Dover Publications' two-volume reprint (1993) of the Yule-Cordier edition is a splendid read (although only part of Polo's time was spent in Beijing) because of its entertaining introduction and footnotes by famous explorers attempting to follow his route. **Ray Huang**'s ironically titled *1587, A Year of No Significance* (Yale University Press, 1982) is an account of the Ming dynasty in decline; written in the first person, it paints a compelling picture of the well-intentioned Wanlì emperor trapped by a vast, impersonal bureaucracy. The parallels with the present regime are striking. **Lord Macartney**'s *An Embassy to China* (J. L. Cranmer-Byng [Ed.], Longman, 1962) gives a detailed account of Qing China and particularly Beijing at the end of the 18th century. This should be compulsory reading for modern businesspeople, as it prefigures WTO negotiations and the expectations of what will arise from them. Macartney's prediction that the Chinese would all soon be using forks and spoons is particularly relevant. **Hugh Trevor-Roper**'s *Hermit of Peking* (Eland Press, 1976), part history, part detective story, uncovers the life of Sir Edmund Backhouse, resident of Beijing from the end of the Qing dynasty into the

Republic, who knew everyone in the city at the beginning of the century, and who deceived them all, along with a generation of China scholars, with his fake diary of a Manchu official at the time of the Boxer Rebellion. A serviceably translated bilingual edition of **Lao She**'s *Teahouse* (Chinese University Press, 2004) succinctly captures the flavor of life in Beijing during the first half of the 20th century. The helplessness of the characters in the face of political movements is both moving and prophetic. **John Blofeld**'s *City of Lingering Splendour: A Frank Account of Old Peking's Exotic Pleasures* (Shambhala, 1961) describes the seamier side of Beijing in the 1930s, by someone who took frank enjoyment in its pleasures, including adventures in "the lanes of flowers and willows"—the Qian Men brothel quarter. In the same period, **George Kates,** an American, lived more decorously in the style of a Chinese gentleman-scholar in an old courtyard house of the kind now rapidly vanishing, and gives a sensitive and very appealing portrait of the city in *The Years That Were Fat* (Harper, 1955; reprinted by Oxford University Press, 1988). **Ann Bridge,** the wife of a British diplomat in Beijing, wrote novels of life in the capital's Legation Quarter in the 1930s (cocktail parties, horse racing, problems with servants, love affairs—spicy stuff in its day, and best-selling, if now largely forgotten). *Peking Picnic* (Chatto and Windus, 1932; reprinted Virago, 1989) features a disastrous trip to the outlying temples of Tanzhe Sì and Jietai Sì (but one well worth undertaking yourself). *The Ginger Griffin* (Chatto and Windus, 1934; reprinted by Oxford University Press, 1985) offers the adventures of a young woman newly arrived in the city, who attends the horse races and who has a happier ending.

David Kidd, another American, lived in Beijing for a few years before and shortly after the Communist victory of 1949, and gives an account of the beginning of the city's destruction in *Peking Story* (Eland Press, 1988; originally *All the Emperor's Horses,* John Murray, 1961). Perhaps the best example of the "hooligan literature" of the late 1980s is *Please Don't Call Me Human* (No Exit Press, 2000) by **Wang Shuo.** There's little plot to speak of, but it's a devastating and surreal parody of Chinese nationalism, all the more poignant as the Olympics draw near. *Red China Blues* (Anchor Books, 1997), by **Jan Wong,** is one of our all-time favorite memoirs. Wong initially came to Beijing as a young and fervent Maoist in 1972 and became one of only two international students allowed to study at Beijing University during the height of the Cultural Revolution. Years later, she returned, older and wiser, as an international correspondent for the *Globe and Mail* in 1988, just in time to witness and report on the Tian'an Men protests of 1989. *Black Hands of Beijing* (John Wiley, Inc., 1993), by **George Black and Robin Munro,** is the most balanced and least hysterical account of the Tian'an Men protests of 1989, putting them in the context of other, better-planned movements for social change, all of which suffered in the fallout from the chaotic student demonstrations and their bloody suppression. Only one of **Tim Clissold**'s tales in *Mr. China* (Constable & Robinson, 2004) is set in Beijing, and the naivety of the author is at times breathtaking, but his account of setting up joint-ventures from the mid-1990s onwards is frank testimony that should be read by anyone considering doing business in China.

M.A. Aldrich's *The Search for Vanishing Beijing* (Hong Kong University Press, 2006) is a comprehensive narrative of Beijing. The work includes stories by Marco Polo and Bernard Shaw, as well as commentary from Ming and Qing-era travel guides. **Frances Wood**'s *Forbidden City* (British Museum Press, 2005) is a short and thoroughly entertaining introduction to Beijing's main attraction.

Peter Hessler was the Beijing-based *New Yorker* correspondent for several years. His second book, *Oracle Bones* (HarperCollins, 2006), is an insightful look into the lives of young Chinese migrants and colorful personalities from old and new Beijing.

For those looking for an atypical story about modern China, **Rachel DeWoskin** gives an entertaining account of her time as the star of a popular Chinese television drama in the early 90s in her novel *Foreign Babes in Beijing* (W.W. Norton, 2006).

3

Suggested Itineraries

Seeing Beijing in a day? You must be kidding. It is technically possible to see the big-name attractions—the **Forbidden City, Temple of Heaven, Summer Palace,** and **Great Wall**—in as little as 3 days, but you'll need at least a week to get any sort of feel for the city.

But if a day is all you have, we want to help you make the most of it by providing a ready-made itinerary that allows you to have a satisfying trip.

We've left the Great Wall out of the itineraries below, as it requires a full day in itself, or better yet, an overnight stay to allow for spectacular late afternoon and early morning photography (see chapter 11 for details). The traffic in Beijing means that the only sensible way to tour the city is to tackle the sights in groups. We take you to the central sights on the first day, the north of town on the following day and to the less-visited south of town on the third day.

1 The Best of Beijing in 1 Day

Fortunately for the harried tourist, when the Mongol founders laid down the Beijing (then Khanbalik) city grid, it was on a north–south axis, making navigation straightforward and grouping the key landmarks in a central location. The main downside, for which Kublai Khan cannot be blamed, is that there are few dining options en route, so we recommend that you eat a hearty breakfast at your hotel. *Start: There should be a Temple of Heaven metro stop by the time you read this. If things fall behind schedule, take a cab to the north gate (Bei Tian Men).*

❶ Temple of Heaven (Tiān Tan Gong Yuan) ✸✸
Just after dawn you'll find regular park goers practicing *taijiquan,* kung fu, group dancing, or giant calligraphy on this huge park's greenery and paved walkways. As you walk through the grounds, in addition to the music providing background tunes for the dancers, you'll probably hear birds and crickets chirping happily through their cages as their owners (mostly retired elderly men) take them out for walks. Don't miss **Qinian Dian (Hall of Prayer for Good Harvests).** Its history dates back to 1420, but the current structure is a replica built in

1889 when the original burned to the ground. The circular wooden hall, with its triple-layered cylindrical blue-tiled roof, is perhaps the most recognizable emblem of Chinese imperial architecture outside of the Forbidden City. The main hall is 38m (125 ft.) high and 30m (98 ft.) in diameter and—here's the kicker—it was constructed without a single nail. See p. 127.

Ride the metro to:
❷ Tian'an Men Square (Tian'an Men Guangchang) ✸
Set on the site of the former Imperial Way, the broad square is also a recent creation,

dating from the 1950s when Mao, encouraged by his Soviet advisors, ordered the clearing away of the old government ministries. There were plans to "press down" the "feudal" Forbidden City by surrounding it with high-rise buildings and smokestacks, but the fledgling republic lacked the resources to carry out the plan.

To your left looms the **Great Hall of the People,** to your right is the **National Museum**—neither worth a visit if you're pressed for time. Impressive in its vastness, there's little to do in the Square unless you plan to cut short your tour by unfurling a protest banner. See p. 120.

Walk to the southern end of the Square to:

❸ Chairman Mao's Mausoleum (Mao Zhuxi Jinian Guan) ✦

Built on the site of Da Qing Men (Great Qing Gate) this hastily constructed building is unimpressive in itself, but what makes this site compelling is the genuine reverence of local visitors for The Great Helmsman. It makes for a memorable 15 minutes of people-watching. *Note:* The Mausoleum is closed Sundays. See p. 121.

Walk north, taking the underpass to:

❹ Tian'an Men (Gate of Heavenly Peace)

Climb to the dais above Mao's portrait for a view south along the former Imperial Way. Beyond **Qian Men (Front Gate)** you may spy the newly reconstructed **Yongding Men.** It's not in the same spot as the original, but it is one of the first steps in a plan to revamp the north–south axis. A boulevard connecting to Olympic Park in the north of town is underway, with input from Albert Speer, Jr., who

also happens to be the son of Hitler's personal architect.

A less traditional structure is apparent to your right: The National Theatre resembles a UFO that made an emergency landing in a pond. See p. 120. Continue north, through the gate to:

❺ Forbidden City (Gu Gong) ✦✦✦

The majority of visitors to Beijing's main attraction rent their audio tour and rush through the central route without ducking into the eastern and western axes. This is a mistake. The most charming and intriguing parts of the Forbidden City are located away from the main tourist route. Allow at least 3 hours, and do not miss newly opened sights, particularly the **Wuying Dian** (west side) and **Juanqin Zhai** (northeast side). See p. 122.

TAKE A BREAK
After a slew of bad publicity (which downplayed the fact that Forbidden City officials originally invited the global chain to set up shop here to help offset costs), the Starbucks that once occupied a small corner space east of Qianqing Men closed its doors in mid-2007. In its place are a bunch of identical kiosks selling Nescafé, Coke, and Lipton ice tea. Thank goodness they drove out the capitalist beverage makers! Still, it's better than nothing, and this is a good place to grab some bench space and do a little people watching while you rehydrate with a bottle of ice cold water or cool off with an ice cream.

If you wish to also get an aerial view of the Forbidden City, proceed to Jing Shan Gongyuan (p. 138), immediately opposite the north entrance to the Forbidden City.

2 The Best of Beijing in 2 Days

If you've survived "The Best of Beijing in 1 Day," you'll find your second full-day tour takes in a different side of Beijing. Today we'll take you to the Lake district, our favorite city retreat, and a couple of impressive temples for good measure. *Start: Bei Hai Gong Yuan.*

Suggested Beijing Itineraries

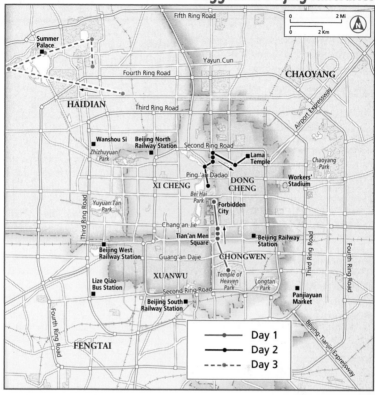

❶ Bei Hai Gongyuan (Bei Hai Park) ✦

After all the grandeur you've just sampled, you'll find that this park, set around a lake carved out in the 12th century, provides a welcome change. On the south side of the park, **Qiong Dao,** an islet topped by a white dagoba built to commemorate the visit of the first Dalai Lama to the capital in 1651, is worth a quick look.

The north side of the park is more interesting, so catch a boat from the islet to the opposite side of the lake. Don't miss **Daci Zhenru Bao Dian;** this Buddhist hall is one of the most impressive structures in Beijing. See p. 138.

Emerging from the north of the park, turn right and cross at the first set of lights to:

❷ Qian Hai Hou Hai (The Lake District) ✦✦✦

Qian Hai and Hou Hai's banks, now overflowing with alfresco bars, cafes, and the odd curio shop, were once exclusive areas for nobles and merchants. Prior to 1911, only people with connections to the imperial family were permitted to maintain houses and conduct business here. The present-day commercial fare on the main banks can be wearying, but the area's back alleys are still ripe for exploration. Walk northeast along Qian Hai Nanyan until you come to Yinding Qiao (Silver Ingot Bridge), the bridge that marks the boundary between Qian Hai and Hou Hai. From here you can watch the boats drifting along below, several of which come complete with zither players strumming out classics such as *Moonriver* for foreign passengers. If you want your own Sino-Western serenade, you can rent boats with musicians from the small dock near the Lotus Lane entrance.

Cross Yinding Qiao and turn right to:

> **TAKE A BREAK**
> **Nuage** has the best cup of coffee the Lake District has to offer. They are the second restaurant on the left (set back a bit from the road), behind No Name bar. They serve traditional Vietnamese drip coffee coupled with a gorgeous rooftop view of the Drum and Bell Towers (℡ 010/6401-9581).

Retrace your steps to Yinding Qiao, turning right at the bridge. Take your first right onto:

❸ Tobacco Alley (Yandai Xiejie)

This little street is packed with cafes and small stores selling various trinkets, clothing from minority regions, and reproductions of Cultural Revolution memorabilia. Street vendors set up shop on the already narrow pathway and often sell fresh lollipops blown into animal shapes, or candied fruit kebabs.

Follow the alley until it ends at the main road. Walk ½ block directly north (left) to:

❹ Drum Tower (Gulou)

The Drum and Bell Towers lie on the northern part of the north–south axis that runs the length of central Beijing, through the center of the Forbidden City. You only need to climb up one tower's steep set of stairs, and your best bet is the Drum Tower. The upper chamber has replicas of traditional drums, which are showcased in performances several times per hour. Outside, a clear day provides a fantastic view of Hou Hai Lake to the west. See p. 161.

Take a ¥10 ($1.35/65p) cab east to:

❺ Yong He Gong (Lama Temple) 👍👍👍

Though often referred to as the Lama Temple, Yong He Gong actually translates as "The Palace of Peace and Harmony." But being one of Beijing's top tourist attractions, this temple is rarely peaceful. Try to ignore the crowds and roam around the many courtyards at a leisurely pace, exploring the temple's impressive offerings, such as a 6m (20-ft.) bronze statue of Tsongkapa (1357–1419), founder of the now dominant school of Tibetan Buddhism, housed in **Falun Dian (Hall of the Wheel of Law).** You'll find the temple's most prized possession in the last of the major halls, **Wanfu Ge (Tower of Ten Thousand Happiness).** There, standing 18m (59 ft.) tall, is the ominous Tibetan-style statue of Maitreya (the future Buddha), which was carved from a single piece of white sandalwood and was transported all the way from Tibet as a gift to Qianlong from the seventh Dalai Lama. See p. 137.

Exit Yong He Gong, cross the street and walk south for less than half a block. Turn right onto the street marked by a traditional Chinese arch. Walk for about 5 minutes to:

❻ Confucius Temple (Kong Miao) 👍

On a tree-shaded street lies China's second largest Confucius Temple. Two stelae at the front instruct you to park your horse in six different languages. The Temple is the busiest before national university entrance examinations, when students and parents descend in droves to seek out the Great Sage's assistance. Students make a beeline for the main hall, **Dacheng Dian.** They throw their incense on the shrine rather than burn it because of fire regulations. See p. 134.

3 The Best of Beijing in 3 Days

It's time to get away from the city center. For the third full-day tour, we take you to the far northwest corner of Beijing. The district is home to China's top two universities, the self-styled Harvard and M.I.T. of China, as well as the Beijing Foreign Language and Culture University (BLCU), where you can find foreign students from all over the world learning Chinese. Nestled amongst all the student bars and Wi-Fi cafes are a couple of imperial playgrounds. **Start:** *Take a cab to the east gate of Peking University (Beida Dong Men).*

❶ Peking University (Beijing Daxue or "Beida")

This is China's most famous university and its campus has seen plenty of action in its hundred-odd years. Beida, as the university is commonly known, was traditionally home to student activists, including some of the leaders of the infamous Tian'an Men demonstrations of 1989 (ironically, the campus has a road called Minzhu Lu, Democracy Road). You can ponder the campus' historical significance from the rocky seats surrounding Weiming Lake. Better yet, if you're visiting in winter, rent some skates and take a spin around the frozen lake.

Exit from the east gate and walk 800m (½ mile) north to the major T-intersection marked by the west gate of Tsinghua University (gaggles of Chinese tourists will be taking their photos here). Turn left and walk 400m (¼ mile) to:

❷ The Old Summer Palace (Yuan Ming Yuan) 🏮🏮

If pushed for time, just visit the northeast side of the park, which is home to the remnants of the **Xi Yang Lou (Western Mansions).** These buildings were razed by British and French forces in 1860, a year before Cixi rose to Empress Dowager status. They featured spectacular fountains and housed magnificent European art, but it could have been worse—the Anglo-French forces considered destroying the Forbidden City. See p. 140.

Head to the park's east gate, beside the parking lot, to find:

> **TAKE A BREAK**
> It's worth coming to **Mima (Zuo You Jian)** 🏮 just to enjoy the architecture: The cafe consists of a minimalist loft with an outdoor maze of rice paper domes, punctuated by clusters of bamboo. Don't miss the original bathroom design. Mima serves simple snacks and cold beer. (✆ **010/8268-8003**).

Give your feet a rest and take a cab to:

❸ Summer Palace (Yi He Yuan) 🏮🏮🏮

Later in her rule, Cixi spent a considerable amount of time in this watery imperial playground, even setting up her own photographic studio. Modeled on Hangzhou's West Lake, the complex was ransacked by foreign troops in 1860 and 1900, and restored under Cixi's orders, on the first occasion with funds earmarked for the navy. The lake is the gem of the palace: Escape the crowds for an hour or so by hiring a boat, or in winter a pair of skates. On land, allow 3 hours for a cursory look around.

Proceed to the south exit to join a rusty "imperial yacht." See p. 130.

A short cab ride north brings you to:

❹ Fragrant Hills (Xiang Shan) 🏮

This outdoor playground has been around since 1168. It covers 160 hectares and the highest peak is supposed to look like an incense burner. Take the chairlift to the top for a leisurely purview over

Beijing's northwest district for ¥30 ($4/£2) one-way, ¥50 ($6.65/£3.35) return. The multitude of pools, pavilions, temples, villas, and ancient trees make it an idyllic picnic spot, far removed from the din of the city traffic. In 1949, Mao Zedong stayed here while commanding the battle of crossing the Yangtze River, which clinched victory over the Nationalist forces. The building that played witness to this shining moment of Communist history is now maintained as a shrine.

Take a cab to the Wudaokou metro stop.

TAKE A BREAK
You are now in Wudaokou, a coffee shop/bar/bookstore area that has sprung up around the metro stop of the same name. It is a veritable hub of intellectual activity where all the foreign students come to hang out, study, and party. **Sculpting in Time** (Building 12, Huaqing Jiayuan, Chengfu Lu, south of the metro on the street that runs parallel to the tracks; *℃* **010/8286-7025**) is a cafe in the heart of this youthful area. It serves some excellent coffee with free wireless Internet to boot.

Take the metro one stop to Da Zhong Si and explore:

❺ Da Zhong Si

This Qing temple now houses the Ancient Bell Museum (Gu Zhong Bowuguan). It was once known as Juesheng Si (Awakened Life Temple), but clearly there wasn't enough awakening going on, so a 47-ton bell was transported here on ice sleds in 1743. The third hall on the right houses clangers garnered from around Beijing. Some were donated by eunuchs wishing the relevant emperor long life, with hundreds of donors' names scrawled on their sides. But frustratingly, none of this is fleshed out in the museum. The main attraction is housed in the rear hall—a big bell carved inside and out with 230,000 Chinese and Sanskrit characters. It tolls once a year, on New Year's Eve. Visitors rub the handles of Emperor Qianlong's old washbasin, and climb up narrow steps to make a wish while throwing coins through a hole in the top of the bell. But it is no longer the "King of Bells"—that honor now goes to the 50-ton bell housed in the Altar to the Century (Zhonghua Shiji Tan), constructed in 1999 to prove that China could waste money on the millennium, too.

Navigate the confusion of the metro system by changing trains twice to get to the Wangfujing stop. Get out here to explore:

❻ Wangfujing Dijie

In contrast to today's first destination, this pedestrian mall is "new China," the side the regime is desperate for you to see. Those with weary legs may wish to duck into **Oriental Plaza** for coffee and air-conditioned comfort, while the energetic can sample part of our Walking Tour of Wangfujing (p. 161).

Be sure to reach your final destination before sunset.

WINDING DOWN
With nothing but air between you and the Forbidden City, the rooftop bar **Palace View Bar (Guan Jing Jiuba)** ✷✷ offers a magical spot to view Beijing's pollution-enhanced sunset. Open June through October. In the Grand Hotel (*℃* **010/6513-7788**, ext. 458). See p. 194.

4

Getting to Know Beijing

As early as the 1920s, guidebook writers complained that as quickly as they could write about one of Beijing's historic buildings, it was pulled down.

Today we face the same problem with bars, clubs, and restaurants, whose lifetimes seem even shorter than the Chinese government's swiftness to suppress dissent. Whole streets and city blocks are often bludgeoned into oblivion almost overnight. Similarly, new neighborhoods are being set up as quickly as they are torn down. Once-barren areas north of the city have been transformed with the ultra-modern athletic stadiums of

Olympic Green and Olympic Forest Park.

The choices of what to do and see in a city already packed with pleasures increase all the time. This chapter deals with everything you need to know to get yourself around Beijing, a city better supplied with taxis and public transport than almost any counterpart in Europe. Beijing's layout is simple, and navigation is mainly by landmark. The only confusion lies in the fact that any landmark may well be razed by the time you reach the city, taking two or three of our favorite restaurants with it.

1 Orientation

ARRIVING

Beijing's Capital Airport (Shoudu Jichang), is one of three airports in the city but the only one to see foreigners. It now handles all international and nearly all domestic flights. It's located 25km (16 miles) northeast of the city center (© **010/6457-1666,** information in Mandarin only; © **010/6601-3336** domestic ticketing; © **010/6601-6667** international ticketing). A splashy new airport terminal, designed by architect Lord Norman Foster, will open in 2008.

Health declaration and **immigration forms** are usually supplied in-flight or are available as you approach the immigration counters, which typically take 10 to 15 minutes to clear on arrival. Have the forms completed and your passport ready.

There are no longer **Customs declaration forms,** and foreigners are rarely stopped. Immediately after Customs, you may be asked to put your larger bags through an **X-ray machine,** which may or may not be photo-safe.

There are signposted **money-changers** (branches of various Chinese banks, all of which can help you), several ATMs accepting foreign cards (at arrivals level and departures level), and even automated money-changing machines. Exchange rates are the same here as everywhere else, although this may change eventually. Exchange as much currency as you think you'll need, and try to get at least ¥100 in ¥10 notes.

TRAINS Twice-weekly Trans-Siberian services from Moscow (one via Ulan Bator in Mongolia, and one via Harbin), weekly services from Ulan Bator only, and services from Pyongyang in North Korea (which you'll only take if on a pre-arranged tour) all

Beijing

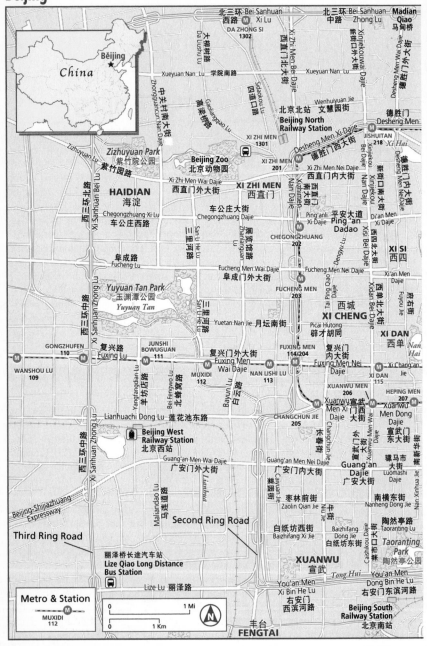

China

Běijīng

北三环 Bei Sanhuan 西路 Xi Lu

北三环 Bei Sanhuan 中路 Zhong Lu

Madian Qiao 马甸桥

新街口外大街 Xinjiekouwai Dajie

DA ZHONG SI 1302

大柳树路 Da Liushu Lu

Zhongguancun Nan Dajie 中关村南大街

高粱桥路 Gaoliangqiao Lu

Xueyuan Nan Lu 学院南路

Sidaokou Lu 四道口路

西直门北大街 Xi Zhi Men Bei Dajie

Xueyuan Nan Lu 学院南路

Desheng Men Wai Dajie 德胜门外大街

Desheng Men 德胜门

Zizhuyuan Lu 紫竹院路

Zizhuyuan Park 紫竹院公园

Beijing Zoo 北京动物园

北京北站 Beijing North Railway Station

Wenhuiyuan Jie 文慧园街

JISHUITAN 218 Xi Hai 西海

紫竹园路 Zizhuyuan Lu

HAIDIAN 海淀

Xi Zhi Men Wai Dajie 西直门外大街

XI ZHI MEN 西直门

XI ZHI MEN 1301

XI ZHI MEN 201

Desheng Men Xi Dajie 德胜门西大街

德胜门内大街 Desheng Men Nei Dajie

西直门内大街 Xi Zhi Men Nei Dajie

新街口南大街 Xinjiekou Nan Dajie

新街口北大街 Xinjiekou Bei Dajie

XI SI 西四

Xizhimen Nan Dajie 西直门南大街

Chegongzhuang Xi Lu 车公庄西路

车公庄大街 Chegongzhuang Dajie

San Li He Lu 三里河路

Zhanlanguan Lu 展览馆路

Ping'anli Xi Dajie 平安里西大街

Ping'an Dadao 平安大道

Di'an Men 地安门

西四北大街 Xisi Bei Dajie

Fucheng Lu 阜成路

CHEGONGZHUANG 202

Fucheng Men Wai Dajie 阜成门外大街

Fucheng Men Nei Dajie 阜成门内大街

Dengshi Lu 灯市口

Xi'an Men Dajie 西安门大街

Fuyou Jie 府右街

Yuyuan Tan Park 玉渊潭公园 Yuyuan Tan

FUCHENG MEN 203

San Li He Lu 三里河路

Yuetan Nan Jie 月坛南街

Picai Hutong 辟才胡同

西城 XI CHENG

Xidan Bei Dajie 西单北大街

XI SI 西四

XI DAN 西单

Nan Hai 南海

GONGZHUFEN 110

JUNSHI BOWUGUAN 111

Fuxing Lu 复兴路

Yangfangdian Lu 羊坊店路

复兴门外大街 Fuxing Men Wai Dajie

FUXING MEN 114/204

复兴门内大街 Fuxing Men Nei Dajie

Xi Chang'an Jie 西长安街

WANSHOU LU 109

Xi Sanhuan Zhong Lu 西三环中路

Xi Sanhuan Bei Lu 西三环北路

Wanfeng Lu 万丰路

Fuxing Men Wai Dajie 复兴门外大街

MUXIDI 112

NAN LISHI LU 113

NAN LISHI LU 113

Bayun Lu 白云路

XI DAN 115

XUANWU MEN 206

Xuanwu Men Xi Dajie 宣武门西大街

HEPING MEN 207

Lianhuachi Dong Lu 莲花池东路

CHANGCHUN JIE 205

Xuanwu Men Dong Dajie 宣武门东大街

Beijing West Railway Station 北京西站

Guang'an Men Wai Dajie 广安门外大街

Guang'an Men Nei Dajie 广安门内大街

Xuanwu Men Wai Dajie 宣武门外大街

Guang'an Dajie 广安大街

Guang'an 广安门

Beijing-Shijiazhuang Expressway 北京-石家庄

Maliandao Lu 马连道路

马连道北路 Maliandao Bei Lu

Lianhua 莲花

广安门外大街 Guang'an Men Wai Dajie

广安门内大街 Guang'an Men Nei Dajie

Caiyuan Lu 菜园路

Zaolin Qian Jie 枣林前街

枣林前街 Zaolin Qian Jie

Luomashi Dajie 骡马市大街

南横东街 Nanheng Dong Jie

Second Ring Road

Baizhifang Xi Jie 白纸坊西街

Baizhifang Dong Jie 白纸坊东街

Caishikou Dajie 菜市口大街

Taoranting Lu 陶然亭路

Third Ring Road

丽泽桥长途汽车站 Lize Qiao Long Distance Bus Station

白纸坊东街 Baizhifang Dong Jie

XUANWU 宣武

Taoranting Park 陶然亭公园

You'an Men 右安门

Tong Hui

You'an Men Xi Bin He Lu 右安门西滨河路

You'an Men Dong Bin He Lu 右安门东滨河路

右安门东滨河路

Beijing South Railway Station 北京南站

Lize Lu 丽泽路

丰台 FENGTAI

Metro & Station

MUXIDI 112

0 ———— 1 Mi

0 ———— 1 Km

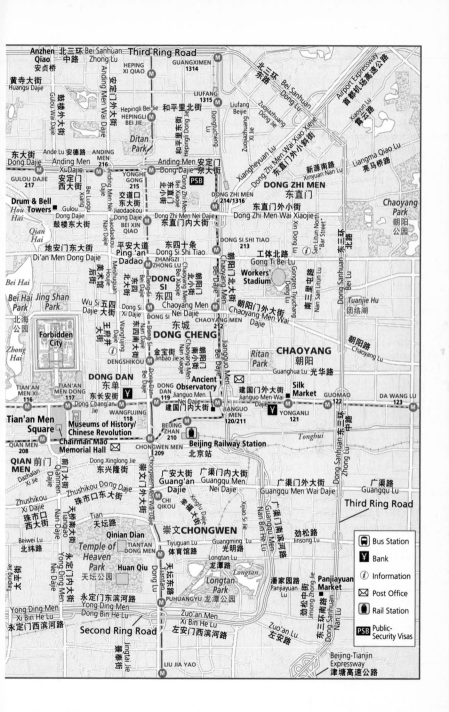

arrive at **Beijing Zhan,** Beijing's original main railway station, built with Soviet assistance in the late 1950s to replace one built by the British in 1901. Twice-weekly trains from Hanoi in Vietnam, and trains from Kowloon in Hong Kong which run on alternate days, arrive at the new and far larger but already disintegrating **Xi Ke Zhan** (also known as Beijing Xi Zhan), the West Station. Neither station has any currency exchange facility or ATM, although there are banks and ATMs accepting foreign cards 5 minutes' walk north of Beijing Zhan, at Citibank next to the Beijing International Hotel, and at the Hongkong and Shanghai Bank (HSBC) on the north side of the COFCO shopping complex.

Domestic train services from Shanghai and most stations to the south, southeast, east, and northeast arrive at Beijing Zhan, which has its own metro station (210) on the circle line, with entrances across the forecourt to the right and left as you leave the railway station. The West Station will gain its own metro connection in a few years' time.

GETTING INTO TOWN

TAXIS   You will be pestered by **taxi** touts as soon as you emerge from Customs. *Never* go with these people. The signposted taxi rank is straight ahead and has a line that mostly works, although a few people will always try to cut in front of you. Line up at the two-lane rank, and a marshal will direct you to the next available vehicle as you reach the front of the line. Rates are clearly posted on the side of each cab. All cabs are ¥2 (25¢/15p) per kilometer. After 15km (9⅓ miles), rates increase by 50%. If you only want to go to the hotels (such as the Kempinski, Hilton, or Sheraton) in the San Yuan Qiao area, where the Airport Expressway meets the Third Ring Road, your taxi driver may be a bit grumpy, but that's his bad luck.

Expect to pay around ¥80 ($11/£5.35) to reach the eastern part of the city and around ¥100 ($13/£6.65) to reach the central hotels. These estimates include the meter rate and a ¥10 ($1.35/65p) expressway toll, which you'll see the driver pay en route. Fares to the central hotels will increase significantly if you travel during rush hours (8–9am and 3:30–7pm). For most of the day, you can reach hotels on the Third Ring Road within about 30 minutes, and central hotels in about 45 minutes—the latter trip may rise to more than an hour during rush hours. Make sure you read the box "Ten Tips for Taking Taxis Around Town," in this chapter.

HOTEL SHUTTLES   If you book a hotel room in advance, ask about shuttle services. Some hotels, such as the Kempinski, offer guests free transportation with a regular schedule of departures. The Peninsula Palace Hotel will send a Rolls-Royce for you, but for a fee.

AIRPORT BUSES   Air-conditioned services, run by two different companies, leave from in front of the domestic arrivals area. The Airport Shuttle Bus runs five routes; the most useful, Line 2 to Xidan, runs every 10 minutes from 7am to last arrival. The fare is ¥16 ($2.15/£1.05). Destinations include San Yuan Qiao (near the Hilton and Sheraton hotels), the Dong Zhi Men and Dong Si Shi Tiao metro stations and the CAAC ticket office in Xidan. Lines 1 through 5 all pass through San Yuan Qiao, but only Line 2 lets off passengers at a location convenient for picking up taxis to continue to other destinations. Most hotels in the center of the city can be reached by taxi for under ¥20 ($2.65/£1.35) from there. If you're staying in the university district, save yourself a bundle and take Line 5 to Zhongguancun Bridge. From there it is a ¥10 to ¥20 ($1.35–$2.65/65p–£1.35) taxi ride to most of the major universities. For more detail on the airport buses and where they stop, check out the airport's website (www.bcia.com.cn/en/passengers_Land_airport_page.html).

There is also a Kong Gang Bus for ¥1 to ¥3 (13¢–40¢/6p–20p) available at the exit of both terminal buildings. It stops at destinations very close to the airport (Ying Hua Yuan, Guo Tai Guang Chang, and the Airport Hotel).

EXPRESS TRAIN   The airport train line to Dong Zhi Men has been under construction for years. If everything goes according to plan, a new express train will run from Beijing Capital International Airport to Dong Zhi Men, where passengers can disembark and have direct access to the city's existing metro system. At time of writing, the officials from the Beijing Subway Operation Company confirm the train will be up and running by June 30, 2008 (i.e. *just* in time for the 2008 Olympics).

DEPARTING BEIJING

Check with your airline for the latest advice, but for international flights make sure you are at the airport *at least* 1½ hours before departure; 1 hour for domestic flights. As you face the terminal, international departures are to the right, and domestic to the left. Departure tax for international and domestic flights is now included in the price of your ticket. Before joining lines for emigration, pick up and complete a departure card. Have your passport, departure card, and boarding card ready.

TRAVELING BEYOND BEIJING

BY PLANE   There are daily **direct flights** from Capital Airport to nearly every major Chinese city, including Shanghai for around ¥1,130 ($151/£75), Guangzhou for ¥1,700 ($227/£113), Xi'an for ¥1,050 ($140/£70), Chengdu for ¥1,440 ($192/£96), and Lhasa for ¥2,430 ($324/£162). Prices vary widely, according to season and your bargaining skills, and may be reduced to half the amounts quoted here. Much Chinese domestic flying is done on a walk-up basis, but the best discount is never available at the airport. The aviation authority officially permits the airlines to discount to a maximum of 40% on domestic flights, but discounts of 50%, sometimes even more, are not uncommon at ticket agencies.

Tickets for domestic flights (and international flights) on Chinese airlines are best purchased through a travel agent, such as **Airtrans** (next to the Jianguo Hotel; ✆ 010/6595-2255), or in one of two main ticketing halls: the Aviation Building (Minhang Dalou; ✆ **010/6601-7755;** fax 010/6601-7585; 24 hr.) at Xi Chang'an Jie 15, just east of the Xidan metro station; or at the Airlines Ticketing Hall (Minhang Yingye Dating; ✆ **010/8402-8198;** fax 010/6401-5307; 8am–8:30pm), at Dong Si Bei Dajie 394. Both ticketing halls accept credit cards and offer discounts similar to those of an agent.

Ctrip and eLong are two companies that offer excellent prices on domestic and international tickets through their online websites www.english.ctrip.com and www.elong.net. You can book flights online and pay for tickets in cash upon delivery. You can also pay by credit card (expect a 3%–5% surcharge) after faxing through a credit card authorization form. If you hate the internet, both companies have English-speaking agents that can walk you through the booking and payment process.

Booking from overseas via websites offering tickets for Chinese domestic flights, most of which do not appear on international ticketing systems, is *always* a mistake. You'll nearly always be charged the full price (which is generally only paid by a handful of people traveling at peak times at the last minute), and probably a booking fee, too.

Most hotels can arrange tickets for flights on **foreign airlines,** but they tend to levy hefty service fees. The airline offices themselves do not usually attempt to match the prices offered by agents, but are merely a source of the price to beat elsewhere. Special offers are often published in the monthly expat magazines *that's Beijing* and *Time Out,* but sometimes agents undercut even these, or they bend the rules on advance booking requirements to give an advance-purchase price at the last minute.

BY TRAIN   The main railway stations are **Beijing Railway Station (Beijing Zhan;** *(C)* **010/5182-1114)** and **West Station (Xi Ke Zhan;** schedule information *(C)* **010/ 5182-6253).** Tickets can be purchased at these stations for any train leaving Beijing up to 4 days in advance, and during the busiest seasons up to 10 days in advance. It is possible to buy **round-trip tickets** *(fancheng piao)* to major destinations like Shanghai or Xi'an up to 12 days in advance, subject to availability. There are now 19 brand new **Z trains** directly connecting with other cities, which depart at night and arrive early the following morning. Cities served are: Changchun, Changsha, Harbin, Hangzhou, Hefei, Nanjing, Shanghai (five trains), Suzhou, Wuhan (four trains), Xi'an, and the newly opened railway station in Yangzhou. All compartments are spanking new, and staff is more enthusiastic than on other services. Television screens have been installed in soft-sleeper compartments, which may disturb your night's rest. Tickets for Z trains may be purchased 20 days in advance.

   Satellite ticket offices *(tielu shoupiao chu)* scattered throughout the city charge a negligible ¥5 (65¢/35p) service fee; convenient branches are just inside the main entrance of the Sanhe Baihuo (department store), south of the Xin (Sun) Dong An Plaza on Wangfujing Dajie (9am–9pm); at the Shatan Shoupiao Chu further north at Ping'an Dadao 45, west of Jiaodaokou Nan Dajie (8am–6pm; *(C)* **010/6403-6803**); and at the Gongti Dong Lu Shoupiao Chu (*(C)* **010/6509-3783)** in San Li Tun, opposite and slightly south of the Workers' Stadium east gate. Tickets for all trains from Beijing can also be booked free of charge at Beijing South Station (Beijing Nan Zhan; *(C)* **010/6303-0031)** and at Beijing North Station (Beijing Bei Zhan, *(C)* **010/6223-1003),** which is more conveniently located just north of the Xi Zhi Men metro station. Ordinary travel agents without computers on the railway system will usually also handle rail-ticket bookings. The fee per ticket should be no more than ¥20 ($2.65/ £1.35), including delivery to your hotel, although some agencies like to take foreign visitors for a ride in more than one sense. Ticket desks in hotels may charge up to ¥50 ($6.65/£3.35) per ticket. Mandarin speakers can check train times and book tickets using one of several hot lines (*(C)* **010/9510-5105,** 010/5165-3050, or station numbers below).

   At **Beijing Railway Station (Beijing Zhan;** *(C)* **010/5182-1114),** the best place to pick up tickets is the "ticket office for foreigners" inside the soft-berth waiting room on the ground floor of the main hall, in the far left corner (5:30am–11pm). Tickets for both versions of the **Trans-Siberian,** the Russian K19 via Manchuria (Sat 10:56pm) and the Chinese K3 via Mongolia (Wed 7:40am), must be purchased from the CITS international railway ticket office inside the International Hotel (Mon–Fri 8:30am–noon and 1:30–5pm, weekends 9am–noon and 1:30–4pm; *(C)* **010/6512-0507)** 10 minutes' walk north of the station on Jianguo Men Nei Dajie (metro: Dong Dan). Both trains travel to Moscow for ¥2,512 ($335/£167) soft sleeper, but only the K3 passes through Mongolia and stops in Ulan Batar for ¥845 ($113/£56). There is a separate train, the K23, which goes to Ulan Batar (Sat 7:40am).

   At the **West Station (Xi Ke Zhan;** schedule information *(C)* **010/5182-6253),** the best ticket outlet is not the main ticket hall but a second office inside the main building, on the second floor to the left of the elevators (signposted in English); this is also where you go to purchase tickets for the **T97 express to Kowloon/Jiulong** (Departs daily at noon; 25 hr.; ¥962/$128/£64 soft sleeper, ¥619/$83/£41 hard). The West Station is also the starting point for **trains to Hanoi,** but you have to buy tickets (Departs at 4:15pm Mon and Fri; 34 hr.; ¥1,100/$147/£73 soft sleeper only) at a "travel service" booth (9am–4:30pm; ✆ **010/6398-9485**) inside the Construction Bank on the east side of the station complex. The nearest **airport shuttle** stops at the Aviation Building in Xidan (see above), reachable by bus no. 52 from the station's east side. The taxi rank is on the second floor.

Warning: Larger baggage is X-rayed at the entrances to most Chinese railway and bus stations. Keep film in your hand baggage.

VISITOR INFORMATION

The Beijing Tourism Administration maintains a 24-hour **tourist information hot line** at ✆ **010/6513-0828.** Staff actually speak some English, so it's unfortunate that they rarely have the answers to your questions, and simply refer you on to CITS. Hotel concierges and guest relations officers are at least close at hand, although they often have little knowledge of the city, will be reluctant to work to find the answers if they can convince you to do something else instead, and, when they do find the answer to a question, they do not note it down for the next time a guest asks. Beware of strong recommendations to visit dinner shows or other expensive entertainments, as they are often on a kickback.

You can also try the new BTA-managed **Beijing Tourist Information Centers (Beijing Shi Luyou Zixun Fuwu Zhongxin)** located in each district and all marked with the same aqua-blue signs. The most competent branch is in Chaoyang, on Gongti Bei Lu across from the City Hotel and next to KFC (✆ **010/6417-6627;** fax 010/6417-6656; cylyxx@163.com; daily 9am–5pm). Free maps are available at the door, and staff can sometimes be wheedled into making phone calls. Ignore the extortionist travel service.

For the most current information on life in Beijing, particularly restaurants and nightlife, see the intermittently accurate listings in the free English-language expat-produced monthlies *that's Beijing* or *Time Out* (largely translated from a vastly superior Chinese language magazine), available in hotel lobbies and at bars in the major drinking districts (see chapter 10 for these). Online, *City Weekend* (www.cityweekend.com.cn) manages to update its website with fair regularity. The e-mail newsletter *Xianzai Beijing* (see www.xianzai.com for more information) provides a list of each week's events, as well as special hotel, air ticket, and restaurant offers.

CITY LAYOUT & HISTORY

Modern Beijing stands on the site of the capital founded in 1271 by the Mongols, when the territory of modern-day China was merely a part of a far larger Mongol empire. Known to the Mongols as Khanbalik and to their Chinese subjects as Da Du or "Great Capital," it lay on a plain with limited and bitter water supplies, handy for the steppe from which the Mongols had emerged, but well away from the heartlands of the Han, as the main ethnic Chinese group still call themselves. When, in 1368, the Mongol Yuan dynasty was expelled, the foreigner-founded capital was abandoned for Nanjing, the "Southern Capital." The third Ming emperor, who had formerly been in charge of resisting fresh Mongol advances from the north, returned the city to capital status in 1420, renaming it Beijing, or "Northern Capital."

Although retaining much of the plan and grid of the Mongol founders, the emperor remodeled the city extensively, creating a secondary, broader walled extension to the south of the Mongol original. Many of the capital's major monuments date from this period, and its most extensive, the Forbidden City, right at the city's heart, is the one around which the remainder of the capital is still more or less arranged. The key ceremonial halls lie on a nearly north–south axis (actually aligned on the Pole Star), which bisects the city. Most north–south streets parallel this, and main east–west routes cross them at right angles. There are very few major streets running diagonally. The grid created was originally filled in with a maze of lanes peculiar to Beijing and to a handful of other northern cities, called *hutong* (both singular and plural), derived from a Mongol word. But most of these narrow streets have now been destroyed.

In 1644 the Ming dynasty was overthrown by a peasant rebellion, and the peasants were driven out shortly afterwards by invading Manchu forces from beyond the Great Wall to the northeast. China was absorbed into the Qing empire, and foreigners ruled from Beijing until the Qing abdication of 1912. Including occupation by foreign forces in 1860 and from 1900 to 1901, and Japanese occupation during World War II, Beijing has been under foreign control for more than half of its existence.

Beijing was once a set of walls within walls. The Qing took over the walled Forbidden City and the walled Imperial City within which it sat, and their followers took over the remainder of the northern section of the walled city. This area was known to other foreigners as the Tartar City, while the broader but separate walled section to the south of the Qian Men (Front Gate) became the Chinese City—the Chinese quarter of Beijing.

The enemy was now within the gates, and the outer city walls were neglected, but the Qing built many temples and palaces, leaving the city's basic grid largely unchanged while building extensive gardens to the northwest.

With the exception of a limited number of Russians and small groups of missionaries, some of whom were allowed to erect churches, Beijing remained free of Western influence or a Western presence until 1860, when emissaries sent to complete ratification of a treaty forced on the Qing at the end of the Second Opium War by the British and French were put to death or imprisoned. British troops, led by Lord Elgin, torched the vast area of palaces and gardens to the northwest of the city, of which now only fragments remain at the Summer Palace and Old Summer Palace. French troops opposed razing such magnificent buildings, and were content simply to loot them.

For the first time, Western powers were allowed to station ministers in Beijing, and accommodation was allocated to them just inside the Tartar City, east of the Qian Men and what is now Tian'an Men Square. At the end of the 19th century, resentment at the expansion of foreign influence in China led to attacks on Chinese who had converted to Christianity, destruction of railway lines and foreign property, and eventually to a siege of the Legation Quarter during which the attackers razed much of the surrounding housing, a fabulous library of ancient learning, and part of the Qian Men. The siege was only lifted 2 months and many deaths later by the forces of eight allied powers who marched from the coast. Imperial troops, Boxers, Beijing residents, and foreign troops indulged in an orgy of looting and destruction, which supplemented the burning of shops selling foreign goods and the destruction of churches already accomplished by the Boxers. The Legation Quarter subsequently became a further walled enclave, with many foreign banks, offices, and legation (embassy) buildings. In the early 20th century it was still the only area with paved roads and proper drainage and sewerage in an otherwise notably malodorous city.

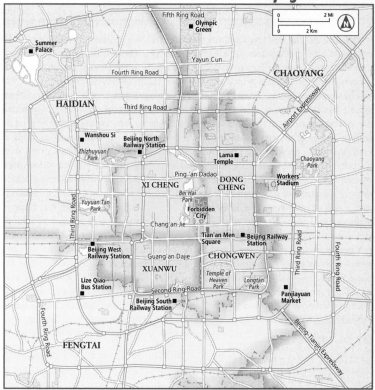

The churches were rebuilt (and still stand), but the temples that had been collateral damage were mostly left in ruins. The Qing were in decline, and after their fall in 1912, much else went into decline, too; ancient buildings being the victims of neglect or casual destruction. This process continued during the 1911/1912 to 1949 Republic and accelerated following the Communist Party victory and the creation of the People's Republic of China.

Signs at the Old Summer Palace and elsewhere harp on foreign destruction in 1860 and 1900, but since 1949 the Chinese themselves have almost completely demolished their city. Temples have been turned into housing, warehouses, industrial units, offices, and police stations. The slender, walled space south of the Tian'an Men was smashed open to create the vast expanse of the modern square, lined by hideous Soviet-influenced halls of rapidly down-at-heel grandeur. The city walls and most gate towers were pulled down to allow the construction of the Second Ring Road and the first metro line. Areas of traditional courtyard houses were pulverized for the construction of shabby six-story concrete dormitory blocks. Political campaigns against all traditional culture led to the defacing, damage, or destruction of many ancient buildings and their contents, particularly during the 1966 to 1976 Cultural Revolution.

The *hutong*, once "numberless as the hairs on an ox," will soon be no harder to count than your fingers and toes, because China's increasing wealth has seen the government trying to turn the capital from a sleepy backwater into a city of international standing. The broad boulevards apparently required by Marxist theory have become ever more numerous, and the last few years have seen several new routes blasted across the city. An assortment of often hideous towers representing no particular style or culture but sometimes with cheesy Chinese toppings have sprung up within the vanished city walls, dwarfing the Forbidden City and the few older buildings which remain.

The awarding of the 2008 Olympics to Beijing has delivered the coup de grâce. Whole blocks of housing disappear every few weeks as developers, hand-in-glove with the government, expel residents. Developers race to destroy the remaining halls of ancient and largely forgotten temples before those charged with preserving them can catch up, although a few are given ham-fisted restoration and reopened to the public for a fee. A third, fourth, fifth, and now a sixth ring road have dropped like nooses around the neck of the old city center, inevitably leading to road-widening schemes through the heart of the remaining *hutong*. Demolition of the ancient Da Zhalan district is well advanced, and the latest scheme is to widen De Sheng Men Nei Dajie into a 50m-wide (164-ft.) road, which will plunge right through the heart of the Back Lakes area. The authorities are determined that by 2008 we should be impressed by the city's modernity, and all but the basic grid of the Yuan and Ming plan will have been swept away for shiny towers and gridlock. The most noticeable buildings will be those most alien to China—a three-venue National Grand Theatre resembling a flying saucer which has landed in a lake, under construction in the heart of the city just west of Tian'an Men Square and designed by Frenchman Paul Andreu; and the vast venues for the Beijing Olympics including the $100-million National Swimming Center.

MAIN STREETS

The main west-to-east artery of interest to visitors runs across the top of Tian'an Men Square, past the Tian'an Men (Gate of Heavenly Peace) itself. It changes names several times, but is most importantly Xi Chang'an Jie to the west of the square, Dong Chang'an Jie to the east, then Jianguo Men Nei Dajie until it crosses the Second Ring Road, when it becomes Jianguo Men Wai Dajie. Compass points such as *xi* (west) and *dong* (east) turn up very frequently in street names, as do words such as *men* (gate), *nei* (inside), and *wai* (outside). Metro Line 1 runs under this route, passing several major hotels and shopping areas. The Xi Dan Bei Dajie and Wangfujing Dajie shopping streets run north from this route. The Second Ring Road runs around the combined outer perimeter of the old city walls they replaced, still showing the bulge of the wider Chinese City to the south and, depending on the time of day, usually provides a quicker route around the city center than going though it. Further out and quicker still, the Third Ring Road, which links with the airport expressway and routes to the Summer Palace, is the site of several major long-distance bus stations, numerous upmarket joint-venture hotels, and important restaurants. Beware the taxi driver who suggests using the Fourth or Fifth Ring Roads. Speeds on these routes are higher, but the kilometer count for getting round the city will also be significantly greater, and so will the cost.

FINDING AN ADDRESS

Maps of Beijing are rarely accurate—the cartographers don't seem to feel it necessary to do more than sketch the main roads—and the smashing of new routes across and around the city is so rapid they can't keep up. Although some claim to issue half a dozen editions a year, the presence of *zui xin* or "newest" on the map cover is only an indication that the characters *zui xin* have been put on the cover. Bilingual maps, or maps with Romanized Chinese, tend to be less accurate to start with, and are printed less often. Regardless of this, **always buy a map,** available from vendors at all arrival points and at all bookstores, for around ¥5 (65¢/35p). The small pages of this book cannot give you a detailed picture of any area, but the characters on the maps, map keys, and in the text of chapters 5 and 6 can be used to help you find your way around the Chinese map. The staff at your hotel can mark where you are and where you want to go, and you can compare the street-name characters with those on the road signs so you can keep track of your route. There's no question of really getting lost, and you can always flag down a cab and show the driver the characters for where you want to go. Street numbers are given in this book: odd numbers indicate the north or west side of the street, while an even-numbered residence will be on the south or east side, but otherwise no one uses them. Navigation is by street name and landmark.

NEIGHBORHOODS IN BRIEF

Citywide architectural uniformity makes the boundaries of Beijing's official districts rather arbitrary, so we've avoided them in favor of maps showing in more detail the areas of most interest to visitors for their clusters of accommodations, restaurants, and attractions. Beyond the districts listed below, the metropolitan area stretches far into the countryside, adding perhaps another five million people to the urban population of around 10 million.

Dong Cheng

Dong Cheng (East City) occupies the eastern half of the city center, spreading north and east from the southwest corner of Tian'an Men Square until it reaches the Second Ring Road, and occasionally spills over it. It includes the square itself, the Forbidden City, major temples such as the Yong He Gong (Lama Temple) and Confucius Temple, and the major shopping streets of Wangfujing and Dong Dan. It's essentially the eastern half of the Qing-era Tartar City, north of the wall separating it from the Chinese City, of which the twin towers of the Qian Men (Front Gate) are the most significant remaining fragments.

Xi Cheng

The western half of the old Tartar City, Xi Cheng spreads farther west beyond the line of the original city wall at the Second Ring Road. It is home to Zhong Nan Hai, the off-limits central government compound otherwise known as the new Forbidden City, Bei Hai Gongyuan, and the Bai Ta Si (White Dagoba Temple). The Shicha Hai (Back

Lakes) and Di'an Men area within Xi Cheng, with its string of lakes and relatively well-preserved *hutong*, is where the last fading ghosts of (pre-1949) Old Beijing reside. It's popular among writers, musicians, foreigners teaching in Beijing, and other younger expatriates who haunt a collection of trendy, nameless bars and cafes at the waters' edge. Several minor sights here provide the excuse for a day's wandering.

Chaoyang

Part urban, part suburban, Chaoyang sprawls in a huge arc around the northeast and eastern sides of the city, housing the two main diplomatic compounds (and a third new one on the way), the San Li Tun and Chaoyang drinking districts, and the newly coined CBD (Central Business District) around the China World Trade Center. This is the richest district in Beijing, the result, according to some, of the district's good *fengshui*.

The South

If Chaoyang has Beijing's best *fengshui*, the old Chinese City south of the Qian

Men, made up of Chongwen (east) and Xuanwu (west), both enclosed by the suburban sprawl of Fengtai to the south and southwest, has the worst. Squalid since its construction in the Ming dynasty, this is where you'll find the city's grittiest *hutong* and some of its best bargains on fake antiques, as well as Ming architectural jewels such as the Temple of Heaven (Tian Tan).

Haidian and Yayun Cun

Sprawling to the northwest, Haidian is the university and high-tech district, referred to hopefully in local media as "China's Silicon Valley" and home to the Summer Palace. Directly north of town is Yayun Cun (Asia Games Village), home to Beijing's best new Chinese restaurants, and site of many Olympic venues.

2 Getting Around

The major street layouts in Beijing are often well planned: sidewalk for pedestrians, a fenced-off bike lane, two lanes for cars, another bike lane, and then sidewalk again. This is one of the benefits of the hideous boulevardization, or would be if only the inhabitants used these layouts properly. However, cars are parked on the pavement, usually at an angle so as to drive pedestrians into the bike lanes, and even pushbikes are usually parked so as to cause quite unnecessary obstruction to pedestrians. So the pedestrians are forced to get in the way of the cyclists, who are anyway going in both directions in the lanes on each side of the road, as well as along the edges of the lanes for cars, often in the wrong direction. Meanwhile, cars come along the bike lanes, also often in the wrong direction, so as to get access to the pavements and drive at a few pedestrians before parking.

Although residents quickly become inured to all this madness, and although if visitors use taxis and buses they are unlikely to get injured, they'll certainly see a few accidents and injuries. The best way to get around the city is by metro or by taxi, or often by a combination of the two.

BY METRO

The Beijing metro system *(ditie)* is undergoing a process of rapid expansion. This is leading to traffic snarls at ground level, which make using the existing four lines (two underground, two light rail or *chengtie*) essential. Although other cities have involved foreign companies in the construction of up-to-date rolling stock, Beijing seems to have stuck to a locally made product, which is slow and squeaky. And whereas other cities have switched to modern electronic gates to read your ticket, Beijing has stuck with a paper ticket system and lots of staff to check the tickets.

Eventually there will be 15 metro and light-rail lines, but for now the system consists of the **Circle Line** (sometimes known as **Line 2**), which follows the upper portion of the Second Ring Road, cutting across under Qian Men, effectively following the line of the Tartar City walls that were demolished to make its construction possible (the Dongnan Jiaolou, home to the Red Gate Gallery, was spared because the metro takes a turn at that point). **Line 1** runs from Pingguo Yuan in the west, the site of Capital Iron and Steel and other heavy industry which are the sources of much of Beijing's pollution, right across town beneath Chang'an Jie and its extensions to Si Hui Dōng in the east. **Line 8** extends Line 1 into the eastern suburbs. The light-rail **Line 13** swings in a suburban loop to the north, from the Circle Line's Xi Zhi Men to Dong Zhi Men stations. Several other lines, such as north–south **Line 5**, and one to the airport, should be completed by the time you read this. Stations are numbered (see Beijing metro map), signs on platforms tell you which station is the next in each direction, and English announcements are made on trains, so navigation is not difficult.

For now, ticket booths are below ground, and a ticket costs ¥3 (40¢/20p) for a ride anywhere from any Circle Line or Line 1 station to any other on those two lines, with free interchange. Because there's a fair bit of pushing and shoving at the ticket counters, buy a few tickets at one time (just hold up a number of fingers), but note that the two lines have different colored tickets, and you must use the right color as you start your journey. A ticket allowing you to start from or switch to Line 13, a *huancheng piao*, is ¥5 (65¢/35p), ¥4 (55¢/25p) for Line 8. Alternatively, you can buy an electronic card that can be used for subway and bus rides. The metro card, officially known as the "Municipal Administration and Communication Card" (Shizheng Jiaotong Yikatong) can be bought for a ¥40 ($5.35/£2.65) minimum, including ¥20 ($2.65/£1.35) for deposit.

Entrances are not clearly marked. Find them on maps, marked with a D (for *ditie*) in a circle, and look for the same sign at entrances. Escalators are up only, staircases are long, and there are no elevators. Those with limited mobility should stay on the surface.

BY TAXI

Beijing's rapid conversion from a city for bicycles to one for cars has brought the inevitable traffic jams. Get on the road well before 7:30am to beat the rush, or forget it until about 10am. The city's arteries start to clog again about 3pm, and circulation slows to a crawl until 7:30pm. Take the metro to the point nearest your destination and jump in a cab from there.

By the time you reach Beijing, the cheap but poorly air-conditioned **Xiali** rattletraps should be a thing of the past. There are now essentially two fare types available, with their per-kilometer rates posted on the side window.

The red **Fukang,** a Citroën joint-venture built in Wuhan on the Yangzi River, are slightly older than the green or yellow **Xiandai** (Hyundai, a Beijing-based joint venture). The Xiandai have better air-conditioning and are much roomier. Both have an initial charge of ¥10 ($1.35/65p) which includes 3km (2 miles), and each subsequent kilometer is ¥2 (25¢/15p), ¥3 (40¢/20p) after 15 kilometers.

There are a mix of old and new **Santana** and **Jetta** cabs built in various Volkswagen joint ventures around China. They're similar to popular Volkswagen models in the West and are equally solid. Occasionally, there are larger vehicles charging as much as ¥3 (40¢/20p) per kilometer. Some of these have dodgy meters and hang around larger hotels where corrupt bellhops call them for you. Always follow the advice in the box "Ten Tips for Taking Taxis Around Town," below.

All taxis are metered. But on the front of the meter they also have a button, for one-way trips out of town, which is pushed regardless of the type of trip to be taken. This causes the rate per kilometer to increase by 50% after 15km (9 miles). If you are hiring the vehicle to take you somewhere, wait, and bring you back, or to run you around town all day, then you should insist that the button is not pushed. As elsewhere in the world, the meter also ticks over slowly when the vehicle is stationary or moving very slowly.

Between 11pm and 5am the meter starts at ¥11 ($1.45/75p) and rates increase to ¥2.40 (30¢/15p) per kilometer, ¥3.40 (45¢/25p) after 15 kilometers.

Consider taking taxis for **trips out of town.** Your hotel's transport department would love for you to take one of their cars for the day—and they would love to separate you from up to ¥1,200 ($160/£80) for a trip you can bargain for yourself for ¥400 ($53/£27), which is what most drivers take in each day. Even after overhead, this

Tips   Ten Tips for Taking Taxis Around Town

1. **Never** go with a driver who approaches you at the airport (or railway stations). Leave the building and head for the rank. As with everywhere else in the world, airport taxis are the most likely to cause trouble. Drivers who approach you are usually *hei che*—illegal and meterless "black cabs."
2. Cabs waiting for business outside major tourist sights, especially those whose drivers call out to foreigners, should be avoided, as should cabs whose drivers ask you where you want to go before you even get in. Always flag down a passing cab, and nine times in ten the precautions listed here will be unnecessary.
3. If you're staying in an upmarket hotel, do not go with taxis called by the doorman or waiting in line outside. Even at some famous hotels, drivers pay kickbacks to the doormen to allow them to join the line on the forecourt. Some cabs are merely waiting because many guests, Chinese and foreign alike, will be out-of-town people who can be easily misled. Instead, flag down a passing cab for yourself. Take the hotel's business card to show to a taxi driver when you want to get back.
4. Better hotels give you a piece of paper with the taxi registration number on it as you board or alight, so that you can complain if something goes wrong. Often you won't know if it has, of course, and there's no guarantee that anything will happen if you complain to the hotel, but hang onto it anyway.
5. Look to see if the supervision card, usually with a photo of the driver and a telephone number, is prominently displayed, as regulations require. If it isn't, you may have problems. Choose another cab.

puts them well above the average Beijing resident in income, but they often work 12 hours a day, 7 days a week to obtain it, and the vehicle often works 24 hours, with a separate driver on the night shift. They are also squeezed by the taxi companies. So a trip out of town is a welcome change, and better than spending much of the day cruising the city empty. But the rate you pay should be well under the official per-kilometer rate, and a price should be negotiated. Again, deal with drivers stopped at random and not those targeting foreigners or better hotels, and begin getting quotes the day before you want to travel. The lack of a common language need not deter you, as long as you have the characters for the name of your destination and can write down the start and return times. Prices can be negotiated using pen and paper or a calculator. ¥400 ($53/£27) for a round-trip of around 200km (124 miles) is fine. You should also be prepared to pay road tolls and parking fees (probably in total no more than about ¥60/$8/£4), and it's a nice gesture to buy the driver lunch.

BY BUS

Unless you are on the tightest of backpacker budgets and are traveling alone, your first choice for getting around town is the metro, your second choice is taxi, and your last resort should be the bus, although the introduction of dedicated bus lanes will make them more appealing. Most buses have conductors who'll need to know your

6. Can you clearly see the meter? If it's recessed behind the gear stick, or partly hidden by an artfully folded towel, for example, choose another cab.

7. Always make sure you see the meter reset. If you didn't see the flag pushed down, which shouldn't happen until you actually move off, then you may end up paying for the time the cab was in the rank. This is a particularly popular scam outside better hotels.

8. If you are by yourself, sit in the front seat. Have a map with you and look as if you know where you are going (even if you don't).

9. Rates per kilometer are clearly posted on the side of the cab and vary by vehicle type. The flag drop of ¥10 ($1.35/65p) includes 2km (1¼ miles), after which the standard kilometer rate begins. But in Beijing, after 15km (9 miles), the rate jumps by 50% if the driver has pushed the "one-way" button on the front of the meter. This button is for one-way trips out of town and usually should not be pushed, but always is. As a result, it's rarely worthwhile to have a cab wait for you with the meter running and take you back.

10. Pay what's on the meter, and don't tip—the driver will insist on giving change. Always ask for a receipt *(fa piao)*. Should you leave something in a cab, there's a remarkably high success rate at getting even valuable items back if you call the number on the receipt and provide the details. You'll need the assistance of a Mandarin speaker.

destination in order to work out how much to charge. Sometimes fees are payable into a slot at the front of the bus with no change given. Regular buses charge a flat fare of ¥1 (15¢/5p), while air-conditioned buses charge ¥2 (25¢/15p) and up. Entrance and exit doors are marked with the *shang* and *xia* characters respectively (see appendix B).

BY PEDICAB
Unless you are competent in Mandarin and obviously familiar with the city, a ride in a pedicab will always end in grief, and arguments over the agreed fare ("No! Thirty *dollars!*"). A taxi is cheaper, quicker, and less stressful, and it won't make you look like an idiot tourist.

BY BICYCLE
There used to be considerable charm in being one fish in a vast shoal of bicycles, but cycling is now ill-advised for the timid (or sensibly cautious). But enthusiasts for two-wheeled travel will certainly find that at some times of day they can get around more quickly than anyone else. Many upmarket hotels will rent you a bicycle for around ¥80 to ¥100 ($11–$13/£5.35–£6.65) for the day, however a *new* bike may be purchased for as little as ¥130 ($17/£8.65), so if you're going to be using a bike for a few days, buying one is a better deal. Don't expect sophisticated accessories such as gears on rental

bikes or bikes purchased for these prices. Flat Beijing does not require them anyway. Budget accommodations and some bike enclosures next to metro stops charge a more appropriate ¥10 ($1.35/65p) for the day. Check the bike's condition carefully, especially the brakes and tires. Sidewalk bicycle-repair operations are everywhere and will make repairs for a few yuan, if worst comes to worst. Always park the bike in marked and supervised enclosures, using the lock, which is built in or provided, or expect the bike to be gone when you get back. The parking fee is usually ¥0.20 (3¢/1p).

ON FOOT

The vast width of Beijing's boulevards makes maps deceiving. Blocks are long, and everything is farther away than it seems. Save your feet for getting around temples, palaces, and markets, which can be very extensive, or for the walking routes in chapter 8. Use pedestrian underpasses and footbridges wherever available, or be prepared to adopt the matador approach of the locals, letting cars sweep past you to either side as you wait for the opportunity to cross to the next lane. Traffic turning right at lights does not give way to pedestrians, nor does any other traffic unless forced to do so by large groups of people bunching up to cross the road.

BY CAR

The rule of the road is "me first," regardless of signs, traffic lights, road markings, safety considerations, or common sense, unless someone with an ability to fine or demand a bribe is watching. In general, the bigger your vehicle, the more authority you have. Maximum selfishness in the face of common sense characterizes driving in general, and there is no maneuver so ludicrous or unexpected that someone will not attempt it. Residents have time to adapt—visitors do not. Our strong advice is to forget it, and take a taxi.

FAST FACTS: Beijing

Airport See "Arriving" under "Orientation" at the beginning of this chapter.

American Express Beijing: Room 2313–14, China World Tower 1, China World Trade Center; ✆ 010/6505-2639. After hours: U.S. hot line ✆ 001336/668-6809. Emergency card replacement: 00852/1220-62796. Stolen traveler's checks: 010800/744-0106 (toll-free).

Area Codes In mainland China, area codes begin with a zero, which must be dropped when calling China from abroad. The whole area code can be dropped when calling another number in the same area.

Babysitters Babysitting services are widely available in hotels but are usually carried out by regular members of the housekeeping staff. Don't expect special qualifications, but do expect your children to be spoiled rotten.

Banks, Currency Exchanges & ATMs Larger branches of the **Bank of China** typically exchange cash and traveler's checks on weekdays only, from 9am to 4pm, occasionally with a break for lunch (11:30am–1:30pm). Most central is the branch at the bottom of Wangfujing Dajie, next to the Oriental Plaza. Other useful branches include those at Fucheng Men Nei Dajie 410; on Jianguo Men Wai Dajie, west of the Scitech Building; in the Lufthansa Center, next to the Kempinski Hotel; and in Tower 1 of the China World Trade Center. Outside the airport, Bank of China **ATMs** accepting international cards 24 hours a day are now widespread, and include those outside the Wangfujing Dajie branch mentioned above. Others exist farther north on Wangfujing Dajie, outside the Xin (Sun) Dong An Plaza; on the left just inside the Pacific Century Plaza on Gongti Bei Lu east of San Li Tun (only 9am–9pm); and adjacent to the Bank of China branch next to the Scitech Building (see above; also 24 hr.). The Citibank ATM east of the International Hotel, and the Hongkong and Shanghai Bank machine at the entrance to COFCO Plaza, roughly opposite each other on Jianguo Men Nei Dajie, are Beijing's most reliable. There are also six ATMs at the airport. See "Money" in chapter 2 for further details on using ATMs.

Books   The best selection of English-language books in Beijing can be found at the clearly marked **Foreign Languages Bookstore** (Waiwen Shudian; 9am–8:30pm) at Wangfujing Dajie 235, opposite the Xin (Sun) Dong An Plaza. Look on the right side of the first floor for China-related nonfiction, glossy *hutong* photo books, cookbooks, the full range of Asiapac's cartoon renditions of Chinese classics, and even Frommer's guides. Cheap paperback versions of a huge chunk of the English canon, as well as a number of contemporary works, are sold on the third floor. **The Bookworm** (p. 195) in San Li Tun carries a smaller but more daring collection of fiction, and also houses Beijing's most intriguing library of English-language materials. They also have an extensive selection of US and UK magazines. **Charterhouse** in megamall The Place has a large, but rather random selection of English-language books. They have plenty of travel guides and a decent selection of international magazines.

Business Hours   Offices are generally open 9am to 6pm, but closed Saturday and Sunday. All shops, sights, restaurants, and transport systems offer the same service 7 days a week. Shops are typically open at least 8am to 8pm. Bank opening hours vary (see "Banks, Currency Exchanges & ATMs" above).

Car Rentals   Because of the many driving hazards in Beijing, renting a car is not recommended for visitors. Taking taxis is cheaper and easier. If you must, **Hertz** (www.hertz.net.cn) has offices inside the Lufthansa Center (✆ 010/6462-5730) and the Zuo Jia Zhuang (✆ 010/8454-1868), open 9am to 7pm weekdays, 9am to 5pm on weekends. Daily rates start from ¥320 ($43/£21) per day for Jettas, and free mileage is restricted to 180km (112 miles) per day (300km/186 miles for Hertz members). **Avis** (16, 1/F 1 Dongzhimen Nei Dajie; ✆ 010/8406-3343) is another good option. For a cheap local rental company, try **Beijing Shou Qi Zuhuo Youxian Zeren Gongsi** (4 Chui Yang Liu Zhong Jie; ✆ 010/6775-0039). The big snag is that a Chinese driver's license and a residence permit is required, something no short-term visitor will be able to arrange. Your passport, a business card, and a whopping ¥20,000 ($2,667/£1,333) credit card deposit are required the first time you rent a vehicle. The fleet is fairly battered (locals rent cars when learning to drive), and it's often difficult to obtain a vehicle on weekends.

Currency   See "Money" in chapter 2.

Doctors & Dentists   For comprehensive care, the best choice is **Beijing United Family Hospital** (Hemujia Yiyuan; ✆ 010/6433-3960) at Jiangtai Lu (2 blocks southeast of the Holiday Inn Lido); it is open 24 hours, is staffed with foreign-trained doctors, and has a pharmacy, dental clinic, in- and out-patient care, and ambulance service. Other reputable health-service providers, both with 24-hour ambulance services, are the **International Medical Center** ((C) 010/6465-1561), inside the Lufthansa Center; and the **International SOS Clinic and Alarm Center** ((C) 010/6492-9111), in Building C of the BITIC Leasing Center.

Driving Rules "I'm bigger than you, so get out of my way," sums it up. See "By Car" above.

Drugstores Bring supplies of your favorite over-the-counter medicines with you, as supplies of well-known Western brands are unreliable and sometimes fake. The real thing can be found in the lobbies of international five-star hotels. Better still, branches of **Watson's** (on the first floor of Full Link Plaza at Chaoyang Men Wai Dajie 19, 10:30am–9:30pm; and in the basement of the Oriental Plaza at the bottom of Wangfujing Dajie 1, 10am–10pm) stock most common remedies and toiletries, mostly in the British versions. For more specific drugs, try the pharmacy in the Beijing United Family Hospital or the International SOS Clinic (see "Doctors & Dentists" above).

Electricity The electricity used in all parts of China is 220 volts, alternating current (AC), 50 cycles. Most devices from North America, therefore, cannot be used without a transformer. The most common outlet takes the North American two-flat-pin plug (but not the three-pin version, or those with one pin broader than the other). Nearly as common are outlets for the two-round-pin plugs common in Europe. Outlets for the three-flat-pin (two pins at an angle) used in Australia, for instance, are also frequently seen. Most hotel rooms have all three, and indeed many outlets are designed to take all three plugs. Adapters are available for only ¥8 to ¥17 ($1.05–$2.25/55p–£1.15) in department stores. Shaver sockets are common in bathrooms of hotels from three stars upwards. British-style three-chunky-pin plugs also often occur in mainland joint-venture hotels built with Hong Kong assistance, but hotels of this caliber will have adapters available.

Embassies & Consulates Beijing has two main embassy areas—one surrounding Ritan Gongyuan north of Jianguo Men Wai Dajie, and another in San Li Tun north of Gongti Bei Lu. A third district, future home of the new U.S. Embassy, has sprouted up next to the Hilton Hotel outside the north section of the East Third Ring Road. Embassies are typically open Monday through Friday from 9am to between 4 and 5pm, with a lunch break from noon to 1:30pm. The **U.S. Embassy** is due to move in 2008, but for now it's in Ritan at Xiushui Dong Jie 2 ((C) 010/6532-3431 or, after hours, 010/6532-1910; fax 010/6532-4153). The **Canadian Embassy** is at Dong Zhi Men Wai Dajie 19 ((C) 010/6532-3536; bejing-cs@ international.gc.ca). The **British Embassy** consular section is in Ritan at Floor 21, North Tower, Kerry Centre, Guanghua Lu 1 ((C) 010/8529-6600, ext. 3363; fax 010/8529-6081). The **Australian Embassy** is in San Li Tun at Dong Zhi Men Wai Dajie 21 ((C) 010/5140-4111; fax 010/6532-4605). The **New Zealand Embassy** is in Ritan at Dong Er Jie 1 ((C) 010/6532-2731, ext. 220; fax 010/6532-4317).

Emergencies No one speaks English on emergency numbers in China, although your best bet will be (C) **110**. Find help nearer at hand.

Etiquette & Customs **Appropriate attire:** Wear whatever you find comfortable. Some of the diaphanous or apparently spray-on dressing of younger women is more likely to surprise you than your attire will surprise them. Foreigners are stared at regardless of what they wear. Swimwear should tend towards the conservative by Western standards—shorts rather than briefs for men, swimsuits rather than bikinis for women—but not if you are using pools in deluxe hotels with plenty of foreign guests. Business attire is similar to that of the West. For most visitors, opportunities to dress up formally are few, and there are no restaurants or hotels absolutely requiring jacket or tie.

Greetings and gestures: The handshake is now used as it is in the West, although there's a tendency to hang on longer. Bring business cards if you have them, as an exchange of cards almost always follows. Present yours with two hands, and then hold the one you're given with two hands. If you can speak even two words of Mandarin, you will be told that you speak very well. But even if you are fluent, this is something you should deny.

Avoiding offense: However great the provocation, do not lose your temper and shout at someone in public or cause them to experience public shame (loss of face). Even flatly contradicting someone in front of others (so he loses face) is also best avoided if harmony is to be maintained. Instead, complain calmly and privately, and directly to a superior if you wish. Punctuality is very important in China, and the traffic situation in most cities makes that difficult, so allow plenty of time.

Eating and drinking: Master the use of chopsticks before you go. Suggestions that the food is lacking in some way, made by the host, should always be greeted with firm denials. Serve yourself from main dishes using the spoon provided, then eat with chopsticks. Do not leave them sticking up out of your bowl. Your cup of tea will constantly be topped up—when you want no more, leave it full. There's a great deal of competitive drinking at banquets, which is done by the simultaneous drinking of toasts in *bai jiu* (Chinese spirits), to cries of *"Gan bei!"* ("dry cup"—down in one). Avoid participation by drinking beer or mineral water instead, but if toasts of welcome are made, be sure to make one in reply. Dining tends to happen early, and at the end of the meal everyone disappears quickly. If you are invited to eat at someone's home, be sure to take off your shoes at the entrance (your host's protestations that it's not necessary are merely polite).

Holidays See "Holidays" under "When to Go" in chapter 2.

Hot Lines Hot lines and all kinds of telephone booking and information numbers are given throughout this book. But in almost no cases will English be spoken at the other end. Ask English-speaking staff at your hotel to find answers to your questions and to make any necessary calls on your behalf.

Information See "Visitor Information" earlier in this chapter.

Internet Access Internet bars in Beijing are subject to numerous regulations (no one under 18, no smoking) and are restricted in number. The best bet for affordable Internet access is any of the city's various **youth hostels**; the cost is usually ¥10 ($1.35/65p) per hour. There are two conveniently located Internet bars on the third floor of the Lao Che Zhan (Old Train Station) shopping center next to Qian Men. **Qianyi Wangluo Kafeiwu** (© **010/6705-1722**) is open from 9:30am to 11pm and charges ¥20 ($2.65/£1.35) per hour in a cafe setting with a full coffee menu. A simpler, nameless place next door, open from 9am to midnight, charges ¥6 (80¢/40p) per hour. **Moko Internet Cafe (Moke Wangba; ℂ 010/6252-3712)** on Dong Si Dajie, just south of the Dong Si Mosque, is open from 8am to midnight. Rates are ¥10 ($1.35/65p) per hour downstairs, ¥4 (55¢/25p) upstairs, or free for the first hour if you spend ¥12 ($1.60/80p) in the cafe. The basement of East Gate Plaza, just south of Oriental Kenzo on Dong Zhong Jie (metro: Dong Zhi Men, exit C) houses **Yuntian Wangluo (ℂ 010/6418-5815)** open 8am to 10pm, ¥4 (55¢/25p) per hour.

Language   English is rare in Beijing. If you're staying at a reputable five-star hotel, use their well-trained, English-speaking staff to help you with phone calls and bookings. Almost no information, booking, complaint, or emergency lines in Beijing have anyone who speaks English.

Legal Aid   If you get on the wrong side of what passes for the law in China, contact your consulate immediately.

Liquor Laws   With the exception of some minor local regulations, there are no liquor laws in Beijing. Alcohol can be bought in any convenience store, supermarket, restaurant, bar, hotel, or club, 7 days a week, and may be drunk anywhere you feel like drinking it. If the shop is open 24 hours, then the alcohol is available 24 hours, too. Closing times for bars and clubs vary according to demand, but typically it's all over by 3am.

Lost & Found   Be sure to contact all of your credit card companies the minute you discover your wallet has been lost or stolen. Your credit card company or insurer may require a police report number or record of the loss, although many Public Security Bureaus (police stations) will be reluctant to do anything as energetic as lift a pen. Most credit card companies have an emergency toll-free number to call if your card is lost or stolen: In **mainland China,** Visa's emergency number is ℂ **010/800-744-0027** (Northern China); American Express cardholders and traveler's check holders should call ℂ **010/800-744-0106;** MasterCard holders should call the US hotline collect at ℂ **636/722-7111.** Diners Club members should call Hong Kong at ℂ **852/2860-1800,** or call the U.S. collect at ℂ **416/369-6313.** Also see "Emergency Cash" under "Money" in chapter 2.

Mail   Sending mail from China is remarkably reliable, although sending it to private addresses within China is not. Take the mail to post offices rather than dropping it in a mail box. Some larger hotels have postal services on-site. It helps if mail sent out of the country has its country of destination written in characters, but this is not essential. Hotel staff will often help. Letters and cards written in red ink will occasionally be rejected, as this carries very negative overtones. Costs are as follows: Overseas mail: **postcards** ¥4.20 (55¢/30p), **letters under 10g** (.35 oz.) ¥5.40 (70¢/35p), **letters under 20g** (.70 oz.) ¥6.50 (85¢/45p). EMS (**express parcels** under 500g/18 oz.): to the U.S. ¥180 to ¥240 ($24–$32/£12–£16); to Europe ¥220 to ¥280 ($29–$37/£15–£19); to Australia ¥160 to ¥210 ($21–$28/£11–£14). **Normal parcels** up to 1kg (2.2 lb.): to the U.S. by air ¥95 to ¥159 ($13–$21/£6.35–£11), by sea ¥20 to ¥84 ($2.65–$11/£1.35–£5.60); to the U.K. by air ¥77 to ¥162 ($10–$22/£5.15–£11), by sea ¥22 to ¥108 ($2.95–$14/£1.45–£7.20); to Australia by air ¥70 to ¥144 ($9.35–$19/£4.65–£9.60), by sea ¥15 to ¥89 ($2–$12/£1–£5.95). Letters and parcels can be registered for a small extra charge. Registration forms and Customs declaration forms are in Chinese and French.

Maps Purchasing city maps as you go is absolutely essential, even though few are bilingual. These are available at bus and railway stations and at airports for around ¥5 (65¢/35p). Get your hotel staff to circle the characters for your hotel on the map, and the characters for the main sights you plan to see. You can then jump in a taxi at any point, show the driver the characters for where you want to go, and keep an eye on the route he/she takes.

Newspapers & Magazines Sino-foreign joint-venture hotels in the bigger cities have a selection of foreign newspapers and magazines available, but these are not otherwise on sale. The government distributes a propaganda sheet called *China Daily,* usually free at hotels. Beijing also supports a number of self-censoring entertainment magazines usually produced by resident foreigners. Nevertheless, these do have intermittently accurate entertainment listings, as well as restaurant reviews. See "Visitor Information" earlier in this chapter.

Police Known to foreigners as the PSB (Public Security Bureau, *gong'an ju*), this is only one of several different bureaus in mainland China. The police (*jingcha*) are quite simply best avoided—honestly, they are looking to avoid doing any work. Ideally, any interaction with the police should be limited to visa extensions. If you must see them for some reason, approach your hotel for assistance first, and visit the office listed under "Visa Extensions," under "Entry Requirements & Customs" in chapter 2, where you are likely to find an English speaker of sorts.

Post Office There are numerous post offices across the city, including one a long block north of the Jianguo Men metro station on the east side of Jianguo Men Bei Dajie (8am–6:30pm), one inside the Landmark Tower (next to the Great Wall Sheraton), one next to the Friendship Store on Jianguo Men Wai Dajie, one on Gongti Bei Lu (opposite the Workers' Stadium), the main office on Jianguo Men Nei Dajie on the corner of Beijing Zhan Kou leading to Beijing Station (almost opposite the International Hotel), and the EMS Post Office (Beijing Youzheng Sudi Ju) at the corner of Qian Men Dong Dajie and Zhengyi Lu. There is a **FedEx** (© **800/988-1888** toll free from a land line, or 400/889-1888 from cell phone with local call charges) office in Oriental Plaza, Room 01-05A, No. W1 Office Building. **DHL** has branches in the China World Center and COFCO Plaza, and **UPS-Sinotrans** has a useful branch in the Scitech Building at Jianguo Men Wai Dajie 22.

Restrooms Street-level public toilets in China are common, many detectable with the nose before they are seen. Entrance fees have been abolished in Beijing, but someone may still try to charge you for toilet paper ¥0.20. In many cases you merely squat over a trough. Use the standard Western equipment in your hotel room, in department stores and malls, and in branches of foreign fast-food chains. This is the principal benefit of the presence of so many branches of McDonald's.

Safety See "Health & Safety" in chapter 2.

Smoking The government of China is the world's biggest cigarette manufacturer. China is home to 20% of the world's population but 30% of the world's cigarettes. About one million people a year in China die of smoking-related illnesses. Nonsmoking tables in restaurants are almost unheard of, and NO SMOKING signs are favorite places beneath which to smoke, especially in elevators. Smokers are generally sent to the spaces between the carriages on trains, but they won't bother to go there if no one protests. You'll find the same attitude on air-conditioned buses.

Taxes Service charges mostly only appear in Sino-foreign joint-venture hotels, and range from 10% to 15%. Airport departure taxes are now included in the cost of your ticket.

Telephone The international country code for mainland China is **86.**

To call China:

1. Dial the international access code: 011 in the U.S., 00 in the U.K., for example.
2. Dial the country code: 86 for China.
3. Dial the city code, omitting the leading zero, and then dial the number. To reach Beijing from the U.S., you would dial 011-86-10-plus the 8-digit number.

To call within China: For calls within the same city, omit the city code, which always begins with a zero when used (010 for Beijing, 020 for Guangzhou, for example). All hotel phones have direct dialing, and most have international dialing. Hotels are only allowed to add a service charge of up to 15% to the cost of the call, and even long-distance rates within China are very low. To use a public telephone you'll need an IC (integrated circuit) card *("aicei" ka)* available from post offices, convenience stores, and street stalls, available in values beginning at ¥20 ($2.65/£1.35) (wherever you can make out the letters "IC" among the Chinese characters). A brief local call is typically ¥0.30 to ¥0.50 (4¢–7¢/2p–3p). Phones show you the value remaining on the card when you insert it, and count down as you talk.

To make international calls: First dial 00 and then the country code (U.S. or Canada 1, U.K. 44, Ireland 353, Australia 61, New Zealand 64). Next dial the area or city code, omitting any leading zero, and then dial the number. For example, if you want to call the British Embassy in Washington, D.C., you would dial 00-1-202-588-7800. Forget bringing access numbers for your local phone company—you can call internationally for a fraction of the cost by using an IP (Internet Protocol) card *(aipi ka),* available wherever you see the letters "IP." You should bargain to pay less than the face value of the card—as little as ¥40 ($5.35/£2.65) for a ¥100 ($13/£6.65) card from street vendors. Instructions for use are on the back, but you simply dial the access number given, choose English from the menu, and follow the instructions to dial in the number behind a scratch-off panel. Depending on where you call, ¥50 ($6.65/£3.35) can give you an hour of talking. If using a public phone, you'll need an IC card (see above) to make the call. In emergencies, dial 108 to negotiate a collect call, but again, you'll need help from a Mandarin speaker.

For directory assistance: Dial 114. No English is spoken, and only local numbers are available. If you want numbers for other cities, dial the city code followed by 114—a long-distance call. You can text the name of the establishment you are looking for (in English) to 85880, and for a small fee, the address will return in Chinese, ready to show to your taxi driver.

For operator assistance: Just ask for help at your hotel.

Toll-free numbers: Numbers beginning with 800 within China are toll-free, but calling a 1-800 number in the States from China is a full tariff international call, as is calling one in Hong Kong from mainland China, or vice versa.

Time Zone The whole of China is on Beijing time—8 hours ahead of GMT (and therefore of London), 13 hours ahead of New York, 14 hours ahead of Chicago, and 16 hours ahead of Los Angeles. There's no daylight saving time (summer time), so subtract 1 hour in the summer.

Tipping In mainland China, as in many other countries, there is *no tipping,* despite what tour companies may tell you (although if you have a tour leader who accompanies you from home, home rules apply). Until recently, tipping was expressly forbidden, and some hotels still carry signs requesting you not to tip. Foreigners are overcharged at every turn, and it bemuses Chinese that they hand out free money in addition. Chinese never do it themselves, and indeed if a bellhop or other hotel employee hints that a tip would be welcome, he or she may be fired. Waitresses may run out of restaurants after you to give you change, and all but the most corrupt of taxi drivers will insist on returning it, too. In China, the listed price or the price bargained for is the price you pay, and that's that.

Water Tap water in mainland China is not drinkable, and should not even be used for brushing your teeth. Use bottled water, widely available on every street, and provided for free in all the better hotels.

Weather For daily weather forecasts, check *China Daily* or CCTV 9, China Central Television's English channel (broadcast in most hotels). There is also a weather hot line (© 121); dial 6 after a minute or so for the report in English for ¥3 (40¢/20p) per min, charged to your hotel room.

5

Where to Stay

There are two types of hotel in mainland China: the **Sino-foreign joint-venture** hotels with familiar brand names, and **Chinese-owned and -managed** hotels. At the four- and five-star levels (see below for details on local star ratings), the Chinese-owned and -run hotels want you to think they are on par with the joint ventures. At lower levels they can range from indescribably battered and grubby to friendly, clean, and comfortable. (***Note:*** We awarded the star ratings shown at the beginning of each review in this chapter. Our 0–3 star scale does not coincide with the Chinese star-rating system.)

Your **first choice** at the four- or five-star level should be a familiar brand name, or a property from one of the Asian luxury chains. In most cases, the buildings are Chinese-owned, and the foreign part of the joint venture is the management company, which supplies worldwide marketing efforts, staff training, and senior management, while ensuring conformity with brand standards (never entirely possible; you'll generally find 90% of what you'd expect from the same brand at home).

Your **second choice** should be a wholly Chinese-owned and -run hotel with foreigners in senior management whose main purpose is to be there and make sure that things actually happen. But in both types of hotel, the general manager may have far less idea than he thinks he has of what's going on: The transport department uses hotel vehicles for private hires to make money on the side; the

human resources manager rejects applicants whose experience may be threatening and makes a good income from bribes (to ensure that the housekeeper's nephew gets a job in security, for instance); the front office manager institutes a system of fines, and pockets them himself; or the doormen charge taxis to be allowed to wait in the rank.

Entirely **Chinese-owned and -run** hotels at four- and five-star levels usually have only one thing in common with their counterparts: They charge the same (or, at least, attempt to do so), but you'll rarely get value for your money. At the four-star level and below, the best choice is almost always the newest hotel—teething troubles aside, most things will work, staff will be eager to please (if not quite sure how), rooms will be spotless, and rates can be easily bargained down, since few hotels spend any money on advertising. The aim is to find sweetly inept but willing service rather than the sour leftovers of the *tie fanwan* (iron rice bowl) era of guaranteed employment, for whom everything is too much effort.

A drawback for all hoteliers is that the government requires them to employ far more people than they need, and it's nearly impossible to obtain staff with any experience in hotel work. The joint-venture hotels are the training institutions for the rest of the Chinese hotel industry, which steals their local staff as soon as possible. Lower-level hotels are run by half-understood rules, with which there's half-compliance, half the time. A hotel may have designated nonsmoking rooms, but that doesn't mean they don't have ashtrays in them.

Until recently throughout China, only hotels with **special licenses** were allowed to take foreign guests. This requirement has now vanished from Beijing. In theory, all hotels with such licenses have at least one English speaker, usually of modest ability.

The Chinese **star-rating system** is meaningless. Nationwide, five-star ratings are awarded by a central authority, but four-star and lower ratings depend upon local standards, and both depend upon compliance with a checklist, but more crucially, with banqueting the inspectors. (Inspectors have no idea how to run a hotel anyway.) In general, Chinese hotels receive almost no maintenance after they open. There are Chinese "five-star" hotels in Beijing which have gone a decade without proper redecoration or refurbishment. Foreign managements force the issue with building owners, but it's rare for standards to be maintained. A new three-star will usually be better than an old four-star.

Outside of joint-venture hotels, don't rely on finding **amenities;** even if we list them in this book, there's no guarantee that you'll find them fit to use. Salons, massage rooms, nightclubs, and karaoke rooms are often merely the bases for other kinds of illegal entertainment (for men). Fitness equipment may be broken and inadequately supervised, and Jacuzzis may have more rings than a sequoia, so proceed with care.

You may receive unexpected **phone calls.** If you are female, the caller may hang up without saying anything, as may be the case if you are male and answer in English. But if the caller persists and is female, and if you hear the word *anmo* (massage), then what is being offered needs no further explanation, but a massage is only the beginning. Unplug the phone.

Almost all rooms, however basic, have the following: A telephone whose line can usually be unplugged for use in a laptop; air-conditioning, which is either central with a wall-mounted control or individual to the room with a remote control, and which may double as a heater; a television, usually with no English channels except CCTV 9 and possibly an in-house movie channel using pirated DVDs or VCDs; a thermos of boiled water or a kettle to boil your own, usually with cups (wash before using) and free bags of green tea; and an array of switches, which may not control what they say they control, found near the bed. The bathrooms have free soap and shampoo, and in better hotels a shower cap and toothbrush/toothpaste package.

Ordinary Chinese hotels usually contain a *biaozhun jian,* or "standard room," which means a room with twin beds or a double bed, and with a private bathroom. In older ordinary hotels, double beds may have only recently been installed, the switches are all in the wrong place, and the room is now referred to as a *danren jian* or single room. Nevertheless, two people can stay there and the price is lower than for a standard room with twin beds.

Foreign **credit cards** are increasingly likely to be accepted in three-star hotels and above, but never rely on this. Most hotels accepting foreigners will exchange foreign currency (cash) on the premises; some may not accept traveler's checks. Almost all hotels require **payment in advance,** plus a deposit *(yajin),* which is refundable when you leave. Some hotels add a 5% to 15% **service charge** on top of their room rates (our listings indicate where this is done).

Keep all **receipts** you are given. To get your deposit back, you may need to hand over the receipt for your key when you check out, and since staff occasionally forget to enter payments in computers or ledgers, you may need receipts to prevent yourself from being charged twice.

To **check in** you'll need your passport, and you must complete a registration form (which will be in English). Always inspect the room before checking in. You'll be asked how many nights you want to stay, and you should always say just 1, because if you say 4, you'll be asked for 4 nights' money in advance (plus a deposit), and because it may turn out that the hot water isn't hot enough,

the karaoke rooms are above your head, or a building site behind the hotel starts work at 8am sharp. Once you've tried 1 night, you can pay for more.

When you **check out,** the floor staff will be called to verify that you haven't stolen anything. This step may not happen speedily, so allow extra time.

Children 12 and under stay free. Hotels will add an extra bed to your room for a small charge, which you can bargain down.

SAVING ON YOUR HOTEL ROOM

The **rack rate** is the maximum rate that a hotel charges for a room. In China these rates are nothing more than the first bid in a bargaining discussion, designed to keep the final price as high as possible. You'll almost never pay more than 90%, usually not more than 70%, frequently not more than 50%, and sometimes as little as 30% of this first asking price. To lower the cost of your room:

- **Do not book ahead.** Just show up and bargain. In China this applies to the top class joint-venture names as much as all the others. The best price is available over the counter, as long as there's room. For most of the year there are far more rooms than customers at every level. The low hotel seasons are winter (especially around Chinese New Year as this is time spent with the family and not in hotels) and late summer (excluding the 2008 Olympics). For ordinary Chinese hotels you may well pay double by booking ahead, and there's no guarantee that your reservation will be honored if someone else arrives before you, cash in hand. E-mail is almost never answered, and faxes get ignored. Chinese mostly just show up and bargain.
- **Book online.** If you want to reserve a room in a particular joint-venture hotel during a busy period, look at its website for rates. Major hotel chains operating in China often have their best *published* rate on their websites. However, these rates fluctuate constantly according to demand, and are sometimes linked to inventory systems that alter prices at frequent intervals, sometimes hourly. Prices for any time of year quoted far in advance will always look uninviting. Rates are much cheaper nearer the time, unless some major event (e.g., the Olympics!) is taking place. Ordinary hotels, if they have a website, will just quote rack rates.
- **Dial any central booking number.** Contrary to popular wisdom, as the better hotels manage their rates with increasing care, the central booking number is likely to have a rate as good as or better than the rate you can get by calling the hotel directly, and the call is usually toll-free.
- **Avoid booking through Chinese hotel agencies and websites specializing in Chinese hotels.** You'll obtain the same discount if you contact the hotels directly. In fact, you can usually beat the agency's discount because you won't be paying their markup (usually at least 10%). Many agencies have no affiliations with hotels, and simply jump on the phone to book a room.

The Olympic Rates

The advice above is for regular tourist seasons. The Olympics is a whole other ball game. If you are traveling to Beijing specifically for the 2008 Olympics be sure to book far, *far* in advance. Regular summer discounts will not be in effect for the XXIX Olympiad. Most of the top hotels around town are already booked solid, hosting government officials or sponsor companies. Try your luck at the small, independent hotels or look into subletting an apartment (try the classifieds section of *that's Beijing*'s website, www.thatsbj.com). Wherever you end up, you should be prepared to pay premium rates.

HOW TO CHOOSE THE LOCATION THAT'S RIGHT FOR YOU

On short visits, the best option is to stay in the **city center,** within walking distance of the Forbidden City and Tian'an Men Square, on Wangfujing Dajie or nearby. The range of accommodations in this area—from super-luxury to rock-bottom—is unmatched.

The greatest luxury and highest standards of service can be found in **Chaoyang,** near the two main diplomatic areas just outside the East Second Ring Road. The district's southern half, also known as the CBD (Central Business District), is filled almost exclusively with high-end hotels and is the city's glitziest shopping area. The north boasts proximity to the airport and the dining and nightlife options of San Li Tun.

A wide variety of mid-range and budget accommodations options are offered in the **southern districts** of Xuanwu (southwest) and Chongwen (southeast). Hotels here offer convenient access to the metro line, Beijing Railway Station, and Beijing West Railway Station.

A district that has blossomed markedly in the past few years, the **Back Lakes (Hou Hai** or **Shicha Hai)** area is the most picturesque place to stay. Here you'll find interesting cafes, narrow lanes called *hutong,* and a last glimpse of Old Beijing.

The **western** part of the city, where most universities are located, is the least charming area to park your luggage, but hotels are generally cheaper and are near the Summer Palace.

1 Best Hotel Bets

- **Best Newcomer:** It's a hard call given how many new hotels have popped up in the lead-up to the Olympics, but one of our tried-and-tested favorites is **The Ritz Carlton, Financial Street.** Though the hotel caters to a business crowd, the homey touches makes it feel more like a boutique, with the Ritz's trademark impeccable service and the best Italian restaurant in town to boot. See p. 77.
- **Most Relaxed Atmosphere:** Located down an unassuming alley, the **Hotel Côté Cour S.L.** is the best of a glut of courtyard accommodations that have flooded Beijing. The private garden and a modern, airy lounge are fantastic places to unwind. The old *hutong* neighborhood where the hotel is located is as uncommercial as Beijing gets—it's simply bicycles and one-level courtyard homes here, with the odd dog and rickshaw thrown in. See p. 68.

- **Best Whiff of Old Beijing:** Located on a bustling street in the *hutong,* **Gu Xiang 20** is located in a neighborhood that combines old Beijing with hip bars and clothing shops, just a short walk away from Hou Hai Lake. The modern rooms with Chinese fretwork and nice views of the *hutong* give you a taste of old Beijing, without having to live like an old Beijinger. See p. 69. If you prefer to live more locally—and that means with a squat toilet—try the nearby Hutonger. See p. 69.
- **Best Hotel Garden:** The **Bamboo Garden Hotel**'s three courtyards are filled with rockeries, stands of bamboo, and other green leafiness. A traditional Chinese garden stretches away behind the otherwise modern **Shangri-La Beijing Hotel** to its tennis courts at the rear. See p. 68 and 77, respectively.
- **Best Business Hotel:** That 90% of **China World Hotel**'s guests are there for business comes as no surprise. It's part of a vast shopping complex offering a full-scale business center and top-notch executive floors, state-of-the-art conferencing facilities, free wireless connectivity in public areas, Beijing's finest European restaurant, a specialist wine store, and a supermarket. It sits right above a metro stop and the east Third Ring Road. See p. 70.
- **Best Design:** In a city full of bland, monolithic hotels, **Hotel Kapok** stands out from the rest with its innovative exterior that looks like a lantern lit up at night. It's also conveniently located a block away from the Forbidden City. See p. 66.
- **Best Health & Fitness Facilities:** The health club and spa at the **St. Regis Beijing** is the capital's most luxurious by far, but the most extensive facilities, including a running track and courts for almost everything, can be found at the **Kerry Centre Hotel.** See p. 71 and 70, respectively.
- **Best Pool:** The pool at the **Grand Hyatt** is very kitsch and out of keeping with the tastefully understated modern but comfortable design of the remainder of the hotel. A small lagoon buried among mock-tropical decor beneath a ceiling of electric stars, it's worth visiting even if you have no plans to swim, and it has plenty of space if you do. See below.
- **Best for Children:** The **Westin Beijing, Financial Street** pays special attention to young kids with cribs available in rooms and highchairs (rare in China) in the restaurants; a kids' center offers babysitting. See p. 77. The **Kerry Centre Hotel** also has a supervised play area for children, a wide range of sports facilities, and a pool for the older ones. See p. 70.

2 Beijing City Center, around Wangfujing Dajie

VERY EXPENSIVE

Grand Hyatt Beijing (Beijing Dongfang Junyue Dajiudian) 北京东方君悦大酒店 *✹✹* The Grand Hyatt is unrivaled for location: directly over the Wangfujing metro station, attached to one of the city's best indoor malls, at the foot of the capital's most famous shopping street, and within walking distance of the Forbidden City. Standard rooms are spacious, with soft carpets and desks equipped with buttery leather chairs. Bathrooms are a bit on the small side, but do have separate shower units. They recently extended the reception area, which is a good thing because check-in time can be hectic. Thankfully, service is fantastic and reception staff are quick to make eye contact, apologize for the wait, or quickly wave you over when they are free. The palatial lobby is a popular meeting place, with live music in the evenings and Beijing's best chocolate shop at one end. The vast swimming pool has a mock-tropical decor, with rock caves and a ceiling of electric stars—it's very kitsch and un-Hyatt but worth a visit even if you have no plans to swim. Some of Beijing's best restaurants—including Noble Court and Made in China (p. 87)—are scattered throughout.

Dong Chang'an Jie 1 东长安街1号 (within the Oriental Plaza complex at the foot of Wangfujing Dajie); see map p. 108. ℭ **800/633-7313** in the U.S. and Canada, 0845/888-1226 in the U.K., 1800/13-1234 in Australia, 0800/44-1234 in New Zealand, or 010/8518-1234. Fax 010/8518-0000. www.beijing.grand.hyatt.com. 825 units. ¥3,800 ($507/£253) standard room (discounts up to 60% during the low season), plus 15% service charge. AE, DC, MC, V. Metro: Wangfujing (118, exit A). **Amenities:** 5 restaurants (Beijing, Cantonese, Italian, Japanese, International); cafe; bar; indoor resort-style pool (50m/164 ft.); children's pool; fitness center with latest equipment; Jacuzzi; sauna; business center; shopping arcade; 24-hr. room service; massage; solarium. *In room:* A/C, satellite TV, dataport, broadband, minibar, hair dryer, safe, scale.

The Peninsula Beijing (Wangfu Fandian) 王府饭店 ⟨★★★   The range of accommodations choices in Beijing is now so vast that no hotel can claim to be the absolute best, but if a choice had to be made, it would be the Peninsula. Most international hotel management agencies are forced to work with Chinese parent companies, which typically hold the majority stake and are interested in squeezing their properties, rather than investing in staff training or renovations. The Peninsula is owned by its parent company, and it shows. Service is impeccable, and helpful touches abound: Braille on all signs; a user-friendly bedside control panel which displays the outside temperature and humidity; and tri-level mood lighting. In the exclusive shopping arcade is Jing, one of the city's best fusion restaurants.

Jinyu Hutong 8 金鱼胡同8号 (1 block east of Wangfujing Dajie); see map p. 108. ℭ **866/382-8388** (toll-free from U.S.) or 010/8516-2888. Fax 010/6510-6311. www.peninsula.com. 525 units. ¥2,850 ($380/£190) standard room (discounts up to 50% during the low season), plus 15% service charge. AE, DC, MC, V. **Amenities:** 2 restaurants (fusion, Cantonese); cafe; indoor pool; fully equipped fitness center; saunas and steam rooms; 24-hr. concierge; tour desk; Rolls-Royce and Mercedes limousines; business center; shopping arcade (with ATM and bank); Clarins Beauty Institute; 24-hr. room service; massage; babysitting; same-day dry cleaning/laundry service. *In room:* A/C, 42-in. plasma TV/DVD, silent fax, free Wi-Fi and broadband, minibar, hair dryer, safe.

Raffles Beijing (Beijing Fandian Laifoshi) 北京饭店莱佛士 ⟨★★   If you're looking for a slice of Old World charm, look no further than Raffles Beijing. The hotel took over management of this historic building and lovingly restored it with wood paneled floors and sparkling chandeliers. Rooms feature marble entrances, wood panel floors, and Oriental rugs. All rooms in the historic building are decorated differently. Personality suites are named for famous historical characters. The Li Zongren (a former general for Chiang Kai Shek and later a Communist sympathizer) suite has a four-poster bed on a raised platform, Chinese bric-a-brac, and a huge bathroom that has two separate entrances. Mounted black and white photos of old Beijing adorn the walls. The huge plasma TV is a bit out of place, and cheekily encased in an early-20th-century-esque gold frame. Rooms facing south look out onto Chang'an Jie, one of Beijing's main thoroughfares. Sadly, none of the rooms have balconies. Certain amenities are also inconveniently located in a separate building—you have to walk by a Japanese restaurant and a vaulted atrium to get to the pool and health club. Business travelers who don't need the historic decor might want to check out the contemporary executive suites housed in the same building as the pool and gym.

Dong Chang'an Jie 1 东长安街1号 (1 block west of Oriental Plaza). ℭ **800/768-9009** (toll-free from U.S.) or 010/6526-3388. Fax 010/8500-4380. www.beijing.raffles.com. 171 units. ¥3,800–¥4,700 ($507–$627/£253–£313) doubles (discounts up to 40% during the low season), plus 15% service charge. AE, DC, MC, V. Metro: Wangfujing (118, exit A). **Amenities:** 3 restaurants (Chinese, French, afternoon tea); bar; indoor pool; fully equipped fitness center; saunas and steam rooms; 24-hr. concierge; tour desk; business center; 24-hr. room service; massage;

babysitting; same-day dry cleaning/laundry service. *In room:* A/C, LCD TV, fax and DVD upon request, free Wi-Fi and broadband, minibar, hair dryer, safe.

The Regent Beijing (Beijing Li Jing Jiu Dian) 北京丽晶酒店 ✪ In the five-star hotel ghetto of Wangfujing, this latest addition to the neighborhood would give the nearby Peninsula and Grand Hyatt some stiff competition if it weren't for the less-than-impressive service. The staff, in a throwback to China of the early 1980s, are surprisingly gruff and unattuned to English-speaking guests. But if it's pure hardware you're going for, The Regent, which opened in 2007, sparkles with newness and fine amenities. The rooms, spacious and decorated in wood, beige, and purple tones, have an understated elegance with nice Chinese antique accessories—and flatscreen TVs to boot. The beige marble bathrooms have freestanding bathtubs that are some of the most comfortable in Beijing and separate shower stalls. The hotel is full of resort-like amenities, like the fantastic Serenity Spa, and the health club, which features a 32-meter long swimming pool that laps along its edges like a tide. An impressive lobby lounge atrium and several top-notch restaurants round out the package.

Jin Bao Jie 99 金宝街99号. ✆ **800/545-4000** or 800/610-8888 toll free in the US, 010/8522-1888 from China. Fax 010/8522-1818. www.regenthotels.com. 499 units. ¥3,200 ($427/£213) standard room (discounts up to 40% during the low season), plus 15% service charge. AE, DC, MC, V. Metro: Wangfujing (118, exit A). **Amenities:** 5 restaurants (Chinese, Italian, International); cafe; bar; indoor pool; health club; business center; tour desk; 24-hr. room service; spa; babysitting; same-day dry cleaning/laundry service; executive-level rooms; nonsmoking floor; currency exchange. *In room:* A/C, satellite TV, dataport, broadband, minibar, hair dryer, safe.

EXPENSIVE

Crowne Plaza Hotel (Guoji Yiyuan Huangguan Fandian) 国际艺苑皇冠饭店 ✪
This hotel recently completed a massive renovation that has left them awash in sparkling white marble and public spaces with plenty of natural light. Standard double rooms are a bit on the small side, but they come with swanky new flatscreen TVs and decent-size bathrooms. The beige and cream decor is soothing, but the carpets don't *quite* hide the stains. The location at the north end of Wangfujing, the city's popular shopping district, is pretty well near perfect. They are also far more affordable than The Peninsula hotel around the corner.

Wangfujing Dajie 48 王府井大街48号 (corner of Dengshi Kou Dajie); see map p. 108. ✆ **877/932-4112** in the U.S. and Canada, 1800/36-300 in Australia, 0800/80-1111 in New Zealand, 0800/917-1587 in the U.K., or 010/5911-9999. Fax 010/5911-9998. www.sixcontinentshotels.com. 395 units. ¥1,180 ($157/£79) standard room, plus 15% service charge. AE, DC, MC, V. Metro: Wangfujing (118, exit A). **Amenities:** 2 restaurants (Cantonese, Western); bar; tiny indoor pool; small health club with old equipment; underwhelming Jacuzzi, sauna, and solarium; concierge; business center; salon; 24-hr. room service; babysitting; same-day dry cleaning/laundry service. *In room:* A/C, satellite plasma TV, broadband/dataport, minibar, hair dryer, iron, safe.

Hotel Kapok (Mumian Hua Jiudian) 木棉花酒店 ✪ Just yards away from the Forbidden City, this hotel claims to be the first legitimate boutique hotel in Beijing. The hotel gets accolades for innovative design—the exterior looks like a lantern when it's lit up at night, and the lobby features an atrium with a cascading series of lights that resemble rain. Glass walls (with curtains) separate the bathroom from the bedroom, and the some rooms have access to small, private gardens. But keep in mind that it's still a Chinese-managed hotel: Beds are hard and service can be lacking.

Donghuamen Dajie 16 东华门大街16号; see map p. 108. ✆ **010/6525-9988** Fax 010/6525-0988. www.hotelkapok.com. 89 units. ¥2,180 ($291/£145) standard room, ¥3,180 ($424/£212) suite (discounts up to 50% in the low season), plus 15% service charge. AE, DC, MC, V. **Amenities:** Restaurant (Western); bar; fitness center; business center; Wi-Fi; tour desk; 24-hr. room service; sauna; laundry service; nonsmoking floor. *In room:* A/C, satellite TV, broadband, minibar, hair dryer, safe.

Park Plaza Beijing (Beijing Li Ting Jiu Dian) 北京丽亭酒店 (*Value*)   Sitting next to its sister hotel The Regent, the Chinese four-star Park Plaza is one notch below in price and grandeur, but it's a good value for the business or leisure guests looking for comfortable rooms in a great location without the opulent amenities. Rooms, decorated in wood and beige tones, are a bit cramped but do the job just fine. The hotel is often booked to capacity and is popular with Western business travelers.

Jin Bao Jie 97 金宝街97号. © 010/8522-1999. Fax 010/8522-1919. 216 units. ¥1,784 ($238/£119) standard room, ¥2,839 ($379/£189) suite (discounts up to 50% in the low season), plus 15% service charge. AE, DC, MC, V. Metro: Wangfujing (118, exit A). **Amenities:** 2 restaurants (Japanese, Western); bar; fitness center; business center; babysitting; tour desk; 24-hr. room service; sauna; massage; same-day dry cleaning/laundry service; executive-level rooms; nonsmoking floor; currency exchange. *In room:* A/C, satellite TV, broadband, minibar, hair dryer, safe.

MODERATE

Haoyuan Binguan 好园宾馆 (*）   Located down a lane just off one of Beijing's trendiest shopping streets, the 19-room Haoyuan is among the most exclusive of the city's popular courtyard-style hotels. Red doors hung with lanterns and flanked on either side by stone lions mark the entrance. Inside is a neatly restored Qing-era house, with a small unadorned courtyard in front and a sublime larger courtyard at the back, decorated with flowers and tree-shaded, stone chess tables. Larger rooms in the rear courtyard are furnished with canopy beds and custom-made Ming reproduction furniture. A bonus for fans of Communist Party history: The house once belonged to Hua Guofeng, Party chair after Mao, who aped the Great Helmsman's coiffure but didn't gain his stature.

Shijia Hutong 53 史家胡同53号 (blue sign points way on Dong Dan Bei Dajie); see map p. 108. © 010/6512-5557. Fax 010/6525-3179. 19 units. ¥668 ($89/£45) standard room (discounts rare, even in winter). AE, DC, MC, V. **Amenities:** Restaurant (Chinese/Western); bike rental; tour desk; laundry service; free Wi-Fi. *In room:* A/C, satellite TV, fridge, hair dryer.

INEXPENSIVE

Days Inn Joiest Beijing (Beijing Zhong Xindai Si Jiudian) 北京中欣戴斯酒店 (*Finds*)   This hotel is about two blocks away from being in an ideal location. It is north of the Temple of Heaven and south of Tian'an Men Square, but not quite walking distance to either. It is, however, brand new and an excellent budget option. Rooms are outfitted with light wood furniture, IKEA-esque furnishings, and bedspreads in beige and white. Bathrooms are spotless and come with a shower cubicle, though no bathtubs. Staff is friendly, but English service is uneven.

Zhushikou Dong Dajie 14 珠市口东大街14号 (north of Temple of Heaven). © 010/6707-7799. Fax 010/6707-7798. 245 units. Doubles ¥369–¥389 ($49–$52/£25–£26); ¥719 ($96/£48) suite. AE, DC, MC, V. **Amenities:** Restaurant; bar; limited business center; laundry service; currency exchange. *In room:* A/C, satellite TV, broadband, safe.

Saga Youth Hostel (Shijia Guoji Qingnian Lushe) 实佳国际青年旅社   Opened in May 2002 in one of Beijing's most famous *hutong,* the Saga is a favorite among savvy backpackers. The view west from the third-floor balcony across well-preserved old courtyard houses is a joy, especially at sunrise. To the east, alas, hastily built monstrosities are rising from the rubble of Old Beijing. Sunnier dorm rooms on the third floor are preferable, although their proximity to the kitchen means an early night's sleep is not guaranteed. The large, clean, communal kitchen is a huge plus, and staff is incredibly helpful. Unfortunately, the cost of popularity shows in the bathrooms, which are tatty.

Shijia Hutong 9 史家胡同9号 (west of intersection with Chaoyang Men Nan Xiao Jie; see map p. 108. ☎ 010/6527-2773. Fax 010/6524-9098. www.hostelworld.com. 24 units, 12 with in-room shower. ¥218 ($29/£15) twin; ¥65 ($8.65/£4.35) dorm bed. No credit cards. Bus: 713 from Beijing Zhan [210, exit B] to Lumicang. **Amenities:** Cafe; travel service; self-service laundry; cheap Internet access; self-service kitchen; table soccer. *In room:* A/C, no phone.

3 Back Lakes & Dong Cheng

EXPENSIVE

Hotel Côté Cour S.L. 🕿🕿 This new courtyard hotel, down an unassuming alley, is the best of the bunch of a crop of new courtyard accommodations that have flooded the Beijing market. Lime green walls, Chinese antiques, and funky tiled bathrooms make this a charming boutique experience. The outdoor garden is a great place to unwind and read if you happen to be staying in Beijing's more pleasant months; otherwise, head to the airy lounge decorated with contemporary art, where free breakfast and cappuccinos are served.

Yanyue Hutong 70 演乐胡同70号.☎ 010/6512-8020. Fax 010/6512-7295. www.hotelcotecoursl.com. 14 units, ¥1,295 ($173/£86) standard room. AE, DC, MC, V. **Amenities:** Restaurant (Chinese); bar; lounge; laundry service; same-day dry cleaning; nonsmoking floors. *In room:* A/C, satellite TV, broadband, Wi-Fi, hair dryer, safe.

Red Capital Residence (Xin Hong Zi Julebu) 新红资俱乐部 🕿 When Communist Party elders in Zhong Nan Hai decided it was time to upgrade their decor to IKEA, they were surprised to find old China hand Lawrence Brahm desperate to obtain their clapped-out furniture. Art Deco furnishings steal the show at this Cultural Revolution–themed *siheyuan*, set around a tiny central courtyard which conceals a homemade bomb shelter, now converted into a somewhat claustrophobic wine bar. It may be a tad museum-like, pretentious even, but if you can't resist the chance to curl up with a book in stuffed armchairs once used by Marshal Peng Dehuai and Premier Zhou Enlai, then this boutique hotel is worth the outlay. The two Concubine's Private Courtyards, fitted with ornate Qing dynasty beds, are the most romantic rooms in the capital. Book well in advance.

Dong Si Liu Tiao 9 东四六条9号 (walk a long block west from metro, turn left into Chao Nei Bei Xiao Jie, and take 4th turn on right); see map p. 108. ☎ 010/8403-5308. Fax 010/6402-7153. www.redcapitalclub.com.cn. 5 units, shower only. $150 single room; $190 double room, plus 15% service charge. AE, DC, MC, V. Metro: Dong Si Shi Tiao (213, exit D). **Amenities:** Cigar lounge; underground wine bar; laundry service. *In room:* A/C, satellite TV, safe.

MODERATE

Bamboo Garden Hotel (Zhu Yuan Binguan) 竹园宾馆 🕿 Said to be the former residence of the infamous Qing dynasty eunuch, Li Lianying, Bamboo Garden was the first major courtyard-style hotel in Beijing and is among the most beautiful. It's slightly more luxurious than the Lusong Yuan (see below), but with less character. Rooms border three different-size courtyards; each filled with rock gardens, clusters of bamboo, and covered corridors. Standard rooms in two multi-story buildings at opposite ends of the complex are decorated with Ming-style furniture and traditional lamps that cast pleasant shadows on the high ceilings. A restaurant looks out over the rear courtyard.

Xiaoshi Qiao Hutong 24 小石桥胡同24号 (3rd *hutong* on right walking south from metro stop); see map p. 108. ☎ 010/6403-2229. Fax 010/6401-2633. 44 units. ¥580–¥680 ($77–$91/£39–£45) standard room (discounts rare). AE, DC, MC, V. Metro: Gu Lou Dajie (217, exit B). **Amenities:** Restaurant (Chinese); bar; concierge; travel service; business center; salon; laundry service; currency exchange. *In room:* A/C, satellite TV, fridge.

Gu Xiang 20 (Gu Xiang Er Shi) 古巷20 ✿ Newly opened in 2007, this intimate hotel located on a bar-lined alley in the *hutong* boasts modern rooms decorated with Chinese antiques and flat-screen TVs. Beds are dark wood, and long, emperor-style calligraphy tables serve as desks. Rooms on the third floor are larger and some come with their own balconies with views overlooking the rooftops of traditional courtyard houses nearby. They're well worth the upgrade. The English service is uneven, but everyone is super friendly.

Nanluogu Xiang 20 南锣鼓巷20号 (about 200m south of north entrance of Nanluogu Xiang); see map p. 108. ☎ 010/6400-5566. Fax 010/6400-3658. www.guxiang20.com. 28 units. Doubles ¥500–¥1,280 ($67–$171/£33–£85). AE, DC, MC, V. **Amenities:** Restaurant; bar; room service; limited business center; dry cleaning/laundry service; rooftop tennis court. *In room:* A/C, satellite TV, free Wi-Fi, minibar, fridge.

Lusong Yuan Binguan 吕松园宾馆 ✿✿ The Lusong Yuan, set on the site of a Qing dynasty general's residence down a quaint *hutong* north of Ping'an Dadao is a thoroughly charming courtyard hotel. Smaller and more intimate than the Bamboo Garden, with more traditional rooms, it wins with the details—bright paneled ceilings in the hallways, faux rotary phones in-room, and Chinese-style wall-mounted lamps over the beds. A few rooms open directly onto quiet, semi-private courtyards, adorned with potted plants and presided over by white stone busts of "the father of modern China" (Sun Yat-sen) and "the father of modern Chinese literature" (Lu Xun). A tea-house with stone floors and low-backed Ming-style chairs is next to the lobby. Avoid the airless dorms in the basement.

Banchang Hutong 22 板厂胡同22号 (walking north from Di'an Men Dong Dajie on Jiaodaokou Nan Dajie, 2nd *hutong* on left); see map p. 108. ☎ 010/6404-0436. Fax 010/6403-0418. www.the-silk-road.com. 59 units. ¥1,100 ($147/£73) standard room (discounts up to 40% during the low season). AE, DC, MC, V. **Amenities:** Restaurant (Chinese); laundry service; limited currency exchange; Internet access. *In room:* AC, TV.

Qomolangma Hotel (Zhumulangma Biguan) 珠穆朗玛宾馆 ✿ At the rear of the Qomolangma Hotel is a vast courtyard containing four other separate and private courtyards. Make sure to request a room here, rather than in the street-facing building, which is a completely unimpressive hotel. Courtyard rooms are furnished with traditional Chinese furniture, and the deluxe suites come with big bathtubs. The restaurant hosts free Tibetan song and dance performances Friday nights from 7 to 8pm.

Gulou Xi Dajie 149 古楼西大街149号 (northwest of Drum Tower). ☎ 010/6401-8822. Fax 010/6401-1330. www. qomolangmahotel.com. 65 units. Doubles ¥518–¥1,000 ($69–$133/£35–£67). AE, MC, V. **Amenities:** Restaurant (Tibetan); same-day dry cleaning/laundry service; exercise room (currently being renovated, should be done by the time you read this); business center. *In room:* AC, satellite TV, fridge, free broadband, hair dryer.

INEXPENSIVE

Hutonger (Hutong Ren) 胡同人 *(Finds)* Super-cozy rooms with loft beds greet you at this tiny gem tucked in the *hutong*. The location is excellent, about a stone's throw away from the most popular, cafe-lined *hutong* in Beijing. Rooms are set up with desks and sofas on the main floor and small ladders that lead to beds perched on cozy over-hanging lofts. But be forewarned, perhaps in an effort to convey an "authentic" *hutong* experience, each room is equipped with a squatter toilet! Noise may be a problem since all rooms are adjacent to the small bar and restaurant, but this place gets kudos for character—an old tree sprouts out of one corner of the kitchen.

Ju'er Hutong 71 菊儿胡同71号 (down a small lane east of Nanluogu Xiang). ☎ 010/8402-5238. Fax 010/8402-5238. 5 units. Doubles ¥180–¥280 ($24–$37/£12–£19). **Amenities:** Bar, Wi-Fi. *In room:* A/C, satellite TV.

Peking Downtown Backpackers Accommodation (Dong Tang Qingnian Lushe) 东堂清旅社 ⭐ This is by far the best hostel in Beijing and it's in a fabulous location. They have bargain basement dorm rooms for ¥55 to ¥75 ($7.35–$10/£3.65–£5) as well as private singles and doubles. The bathroom has that annoying layout with a toilet placed smack in the middle of the shower area, but it is very clean and the folks manning the reception desk speak excellent English.

Nanluoguxiang 85 南锣鼓巷85号; see map p. 108. ☎ 010/8400-2429. Fax 010/6404-9677. downtown@ backpackingchina.com. 20 units. Doubles ¥130–¥170 ($17–$23/£8.65–£11) includes breakfast. **Amenities:** Restaurant (Western); laundry service; Internet access, free airport pick-up if you're staying over four days (you pay the ¥20/$2.65/£1.35 toll fees). *In room:* AC. No credit cards.

Qilu Fandian 齐鲁饭店 *Value* The bland, white-tiled exterior promises little, but the rooms are a pleasant surprise—freshly painted and carpeted and containing firm mattresses. Best of all, you're within sight of the delightful Shicha Lakes area and the north gate of Bei Hai. The friendly staff speak little English, but are willing to try. Owned by the Women's Federation, the hotel hosts mostly business travelers. An excellent vegetarian restaurant is attached.

Di'an Men Xi Dajie 103, Xi Cheng Qu 地安门西大街103号; see map p. 108. ☎ 010/6618-0966. Fax 010/6618-0969. 126 units. ¥378–¥428 ($50–$57/£25–£29) standard rooms (discounts up to 40% during the low season). MC, V. Bus: 810 from Jishui Tan metro to Bei Hai Hou Men. **Amenities:** 2 restaurants (Szechuan, vegetarian); concierge; business center; dry cleaning/laundry service. *In room:* A/C, TV.

4 Chaoyang

VERY EXPENSIVE

China World Hotel (Zhongguo Dafandian) 中国大饭店 ⭐⭐⭐ China World is the city's top business hotel. It has an enviable location in the heart of the Central Business District. The attached China World shopping mall is one of the best in town, with luxury boutiques, a well-stocked supermarket, and an ice rink. Standard rooms are spacious with marble bathrooms and separate shower units. Closets have fantastic shelving units for those who prefer to get things out of the suitcase. Get a corner room if you can—they're the same price, but bigger. For a real bargain, book yourself into a premier room—it's the same size as an executive suite, but minus a dividing wall between the sitting area and bedroom. For wine lovers, in-house restaurant Aria was recently tapped by the Wine Spectator for having one of the best wine lists in the world. The menu has about 450 bottles and sommeliers are on hand to help out with choices.

Jianguo Men Wai Dajie 1 建国门外大街1号 (at intersection with E. Third Ring Rd.). Metro: Guomao (122, exit A). ☎ 010/6505-2266. Fax 010/6505-0828. www.shangri-la.com. 716 units. ¥3,300 ($440/£220) standard room (discounts up to 60% during the low season), plus 15% service charge. AE, DC, MC, V. **Amenities:** 4 restaurants plus several more in attached mall; indoor pool (25m/82 ft.); golf simulator; 3 indoor tennis courts; full-service health club; separate spa with aromatherapy; concierge; business center; shopping complex; salon; 24-hr. room service; same-day dry-cleaning/laundry service; executive-level rooms; nonsmoking rooms; currency exchange; Wi-Fi in executive rooms. *In room:* A/C, satellite TV, broadband, minibar, hair dryer, safe.

Kerry Centre Hotel (Beijing Jiali Zhongxin Fandian) 北京嘉里中心饭店 ⭐⭐ *Kids* The Kerry Centre is our top choice for a hotel in the Central Business District. Where nearby China World (also a Shangri-La hotel) plays instrumental versions of Carpenters classics, Kerry Centre has hip lounge music in public areas. Standard rooms are decorated in textured, solid colors of gold and dark green, with maroon accent pillows. Bathrooms are small and rather awkwardly laid out, with tubs jammed

Deluxe Hotels on the Horizon

When we arrived in the capital a decade ago, we could count the number of five-star hotels on one hand. Now we couldn't keep track of all the five-stars even if we used both of our hands and feet. A few of the most anticipated five-star hotels hadn't opened by press time, including the **Park Hyatt Beijing** (✆ **010/8567-1234;** 4/F Yintai Office Tower Jianguo Men Wai Dajie; www. beijing.park.hyatt.com), which occupies the top half of one of the city's tallest skyscrapers and features the highest restaurant in the city with 360-degree views of its surrounding Central Business District. Also set to open is the capital's second **Ritz Carlton** (✆ **010/6501-8888;** 6A Xi Da Wang Lu; www. ritzcarlton.com) which, like the Park Hyatt, is located in the bustling Central Business District. Right next to the Ritz Carlton looms the **JW Marriott** (✆ **010/ 6501-8188;** Jian Guo Lu 83; www.marriott.com). Just north and slightly west, the **Mandarin Oriental** (✆ **010/6505-2806;** Dong San Huan Zhong Lu 32; www. mandarinoriental.com), located in the twisting steel structure known as Rem Koolhaus' CCTV Tower, plans to open just weeks before the Olympics.

---

into the corner and toilets tucked behind the door. Executive floors have far roomier bathrooms and added luxuries like free broadband or Wi-Fi Internet, Bose CD players, huge plasma TVs, and DVD players. They also have the best health club in town, including a spacious gym with the latest equipment, a 35m (115-ft.) indoor lap pool and two Jacuzzis, two indoor tennis courts, and even a short outdoor jogging path. Their restaurant Horizon is popular for its scrumptious ¥168 ($22/£11) dim sum lunch buffet for two, and Centro is a popular gathering spot for proper cocktails and a night of people watching.

Guanghua Lu 1光华路1号 (on west side of Kerry Centre complex, north of Guomao metro). Metro: Guomao (122, exit A). ✆ 010/6561-8833. Fax 010/6561-2626. www.shangri-la.com. 487 units. ¥3,000 ($400/£200) standard room (discounts up to 50% during the low season), plus 15% service charge. AE, DC, MC, V. **Amenities:** 2 restaurants; bar; indoor pool; indoor basketball/tennis/badminton courts; fitness center; children's play area; concierge; tour desk; business center; shopping arcade; 24-hr. room service; same-day dry-cleaning/laundry service; executive-level rooms; 5 nonsmoking floors; currency exchange; roof-top track for running and in-line skating; sun deck. In room: A/C, satellite TV, broadband, minibar, hair dryer, safe.

St. Regis Beijing (Beijing Guoji Julebu Fandian) 北京国际俱乐部饭店 ✮✮

When the St. Regis reopens in late spring 2008 after an extensive 8-month renovation, it should once again be at the top of the game. No hotel in Beijing can rival the on-call personalized butler service of the St. Regis, which boasts the highest staff-to-guest ratio in China. Almost unnerving attention is paid to your individual needs, down to what side of the bed you sleep on for turndown service, and what fruit you take from the fruit bowl. The white marble lobby, with its towering palms and afternoon tea, is the city's most elegant, and the health club is world class, with a spa drawing on waters from a mile under ground. Danieli's on the second floor is one of the city's finest Italian restaurants, and the Press Club Bar is a stylish, clubby watering hole.

Jianguo Men Wai Dajie 21 建国门外大街21号 (southwest of Ritan Park); see map p. 117. ✆ 010/6460-6688. Fax 010/6460-3299. www.stregis.com/beijing. 273 units. ¥2,700 ($360/£180) standard room, plus 15% service charge. AE, DC, MC, V. Metro: Jianguo Men (120/211, exit B, 1 block away). **Amenities:** 5 restaurants (Cantonese, American, Japanese, Italian, International); bar; gorgeous indoor pool (25m/82 ft.); putting green and driving area; well-equipped exercise room; spa; concierge; business center; salon; 24-hr. room service; same-day dry cleaning/

laundry service; nonsmoking rooms; cigar and wine-tasting rooms; currency exchange; 24-hr. butler service; squash courts; billiards room. *In room:* A/C, satellite TV/DVD, broadband, minibar, hair dryer, safe.

EXPENSIVE

Hilton Beijing (Beijing Xierdun Fandian) 希尔顿饭店 ⨘ What a difference a renovation can make. Once saddled with some of the most tired guest rooms in the capital, the Hilton's newly overhauled rooms now sport attractive carpets, stylish and functional glass desks, and ultracomfortable beds. The new marble bathrooms are spacious, with separate shower units and deep tubs. A sleek atrium bar, with Chinese-inspired bird cages, was recently added.

Dongfang Lu 1东方路1号 (east side of N. Third Ring Rd., north of Xiaoyun Lu). ℂ **010/5865-5000.** Fax 010/5865-5800. www.beijing.hilton.com. 377 units. ¥2,200 ($293/£147) standard room (discounts up to 40% during the low season), plus 15% service charge. AE, DC, MC, V. **Amenities:** 3 restaurants; bar; indoor pool; small outdoor tennis court; squash court; fitness club; Jacuzzi; sauna; bike rental; concierge; tour desk; business center; salon; 24-hr. room service; in-room massage; babysitting; same-day dry-cleaning/laundry service; 2 squash courts; valet. *In room:* A/C, satellite TV, broadband, minibar, hair dryer, safe.

Jianguo Hotel (Jianguo Fandian) 建国饭店 This four-star property, opened in 1982, was the first joint-venture hotel in Beijing. It's one of the few older hotels to have kept up standards with constant refurbishment and comprehensive staff training. The ground floor contains the best rooms, with French windows opening onto small patios alongside goldfish-stocked pools. Despite being on a bustling street, rooms are quiet. A popular meeting place for expats and business visitors, the large lobby offers afternoon tea, a string quartet every evening, and an orchestra during Sunday morning coffee. Justine's, Beijing's first serious French restaurant, now faces massive competition but is still worth a visit, particularly for the set-price Sunday lunch.

Jianguo Men Wai Dajie 5 建国门外大街5号 (east of Silk Market); see map p. 117. ℂ **010/6500-2233.** Fax 010/6500-2871. www.hoteljianguo.com. 449 units. ¥1,652 ($220/£110) standard room, plus 15% service charge. AE, DC, MC, V. Metro: Yong'anli (121, exit B). **Amenities:** 3 restaurants (Chinese, French, International); bar; indoor pool; fitness center; Jacuzzi; sauna; concierge; tour desk; business center; shopping arcade; salon; 24-hr. room service; same-day dry cleaning/laundry service; executive-level rooms; currency exchange. *In room:* A/C, satellite TV, broadband/dataport, minibar, hair dryer, safe.

Traders Hotel Beijing (Guomao Fandian) 国贸饭店 ⨘ The greatest advantage to staying in this efficient and well-run Shangri-La four-star hotel is access to the five-star health club facilities in the China World Hotel next door. (These two sister hotels are joined by an underground shopping center.) Otherwise, Traders is a straightforward business hotel, with slightly small and plain but nicely outfitted rooms, unobtrusive service, and easy access to the metro. The only major drawback is the tiny bathrooms, but this is compensated for by reasonably low room rates. The West Wing has the slightly nicer (and more expensive) rooms.

Jianguo Men Wai Dajie 1 建国门外大街1号 (behind China World Hotel); see map p. 117. ℂ **010/6505-2277.** Fax 010/6505-0818. www.shangri-la.com. 560 units. ¥1,350 ($180/£90) standard room, plus 15% service charge. AE, DC, MC, V. Metro: Guomao (122, exit A). **Amenities:** 2 restaurants (Cantonese, Western); bar; small exercise room; Jacuzzi; sauna; concierge; business center; shopping complex; salon; 24-hr. room service; same-day dry cleaning/laundry service; executive-level rooms; nonsmoking rooms; currency exchange. *In room:* A/C, satellite TV, free broadband, minibar, hair dryer, safe.

INEXPENSIVE

Gongti Youth Hostel (Gongti Qingnian Lushe) 工体青年旅社 *Value* Located inside the Workers Stadium, in the heart of the San Li Tun bar area, this well-run YHA offers a quiet location above a three-star hotel (The Sports Inn), a view over

pleasant gardens and a lake, and relatively new facilities. The fourth-floor rooms (not ideal if you have lots of luggage) are agreeably curved, and all face southeast. If you crave privacy, there are single rooms. The problems facing this YHA are common to all youth hostels in Beijing: There are not enough hostels to meet demand, so they're frequently overbooked (particularly in summer); turnover is high, as other hotels poach their well-trained staff; and they rely on the state-run parent hotel for housekeeping, which often leads to messy bathrooms.

Gongren Tiyuchang 9 Tai 工人体育场9台; see map p. 117. ⓒ 010/6552-4800. Fax 010/6552-4860. 38 units, communal bathrooms/showers. Dorm beds from ¥60 ($8/£4); ¥120 ($16/£8) single room. Discounts for YHA members. No credit cards. Metro: Dong Si Shi Tiao (213, exit B), 3 long blocks east. **Amenities:** Bike rental; travel service; self-service kitchen and laundry; Internet access; reading room. In room: A/C, TV, no phone.

Zhaolong Qingnian Luguan 兆龙青年旅馆
Whether proximity to the San Li Tun bar area is a plus or a minus is open to question, but the Zhaolong is a quiet alternative to the madness of its better-known cousin, Poacher's. Most guests are Chinese backpackers or foreigners conversant in Chinese. Doors close at 1am to discourage revelers. Twins and dorms are simple and clean; neither has an in-room bathroom, but common showers are adequate. Facilities are minimal. Proximity to the East Third Ring Road means convenient bus access to all parts of town.

Gongti Bei Lu 2 工体北路2号 (behind Great Dragon Hotel); see map p. 117. ⓒ 010/6597-2299, ext. 6111. Fax 010/6597-2288. 50 units. ¥160 ($21/£11) twin; dorm beds from ¥60 ($8/£4). AE, DC, MC, V. Bus: 115 from Dong Si Shi Tiao metro to Nongzhanguan. **Amenities:** Bar; access to indoor pool and sauna; travel service; self-service laundry. In room: A/C, no phone.

5 Beijing South

EXPENSIVE

Holiday Inn Central Plaza (Zhonghuan Jiari Jiudian) 中环假日酒店 ⓖⓖ Value
This site was right in the middle of things during the Jin dynasty (1122–1215), but there's nothing central nowadays about the location of this stylish hotel. However, if you're visiting Beijing to be among Chinese people, rather than pampered expatriates, we strongly recommend this hotel. InterContinental Hotels in China often present a bland, cut-price version of luxury (such as the Downtown and Lido Holiday Inns), but this Zenlike hotel is a startling exception. Credit must be given to the local designer, who has achieved the architectural Holy Grail: minimalism without coldness. Service is equally to the point. Set in a residential area, Beijing's Muslim quarter is a short walk to the east, a lively strip of restaurants near Baoguo Si lie to the north, and it's also handy to both of Beijing's main railway stations.

Caiyuan Jie 1 菜园街1号; see map p. 112. ⓒ 800/830-6368 or 010/8397-0088. Fax 010/8355-6688. 322 units. Standard rooms ¥1,660 ($221/£111), plus 15% service charge (discounts up to 50% during the low season). AE, DC, MC, V. Bus: 395 from Changchun Jie metro (205; exit A). **Amenities:** 2 restaurants (Cantonese, International); cafe; bar; indoor pool; well-equipped exercise room; yoga room; concierge; tour desk; business center; 24-hr. room service; same-day dry cleaning/laundry service; executive-level rooms; currency exchange. In room: A/C, satellite TV, broadband, minibar, hair dryer, safe.

The Marco Polo (Mage Boluo Jiudian) 马哥孛罗酒店 ⓖ Value
Although not among the main clusters of foreign hotels, the Marco Polo is as close to the center of things as any of them, and is quieter and better connected than most. (The location—just south of the No. 1 Line's Xi Dan station and north of the Circle Line's Xuanwu Men station—enables guests to get in and out during the worst of rush hour.) The lobby, sumptuously decorated with white marble and gold friezes, is stylish yet of

Finds In the Red Lantern District

Southwest of Qian Men, beyond the mercantile madness of Da Zhalan, is where you'll find the remains of Beijing's once-thriving brothel district, **Ba Da Hutong** (eight great lanes). Prior to the Communists' elimination of prostitution in the 1950s (and its rapid reemergence since the 1980s), government officials, foreign diplomats, and other men of means would come here to pay for the pleasures of "clouds and rain."

The transaction was not always lurid. The women were closer to courtesans, akin to Japanese geishas, and their customers often paid simply for conversation and cultured entertainment. Popular guidebooks were published advising on the etiquette for wooing courtesans. Although the promise of another brand of entertainment always lurked in the background, and many of the women who worked south of Qian Men were kidnapped from other provinces, the dynamic was not half as base as its modern counterpart's.

Many wonderful old bordellos still stand, although local tour groups are forbidden to take tourists to the area or even mention it. Most buildings were converted into apartments or stores, but a few were restored and turned into cheap hotels. While those who can afford it will prefer to stay in a more luxurious hotel further north, travelers on a budget would be hard-pressed to find affordable accommodations with so much character.

Among the best restored of the old brothels is **Shanxi Xiang Di'er Binguan** 陕西巷第二宾馆 (☎ 010/6303-4609), at the north end of Shanxi Xiang (once home to the most upmarket bordellos), a poorly marked and malodorous lane a few minutes' walk south of Da Zhalan. As with most buildings of its kind, it is recognizable by its multi-story height (rare in a neighborhood made up of single-floor houses) and by the glass that divides its roof, designed to let light into the central courtyard while blocking an outsider's

a modest enough scale to suggest the atmosphere of a discreet boutique hotel. The medium-size rooms are well-appointed, although bathrooms are somewhat cramped. Cafe Marco features buffet or a la carte dishes from the Mediterranean, Middle East, Southeast Asia, and China in honor of the routes the great traveler took himself.

Xuanwu Men Nei Dajie 6 宣武门内大街6号 (south of Xi Dan metro stop); see map p. 112. ☎ 010/6603-6688. Fax 010/6603-1488. www.marcopolohotels.com. 296 units. ¥2,080 ($277/£139) standard room (discounts up to 70% during the low season), plus 15% service charge. AE, DC, MC, V. Metro: Xi Dan (115, exit E). **Amenities:** 2 restaurants (Cantonese, Cafe Marco); bar; indoor pool; fitness center; concierge; tour desk; business center; salon; 24-hr. room service; same-day dry cleaning/laundry service; executive-level rooms; currency exchange. *In room:* A/C, satellite TV, expensive broadband, minibar, hair dryer, safe.

MODERATE
City Central Youth Hostel (Chengshi Qingnian Jiudian) 城市青年酒店 ★★ Value
Housed in the old post office building, this newly opened hostel cum hotel has an unbeatable location directly opposite Beijing railway station. The manager was inspired by a visit to Sydney Central YHA, and has attempted to create a replica here. Standard rooms on the fifth and sixth floor are minimalist and clean, with none of the sleaze

view of the activities taking place inside. Far nicer than the late-night barber shops and karaoke parlors where Beijing's working girls now do business, the hotel is spacious and lavishly decorated, with red columns and walls supporting colorfully painted banisters and roof beams, the latter hung with traditional lanterns. The rooms, arranged on two floors around the courtyard, are tiny and windowless, as befit their original purpose, but now have air-conditioning, TVs, and bathrooms for ¥100 ($13/£6.65) per night. To reach the hotel, walk east from Far East Youth Hostel (see above) and turn left down the second *hutong* on the right.

The 200-year-old **Qian Men Changgong Fandian** 前门长工饭店 (©**010/6303-2665**), at Yingtao Xiejie 11 樱桃斜街11号, is less well maintained than the Shanxi Xiang Di'er but closer to the city center and far grander inside. The tell-tale roof peeks over the rest of the street but the facade has been pasted over with anonymous white tile, which makes the elaborate interior more surprising. A large sign by the door describes the building's history as a "black meeting hall." Beyond is a large, high-ceilinged central courtyard surrounded by green walls with traditional red pillars and banisters. Informal cross-talk performances (a traditional Chinese form of storytelling) and chess games take place in summer. Standard rooms for ¥140 ($19/£9.35) on the first floor are basic and have grotty bathrooms but are still livable, with air-conditioning and TV. The second floor has more luxurious rooms for ¥180 ($24/£12), which are brighter and cleaner with a few pieces of traditional Chinese furniture. A gathering spot for elderly men from the neighborhood, the hotel is worth visiting for its Old Beijing atmosphere even if you don't plan to stay overnight (see "Walking Tour 1: Liulichang & Da Zhalan" in chapter 8). To get here, walk west along Da Zhalan, and take a right at the fork.

associated with other railway hotels (such as the nearby Howard Johnson, whose rooms now sport point-and-choose menus of massage girls), and at a fraction of the expense. Ask for a room on the north side, facing away from the railway station square. Dorm rooms on the fourth floor have double-glazed windows and comfortable bunk beds, but squat toilets are a surprise for the less limber.

Beijing Zhan Qian Jie 1 北京站前街1号; see map p. 112. © 010/6525-8066. Fax 010/6525-9066. www.central hostel.com. ¥288 ($38/£19) standard room; dorm beds from ¥60 ($8/£4). Discounts on dorm beds for YHA members. No credit cards. Metro: Beijing Zhan (210, exit A). **Amenities:** Bar; bike rental; tour desk; self-service laundry and kitchen; supermarket; Internet access; billiards and movie room. *In room:* A/C, TV, free broadband.

Harmony Hotel (Huameilun Jiudian) 华美伦酒店   A stone's throw from Beijing Railway Station, this small and slightly tattered three-star is ideal for those arriving late from the station or looking to catch an early train. Rooms are small for the price and renovations long overdue; however, staff is friendly, and after years of struggling to comprehend the broad accents of Intrepid Tours groups, their English is passable. "Luxury" rooms *(haohua jian)* are nearly double the size of standard rooms and come with bathtubs—well worth the extra ¥100 ($13/£6.65). Ask for a quieter room on an upper floor facing the west side, as the railway area is predictably rowdy.

Suzhou Hutong 59 苏州胡同59号 (from Beijing Zhan metro walk west, taking the 1st right onto Youtong Jie and continuing for 100m/328 ft. northwest); see map p. 112. ✆ 010/6528-5566. Fax 010/6559-9011. 122 units. ¥788 ($105/£53) standard room (discounts up to 25% during the low season). AE, DC, MC, V. Metro: Beijing Zhan (210, exit A). **Amenities:** Restaurant (Cantonese); cafe; bike rental; concierge; tour desk; business center; same-day dry cleaning/laundry service; currency exchange. *In room:* A/C, TV, minibar; fridge.

INEXPENSIVE

Far East Youth Hostel (Yuandong Qingnian Lushe) 远东青年旅社 ✦ *Finds*

Buried deep inside one of the city's most interesting *hutong* neighborhoods, but only a 10-minute walk from both the Heping Men and Qian Men metro stations, the Far East offers comfortable rooms at competitive rates. Even the hallways—partly adorned with faux brick and latticed, dark wood panels—are pleasant. The hostel maintains cheaper dorms behind a courtyard house across the street, but those in the main building are far better. The Far East makes a good choice even if you usually stay at midrange places.

Tieshu Xie Jie 113 铁树斜街113号 (south of Liulichang); see map p. 112. ✆ 010/5195-8561, ext. 3118. Fax 010/6301-8233. 110 units. ¥328 ($44/£22) standard room (often discounted to ¥200/$27/£13); ¥45–¥70 ($6–$9.35/£3–£4.65) dorm bed. AE, DC, MC, V. Metro: Heping Men (207, exit C2). **Amenities:** Restaurant (Chinese); bike rental; tour desk; cheap coin-op laundry; self-catering kitchen; Internet access. *In room:* AC, TV, fridge.

Feiying Binguan 飞鹰宾馆

The Feiying became one of the top budget options in the city after completing a top-to-bottom refurbishment in 2002 and joining Youth Hostelling International. It's the most "hotel-like" YHA you'll find. Standard rooms are bright and well equipped with low, slightly hard, twin beds; bathrooms have proper tubs. Dorms are also nice with in-room bathrooms and brand-new floors. The hotel's best feature is its location, just east of the Changchun Jie metro stop and next to several useful bus stops.

Xuanwu Men Xi Dajie 10 宣武门西大街10号 (down alley east of Guohua Market); see map p. 112. ✆ 010/6317-1116. Fax 010/6315-1165. www.hostelworld.com. 46 units. ¥220 ($29/£15) standard room; ¥60 ($8/£4) dorm bed. Discounts for YHA members. No credit cards. Metro: Changchun Jie (205, exit C1). **Amenities:** Bar; travel service; self-service laundry and kitchen; Internet access; small convenience store. *In room:* A/C, TV.

6 Beijing West, Haidian & Yayun Cun

VERY EXPENSIVE

Marco Polo Parkside (Zhongao Mage Boluo Jiudian) 中奥孛罗酒店 ✦✦

The Olympics National Stadium is about a five-minute walk away from this swank new hotel. Marble entranceways lead the way to plush carpets, generous sized bathrooms with separate shower units, and chic dark wood furniture. Even the decor is slick, with chocolate brown textured velour bed throws and subtle silk-screens. In deluxe rooms, an almond-shaped bathtub sits next to a huge glass window marking the boundary between the bedroom and the bathroom. Too scandalous? Don't worry, the press of a button sends down an electronic curtain. Get a room facing west to see the National Stadium just visible beyond the neighboring high-rises. The hotel was in the middle of their soft opening at time of writing, so we didn't get a chance to pop into the pool, health club, or spa, which were still under construction. Staff are overeager, though still a little unsure of themselves.

Anli Lu 78 安立路78号 (next to Olympic Green, 1km from the National Stadium); see map p. 114. ✆ 010/5963-6688. Fax 010/5963-6500. www.marcopolohotels.com/beijingparkside.html. 315 units. ¥3,000–¥3,200 ($400–$427/£200–£213) superior/deluxe room, plus 15% service charge. AE, DC, MC, V. Metro: Olympic Park. **Amenities:** 3 restaurants (International, Chinese, Korean); bar; indoor pool; health club; spa; concierge; business center; 24-hr. room service; dry cleaning/laundry service; executive-level rooms; nonsmoking floors; currency exchange. *In room:* A/C, satellite TV, free broadband, minibar, hair dryer, safe.

Ritz Carlton, Financial Street (Jinrong Jie Lijia Jiudian) 金融街丽嘉酒店 ★★

Though this hotel caters to a corporate clientele, the place is decorated with homey touches, as if run by a Chinese version of Martha Stewart. The beds are the comfiest in town, and spacious marble bathrooms come with his and her sinks and televisions anchored in front of the bathtub. The basement health club and spa are top-notch, with a luxurious swimming pool that features a giant television screen on one wall and lounge chairs imbedded in the pool that deliver water jet massages. Be sure to dine in Cepe (see p. 103), which serves the city's best upscale Italian fare. The only drawback is the location, which isn't particularly central, even though it's an up and coming business district. The hotel is attached to a chic new shopping center.

1 Jinchengfang Dong Jie 金城坊东街1号 (next to the National Security Council Building); see map p. 114. ✆ 010/6601-6666. Fax 010/6601-6029. www.marriott.com. 253 units. ¥4,000 ($533/£267) standard room (discounts up to 60% during the low season) plus 15% service charge. AE, MC, V. Metro: Fuxing Men (114/204, exit A). **Amenities:** 3 restaurants (International, Italian, Chinese); bar; indoor pool; fitness center; spa; Jacuzzi; sauna; concierge; business center; salon; room service; babysitting services; same-day laundry/dry cleaning; executive-level rooms; currency exchange. *In room:* A/C, satellite TV, Wi-Fi and broadband, minibar, hair dryer, iron, safe with built-in laptop charger, scale.

Shangri-La Beijing Hotel (Xianggelila Fandian) 香格里拉饭店 ★★

It doesn't look like much from the outside, but the Shangri-La is one of the finest hotels in town. It features the new Valley Wing—a luxurious tower of executive rooms decorated in elegant muted beige tones, with access to an indulgent lounge with free breakfast, afternoon cocktails, and canapés. Standard rooms are a good size and comfortably furnished, if less imaginative than rooms at other Beijing hotels in this chain. The Chi Spa, which opened in 2007, offers massages and facials in a calming Tibetan atmosphere. Although off by itself in the northwest, the hotel benefits by having space for a large and lush garden (which includes an outdoor bar and pond), easy access to the Summer Palaces and the Western Hills, and quick routes around Beijing via the third and fourth ring roads.

Zizhu Yuan Lu 29 紫竹院路29号 (northwest corner of Third Ring Rd.); see map p. 114. ✆ 010/6841-2211. Fax 010/6841-8002. www.shangri-la.com. 657 units. $200 standard room (discounts up to 25% during the low season), plus 15% service charge. AE, DC, MC, V. **Amenities:** 3 restaurants (Cantonese, Japanese, International); bar; indoor pool; health club with sauna, solarium, exercise room; concierge; tour desk; business center; 24-hr. room service; same-day dry cleaning/laundry service; executive-level rooms; nonsmoking rooms; currency exchange. *In room:* A/C, satellite TV, free broadband and Wi-Fi, minibar, hair dryer, safe.

The Westin Beijing, Financial Street (Wei Si Ting Da Jiu Dian) 威斯汀大酒店 ★ Kids

One of the newest five-star hotels in Beijing, The Westin caters to business traveler and families, who will find a resort-like atmosphere smack in the middle of Beijing's financial district. The Westin's standard room are decorated plainly in wood, gray, and beige tones but come with luxurious amenities, complete with marble bathrooms with large tubs, flatscreen TVs, Bose radios, and beds so comfortable they're trademarked "The Heavenly Bed." Upgrade to a "relaxation" room, and a bathologist will come to your room to draw you a personalized bath. There's also a spa on the premises that features Chinese reflexology treatments. The hotel has one of Beijing's few poolside bars. A kids' center with babysitting entertains the little ones and gives parents a break.

Airport Hotels

Plenty of hotels, all with free shuttle services, are located near the airport. The most pleasant choice is the **Sino-Swiss Hotel (Guodu Dafandian)**北京国都大饭店 (ℭ **010/6456-5588;** fax 010/6456-1588; www.sino-swisshotel.com). Formerly a Mövenpick, it contains large rooms with two queen-size beds for around ¥856 ($114/£57) after discount. It has a pleasant resort-style pool complex, and regular shuttles go to the airport (every 30 min. from 6:15am to 10:45pm) and downtown. Almost within walking distance of the airport is the very basic **Air China Hotel** (Guohang Binguan; ℭ **010/6456-3440)**国航宾馆, with standard rooms from ¥260 to ¥320 ($35–$43/£17–£21). Slightly nicer rooms can be had at the three-star **Blue Sky Hotel** (Lan Tian Dasha; ℭ **010/8048-9108)**, 15 minutes away in the Konggang Industrial Zone. A standard room costs ¥350 ($47/£23) after discount. Farther from the airport, in northern Chaoyang, the **Holiday Inn Lido** (Lidu Jiari Fandian; ℭ **010/6437-6688;** fax 010/6437-6237; http://beijing-lido.holiday-inn.com) 丽都假日饭店is part of an extensive complex with foreign restaurants and shops. Standard rooms are large but in dire need of refurbishment (¥1,300/$173/£87 after discount), and the coffee served with breakfast is vile

Jin Rong Dajie Yi 9 金融大街乙9号. ℭ **010/6606-8866.** Fax 010/6606-8899. 486 units. ¥2,900 ($387/£193) standard room (discounts up to 55% during the low season), plus 15% service charge. AE, DC, MC, V. Metro: Fuxing Men (114/204, exit A). **Amenities:** 3 restaurants (Chinese, Italian, Western); bar; indoor pool; fitness center; business center; Wi-Fi; shopping complex nearby; tour desk; 24-hr. room service; beauty salon; sauna; same-day dry cleaning/laundry service; executive-level rooms; nonsmoking floor; currency exchange. *In room:* A/C, satellite TV, broadband, minibar, hair dryer, safe.

EXPENSIVE

Beijing Marriott West (Beijing Jinyu Wanhao Jiudian) 北京金域万豪酒店 ✦

The first full-fledged Marriott in Beijing, this hotel offers good value after the discount, although the location is far from the major sights. Along with the Shenyang Marriott (the first Marriott in China), it's among the country's most opulent hotels. The structure was originally an apartment building before Marriott took over, so rooms are immense. Eighty percent have Jacuzzi tubs and all include sumptuous beds and overstuffed chairs. Guests have free access to the attached Bally fitness center.

Xi San Huan Bei Lu 98 西三环北路98号 (in Jinyu Dasha, at intersection with Fucheng Lu); see map p. 114. ℭ 010/6872-6699. Fax 010/6872-7302. www.marriotthotels.com/bjsmc. 155 units. ¥2,800 ($373/£187) standard room (discounts up to 55% during the low season), plus 15% service charge. AE, DC, MC, V. **Amenities:** Restaurant (Western); bar; health club with indoor pool; tennis courts; concierge; business center; salon; 24-hr. room service; same-day dry cleaning/laundry; executive-level rooms; nonsmoking rooms; bowling center; currency exchange. *In room:* A/C, satellite TV, dataport, minibar, hair dryer, iron, safe.

Crowne Plaza Park View Wuzhou (Wuzhou Huangguan Jiari Jiudian) 五洲皇冠假日酒店 (Kids)

From a *fengshui* perspective, the recently opened Wuzhou is unbeatable. It lies close to the north–south axis that runs through the Forbidden City. Far from the expatriate ghettos, the surrounding area has considerable appeal: Yayun Cun is a (relatively) pedestrian-friendly residential area with some of Beijing's best Chinese restaurants (see chapter 6). Within the striking white edifice, you'll find a very North American brand of luxury: *USA Today* delivered to your door and the inevitable Brazilian restaurant. It's all comfortable enough, but we find it a bit bland. Little luxuries are lacking, and service can be indifferent. It's worth upgrading to a "luxury" *(haohua)* room, as bathrooms in the "superior" *(gaoji)* rooms are a bit poky.

Bei Si Huan Lu 4 北四环路4号 (northwest of Anhui Qiao on the N. Fourth Ring Rd.); see map p. 114. ℂ **800/830-2628** or 010/8498-2288. Fax 010/8499-2933. www.crowneplaza.com. 478 units. Luxury rooms ¥1,900 ($253/£127) (discounts up to 25% during the low season), plus 15% service charge. AE, DC, MC, V. Bus: 803 from Anding Men metro (216, exit B). **Amenities:** 3 restaurants (Cantonese, Brazilian, International); bar; indoor pool; exercise room; Jacuzzi; sauna; concierge; business center; 24-hr. room service; massage; same-day laundry/dry cleaning; executive-level rooms; currency exchange. *In room:* A/C, satellite TV, broadband, minibar, hair dryer, iron, safe.

6

Where to Dine

After their first meal in Beijing, most people find themselves saying, "This is not Chinese food." There's none of the lemon chicken you usually get delivered from the Ho-Ho Gourmet back home, the chicken you do get still has its head, and the sauce doesn't drip from it in gelatinous clumps. The rice comes at the end of the meal unless you ask for it early—and there are no fortune cookies.

Of all the vertigo first-time visitors experience in Beijing, the worst spins

The Cuisines

China has between four and ten seminal cooking styles, depending on who you ask, but regional permutations, minority contributions, and specialty cuisines like Buddhist-influenced vegetarian and medicinal dishes push the number into the dozens. Most of these have at least passed through Beijing since privately owned restaurants really took off in the 1980s. Below are summaries of the most consistently popular styles, as well as the cuisines du jour, which may or may not be around next time you visit:

Beijing   This ill-defined cuisine was influenced over the centuries by the different eating habits of successive rulers. Emphasis is on lamb and pork, with strong, salty, and sometimes musky flavors. Staples are heavy noodles and breads rather than rice. *Jiaozi*, little morsels of meat and vegetables wrapped in dough and usually boiled, are a favorite local snack.

Cantonese   The most famous Chinese cooking style, Cantonese tends to be light and crisp, with pleasing combinations of salty and sweet, elaborate presentations, and a fondness for rare animal ingredients at the high end. As with Sichuanese food, real Cantonese puts its American version to shame. It's available in swanky and proletarian permutations.

Home-style (Jiachang Cai)   The most pervasive style in Beijing, home-style food consists of simplified dishes from a variety of regions, primarily Sichuan. It is cheap, fast, and gloriously filling, with straightforward flavors that run the gamut. This is the Chinese equivalent of down-home American cooking, but far healthier and more colorful.

Huaiyang   This ancient style from the lower reaches of the Yangtze River (Chang Jiang) is celebrated for delicate knife work and light, slightly sweet fish dishes. Vegetarian dishes often make interesting use of fruit. The tendency here is to braise and stew rather than stir-fry.

often come from eating. In the past, fear of the food kept many travelers confined to their hotels and a few free-standing Western eateries for sustenance. This is no longer necessary, if it ever was.

Beijing is China's best city for gastronomes. No other Chinese city provides a greater variety of restaurants. Better standards of hygiene have erased the biggest barrier to eating out in the past, making it almost criminal to stay in your hotel. And once you get over the shock of strange flavors, most travelers find the real Chinese food astronomically better than its Western corruption.

Most restaurants in Beijing have very short life spans, creating headaches for guidebook writers and readers. But the volatility is also what makes the city such a wonderful place to eat, as establishments that manage to stick around have generally earned the right to exist.

Beijing has its native cuisine, but it is by no means the dominant one. While there are entire restaurants devoted to producing the city's most famous local dish, Peking roast duck, local diners are fickle and fond of new trends. These sweep through the city like tornadoes through Kansas. A few years ago it was

---

Shanghai These richly sweet, oil-heavy dishes are no longer as trendy as they were a few years ago, but are still easy to find. Shanghainese food tends to be more expensive than fare from Sichuan or Beijing, but affordable Shanghai-style snack shops dot the city. Best are the varieties of *baozi,* or bread dumplings.

Sichuan The most popular of the pure cuisines in Beijing, real Sichuanese is far more flavorful than the "Szechuan" food found in the United States. Main ingredients are vividly hot peppers, numbing black peppercorns, and garlic, as found in classics like *gongbao jiding* (diced chicken with chiles and peanuts). Spicy Sichuan-style hot pot is the city's best interactive food experience.

Southern Minority Cuisine and rare ingredients from Naxi-dominated regions of Yunnan Province are especially fashionable, but Hakka, Dai, Miao, and other ethnic traditions are also well represented. This is some of the city's most interesting food right now, but also its most inconsistent and overpriced.

Uighur Uighur cooking is the more distinctive of Beijing's two Muslim styles (the other being Hui), with origins in remote Xinjiang Province. The cuisine is heavy on lamb and chicken and is justly adored for its variety of thick noodles in spiced tomato-based sauces. Uighurs produce the city's favorite street snack: *yangrou chuan,* roasted lamb skewers with cumin and chile powder.

Vegetarian An increasingly diverse style, the Beijing version of vegetarian cuisine is moving away from its previous obsession with soy- and taro-based fake meat dishes. Decor and quality vary from restaurant to restaurant, but none allow smoking or booze.

Cultural Revolution nostalgia dishes, then fish and sweet sauces from Shanghai, then yuppified minority food from Yunnan, and now the fiery flavors of Sichuan hold sway. Tomorrow it will be something else. Each leaves its mark on the culinary landscape after it has passed, making it possible for visitors to sample authentic dishes from nearly every corner of the country. (For a summary of the most popular cuisines, see "The Cuisines" box below.)

The choices expand well beyond China's borders. Most of Asia and Europe are well represented at close-to-authentic levels. Italian, Russian, French, Indian, and Japanese restaurants are numerous, some of superb quality.

American fast-food outlets are ubiquitous. KFC is the most popular among locals and McDonald's is a close second. Subway, Sizzler, and even A&W are also in the mix. For sandwiches, there are several other choices: Schlotsky's Deli (in the China World Trade Center), and the Kempi Deli (inside the Kempinski Hotel). Among sit-down options are Pizza Hut, T.G.I. Friday's, Henry J. Bean's (in the China World complex), the American-owned Outback Steakhouse, and the Beijing Hard Rock Cafe (check *that's Beijing* for location details).

Beijing frequently ranks among the most expensive cities in which to dine for business travelers, according to the Corporate Travel Index and other sources of such information. While it is possible to spend a lot of money on food in the city, it is also possible to eat, and eat well, for very little. A typical dinner for two at a relatively upscale Chinese restaurant costs ¥80 to ¥140 ($11–$19/£5.35–£9.35), but prices can go much lower with little to no drop in quality.

Main courses in almost every non-Western restaurant are placed in the middle of the table and shared between two or more people. The "meal for two" price estimates in this chapter include two individual bowls of rice and between two and four dishes, depending on the size of the portions, which tends to decrease as prices rise.

Credit cards are generally accepted in most restaurants above the moderately priced level. Hotels frequently levy a 15% service charge, but free-standing restaurants seldom do. Tips are not given; waitresses will often come running out into the street to give your money back if you try to leave one.

Restaurants in this chapter are a mix of established favorites and newer places creative enough or just plain good enough to survive. Beijing's enthusiasm for the wrecking ball can sometimes take down even the most venerable of eating establishments, but new worthies inevitably rise to fill the gap. Most restaurants of note, especially those that cater to foreign clientele, are located in Chaoyang, but excellent establishments exist all over the city. The most picturesque spot to dine in Beijing is around the Back Lakes, north of Bei Hai Park, an area of well-preserved *hutong* (narrow lanes) and idyllic man-made lake promenades that is home to several of the city's most compelling eateries.

Note: For tips on dining etiquette, see "Fast Facts: Beijing" in chapter 4. For more tips and a menu guide to the city's most popular dishes, see "Appendix A: Beijing in Depth" on p. 213.

The price ranges in the reviews below reflect the following equivalents, in terms of main courses: **Very Expensive** ($$$$) = $31 & up; **Expensive** ($$$) = $19 to $30; **Moderate** ($$) = $10 to $18; **Inexpensive** ($) = under $10.

1 Best Dining Bets

- **Best Peking Duck:** Restaurants serving this dish are multiplying around the city, but you should go no further than the Grand Hyatt's **Made in China,** which has been doing the best version of this classic for years. See p. 87.
- **Best Sichuan Cuisine:** Chaotic and crowded, **Chuan Jing Ban Canting,** a restaurant owned by the Sichuan Provincial Government, is the most authentic place for spicy, numbing Sichuanese cuisine in the capital. There's usually a 30-minute wait for dinner, so come either early or late and be sure to order plenty of beer with your meal to cool your tongue. See p. 90.
- **Best Inventive Cuisine: Blu Lobster,** the showcase restaurant of the Shangri-La, brings the modern, inventive dishes of young Irish-born chef Brian McKenna. It's one of the few daring, experimental restaurants in Beijing that rivals those of London and New York. **Whampoa Club Beijing,** opened by ambitious Hong Kong–born chef Jereme Leung, does haute–Northern Chinese cuisine in a sublime dining room that sits under a glass-bottomed goldfish pond. See p. 103 and 103 respectively.
- **Best Hot Pot:** Classy hot pot can be found at **Ding Ding Xiang,** where the Chinese fondue comes in individual-serving pots for diners who'd rather not take the family-style route. Fresh vegetables, an addictive dipping sauce, and yummy steamed buns make this the best hot pot place in town. See p. 99.
- **Best Noodles:** Available in dozens of shapes and sauces, Shanxi-style noodles at the fashionable and aptly named **Noodle Loft** are among the most satisfying in Beijing, and without the crimes of hygiene perpetrated by the more typical noodle joints. See p. 101.
- **Best Karma** (Vegetarian): **Pure Lotus** offers delicious veggie fare in a stylish environment—visit the Holiday Inn Lido location for a particularly meditative, dimmed atmosphere that's perfect for dinner. See p. 104.
- **Best European Cuisine: Cepe** serves tasty Italian fare in stylish surroundings. It's not exactly in a central location, but still attracts devoted diners with its fresh pasta (made daily) and outstanding wine. See p. 103.
- **Best Asian Cuisine** (non-Chinese): Stylish decor and creative rolls make **Hatsune** (p. 93) the best Japanese option in Beijing. Overpriced but superbly decorated, **Nuage** (p. 88) in the Back Lakes offers a lovely view, with lakeside, rooftop dining.
- **Best Wine List:** High import duties and poor selection make life in Beijing tough on wine drinkers. But **The CourtYard,** one of the city's most celebrated restaurants, both for its excellent menu and for its location in a courtyard house overlooking the Forbidden City moat, offers an astonishingly sophisticated wine selection you'd have to go to Hong Kong to equal, with many top wines available by the glass. See p. 86.
- **Best Quintessential Beijing Setting:** Built inside the prayer hall of an old Daoist temple in a sea of crumbling residences near the Back Lakes, **Sansheng Wanwu** eschews the polished gardens and pavilions of the city's other atmospheric restaurants in favor of something far more appropriate: the fast-fading intimacy of one of Beijing's last *hutong* neighborhoods. See p. 89.
- **Best Decor:** The Taiwanese-owned **People 8** gets our vote for best Chinese fusion dishes, with a sublime atmosphere that is romantic, spooky, and stylish. See p. 94. If you're a fan of designer Philippe Starck, head over to **Lan** for a meal in the city's most splashy, nouveau riche Chinese atmosphere. See p. 94.

- **Best Brunch: Vineyard** is a top choice for their weekend brunch. It's bright and airy with a relaxed vibe—a perfect start to the day. The menu carries a good selection of both healthy and calorie-loaded options. See p. 90. For those seeking an indulgent Sunday brunch, head over to the **St. Regis** for their over-the-top buffet featuring champagne, caviar, and oysters. See p. 71. For a buffet extravaganza, visit the **Westin Hotel** (p. 77) for their Sunday champagne brunch, which at ¥298 ($40/£20) is a great deal for its numerous stations offering everything from foie gras and sashimi to chocolate fondue and creative pastries.

2 Restaurants by Cuisine

BEIJING

Beijing Dadong Kaoya Dian ✯✯ (Chaoyang, $$, p. 95)

Made in China (Chang An Yi Hao) (City Center, $$$, p. 87)

Xian'r Lao Man ✯ (Dong Cheng, $, p. 92)

Whampoa Club Beijing (Huang Pu Hui) ✯✯ (Beijing West, $$$$, p. 103)

BELGIAN

Morel's (Molaolongxi Xicanting) ✯✯ (Chaoyang, $$$, p. 94)

BRAZILIAN

Alameda ✯ (Chaoyang, $$, p. 95)

CANTONESE

Horizon (Haitian Ge) ✯ (Chaoyang, $$$, p. 94)

Otto's Restaurant (Richang Cha Canting) ✯ (City Center, $, p. 88)

Paper (Jian) ✯ (Back Lakes, $$$, p. 89)

CONTINENTAL

Blu Lobster (Lan Yun Xi Can Ting) ✯✯ (Haidian, $$$$, p. 103)

DAOIST

Sansheng Wanwu ✯ (Back Lakes, $$$, p. 89)

DUMPLINGS

Xian'r Lao Man ✯ (Dong Cheng, $, p. 92)

EUROPEAN

Vineyard (Putaoyuan'r) ✯ (Back Lakes, $$, p. 90)

FRENCH

Flo (Fu Lou) (Chaoyang, $$$, p. 93)

Jaan (Jia An) ✯ (City Center, $$$$, p. 86)

FUSION

The CourtYard (Siheyuan) ✯✯ (City Center, $$$, p. 86)

Green T. House (Zi Yun Xuan) ✯ (Chaoyang, $$$$, p. 92)

Lan ✯ (Chaoyang, $$$, p. 94)

My Humble House (Dongfang Hanshe) ✯✯ (City Center, $$$$, p. 86)

People 8 (Renjian Xuanse) ✯✯ (Chaoyang, $$$, p. 94)

GUIZHOU

San Ge Guizhouren (Chaoyang, $$, p. 98)

HAKKA

Kejia Cai ✯ (Back Lakes, $, p. 91)

HOME-STYLE (JIACHANG CAI)

Huajia Yiyuan (Dong Cheng, $, p. 91)

Xiangyang Tun (Haidian, $, p. 105)

Xiao Wang Fu (Chaoyang, $$, p. 99)

HONG KONG

Be There or Be Square (Bu Jian Bu San) (City Center, $, p. 87)

Otto's Restaurant (Richang Cha Canting) ✯ (City Center, $, p. 88)

Key to Abbreviations: $$$$ = Very Expensive $$$ = Expensive $$ = Moderate $ = Inexpensive

HOT POT

Ding Ding Xiang (Chaoyang, $, p. 99)

Huangcheng Lao Ma (Chaoyang, $$, p. 97)

Taipo Tianfu Shanzhen ✸✸ (Beijing South, $, p. 101)

HUAIYANG

Kong Yiji Jiulou ✸ (Back Lakes, $, p. 91)

Zhang Sheng Ji Jiudian, ✸✸ (Beijing West, $$, p. 104)

INDIAN

Indian Kitchen (Yindu Xiao Chu) ✸ (Chaoyang, $, p. 99)

Taj Pavilion (Taiji Lou Yindu Canting) (Chaoyang, $$, p. 99)

ITALIAN

Annie's Cafe (Anni Yidali Canting) (Chaoyang, $$, p. 95)

Assaggi (Changshi) ✸✸ (Chaoyang, $$$, p. 93)

Cepe (Yiwei Xuan) ✸✸ (Beijing West, $$$$, p. 103)

Le Cafe Igosso ✸✸ (Chaoyang, $$, p. 97)

JAPANESE

Haiku by Hatsune (Yin Quan Zhi Yu) ✸✸ (Chaoyang, $$$, p. 93)

Hatsune (Yin Quan) ✸✸ (Chaoyang, $$$, p. 93)

JIAOZI

Tianjin Bai Jiao Yuan (Beijing South, $, p. 102)

MALAYSIAN

Cafe Sambal ✸ (Back Lakes, $$$, p. 88)

NORTHEASTERN

Dongbei Hu ✸ (Yayun Cun, $, p. 105)

Xiangyang Tun (Haidian, $, p. 105)

NORTHWESTERN

Xibei Youmian Cun ✸✸ (Yayun Cun, $$, p. 104)

PERSIAN

Rumi (Rumi) ✸✸ (Chaoyang, $$, p. 95)

PIZZA

Hutong Pizza (Back Lakes, $$, p. 90)

SHANXI

Noodle Loft (Mian Ku Shanxi Shiyi) (Chaoyang, $, p. 101)

Xibei Youmian Cun ✸✸ (Yayun Cun, $$, p. 104)

SICHUAN

Chuan Jing Ban Canting ✸✸ (Dong Cheng, $, p. 90)

Lan ✸ (Chaoyang, $$$, p. 94)

Mala Youhuo ✸✸ (Beijing South, $, p. 101)

Source (Dujiangyuan) (Back Lakes, $$$, p. 89)

Yuxiang Renjia ✸ (Beijing South, $, p. 102)

SPANISH

Mare (Da Pa Shi) ✸✸ (Chaoyang, $$, p. 97)

TAIWANESE

Bellagio (Lu Gang Xiaozhen) (Chaoyang, $$, p. 96)

THAI

Serve the People (Wei Renmin Fuwu) (Chaoyang, $$, p. 99)

UIGHUR

Pamer (Pami'er Shifu) ✸ (Beijing South, $, p. 101)

Xiyu Shifu ✸✸ (Yayun Cun, $, p. 105)

VEGETARIAN

Baihe Sushi (Lily Vegetarian Restaurant) ✸ (Beijing West, $$, p. 104)

Pure Lotus (Jing Xn Lian) ✸ (Beijing West, $$, p. 104)

VIETNAMESE
Nuage (Qing Yun Lou) ☞ (Back Lakes, $$$, p. 88)

YUNNAN
Dali Courtyard (Da Li) (Back Lakes, $$, p. 89)

No Name Restaurant (Wu Ming Can Ting) (Back Lakes, $$, p. 106)
Yunnan Jin Kongque Dehong Daiwei Canguan (Haidian, $, p. 90)
Yunteng Binguan ☞ (Beijing South, $, p. 102)

3 Beijing City Center, Around Wangfujing Dajie

VERY EXPENSIVE

Jaan (Jia An) 家安 ☞ FRENCH   The lovely French food here pretty much sticks to traditional lines. Dishes are light, but filling, and resident chef Guillaume Galliot is a stickler for good ingredients—it took him seven months to find a local vegetable supplier that was up to his standards. The menu changes every season. We highly recommend the roasted cod with truffle macaroni cèpe emulsion. The cod melts at the touch of your fork and the sauce is flavorful but not too heavy. The ambience, with generic elevator music, leaves a little something to be desired. The restaurant doesn't really have a space of its own, but is separated from the main lobby by opium bed seating; the narrow layout makes you feel like you're in a brightly-lit hallway that just happens to serve fine food.

Dong Chang'an Jie 1 东长安街1号 (1 block west of Oriental Plaza). ☏ 010/6526-3388. Reservations recommended. Meal for 2 ¥800–¥1,200 ($107–$160/£53–£80). AE, DC, MC, V. Daily noon–2pm; 6:30–10pm. Metro: Wangfujing (118, exit A).

My Humble House (Dongfang Hanshe) 东方寒舍 ☞☞ FUSION   There's nothing humble about this restaurant: The big players have come to town. Perched above Oriental Plaza, the dramatic light-filled atrium sports a slightly sickly bamboo forest on the north side, and a rippling pond to the south, in line with *fengshui* principles. The staff is relaxed and confident, there is a vast amount of space between tables, and the background music complements the experience without becoming a distraction. The superb fare is a mixture of genuine fusion and Hunan-influenced seafood dishes. The menu changes constantly, but the juicy tenderloin Angus beef with black pepper is not to be missed. If there are faults, it's the slim range of wine by the glass, and the inexperience of the bartenders, dumbfounded when asked for a dirty martini.

Dong Chang'an Jie 1 东长安街1号 (west side of Oriental Plaza, podium level); see map p. 108. ☏ 010/8518-8811. Main courses ¥38–¥375 ($5.05–$50/£2.55–£25) with one exception; see abalone reference in review. AE, DC, MC, V. Lunch 11:30am–2:30pm; afternoon tea 2:30–5:30pm; dinner 5:30–10:30pm. Metro: Wangfujing (118, exit A).

EXPENSIVE

The CourtYard (Siheyuan) 四合苑 ☞☞ FUSION   If you read the food magazines, this may be the one Beijing restaurant you know. Owned by a Chinese-American lawyer with family roots in Beijing, the CourtYard serves admirable fare but wins the most accolades for its setting, in a restored courtyard-style house next to the Forbidden City. The house's gray brick exterior still blends with its old Beijing surroundings, but inside is a different world: modernist white and glass, with tall art-hung walls and a beckoning staircase that leads to a contemporary art gallery in the basement. The fare isn't genuine fusion; dishes are recognizably Occidental or Oriental with only token mixing of styles, but they're delectable nonetheless. Foie gras brûlée, cashew-crusted lamb chop, and black cod with tomato marmalade are longtime favorites. The tender grilled chicken breast in lemon grass and coconut curry is superb, justifying rave reviews almost by itself. The wine list is more comprehensive and well thought out than anything this side of Hong Kong, with a surprisingly large number available by the glass. An intimate cigar lounge upstairs, furnished with leather couches, looks out across the Forbidden City's eastern moat.

Donghua Men Dajie 95 东华门大街95号 (10-min. walk, on north side of street); see map p. 108. ℂ **010/ 6526-8883.** Reservations essential. Main courses ¥145–¥245 ($19–$33/£9.65–£16). AE, DC, MC, V. Daily 6–9:30pm. Metro: Tian'an Men East (117, exit B); east side of Forbidden City.

Made in China (Chang An Yi Hao) 长安一号 ★★ BEIJING   This is a restaurant
we regularly visit, for its fantastic Peking duck and its equally enthralling setting—a dining room placed in the middle of an open kitchen, illuminated by the occasional leaping flame from the stove. The Grand Hyatt's showcase restaurant offers traditional northeastern and Beijing dishes in a bustling open-kitchen restaurant. Made in China serves the capital's most palatable *dou zhi* (fermented bean puree), excellent *ma doufu* (mashed soybean) and the ubiquitous *zhajiang mian* (wheat noodles with black bean mince), a dish that has spawned its own chain of restaurants. The Peking duck is the highlight—the presentation and flavors are impeccable. There's the odd fusion twist such as foie gras with sesame pancake, and there are excellent plain dishes such as *tonghao* vegetable with rice vinegar and garlic sauce. Quite unexpected for a Chinese restaurant, Made in China does delicious desserts—the pear champagne and passion fruit sorbet packs a fruity punch. Right next door you'll find the sleek **Red Moon Bar,** perfect for an aperitif.

Dong Chang'an Jie 1 东长安街1号 (inside Grand Hyatt); see map p. 108. ℂ **010/8518-1234,** ext. 3608. Reservations essential. Meal for 2 ¥250–¥350 ($33–$47/£17–£23). AE, DC, MC, V. Daily 7–10:30am; daily 11:30am–2:30pm and 5:30–10:30pm. Metro: Wangfujing (118, exit A).

INEXPENSIVE

Be There or Be Square (Bu Jian Bu San) 不见不散 HONG KONG   This Hong
Kong–style cafe chain, with its hip warehouse-style decor, is the city's most fashionable source of the Westernized Cantonese fare commonly found in the former British colony. All the classics are here: BBQ pork with rice, egg foo yung, beef with rice noodles, and strong milk tea made with condensed milk. There's also a selection of

---

⸨Overrated   Imperial Restaurants

Elaborately presented but seldom appetizing, dishes cooked in Beijing's much-hyped imperial style are one of the city's biggest scams. Famous imperial restaurants **Fang Shan Fanzhuang** in Bei Hai Park and **Li Jia Cai (Li Family Restaurant)** in the Back Lakes area are both set in picturesque surroundings but charge far too much for bad food and are therefore not included in this book. For a better dining experience in either location, pack a picnic. If you really want to drop a hundred bucks on camel paw and soup made from bird saliva, ask the concierge in your hotel to point the way. If you want to enjoy the cuisine of modern Mandarins, we recommend **Chuan Jing Ban** (p. 90) and the **Yunteng Binguan** (p. 102), the restaurants of the Sichuan and Yunnan provincial governments, respectively.

vaguely Western breakfast items, including peanut butter–stuffed French toast. Lines form at lunch, but the efficient staff, all equipped with SWAT-style headsets, make sure the wait is never long.

Level B1 Capital Epoch Plaza (首都时代广场) at Xi Chang'an Jie 88 西长安街88号. (C) **010/8391-4078.** Main courses ¥20–¥50 ($2.65–$6.65/£1.35–£3.35). No credit cards. Daily 9:30am–9:30pm. Metro: Xi Dan (115, exit E).

Otto's Restaurant (Richang Cha Canting) 日昌茶餐厅 *✶* CANTONESE/ HONG KONG   Otto's is authentic Hong Kong prole dining, down to the shouts, smoke, and indecipherable wall-mounted menu. The environment may be jarring and the staff too busy to care, but the food is tremendous. The restaurant specializes in *baozai* (clay pot) rice dishes, best of which is the *lawei huaji baozaifan,* a mix of rice, salty-sweet sausage, and chicken drizzled in soy. Also good, albeit messy, are the *suanxiang jichi* (paper-wrapped garlic chicken wings). Thick glasses of iced coffee sweetened with condensed milk *(bing kafei)* are the perfect remedy for midsummer malaise. New branches are sprouting all over town—notably a 24-hour branch just east of the north entrance to Bei Hai Park.

Dong Dan Dajie 72 东单大街72号 (inside small alley past a movie theater on east side); see map p. 108. (C) **010/ 6525-1783.** Meal for 2 ¥60–¥80 ($8–$11/£4–£5.35). No credit cards. Daily 10am–3am. English menu. Metro: Dong Dan (119, exit A); walk north several blocks. Other branches at Di'an Men Xi Dajie 14 地安门西大街14号, (C) **010/6405-8205** ; 2/F Shanghai Salon上海沙龙2层, (C) **010/6780-4350;** and Hua Yuan Dong Lu 8花园东路8号, (C) **010/8203-8155.**

4 Back Lakes & Dong Cheng

EXPENSIVE

Cafe Sambal *✶* MALAYSIAN   Sambal embraces and surpasses all the clichés of a chic Beijing eatery. It's a cozy courtyard house decorated with antique and modern furnishings, relaxed service, and a well-balanced wine list. And then there's the food, prepared by a charming chef from Kuala Lumpur. You'll need to call a day in advance for the superb double-braised Australian lobster in *nyonya* sauce, or the incredibly fresh chile curry crab, served on a bed of curry leaves, dried shrimp, and chile paste. Try the fried four-sided bean with cashew nut sauce, or the yogurt-based mutton curry. Don't miss the signature dish, Kapitan chicken, a mildly spicy dish with a nutty aftertaste, said to have been invented when Chinese migrants reached Penang during the Ming dynasty. The *kuih dadar,* shredded coconut fried with palm sugar and wrapped in a padang leaf roll, is delectable.

Doufu Chi Hutong 43 豆腐池胡同43号 (walk south along Jiu Gulou Dajie, it's near the corner of the 5th street on left, marked by a red lantern); see map p. 108. (C) **010/6400-4875.** Reservations recommended for dinner. Meal for 2 ¥250–¥400 ($33–$53/£17–£27). AE, DC, MC, V. Daily 11am–midnight. Metro: Gu Lou (217, exit B).

Nuage (Qing Yun Lou) 庆云楼 *✶* VIETNAMESE   Lake views from this restaurant's upstairs windows are matched only by its hallucinatory Hanoi-inspired interior. A long silver dragon snakes up the rear staircase to the main dining room, where the low light from red lanterns flickers on reed curtains and finely crafted wooden tables. The first floor has improbably stylish bathrooms, divided by an elaborate cut-glass pool, and the new rooftop section has breathtaking views of the Back Lakes. Food is not quite as impressive—portions are small and prices inflated—but there are some worthwhile gems. The grilled la lop leaf beef *(ye niurou juan)* is exquisite; and the *phô* (Vietnamese beef noodles in soup) has a smooth, flavorful broth, but at a price 10 times higher than in Vietnam. This is the closest thing Beijing has to a "hot" restaurant in the New York City sense, complete with a long-legged hostess who seems to take pleasure in turning people away. (Make reservations well in advance.) A dance club extends two floors underground.

Qian Hai Dong Yan 22 前海东沿 22号 (east of the Yinding Bridge, at the intersection of Qian Hai and Hou Hai); see map p. 108. ⓒ 010/6401-9581. Reservations required. Meal for 2 ¥300–¥400 ($40–$53/£20–£27). Add an extra 15% service charge for rooftop dining. AE, DC, MC, V. Daily 11am–2pm and 5:30–10pm.

Paper (Jian) 简 ✦ CANTONESE
This stylish restaurant is owned by the proprietor of Bed Bar, one of the hippest bars in town just a few blocks away. It features Chinese food with a modern twist. There's little ordering involved since all meals come in a set menu and feature such goodies as stir-fried eggplant and tiger prawns cooked in tea leaves. The decor is all white and blonde wood—very urban minimalist.

Gulou Dong Dajie 138 古楼东大街138号 (east of the Drum Tower); see map p. 108. ⓒ 010/8401-5080. Set menu (8-course) ¥150 ($20/£10). AE, DC, MC, V. Daily 4–10pm.

Sansheng Wanwu 三生万物 ✦ DAOIST
This restaurant is nestled in half of a defunct Daoist prayer hall, at the back of a crumbling residential cluster east of the Back Lakes. The *hutong* outside has no sign—look for an aged stone archway with the Ming-era temple's name (Guangfu Guan) carved in faded characters at its apex. A narrow path leads from the arch past bemused neighbors to the hall, its beautifully crafted beams and murals brought back to life in early 2003. The manager, who was born in the building and recalls the false roof that hid it from Cultural Revolution vandals, has hired chefs from Qing Cheng Shan in Sichuan, where the Zhengyi school of Daoism developed recipes for longevity and virility. The set meal includes fresh *jiaozi*, accompanied by delicate side dishes like goose liver rolls with hoisin sauce (*e'gan juan*), deep-fried pork with medicinal herbs (*cungu shao*), and sweet gourd-shaped red bean rolls with mountain herbs (*shanyao hulu*). The drink menu features a bracing "immortal's abode" *koumiss (dongtian rujiu)*, made with fermented milk, and the somewhat more appetizing Daoist medicinal tea (*gong cha*).

Yandai Xiejie 37 烟袋斜街37, next to the Lotus Bar (walking south from Drum Tower on Di'an Men Wai Dajie, take your first right onto Yandai Xiejie; walk for about 200m and the archway leading to the restaurant will be on your right). ⓒ 010/6404-2778. Reservations required. Set meal ¥120 ($16/£8). AE, DC, MC, V. Daily 10am till late.

Source (Dujiangyuan) 渡江源 SICHUAN
Frequented by expats, this restaurant in a Chinese courtyard is where you should go if you want to enjoy a quiet Sichuanese meal in style. The set menu, served in courses, can be hit or miss.

Kuanjie Nan Luogu Xiang Banchang Hutong 14 宽街南锣鼓巷板厂胡同14号 (next to Lusong Yuan hotel); see map p.108. ⓒ 010/6400-3736. Lunch or dinner ¥150–¥200 ($20–$27/£10–£13). AE, MC, V. Daily 10:30am–2pm and 5–10:30pm.

MODERATE

Dali Courtyard (Da Li) 大理 ✦ YUNNAN
Romance, romance! Old jazz tunes play in this traditional Chinese courtyard decorated with coal furnaces and art deco furniture. There's no menu—the chef serves up a set meal in courses—so it's perfect for couples or small groups who want to try a range of southwestern Chinese dishes. Items include papaya salad, grilled fish, and stir-fried chicken—all fairly light and healthy. The restaurant is perfect for people who don't like the stress of ordering and

would prefer to concentrate on the ambience. The food is perfectly fine, but nothing will knock you out of the courtyard.

Gulou Dong Dajie, Xiaojingchang Hutong 67 古楼东大街小经常胡同67号; see map p. 108. ✆ 010/8404-1430. Lunch ¥100–¥300 ($13–$40/£6.65–£20), set dinner ¥100–¥300 ($13–$40/£6.65–£20). No credit cards. Daily 11:30am–1:30pm and 6:30–9:30pm.

Hutong Pizza 胡同比萨 PIZZA This hard-to-find pizzeria occupies the site of a former Buddhist nunnery and features untouched murals in the loft. There's no religious theme to the handmade thin-crust pizzas, but if you've arrived from the wilds of China, you may experience something akin to a spiritual experience. The only jarring touch is the presence of green pepper and black olives on an otherwise sublime three-cheese pizza.

Yinding Qiao Hutong 9 银锭桥胡同9号 (from Yinding Qiao walk west, taking the left fork, and then right at T-junction); see map p. 108. ✆ 010/6617-5916. Main courses ¥27–¥109 ($3.60–$15/£1.80–£7.25). No credit cards. Daily 11am–11pm.

No Name Restaurant (Wu Ming Can Ting) 无名餐厅 YUNNAN The demolition of Bai Feng's much-loved No Name Bar is inevitable, but his charming new restaurant has some of its spirit. There are smart touches: Luminous inlaid stones, shimmering waterfalls, and maidenhair ferns create a soothing atmosphere. The minority-chic food is sublime; try the *nongjia shao jian ji* (spicy sautéed chicken fillet), which uses real bird's eye chile, or the delectable grilled lemon grass fish *(daizu xiangmao cao kao yu)*, served wrapped in a lotus leaf. The finest dish is a juicy foil-wrapped beef marinated in mountain herbs *(se shao niurou)*. A range of fresh juices nicely complement the spicy fare, and the bar still makes a mean gin and tonic.

Da Jinsi Hutong 1号大金丝胡同1号 (from Yinding Qiao head west and look for a narrow lane that soon forks right). ✆ 010/6618-6061. Meal for 2 ¥120–¥200 ($16–$27/£8–£13). AE, MC, V. Daily 11am–midnight (kitchen closes at 11pm).

Vineyard (Putaoyuan'r) 葡萄院儿 ✦ EUROPEAN This is one of our favorite new neighborhood haunts—the sunny outdoor patio is a great place to enjoy lunch or Sunday brunch. Their pizza is top notch, and if you're looking for a healthy breakfast, try the granola and fresh yogurt. The cafe also boasts wireless Internet access and a good wine selection. Service takes a sharp nose-dive when the restaurant gets busy, and you may find yourself repeatedly flagging down staff to get your food.

Wudaoying Hutong 31 五道营胡同31号 (just north of the Confucius temple); see map p. 108. ✆ 010/6402-7961. ¥50–¥150 ($6.65–$20/£3.35–£10). MC, V. Lunch & dinner Tues–Sun (closed Mon). Daily 11:30am–midnight; kitchen closes 3–6pm. Metro: Yonghegong (215, exit B).

INEXPENSIVE

Chuan Jing Ban Canting 川京办餐厅 ✦✦ (Value SICHUAN Anyone who has dealt with Chinese officials knows that there is one topic they are all experts on: food. This constantly crowded restaurant occupies the former site of the Qing Imperial examination hall (no traces remain). It is now the headquarters of the Sichuan Provincial Government, and the masses can enjoy the fruits of their rulers' connoisseurship. The spicy *shui zhu yu* consists of sublime, tender fish floating on a bed of crisp bean sprouts, and kids will appreciate the sweet pork with rice crust *(guoba roupian)*. Sichuan standards, such as *mapo doufu* (spicy tofu with chopped meat), are as authentic as the ingredients, which are flown in several times a week. The only evidence you're dining with cadres arrives later in the menu; two pages are dedicated to hard liquor and one to cigarettes.

Gongyuan Tou Tiao 5 贡院头条5号 (from metro, walk 1 block north along the Second Ring Rd., turn left into Dong Zongbu Hutong, Dong Cheng Qu); see map p. 108. © 010/6512-2277. Meal for 2 ¥80–¥140 ($11–$19/£5.35–£9.35). No credit cards. Daily 10:30am–2:30pm and 4:30–9:30pm. English menu. Metro: Jianguo Men (211, exit A).

Huajia Yiyuan 花家怡园 HOME-STYLE   The chef-owner behind this popular courtyard restaurant claims to have created a new Chinese supercuisine, assembled from the best of the country's regional cooking styles. Whether Huacai (his name for the cuisine) will ever spread beyond Beijing remains to be seen, but his long menu is one of the city's most impressive. The new restaurant is slightly less raucous than the recently demolished original, but locals still crowd around tables at night to devour heaped plates of spicy crayfish *(mala longxia)* and drink green "good for health" beer. Try the *larou douya juanbing,* a mix of spicy bacon and bean sprouts rolled in pancakes roast duck–style.

Dong Zhi Men Nei Dajie 235 东直门内大街235号; see map p. 108. © 010/6403-0677. Meal for 2 ¥100–¥120 ($13–$16/£6.65–£8). AE, DC, MC, V. Daily 10am–4am. Metro: Dong Zhi Men (214, exit A).

Kejia Cai 客家菜 ✸ HAKKA   The Hakka, or "guest people" (Kejiaren), are Han who migrated southeast from central China generations ago, but never managed to integrate. Forced by discrimination to live in isolated communities in poor mountainous regions, they kept to their separate culture—and cooking traditions. A historically marginal cuisine, Hakka food has over the past 2 years become the center of epicurean fashion in Beijing. The owner, a local artist, designed this space with a rustic motif: thick wood tables, stone floors, crinkled character-laden wallpaper next to patches of exposed brick, and waitresses in peasant garb. Enjoyable as the dining rooms are, it is the kitchen that keeps lines of customers winding through the door. The cooking style is hard to define vis-à-vis other cuisines available in the city, but ask regular patrons to explain the difference and most give a quick answer: It's good. The *yanju xia* (shrimp skewers served in rock salt) and *lancai sijidou* (diced green beans with ground pork) are both divine, as is the chicken with tea-mushroom soup *(chashugu bao laoji)*. The one dish you'll find on every table is *mizhi zhibao luyu,* a "secret recipe paper-wrapped fish"—tender and nearly boneless, in a sweet sauce you'll want to drink.

Southeast bank of Qian Hai 前海南沿 (50m/164 ft. north of Bei Hai Park north entrance); see map p. 108. © 010/6404-2259. Meal for 2 ¥80–¥100 ($11–$13/£5.35–£6.65). No credit cards. Daily 11am–3:30pm and 5–10:30pm.

Kong Yiji Jiudian 孔乙己酒店 ✸ HUAIYANG   This popular restaurant was named for the alcoholic scholar-bum protagonist of a short story by Lu Xun, the father of modern Chinese literature. It offers an enjoyable dining experience, although it is somewhat weighed down by its own popularity. Service is not what it once was. A small bamboo forest leads to a traditional space outfitted with calligraphy scrolls, traditional bookshelves, and other trappings of Chinese scholarship. The menu, written vertically in the old style, features several hair-raising dishes, including the infamous *zuixia* (drunken shrimp), served still squirming in a small glass bowl filled with wine. Less shocking, and highly recommended, are the *mizhi luyu,* a whole fish deep-fried then broiled in tin foil with onions in a slightly sweet sauce; and the *youtiao niurou,* savory slices of beef mixed with pieces of fried dough. Nearly everyone orders a small pot of *Dongpo rou,* extremely tender braised fatty pork swimming in savory juice, and a plate of *huixiang dou,* anise-flavored beans. Fans of Lu's story will appreciate the wide

---

Moments **Dinner on the Lakes, by Candlelight**

For roughly ¥400 ($53/£27) plus the cost of food, Beijing's ancient roast-meat restaurant **Kaorou Ji** now arranges what may be the most charming dining experience in the city: a meal for up to eight people served aboard a narrow **canopied flat-bottom boat,** staffed by a lone oarsman who guides the craft in a gentle arc around the man-made serenity of Qian Hai and Hou Hai. The entire trip takes roughly 2 hours. A little extra money buys live traditional music and the opportunity to float candles in the lakes after dark falls—a cliché in the making, but who cares? The restaurant is located next to Nuage (p. 88) at Qian Hai Dong Yan 14, and a meal for 2 costs ¥120 to ¥160 ($16–$21/£8–£11); open daily 9am–2pm and 5–9pm. To make boat arrangements, call ℂ **010/ 6612-5717** or 010/6404-2554. *Note:* Boat-rental prices vary from season to season and will probably increase as time goes on.

---

selection of *huangjiu,* a sweet "yellow" rice wine aged for several years, served in silver pots, and sipped from a special ceramic warming cup. Less crowded branches have opened at Yayun Cun (ℂ **010/8480-3966**) and Dong Si Bei Dajie 322 (ℂ **010/6404-0507**). Desheng Men Nei Dajie 德胜门内大街 (next to the octagonal Teahouse of Family Fu on the northwest bank of Hou Hai); see map p. 108. ℂ 010/6618-4917. No reservations. Meal for 2 ¥100–¥140 ($13–$19/£6.65–£9.35). AE, MC, V. Daily 9:30am–2pm and 5–10:30pm.

Xian'r Lao Man 馅老满 ✿ BEIJING/DUMPLINGS   Sixty varieties of dumplings are available at this busy neighborhood hangout, decorated with black and white photos of Beijing and simple Chinese antiques reproductions. With dumpling skins made from high-quality flour and innovative fillings (including cabbage and peanut, or lotus root with pork), this inexpensive restaurant is popular with foreigners and locals alike. We've personally wrapped dumplings in the kitchen as part of a cooking internship, so we can vouch for the cleanliness of the operation!

Andingmen Nei Dajie 252 安定门内大街252 号; see map p. 108. ℂ 010/6404-6944. Meal for 2 ¥50 ($6.65/ £3.35). No credit cards. Daily 10:30am–10:30pm. Metro: Andingmen (216). Another branch at Ya Yuan 5, An Hui Bei Li; ℂ 010/6497-2097.

5 Chaoyang

VERY EXPENSIVE

Green T. House (Zi Yun Xuan) 紫云轩 ✿ FUSION   If you're comfortable with the sentiment that "dining should be part of a lifestyle experience," you'll love this ultra-chic restaurant. If you think that sounds like pretentious twaddle, try Bellagio's, right next door. The restaurant's name changes from purple to green in translation, and dining at Green T. is a similarly psychedelic experience. The imaginatively prepared food is light, with tea-infused flavors, but the cuisine is beside the point. The minimalist decor and attentive service attracts a fashion-conscious crowd. A new branch of the restaurant, called Green T. House Living, opened in 2006 in the outskirts of Beijing, but isn't really worthwhile unless you think an extra dose of pretentiousness is worth the 45-minute drive.

Gongti Xi Lu 6 工体西路6号 (a subtly marked door, on the east side of Bellagio's); see map p. 117. ℂ 010/6552-8310. Reservations essential. Dinner for 2 ¥800–¥1,200 ($107–$160/£53–£80). AE, DC, MC, V. Daily 11am–2:30pm and 6pm–midnight. Other location, known as Green T. House Living紫云轩茶事, far north of the city center at Cuigezhuang Xiang Hegezhuang Cun 318崔各庄乡合各庄村318号. © 0/13601137132. Daily noon–2:30pm and 6pm–midnight.

EXPENSIVE

Assaggi (Changshi) 尝试 ✿✿ ITALIAN   This lovely Italian restaurant recently reopened, much to the delight of Beijing food lovers. The restaurant has a quiet, minimalist sophistication with dim lighting and white furniture. Alfresco dining on their cozy terrace is a must during warmer weather. The staff is attentive and proactive (a rarity in this city), and the food is excellent. Pastas are perfectly al dente and sauces are light and fresh. Our favorite is the walnut penne, a nutty flavored, creamy pasta.

Sanlitun Bei Xiao Jie 1 三里屯北小街1号 (northeast of the German Embassy); see map p. 117. © 010/8454-4508. Main courses ¥60–¥140 ($8–$19/£4–£9.35); prix-fixe lunch ¥60, ¥80, or ¥99 ($8, $11, $13/£4, £5.35, £6.60). AE, DC, MC, V. Daily 10am–11:30pm. Metro: Nong Zhan Guan.

Flo (Fu Lou) 福楼 *Value* FRENCH   This is a branch of the French restaurant empire described by some Paris foodies as the Starbucks of brasseries, but you can only be so picky in Beijing. The restaurant occupies the front of a rather flashy building, all balustrades and staircases, with an (inaudible) nightclub at the rear. The menu offers straightforward French favorites, all done well. Recommended items include the smoked salmon salad with poached egg, pan-fried rib short loin veal with mushrooms, and the chef's specialty, hot goose liver with apple. Reliability and good value may be why it's one of only a handful of free-standing Western restaurants to have survived more than a few years.

Dong San Huan Bei Lu 12 东三环北路12号 (south of the Great Wall Sheraton); see map p. 117. © 010/6595-5139. Main courses ¥90–¥230 ($12–$31/£6–£16); prix-fixe lunch ¥68–¥98 ($9.05–$13/£4.55–£6.55); set dinner menu ¥158 ($21/£11) available Mon–Fri. AE, MC, V. Daily 11am–11pm. Metro: Nong Zhan Guan.

Haiku by Hatsune (Yin Quan Zhi Yu) 隐泉之语 ✿✿ JAPANESE   Haiku is just as sleek, stylish, and popular as her sister restaurant Hatsune (see below). The entrance to the restaurant is a long, mirrored walkway where aspiring models can work on their catwalk strut. Inside, the decor is understated and at times a little too aware of being cool and contemporary—even the sake cups are warped pieces of mini ceramic art. The sushi rolls are similar to those at Hatsune, but the menu is more compact. Choose this restaurant over Hatsune if you're up for late-night drinks at the cool adjacent bar.

Chaoyang Gongyuan Ximen 8 Gongguan Nei Nance 3/F 潮阳公园西门8号公馆内南侧3层 (in what looks like a parking lot across from the Goose and Duck); see map p. 117. © 010/6508-8585, ext. 203. Meal for 2 ¥200–¥250 ($27–$33/£13–£17). AE, DC, MC, V. Daily 6:30–11:30pm.

Hatsune (Yin Quan) 隐泉 ✿✿ JAPANESE   Hatsune is sushi sacrilege via Northern California, with a list of innovative rolls long and elaborate enough to drive serious raw fish traditionalists to ritual suicide. The unconventional attitude is also reflected in the stylish space, high-ceilinged and sleek, with a long glass-and-metal entryway and a rock garden path leading to the bathrooms. Nearly every item on the menu is among the best of its kind in the city, but the rolls are what make this place truly special. With the single exception of the Beijing Roll, a roast duck and "special sauce" gimmick, you simply can't go wrong. The 119 Roll, with bright red tuna inside and out, topped with a divine spicy-sweet sauce, absolutely should not be missed.

Guanghua Dong Lu, Heqiao Dasha C 光华东路和乔大厦C楼 (4 blocks east of Kerry Centre, opposite Petro China building); see map p. 117. © 010/6581-3939. Meal for 2 ¥200–¥250 ($27–$33/£13–£17); Mon–Fri prix-fixe lunch ¥65 ($8.65/£4.35); weekend lunch buffet ¥158 ($21/£11). AE, DC, MC, V. Daily 11:30am–2pm and 5:30–10pm.

Horizon (Haitian Ge) 海天阁 ★ *Value* CANTONESE   The Shangri-La–managed Horizon is one of the finest and more sumptuously decorated Cantonese restaurants in Beijing—and also one of its most reasonably priced. Cantonese is the subtlest of the Chinese cuisines, and this is the real thing, so don't expect the retina-straining colors or tooth-rotting sweet sauces you find at your neighborhood Chinese takeout joint. The menu features shark's fin, bird's-nest soup, and other classic indulgences designed to show off the fatness of your wallet. If instead you let your taste buds lead the way, then the stewed beef and dry bean curd with XO sauce, and the battered king prawns with mustard, should be among your choices. So should the Mandarin fish, deep-fried in the lightest of batters and prettily presented with a delicate sweet-and-sour sauce. The restaurant has also responded to the current obsession with Sichuan food, and the sautéed crab with dried chile is a good choice if you're in the mood for more aggressive flavors. The weekend all-you-can-eat lunch, featuring a respectable selection of dim sum, costs only ¥128 ($17/£8.55) for two.

Guanghua Lu 1, inside Kerry Centre Mall 光华路嘉里中心 (near rear entrance of Kerry Centre Hotel); see map p. 117. ✆ 010/6561-8833, ext. 41. Meal for 2 ¥200–¥300 ($27–$40/£13–£20). AE, DC, MC, V. Daily 11:30am–2:30pm and 5:30–10pm. Metro: Guomao (122, exit A).

Lan 兰 ★ SICHUAN/FUSION   This has become *the* place to be seen in Beijing among the trendy set. European Renaissance-style paintings hang on the wall and cabinets hold wacky items like stacks of canned tuna fish and Mao memorabilia. Designed by Phillip Starck, this flagship of a popular chain of Sichuan restaurants serves decent, if overpriced, dishes. Avoid the fusion fare at all costs, and stick to the basics like the kung pao chicken.

4/F, LG Twins Tower, Jianguomen Wai Dajie Yi 12 建国门外大街乙12号LG双子楼4层; see map p. 117. ✆ 010/5109-6012. ¥200–¥400 ($27–$53/£13–£27). AE, DC, MC, V. Daily 11am–11pm. Metro: Yong'anli (121).

Morel's (Molaolongxi Xicanting) 莫劳龙玺西餐厅 ★★ BELGIAN   Morel's reputation as the best Western restaurant in the city is a holdover from a less competitive era, but this is nevertheless a fine restaurant, with a rare, fanatic devotion to quality. Owned by Belgian Renaat Morel, one of China's most respected European chefs, and run with help from his wife, the restaurant has a casual and cozy feel, its yellow walls and green-and-white checked tablecloths reminiscent of someone's home. The food is simply presented, and side dishes are somewhat limp. However, main courses are supremely done, particularly the wonderful Flemish beef stew with tender chunks of meat, cooked over many hours in a mix of Rodenbach beer, bay leaf, onion, and thyme. Soups change daily and always sell out. The restaurant also has an astounding array of Belgian beers; they now have their own range of purpose-brewed ales. Best of all, however, is the signature Morel's dessert: a near-perfect waffle—save room for it—made in a real waffle iron hand-carried on a plane from Belgium.

Xin Zhong Jie 5 新中街5号 (opposite Worker's Gymnasium north gate); see map p. 117. ✆ 010/6416-8802. Reservations recommended for dinner. Main courses ¥58–¥168 ($7.75–$22/£3.85–£11). AE, DC, MC, V. Tue–Sun 10am till late. Another branch at Liangma Qiao Lu 27 亮马桥路27号 (1 mile east of the Kempinski Hotel). ✆ 010/6437-3939. Metro: Liangma He.

People 8 (Renjian Xuanse) 人间玄色 ★★ CHINESE FUSION   We like the subterranean feel of this elegant restaurant, perfect for a romantic dinner or impressing business clients. A tricky entrance, a labyrinth of stairs and hallways, and a very dark interior lined with bamboo make the walk to the dining room seem like a journey into another world. The light dishes like the miso cod and the sukiyaki (Japanese-style beef cooked in a pot) come in small portions, so order plenty.

Jianguomen Wai Dajie 18 建国门外大街18号 (behind SciTech Hotel); see map p. 117. ✆ 010/6515-8585. ¥250–¥400 ($33–$53/£17–£27). AE, DC, MC, V. Daily 10:30am–2pm; 5:30pm–10pm. Metro: Yong'anli (121).

Rumi (Rumi) 入迷 ✸✸ PERSIAN   This is the only place dishing up Persian food in the city. Be forewarned, however: Alcohol is not served at Rumi, but they make up for it with an extensive offering of fruit juices, milkshakes, and teas. Plus, if you're looking for a buzz, the restaurant offers hookahs—long water pipes with fruit-flavored tobaccos. The portions are generous, grilled meats are seasoned with tasty spices, and the dips and sauces are divine. The bread, which can be on the dry and bland side, could use some sprucing up. Grab a seat on the outdoor terrace if the weather's nice, or otherwise dine in elegance amongst minimalist, off-white decor and vaulted ceilings.

Gongti Bei Lu Jia 1 工体北路甲1号 (across from Pacific Century Place); see map p. 117. ✆ 010/8454-3838. Dinner for two ¥200–¥250 ($27–$33/£13–£17). MC, V. Daily 11am–1am. Metro: Gongti Bei Lu.

MODERATE

Alameda ✸ ⒱ⓐⓛⓤⓔ CONTEMPORARY BRAZILIAN   This glass-walled, airy restaurant serves two-course set lunch and dinner menus at bargain prices. The starter breads—slices of buttered garlic toast and tiny, piping hot cheese puffs—are addictive. Our favorite main courses are the filet mignon with mashed potatoes and the seared red snapper. This place is always packed on the weekends, so call a day or two in advance to make sure you get a table.

Sanlitun Beijie 三里屯北街 (beside the Nali Mall); see map p. 117. ✆ 010/6417-8084. Reservations highly recommended. ¥60 ($8/£4) set lunch; ¥158 ($21/£11) set dinner. V only. Daily noon–3pm, 6–10:30pm. Metro: Gongti Bei Lu.

Annie's Cafe (Anni Yidali Canting) 安妮意大利餐厅 ⒱ⓐⓛⓤⓔ ⓚⓘⓓⓢ ITALIAN   A casual, cozy, and tremendously welcoming Italian bistro tucked among the nightspots at the west gate of Chaoyang Gongyuan, Annie's is the hands-down favorite for affordable Italian fare in Beijing. Wood-fired pizzas are the most popular item, but try baked *gnocchi gratinate* with tomato and broccoli, or the chicken ravioli served with spinach and a fine tomato cream sauce. Appetizers and desserts are just average, the notable exception being the cannoli, a sinful blend of ricotta cheese and dried fruit with a touch of brandy in a fresh shell of fried dough. Annie's staff is bend-over-backward friendly, happy to bring as many baskets of free bread (served with small jars of pesto) as you want.

Chaoyang Gongyuan Xi Men 朝阳公园西门 (west gate of Chaoyang Park); see map p. 117. ✆ 010/6591-1931. Main courses ¥35–¥118 ($4.65–$16/£2.35–£7.85). AE, DC, MC, V. Daily 11am–11pm. Other locations at Jiuxianqiao Jiangtai Lu Shangye Jie 酒仙桥将台路商业街, ✆ 010/6436-3735; Jianguo Lu 88 建国路88号, ✆ 010/8589-8366; Dongsanhuan Lu 16 东三环路16号, ✆ 010/6503-3871.

Beijing Dadong Kaoya Dian 北京大董烤鸭 ✸✸ BEIJING   No hundred years of history or obscure *hutong* location here, just a crispy-skinned and pleasing roast duck that many say is one of the best in town—it rivals that of our favorite place for duck, Made in China, and it's also cheaper. The restaurant claims to use a special method to reduce the amount of fat in its birds, although it seems unlikely that duck this flavorful could possibly be good for you. The birds come in either whole (¥98/$13/£6.55) or half (¥49/$6.55/£3.25) portions and are served in slices with a wide assortment of condiments (garlic, green onion, radish). Place the duck on a pancake with plum

Tips **Where to Buy Picnic Supplies**

Picnicking is the most neglected tradition among travelers in Beijing, considering the city's wealth of picturesque parks and scenic areas. This was once due to a paucity of the necessary components, but the availability of nearly any food item from anywhere now means there is no excuse.

You can purchase basic **groceries** and Chinese-style **snacks** at local markets and the *xiaomaibu* (little-things-to-buy units) found nearly everywhere. Several fully stocked **supermarkets** and a handful of smaller grocers now carry imported wine and cheese, pesto sauce, American junk food, Newcastle Brown Ale, and just about anything else you could want, albeit at inflated prices. Supermarket Olé stocks a good selection of foreign items; find them in the China World Trade Center and the basement of the Ginza Mall at the Dongzhimen metro stop. April Gourmet, opposite On/Off in San Li Tun, has sliced meats, rare Western vegetables, and a full selection of familiar breakfast cereals. Much the same can be found at Jenny Lou's (see chapter 9, p. 178).

Among **delis and bakeries,** the best is the **Kempi Deli** (on the first floor of the Lufthansa building; ✆ **010/6465-3388,** ext. 5741). It offers satisfying crusty-bread sandwiches and a tremendous pastry and fresh baked bread selection that goes for half-price after 9pm. **Mrs. Shannen's Bagels** (✆ **010/8046-4301**) can whip up some mean bagel sandwiches, and if you can't make it to their inconvenient, far northeast suburbs location, they'll deliver.

Recommended picnic spots in the city proper include the **Summer Palace** (p. 130), the **Yuan Ming Yuan** (p. 140), **Ri Tan Park** (p. 140), as well as **Zizhu Yuan Gongyuan** (Purple Bamboo Garden), west of Beijing Zoo. Outside Beijing, sections of the Great Wall provide a dramatic spot for an outdoor meal. Also try the Ming and Qing tombs, Beihai Park, and the Tanzhe and Jietai temples in the western suburbs.

sauce and your choice of ingredients, and then roll and eat. An excellent plain broth soup, made from the rest of the duck, is included in the price. The English picture menu offers a wide range of other dishes, everything from mustard duck webs to duck tongue in aspic, plus a number of excellent *doufu* (tofu) dishes with thick, tangy sauces. Every meal comes with a free fruit plate and dessert. This is one of the few restaurants in Beijing with a nonsmoking room.

Tuanjie Hu Bei Kou 3 团结湖北口3号 (on east side of East Third Ring Rd., north of Tuanjie Hu Park); see map p. 117. ✆ 010/6582-2892. Reservations essential. Meal for 2 (including half-duck) ¥80–¥100 ($11–$13/£5.35–£6.65). AE, DC, MC, V. Daily 11am–10pm. Another excellent location at 1-2/F Nanxincang International Plaza 南新仓国际大厦1-2层 (southwest corner of Dongsishitiao); see map p. 117, ✆ 010/5169-0329. Daily 11am–10pm. Metro: Dongsishitiao (213, exit D).

Bellagio (Lu Gang Xiaozhen) 鹿港小镇 TAIWANESE   Taiwanese food, characterized by sweet flavors and subtle use of ginger, is one of the most appealing to Western palates. Bellagio's team of glam female waitstaff have an unjustified reputation for snooty service. The clientele of the Gongti branch, stumbling out from Babyface and Angel nightclubs, make for amusing people-watching. The decor is all sleek lines and shimmering beads. Don't miss the delicate *shacha niurou*, mustard greens combined perfectly with thinly sliced beef strips. *Taiwan dofu bao*, a tofu clay-pot seasoned with shallots, onion, chile, and black beans, is also remarkable, as is the signature dish, *sanbei ji* (chicken reduced in rice wine, sesame oil, and soy sauce). In summer, don't miss the enormous shaved-ice desserts: One serving is enough for four, but gobble it before it comes tumbling down!

Xiaoyun Lu 35 霄云路35号 (opposite Renaissance Hotel); see map p. 117. ℂ 010/8451-9988. Meal for 2 ¥120–¥200 ($16–$27/£8–£13). AE, DC, MC, V. Daily 11am–4am. Other branches at Gongti Xi Lu 6 工体西路6号 (south of Gongti 100 bowling center); see map p. 117. ℂ 010/6551-3533. Daily 11am–5am; Jian Guo Lu 87 Beijing Shin Kong Place 6F 建国路87号新光天地6楼, ℂ 010/6530-5658, daily 11am–10pm, Metro: Da Wang Lu, exit C; An Hui Bei Li Block 2 Building #4安慧北里2区4号楼, ℂ 010/6489-4300, daily 11am–2am.

Huangcheng Lao Ma 皇城老妈 HOT POT

Upmarket hot pot sounds like a contradiction in terms, but Huangcheng Lao Ma makes it work—and work well. Set inside a huge multi-storied building with a hyperbolic, tile-eave facade and relatively pleasant decor, the restaurant is almost constantly packed. The reason is their special ingredient, "Lao Ma's beef," a magical meat that stays tender no matter how long you boil it. Also popular are the large prawns, thrown live into the pot. The traditional broth is eye-watering spicy; order the split *yuanyang* pot with mild *wuyutang* (water world essence) broth in a separate compartment, or risk overheating your tongue.

Dabeiyao Nan Qingfeng Zha Hou Jie 39 大北窑南庆丰闸后街39 (south of China World Trade Center; south along East Third Ring, take left after crossing river); see map p. 117. ℂ 010/6779-8801. Meal for 2 ¥180–¥200 ($24–$27/£12–£13). AE, DC, MC, V. Daily 11am–11pm. English menu.

Le Cafe Igosso 🌟🌟 ITALIAN

You'd never guess, but a flight of stairs just north of an ugly flyover leads to Beijing's finest Italian restaurant. Start with an aperitif on the second-floor bar, which stocks an impressive range of spirits, before heading up to the small, intimate dining area, with dark wooden floors and furnishings. Service is unobtrusive—quite an achievement in such a small space. Both the chef and the owner are Japanese, so seafood dishes are compelling, particularly their appetizers. The sea bream carpaccio marinated in seaweed has a liquid freshness, and the mustard roast duck is excellent. Move on to pasta for two: From the regular menu, the crab and olive spaghetti is competently delivered, or choose from the handwritten specials menu. Rosemary chicken, served with roast potatoes and fresh rosemary, is the pick of the main dishes. The wine list is simple but adventurous, although selection by the glass is limited. On the right night, this is Beijing's most romantic dining experience.

Dong San Huan Zhong Lu 东三环中路 (700m [2,300 ft.] south of Guomao Bridge on East Third Ring Rd.); see map p. 117. ℂ 010/8771-7013. Weekend reservations essential. Main courses ¥38–¥120 ($5.05–$16/£2.55–£8). AE, MC, V. Daily 11:30am–1am. Metro: Guomao (122, exit C).

Mare (Da Pa Shi) 大怕世 🌟🌟 SPANISH

The huge range of tapas, large wine list, and comfortable dining room make us regulars at this elegant restaurant, decorated to look like a lovely Spanish living room. We love the chicken croquettes, mushroom risotto, and deep-fried baby squid. The chocolate molten cake, flanked by small scoops of hazelnut and vanilla ice cream, is our favorite dessert in town.

Xindong Lu 14 新东路14号 (north of Gongti Bei Lu); see map p. 117. ℂ 010/6417-1459. ¥200–¥300 ($27–$40/£13–£20). AE, DC, MC, V. Daily noon–midnight.

San Ge Guizhouren 三个贵州人 GUIZHOU Southern China's Guizhou Province is one of the country's poorest regions, which lends a certain irony to this restaurant's hip minimalist setting and rich artist clientele. The menu offers a stylish take on the province's Miao minority food with dishes that tend to be spicy, colorful, and slightly rough. Both table-top hot pots—the Miao-style peppermint lamb and the cilantro-heavy dry beef—are highly recommended, as is the flavorful but fatty *jueba chao larou* (bacon stir-fried with brake leaves). ***Note:*** Items listed on the menu as "vegetarian" are not.

Guanghua Xi Lu 3 光华西路3号 (walk north on Dong Da Qiao Lu from Yong'anli metro [121], turn down alley north of Mexican Wave, look for blue sign); see map p. 117. ℂ 010/6502-1733. Meal for 2 ¥80–¥120 ($11–$16/£5.35–£8). AE, DC, MC, V. Daily 11am–2:30pm and 5:30–10pm. Metro: Yong'anli (121, exit B). Other branches at Building 7 Jianwai SOHO 建外SOHO 7楼 (south of Guomao metro [122, exit C]), ℂ 010/5869-0598. Dinner only daily 5pm–10pm; 2/F of Ideal International Plaza on the Fourth Ring Road 北四环理想国际大厦2层, ℂ 010/8260-7670. Daily 10am–10pm; and Building 8 Gongti Xi Lu 工体西路8号, ℂ 010/6551-8517. Daily 24 hours.

Value Chinese on the Cheap

Affordable Chinese food is everywhere in Beijing, and not all of the places that provide it are an offense to Western hygiene standards. As with shopping in this city, high prices don't necessarily guarantee high quality in dining, and cheap restaurants often provide better food than expensive ones. Downmarket dining also offers the best chance to connect with the average Beijing resident.

Most convenient is a stable of adequately clean **Chinese fast-food** restaurants, many of which deliberately try to ape their Western counterparts. Menus typically offer simple noodles, baked goods, and stir-fries. Top chains include Yonghe Dawang 永和大王 (with KFC-style sign) and Malan noodle outlets 马兰拉面 (marked with a Chicago Bulls–style graphic), both with locations throughout the city.

A better option is to visit one of the **point-to-choose food courts** on the top or bottom floor of almost every large shopping center. These typically feature a dozen or so stalls selling snacks, noodles, or simple pre-cooked selections from different regions. Prices are reasonable, making it easy to sample a wide range. Just point to what looks good. The food court in the basement of the Oriental Plaza, requiring purchase of a card you use to pay for food at each stall, is the most extensive. Others can be found in the China World Mall, the Yaxiu Clothing Market, and Xi Dan Baihuo Shangchang north of the Xi Dan metro stop.

One of the most enjoyable local dining areas in Beijing, the legendary 24-hour food street on Dong Zhi Men Nei Dajie known to most as **Ghost Street (Gui Jie** 簋街; the first Chinese character is a homonym for the Chinese word for ghost and actually refers to a vessel, but most Chinese and foreigners alike refer to it as "Ghost Street" or "鬼街"), took a hit from the wrecking ball but is still there in abbreviated form. From the Dong Si Bei Dajie intersection and running east, dozens of small eateries offer hot pot, *mala longxia* (spicy crayfish), and home-style fare through the lantern-lit night.

Serve The People (Wei Renmin Fuwu) 为人民服务 THAI It's a sign of the times that Mao's best-known slogan can be used so frivolously by this chic Thai eatery. In the heart of the San Li Tun diplomatic quarter, you'll find Beijing's finest Thai food at very reasonable prices. The grilled beef salad and green chicken curry are highly recommended, and the *pad thai* (rice noodles with seafood in peanut sauce) is done to perfection. The small but interesting wine list has a limited by-the-glass selection. The temptation to use inappropriate local ingredients (such as cabbage!) plagues other Thai restaurants in the capital, but here the people are given their due.

San Li Tun Xi Wu Jie 1 三里屯西五街1号 (behind German embassy); see map p. 117. ✆ 010/8454-4580. Meal for 2 ¥150–¥200 ($20–$27/£10–£13). AE, DC, MC, V. Daily 10:30am–10:30pm. Metro: Nong Zhan Guan; 1 long block west, right at the stop lights (Sanlitun), then first left.

Taj Pavilion (Taiji Lou Yindu Canting) 泰姬楼印度餐厅 INDIAN One of Beijing's oldest Indian restaurants, the classy small dining room here holds only a few tables, nicely dressed in white linen, with subtle decor refreshingly free of camp. Food and service are both consistently high quality. Recommended dishes include vegetable *kofta* curry (deep-fried vegetables in tomato-based curry sauce), *palak paneer* (spinach with chunks of soft cheese), *rogan josh* (mutton in spicy tomato curry), and chicken *tikka masala* (marinated chicken in rich tomato sauce)—all authentic, thick, and deceptively filling. A second branch recently opened at the Holiday Inn Lido.

L1-28 West Wing of China World Trade Center, Jianguo Men Wai Dajie 1国贸中心; see map p. 117. ✆ 010/6505-5866. Meal for 2 ¥220–¥260 ($29–$35/£15–£17). AE, DC, MC, V. Daily 11:30am–2:30pm and 6:30–10:30pm. Metro: Guomao (122, exit A).

Xiao Wang Fu 小王府 HOME-STYLE NORTHERN CHINESE Xiao Wang serves up tasty, traditional Chinese food in an atmospheric setting—and does a respectable Peking duck. While the food is not particularly imaginative, it does all the standards perfectly well—from kung pao chicken to the spicy Sichuan string beans. We prefer the Ritan Park location, which is slightly pricier, but has a nice alfresco patio and is set within one of Beijing's nicer parks.

North Gate of Ritan Park 日坛路日坛公园北门内. ✆ 010/8561-5985. Meal for 2 ¥200–¥300 ($27–$40/£13–£20). AE, DC, MC, V. Metro: Yong'an Li (121, exit A). Other locations Bldg 2, Guanghua Lu Dongli 光华路东里2号楼, ✆ 010/6591-3255; 15 Qianhai Beiyan 前海北沿15号, ✆ 010/6617-5558.

INEXPENSIVE

Ding Ding Xiang 鼎鼎香 *Finds* HOT POT This Mongolian-style mutton hot pot restaurant is tremendously and justifiably popular for its signature dipping sauce (*jinpai tiaoliao*), a flavorful sesame sauce so thick they have to dish it out with ice cream scoops. Large plates of fresh sliced lamb (*yangrou*) are surprisingly cheap; other options include beef (*niurou*), spinach (*bocai*), and sliced winter melon (*donggua pian*). Reservations strongly recommended.

Dong Zhi Men Wai Dong Jie 14 东直门外东街14号 (opposite Donghuan Guangchang, in alley across from Guangdong Development Bank); see map p. 117. ✆ 010/6417-2546. Reservations highly recommended. Meal for 2 ¥80–¥100 ($11–$13/£5.35–£6.65). DC, MC, V. Daily 11am–midnight. Metro: Dong Zhi Men (214, exit C). Other branches (open from 11am–10pm) at Building 31 Gan Jia Kou Xiaoqu 甘家口小区31号楼, ✆ 010/8837-1327; East Gate Plaza at Dong Zhong Jie 9东中街9号东环广场, ✆ 010/6417-9289; Building 7 Guo Xing Jia Yuan, Shou ti Nan Lu 首体南路国兴家园7号楼, ✆ 010/8835-7775; Jian Guo Lu 87 Beijing Shin Kong Place 6/F 建国路87号新光天地6层, ✆ 010/6530-5997.

Indian Kitchen (Yindu Xiao Chu) 印度消厨 ✿ INDIAN This place has an impressive selection of curries at bargain prices. Set lunch menus for ¥38 ($5.05/£2.55)

Moments Night Market Nosh

Late-night dining is a favorite Beijing pastime, and the most convenient way to experience it is to visit one of the several night markets scattered about the city. This is street food, government regulated but not guaranteed to be clean, so the weak in stomach or courage may want to pass. Gastrointestinal gamble aside, the markets are a vivid and often delicious way to spend an evening.

The markets are typically made up of stalls, jammed side by side, selling all manner of snacks that cost anywhere from ¥0.50 (7¢/3p) to ¥5 (65¢/35p). Most legendary are the little animals on sticks, a veritable zoo of skewers that includes baby birds and scorpions. There are popular markets on **Longfu Si Jie** 隆福寺街 (see chapter 8, p. 164) and **west of the Beijing Zoo** (at the Dongwuyuan Yeshi 动物园夜市), but the most celebrated is the **Donghua Men night market** 东华门夜市, just off Wangfujing Dajie opposite the Xin Dong An Plaza.

With a history supposedly dating back to 1655, the Donghua Men was closed during the Cultural Revolution and reopened in 1984. Previously a charming mish-mash of independent operators each in their own battered tin shacks, it was "reorganized" in 2000. The stalls are all now a uniform red and white, each with identical twin gas burners. Prices have risen into the ¥10 ($1.35/65p) range and the food has fallen a bit in quality. The payoff is an increase in revenues from foreign tourists.

Below are the most common items you'll find for sale at the stalls.

- **Baozi** 包子: Steamed buns typically filled with mixtures of pork and vegetable, but occasionally available with just vegetables, for around ¥3 (40¢/20p) for a basket of five.

- **Jianbing** 煎饼: Large crepe with egg, folded around fried dough with cilantro and with plum and hot sauces, for ¥2 (25¢/15p).

- **Jiaozi** 饺子: Pork and vegetable filling with doughy wrapper, commonly boiled, ¥2–¥4 (25¢–55¢/15p–25p) for 12.

- **Miantiao** 面条: Noodles, commonly stir-fried with vegetables or boiled in beef broth with cilantro, for ¥1–¥3 (15¢–40¢/7p–20p).

- **Xianbing** 馅饼: Stuffed pancakes, usually filled with meat or vegetables, fried golden brown, around ¥2 (25¢/15p).

- **Yangrou chuan** 羊肉串: Lamb skewers with cumin and chile powder, either fried or roasted; also available in chicken *(jirou)*. ¥1 (15¢/7p).

are a steal and attract a loyal following from the nearby embassies. They've got plenty of spicy dishes, but for those with a low spice tolerance, try their lamb or chicken korma, a creamy cashew-based curry that does undeniable damage to the waistline. The decor is casual and unassuming. Service can be uneven.

Sanlitun Bei Xiao Jie 2, 2/F 三里屯北小街2号2层. ℂ 010/6460-9366. Meal for 2 ¥100–¥200 ($13–$27/£6.65–£13). AE, MC, V. Daily 11am–2:30pm and 5:30–11pm. Metro: Nong Zhan Guan.

Noodle Loft (Mian Ku Shanxi Shiyi) 面酷山西食艺 SHANXI   Unheard of outside China and rarely found in such stylish surroundings, Shanxi cuisine is noted for its vinegary flavors, liberal use of tomatoes, and large variety of interesting noodles. The Noodle Loft's interior is ultra-modern in orange and gray, with a large open kitchen featuring giant woks and steamers. An English menu makes ordering easy. Highlights include *yi ba zhua* (fried wheat cakes with chives), *qiao mian mao erduo* (cat's ear-shaped pasta stir-fried with chopped meat), and *suancai tudou* (vinegared potato slices).

Xi Dawang Lu 20 西大望路20号 (from bus stop, walk back 90m [300 ft.]); see map p. 117. ⓒ 010/6774-9950. Meal for 2 ¥80–¥100 ($11–$13/£5.35–£6.65). MC, V. Daily 11am–2:30pm and 5:30–10pm. From Dawang Lu metro stop (123, exit B), take bus No. 11 or 31 for 3 stops, getting off at Jiu Long Shan 九龙山. Other location at Heping Xijie 3 和平西街3号. ⓒ 010/5130-9655. Metro: Hepingli Bei Jie.

6 Beijing South

INEXPENSIVE

Mala Youhuo 麻辣诱惑 *Finds* SICHUAN   Beijing's obsession with Sichuan cuisine seems to have no end, and this restaurant, where locals queue down the street on a Monday night, currently enjoys the most fanatical following. Service is surprisingly friendly for such a busy restaurant, and the mock-village decor is cheesy but fun. The signature dish, *shuizhu yu* (boiled fish with chile and numbing hot peppers) comes in three different varieties, grass carp *(caoyu)*, catfish *(nianyu)*, and blackfish *(heiyu)*. We still prefer the traditional grass carp, but the slightly firmer and less slippery blackfish makes a nice change. For a walk on the culinary wild side, try *mala tianluo,* field snails stewed in chile and numbing hot pepper. Skewers are provided to extract the flesh from the sizable mollusks. Leave the innermost black part to the side, unless you want a serious tummy ache. A nice antidote to all the spice is a clear soup with seasonal leafy greens, *tutang shicai.* A second branch recently opened northeast of Da Zhong Si.

Guang'an Men Nei Dajie 81, Xuanwu Qu 广安门内大街81号 (just south of Baoguo Si); see map p. 112. ⓒ 010/6304-0426. Meal for 2 ¥80–¥140 ($11–$19/£5.35–£9.35). No credit cards. Daily 11:30am–2am. Metro: Changchun Jie (205, exit D1); walk south on Changchun Jie, then turn right (west) at 1st major road. Other branches at Da Zhong Si Taiyang Yuan 大钟寺太阳园, ⓒ 010/8211-9966. Daily 11am–10:30pm; Xi Dan Bei Dajie 176 Chung Yo Store 8/F西单北大街176号中友百货8楼, ⓒ 010/6603-7068, daily 11am–10pm; Xi Dan Bei Dajie 133 Juntai Shopping mall 7F西单北大街133号君太百货7楼, ⓒ 010/8265-6688, daily 11am–10pm; Sky Plaza 3F (300m east of Metro: Dong Zhi Men, exit C) 天恒大厦三层 (东直门地铁C出口向东步行300米), ⓒ 010/8460-8558, daily 11am–midnight; Chong Wen Men Wai Dajie 40 So Show Plaza 7/F 崇文门外大街40号搜秀商城7楼, ⓒ 010/5167-1098, daily 11am–10pm.

Pamer (Pami'er Shifu) 帕米尔食府 *Finds* UIGHUR   Pamer isn't much to look at, but it is clean, and the food it serves is cheaper and better than anything at the more famous Afunti, which is now overrun by tour groups. Cumin-spiced lamb skewers *(yangrou chuan)* are immense and surprisingly low on fat. Also not to be missed are the *nang bao rou* (lamb and vegetable stew served on flat wheat bread) and *shouba fan* (rice with lamb and raisins).

Lianhua Chi Dong Lu 3莲花池东路3号 (north side of Baiyun Qiao; large sign depicts dancing silhouettes); see map p. 112. ⓒ 010/6326-3635. Meal for 2 ¥60–¥100 ($8–$13/£4–£6.65). No credit cards. Daily 11am–2pm and 5:30–9:30pm.

Taipo Tianfu Shanzhen 太婆天府山珍 *HOT POT*   To make the broth for their divine hot pot, this restaurant stews a whole black-skinned chicken with 32 different kinds of mushrooms and lets the mixture reduce for hours. The mushrooms are strained but the chicken stays, served with the by-now vibrant broth in a heavy clay pot kept boiling at your table. Already a fine meal on its own, it gets even better as you add ingredients—lamb *(yangrou)*, beef *(niurou)*, lotus root *(ou pian)*, spinach *(bocai)*, or, best of all, more mushrooms *(shanjun)*. Many of the mushrooms, shown in their uncooked form on a series of posters hung along the walls, are imported from the southern provinces. Good enough to make converts of fungus haters.

At south end of Er Qi Juchang Lu, behind east side of the Chang'an Shangchang 二七剧场路长安商场东侧 (east of metro stop); see map p. 112. ⓒ 010/6801-9641. Meal for 2 ¥120–¥140 ($16–$19/£8–£9.35). MC, V. Daily 10am–11pm. Metro: Muxidi (112, exit B1). Another branch at Anhui Li Er Qu Si Hao Bei Lou 2-3/F, Yayun Cun亚运村 安慧里二区4号北楼2-3层, ⓒ 010/6496-9836.

Tianjin Bai Jiao Yuan 天津百饺园 JIAOZI   No restaurant has managed to fill the vacuum left by the inexplicable closing of Gold Cat, once Beijing's most charming outlet for *jiaozi* (ravioli-like dumplings), but Tianjin Bai Jiao Yuan comes closest. Staff are given to occasional catatonia, and the clichéd red-and-gold interior can't match Gold Cat's old courtyard setting, but the *jiaozi* are just as delicious. The *xiesanxian shuijiao* (dumplings with shrimp, crab, and mushroom filling) and *niurou wan shuijiao* (beef ball dumplings) are treasures, best accompanied by a steaming pot of *chenpi laoya shanzhen bao* (duck, mandarin peel, and mushroom potage). There's also a respectable range of Sichuan dishes, pictured on the menu.

Xin Wenhua Jie 12A 新文化街甲12号 (in alley opposite the Marco Polo); see map p. 112. ⓒ 010/6605-9371. Meal for 2 ¥30–¥60 ($4–$8/£2–£4). No credit cards. Daily 10am–2:30pm and 4:30–9:30pm.

Yunteng Binguan 云腾宾馆 *Finds* YUNNAN   This is a low-key cadre restaurant with exceptionally fresh fare. Even though Yunnan is one of the poorest provinces in China, the Mandarins have their ingredients flown in several times each week. The decor exudes as much warmth as a hospital waiting room, but exceedingly friendly waitstaff more than compensate. The signature dish, *guoqiao mixian* (crossing-the-bridge rice noodles) is worth the trip in itself, a delicious blend of ham, chicken, chrysanthemum, chives, tofu skin, and a tiny egg, all blended at your table with rice noodles in chicken broth. *Zhusun qiguoji* (mushroom and mountain herbs chicken soup) is ideal comfort food, and *zhutong paigu* (spicy stewed pork with mint), while not actually steamed in the bamboo tube it's served in, has hearty, complex flavors. Avoid choosing the enticing mushroom dishes on the picture menu without first checking the price; the Yunteng stocks some fancy fungi.

Dong Huashi Bei Li Dong Qu 7, Chongwen Qu 崇文区东花市北里东区 (follow Jianguo Men Nan Dajie south for 10 min.; on the south side of flyover); see map p. 112. ⓒ 010/6713-6439. Meal for 2 ¥80–¥140 ($11–$19/£5.35–£9.35). MC, V. Daily 11am–1:30pm and 5–10pm. Metro: Jianguo Men (120/211, exit C).

Yuxiang Renjia 渝乡人家 *Finds* SICHUAN   Franchise food in the Chinese capital doesn't carry the same connotations of blandness it does in the United States. Yuxiang Renjia, a constantly crowded chain of restaurants with bright mock-village decor and a talent for producing authentic Sichuan fare, is a case in point. Dishes are slightly heavy on the oil but as flavorful as anything found outside Sichuan itself. The spicy familiar *gongbao jiding* (diced chicken with peanuts and hot peppers) is superb, putting American versions of "kung pao chicken" to shame. They also produce several worthwhile dishes you aren't likely to have tried before, including an interesting smoked duck *(zhangcha ya)* and the "stewed chicken with Grandma's sauce" *(laoganma*

shao ji). Waitstaff sometimes gets overwhelmed, and the impressive decor isn't matched by the hygiene.

Chaoyang Men Wai Dajie 20朝阳门外大街20号(on 5th floor of Lianhe Dasha, behind Foreign Ministry Building 联合大厦); see map p. 112. ☎ 010/6588-3841. Meal for 2 ¥80–¥120 ($11–$16/£5.35–£8). AE, DC, MC, V. Daily 11am–10:30pm, Sat until 10pm only. Metro: Chaoyang Men (212).

7 Beijing West, Haidian & Yayun Cun
VERY EXPENSIVE
Blu Lobster (Lan Yun Xi Can Ting) 蓝韵西餐厅 ✦✦CONTINENTAL   Named for the extremely rare lobsters with natural blue shells, this Shangri-La showcase restaurant is headed by the Irish-born executive chef Brian McKenna, who brings a whimsical, inventive touch to his dishes. He's one of the first chefs in Beijing to play with foam, foie gras, and lobster so well. The tasting menus, with a choice of 6 or 10 courses or 5 courses focusing on foie gras, are the best way to experience the restaurant, done up with sophistication in shades of—you guessed it—blue. McKenna has a special affection for dessert, so save room because he often packs in two, or even three, courses of sweets at the end of an indulgent meal.

Zi Zhu Yuan Lu 29 (first floor of Shangri-La Hotel); see map p. 114. ☎ 010/6841-2211. Meal for 2 ¥2,000 ($267/£133). AE, DC, MC, V. Dinner only. 5pm–1am.

Cepe (Yiwei Xuan) 意味轩 ✦✦ITALIAN   This restaurant serves the best upscale Italian fare in the city. The waitstaff wear sleek pinstripe suits and are incredibly attentive, zipping over to your table at the merest hint of a frown or inquiring look. Lorenzo Maraviglia, the upbeat restaurant manager who used to manage Le Cirque in New York, knows his wines and dishes inside out. Seek him out if you want serious recommendations. This a place to indulge in a leisurely meal. You must order a pasta dish, as the noodles are perfectly al dente and freshly made each morning. We also highly recommend the water buffalo appetizer—it's wrapped in slices of eggplant, lightly fried, and served over a bed of fresh tomato and basil. The decor is contemporary, with an open kitchen housed behind a giant silk screen of a portobello mushroom. There are romantic, semi-private nooks with curtains and leather chaise lounges alongside the back wall. Jazz music and, every now and then, an upbeat Laura Pausini song plays in the background.

Jinchengfang Dong Jie 1 金成坊冻街1号 (inside Ritz Carlton Financial Street Hotel); see map p. 114. ☎ 010/6601-6666. Dinner for 2 ¥600–¥800 ($80–$107/£40–£53). AE, MC, V. Daily 11:30am–3pm; 6–11pm. Metro: Fuxing Men (114/204, exit A).

Whampoa Club Beijing (Huang Pu Hui) 黄浦会 ✦✦BEIJING   Run by rising chef Jereme Leung, this second Whampoa Club follows in the successful footsteps of its sister restaurant in Shanghai, much lauded for its inventive Shanghainese cuisine. This time, Leung focuses on bringing a modern interpretation to the cuisines of Beijing and Shandong, and he pulls it off flawlessly. Highlights from his tasting menus include his bean curd and vegetable roll with foie gras terrine, his oven-baked black cod (which made its debut in Shanghai and is one of the restaurant's best-selling dishes), and his Beijing-style fermented bean paste and pork with handmade noodles. Equally enticing is the setting—the dining room, done in shades of white, blue, and black, sits underneath a glass-bottomed goldfish pond within a traditional Chinese courtyard. One downside is that eating here can be quite pricey.

Jin Rong Jie Jia 23 金融街甲23. ☎ 010/8808-8828. Meal for 2 ¥1,000 ($133/£67). AE, DC, M, V. Lunch & dinner daily 11am–2:30pm and 5:30–10:30pm. Metro: Fucheng Men (203, exit C).

MODERATE

Pure Lotus (Jing Xin Lian) 静心莲 ⊛ VEGETARIAN   The dimmed restaurant, decorated with prayer wheels and Buddhist statues, offers stylish vegetarian food that wows in taste and presentation. Highlights include the pumpkin soup and the vegetarian dumplings. A monk supposedly owns the restaurant, but we suspect that he's more of a businessman given the relatively high prices. The Holiday Inn Lido location is a bit of a trek from central Beijing, but offers a stylish, not-to-be-missed setting.

10 Nongzhanguan Nan Lu (inside Zhongguo Wenlian); see map p. 117. ⓒ 010/8703-6666. Meal for 2 ¥200–¥400 ($27–$53/£13–£27). AE, DC, MC, V. Lunch & dinner daily 11am–11pm. Metro: Gongti Bei Lu. Another branch at 3F, Holiday Inn Lido Hotel, Jiang Tai Lu 6, ⓒ 010/8709-6668.

Xibei Youmian Cun 西贝莜面村 ⊛⊛ (Kids) NORTHWESTERN/ SHANXI   This place is worth the trip out to Yayun Cun in itself. Friendly staff and bright, faux-rural decor make this the best "family restaurant" in Beijing, and the cuisine (a hybrid of Mongolian and Shanxi fare) will have you looking through the picture menu to plan your next visit. The signature dish is *youmian wowo* (steamed oatmeal noodles) served with mushroom (*sushijun retang*) or lamb (*yangrou retang*) broth, with coriander and chile on the side. Familiar *yangrou chuan'r* (mutton skewers with cumin) and yogurt (*suannai*) with honey make excellent side dishes, while the house salad (*Xibei da bancai*) is a meal in itself, crammed with unusual ingredients such as wild greens, radish, and purple cabbage, and topped with a delicious sesame dressing. The one dish you must try is *zhijicao kao niupai* (lotus leaf–wrapped roast beef with mountain herbs). Roast beef will never be the same.

Yayun Cun Anyuan 8 Lou 亚运村安慧北里与慧忠路街角 (corner of Anhui Bei Li and Huizhong Bei Lu); see map p. 114. ⓒ 010/6498-4455. Meal for 2 ¥120–¥200 ($16–$27/£8–£13). AE, DC, MC, V. Daily 10am–1:50pm and 5–9pm.

Zhang Sheng Ji Jiudian 张生记酒店 ⊛⊛ HUAIYANG   It may lack the ambience of Kong Yiji Jiulou, but this branch of Hangzhou's most successful restaurant delivers more consistent Huaiyang fare. Service is no-fuss, and there's a pleasing amount of space between tables and a high ceiling. For starters, try the flavorful *jiuxiang yugan* (dried fish in wine sauce). The recently added *mati niuliu* (stir-fried beef with broccoli, water chestnuts, and tofu rolls) is excellent, and nearly every table carries the signature *sungan laoya bao* (stewed duck with dried bamboo shoots and ham) which has complex, hearty flavors. You can explore the English picture menu without trepidation; Huaiyang cuisine is delicately spiced, and largely eschews endangered species.

Bei San Huan, Zhejiang Dasha 北三环浙江大厦 (west of Anzhen Qiao on North Third Ring Rd.); see map p. 114. ⓒ 010/6442-0006. Meal for 2 ¥100–¥180 ($13–$24/£6.65–£12). AE, DC, MC, V. Daily 11am–2pm and 5–9pm. Metro: Xiongmaohuandao.

INEXPENSIVE

Baihe Sushi (Lily Vegetarian Restaurant) 百合素食 ⊛ VEGETARIAN   Chinese vegetarian restaurants often get bogged down torturing meaty flavors out of gluten, but here you'll find delectable dishes with high-quality ingredients. Start with the hearty *shanyao geng* (yam broth with mushrooms) and the slightly fruity *liangban zi lusun* (purple asparagus salad), followed by *ruyi haitai juan* (vegetarian sushi rolls) and the excellent *huangdi sun shao wanzi* (Imperial bamboo shoots and vegetarian meatballs). When in season, their vegetables are sourced from an organic farm west of Beijing, so ask if they have any organic vegetables (*youji shucai*). Monks dine for free, so you're likely to meet a few from Guangji Si in the evening. Watch your head in the bathroom.

Yi He Yuan Kun Ming Hu Lu 50, 100 meters south to the Xin Jian Gong Men (main gate of Yi He Yuan) 颐和园昆明湖路50号; see map p. 114. ℂ 010/6202-5284. Meal for 2 ¥80–¥140 ($11–$19/£5.35–£9.35). Daily 10am–9pm. Metro: Zhichun Lu. Another branch at Dong Zhi Men Nei Bei Xiao Jie, Cao Yuan Hutong 23东直门内北小街草园胡同23号, ℂ 010/6405-2082.

Dongbei Hu 东北虎 🐾 NORTHEASTERN   Natives of Dongbei (the Northeast) are famously direct, and few hesitate for more than a picosecond before nominating this raucous establishment as the source of Beijing's best Dongbei cuisine. Welcoming staff dressed in florals usher you upstairs past an open kitchen with whole cuts and huge jars of wine on show. Start with the refreshing cold noodle dish, *da lapi,* served in a sesame and vinegar sauce. Your table will groan under the weight of the signature dish, *shouzhua yang pai* (lamb chops roasted with cumin and chile). Filling snacks, such as *tiebingzi* (corn pancakes cooked on a griddle) and *sanxian laohe* (seafood and garlic chive buns), are delicious, as is the sweet and sour battered eggplant *(cuipi qiezi).* So cheap, you won't begrudge the taxi fare out to Yayun Cun.

Anhui Li Er Qu Yi Lou, Yayun Cun 安慧里二区一楼 (300m [984 ft.] east of intersection with Anli Lu); see map p. 114. ℂ 010/6498-5015. Meal for 2 ¥50–¥80 ($6.65–$11/£3.35–£5.35). No credit cards. Daily 11am–10pm.

Xiangyang Tun 向阳屯 HOME-STYLE/NORTHEASTERN   Set in a new courtyard-style complex in northwestern Beijing, this nostalgia restaurant is one of the only venues in the city for *errenzhuan,* a raunchily entertaining style of opera rarely performed outside the frigid northeast. The opera stage sits at one end of the cavernous main hall, decorated in an exaggerated Cultural Revolution–era countryside theme with bright red tables and propaganda-heavy newspapers from the 1960s plastered on the walls. Dishes are large and simple in the northeastern tradition. Good choices are the *Dongbei fengwei dapai* (Northeast-style braised ribs) and the *nongjia xiaochao,* an authentically rural combination of soybeans, green onion, Chinese chives, and bell peppers in a clay pot. Combine a stop here with an afternoon visit to the Summer Palace.

Wanquan He Lu 26 海淀区万泉河路26号 (in Haidian, across from the Zhongyi Yiyuan [Chinese Traditional Medicine Hospital]); see map p. 114. ℂ 010/6264-5522 or 010/6264-2907. Meal for 2 ¥40–¥80 ($5.35–$11/£2.65–£5.35). No credit cards. Daily 10am–11pm. Metro: Wan Liu.

Xiyu Shifu 西域食府 🐾🐾 UIGHUR   Directly opposite Olympic Park you'll find the best Uighur food this side of Turfan. The decor (typical of Yayun Cun) is a nouveau-riche fantasy of arches, Romanesque gold light fittings, and pictures of desert scenes hanging from marble walls, but it's spotless and welcoming, with an imaginatively translated menu. You'll find intriguing dishes, along with authentic Xinjiang favorites. The *da pan ji* (diced chicken, pepper, potatoes, and thick noodles in tomato sauce) is spicy, so when they ask if you like it hot, be honest. The piping-hot *nan* (flat bread) is perfect for sopping up the delicious sauce, and the *shou zhua fan* (rice with lamb and carrot), which often appears as a limp version of fried rice with raisins this far east, is as tasty as anything you'll find in Kashgar. Although spicy mutton skewers with cumin and chile *(yangrou chuan)* ranks as Beijing's most popular dish, too often the spices are heavy, usually to disguise less than fresh meat. Not here.

Corner of Beichen Dong Lu and Datun Lu, Yayun Cun 亚运村北辰东路与大屯路街角; see map p. 114. ℂ 010/6486-2555. Meal for 2 ¥70–¥100 ($9.35–$13/£4.65–£6.65). AE, MC, V. Daily 10:30am–10:30pm. Metro: Olympic Park.

Yunnan Jin Kongque Dehong Daiwei Canguan 云南金孔雀德宏傣族餐馆
Value YUNNAN   The street north of the Minorities University (Minzu Daxue)
was once a claustrophobic *hutong* packed with Uighur, Korean, and Dai restaurants.
Chaps who addressed you as "Hashish" are gone, along with most of the restaurants.
But this holy grail of Dai cuisine remains, offering a superb synthesis of Thai and
Chinese fare. Mirrors, tiled floors, and predictable bamboo furnishings lend it a sterile
feel, but the gracious waitstaff more than compensates. Must-devour dishes include
crispy *tudou qiu* (deep-fried potato balls with chile sauce), delectable *boluo fan* (pine-
apple rice), *zhutong zhurou* (steamed pork with coriander), *zhutong ji* (chicken soup),
and *zha xiangjiao* (deep-fried banana) for dessert. Wash it all down with sweet rice
wine *(mi jiu)*, served in a bamboo cup.

Minzu Daxue Bei Lu 1 民族大学北路1号 (cross footbridge, head right, take the 1st street on your left); see map
p. 114. ✆ **010/6893-2030**. Meal for 2 ¥50–¥100 ($6.65–$13/£3.35–£6.65). No credit cards. Daily 11am–10pm.
Bus: 205 or 106 to Weigong Cun from Xi Zhi Men metro (201, exit A).

7

Exploring Beijing

Sightseeing in Beijing can be an over-whelming prospect. No other city in China, and few other cities in the world, offers so many must-see attractions. It is technically possible to see the big names—the **Forbidden City, Temple of Heaven, Summer Palace,** and **Great Wall**—in as little as 3 days, but you'll want at least a week to get any sort of feel for the city. People spend years here and still fail to see everything they should. For suggested itineraries to help you organize your time, see chapter 3. Sights outside of Beijing require at least half a day. How-ever, the Great Wall requires a full day. (See chapter 11 for details on side trips.) *Note:* Most major sights now charge dif-ferent prices for admission in summer and winter. The summer high season offi-cially runs from April 1 to October 31 and the winter low season from Novem-ber 1 to March 31.

HOW TO SEE BEIJING

Beijing's traffic is appalling. Do *not* plan to see too many sights that are far apart, unless you want your memories of the capital to consist of staring helplessly out of a taxicab window. Regardless of whether you choose to get around by taxi, metro, bus, bike, or foot, plan each day to see sights that are close together.

The best option for reaching sights within Beijing is to take the metro to the stop nearest the attraction you plan on seeing, and duck into one of the many waiting taxis. As an example, the **Summer Palace** is a short ¥15 ($2/£1) cab ride from the new light rail station at Wudaokou. Buses are slow but plentiful and relatively safe, especially if you choose the air-conditioned 800-series buses. Maximum freedom (and usually speed) is realized by hiring a bike for the day. More convenient still is to hire a nor-mal taxi for the day (see section 2, "Getting Around," in chapter 4).

The standard of organized tours in Beijing leaves much to be desired. But if this is your preference, most hotels have offices of Panda Tours and Dragon Tours, which offer overpriced tours to the major attractions (see section 11, "Organized Tours," in this chapter). The advantage is that transport and language barriers are removed, but the freedom to visit smaller attractions and meet locals is sacrificed. The fast pace of these tours can leave you giddy.

The last and least recommended option is to hire a car through your hotel. You will be charged up to five times what you should pay. Aside from convenience, the only conceivable plus is that if you are staying at a foreign-run, luxury hotel, they have a reputation for good service to protect. Organizations such as Panda Tours, which are run by the China International Travel Service, do not.

Beijing City Center

Beijing North Railway Station
北京北站

Beijing Zoo
北京动物园

White Cloud Temple

0   1/2 Mi
0   .5 Km

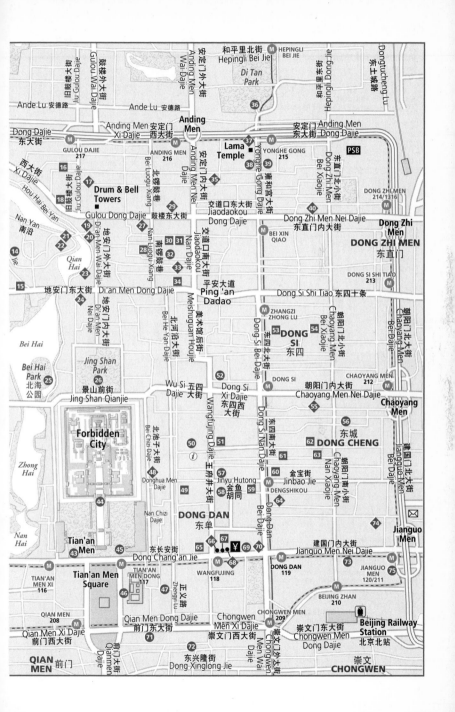

Dongtucheng Lu 东土城路

和平里北街 HEPINGLI
Hepingli Bei Jie BEI JIE

Di Tan
Park

和平里东街 Hepingli Dong Jie

Ande Lu 安德路

Ande Lu 安德路

安定门外大街 Anding Men Wai Dajie

36

Dong Dajie 东大街

安定门 Anding Men 西大街 Xi Dajie

Anding
Men

安定门 Anding Men 东大街 Dong Dajie

GULOU DAJIE
217

安定门内大街 Anding Men Nei Dajie

37

Lama
Temple

雍和宫 YONGHE GONG
215

东直门北大街 Dong Zhi Men Bei Xiaojie

PSB

西大街 Xi Dajie

16

ANDING MEN
216

北锣鼓巷 Bei Luogu Xiang

38

35

雍和宫大街 Yonghe Gong Dajie

DONG ZHI MEN
214/1316

Hou Hai Bei Yan

17

Drum & Bell
Towers

18

旧鼓楼大街 Jiu Gulou Dajie

Gulou Dong Dajie

29

交道口东大街 Jiaodaokou Dong Dajie

东直门内大街 Dong Zhi Men Nei Dajie

Dong Zhi
Men

鼓楼东大街

27

40

DONG ZHI MEN
东直门

Nan Yan 南沿

21

19

地安门外大街 Di'an Men Wai Dajie

30 31

交道口南大街 Jiaodaokou Nan Dajie

BEI XIN
QIAO

22

20

南锣鼓巷 Nan Luogu Xiang

28

32

14 Jie

Qian
Hai

23

33

DONG SI SHI TIAO
213

15

24

地安门东大街 Di'an Men Dong Dajie

34

平安大道 Ping'an Dadao

Dong Si Shi Tiao 东四十条

ZHANGZI
ZHONG LU

53 DONG
SI
东四

54

朝阳门北小街 Chaoyang Men Bei Xiaojie

Bei Hai

Jing Shan
Park

北河沿大街 Bei He Yan Dajie

美术馆后街 Meishuguan Houjie

52

东四北大街 Dong Si Bei Dajie

朝阳门北大街 Chaoyang Men Bei Dajie

Bei Hai
Park
北海
公园

25

26

景山前街 Jing Shan Qianjie

Wu Si 五
四
Dajie 大
街

Dong Si
Xi Dajie
东四西
大街

DONG SI

CHAOYANG MEN
212

Chaoyang
Men

Zhong
Hai

Forbidden
City

北池子大街 Bei Chizi Dajie

王府井大街 Wangfujing Dajie

50

51

东四南大街 Dong Si Nan Dajie

朝阳门内大街 Chaoyang Men Nei Dajie

55

56

东城 DONG
CHENG

62

建国门北大街 Jianguo Men Bei Dajie

Donghua Men
Dajie

48

i

朝阳门南小街 Chaoyang Men Nan Xiaojie

61

63

60

金宝街 Jinbao Jie

49

Jinyu Hutong

DONGSHIKOU

Nan Chizi Dajie

58

金鱼 59
胡同

64

Dong-Dan
Dajie

DONG
DAN
东单

Tian'an
Men

44

43

45

65

66 67

68

¥ 69 70

建国门内大街 Jianguo Men Nei Dajie

Jianguo Men Nei Dajie

74

Jianguo
Men

东长安街 Dong Chang'an Jie
Dong Chang'an Jie

DONG DAN
119

73

JIANGUO
MEN
120/211

75

TIAN'AN
MEN XI
116

Tian'an Men
Square

TIAN'AN
MEN DONG
117

46

47

Zhengyi Lu

WANGFUJING
118

BEIJING ZHAN
210

QIAN MEN
208

正义路 Zhengyi Lu

Qian Men Dong Dajie 前门东大街

Chongwen
Men Xi Dajie

崇文门西大街

CHONGWEN MEN
209

Beijing Railway
Station
北京北站

前门西大街 Qian Men Xi Dajie

71

Qiannen Dajie

Qiannen
Dajie

72

东兴隆街 Dong Xinglong Jie

崇文门外大街 Chongwen Men Wai Dajie

崇文门东大街 Chongwen Men Dong Dajie

崇文 CHONGWEN

QIAN
MEN 前门

Key for Beijing City Center

ACCOMMODATIONS ■

Bamboo Garden Hotel
(Zhú Yuán Bīnguǎn) 16
竹园宾馆

Crowne Plaza Hotel
(Guójì Yìyuàn Huángguān Fàndiàn) 51
国际艺苑皇冠饭店

Grand Hyatt Běijīng
(Běijīng Dōngfāng Jūnyuè Dàjiǔdiàn) 67
北京东方君悦大酒店

Gu Xiang 20
(Gǔ Xiàng Èr Shí) 30
古巷20

Hǎoyuán Bīnguǎn 61
好园宾馆

Hotel Côté Cour S.L. 62

Hotel Kapok
(Mùmián Huā Jiǔdiàn) 49
木棉花酒店

Hutonger
(Hútòng Rén) 28
胡同人

Lǔsōng Yuán Bīnguǎn 34
吕松园宾馆

Park Plaza Beijing
(Běijīng Lì Tíng Jiǔ Diàn) 60
北京丽亭酒店

Peking Downtown Backpackers
Accommodation
(Dōng Táng Qīngnián Lǚshè) 31
东堂青年旅社

The Peninsula Běijīng
(Wángfǔ Fàndiàn) 59
王府饭店

Qílǔ Fàndiàn 15
齐鲁饭店

Qomolangma Hotel
(Zhūmùlǎngmǎ Bīguǎn) 18
珠穆朗玛宾馆

Raffles Beijing
(Běijīng Fàndiàn Láifóshí) 65
北京饭店莱佛士

Red Capital Residence
(Xīn Hóng Zǐ Jùlèbù) 54
东四六条9号

The Regent Beijing
(Běijīng Lì Jīng Jiǔ Diàn) 60
北京丽晶酒店

Ritz Carlton, Financial Street
(Jīnróng Jiē Lìjiā Jiǔdiàn) 13
金融街丽嘉酒店

Saga Youth Hostel
(Shǐjiā Guójì Qīngnián Lǚshè) 63
史家国际青年旅社

Zhōnggòng Běijīng Shì Wěi Bàn
Jīguǎn Zhāodàisuǒ 53
中共北京市委办机关招待所

DINING ◆

Be There or Be Square
(Bú Jiàn Bú Sàn) 70
不见不散

Cafe Sambal 17
豆腐池胡同43号

Cépe
(Yìwèi Xuān) 13
意味轩

Chuān Jīng Bàn Cāntīng 74
川京办餐厅

The CourtYard (Sìhéyuàn) 48
四合苑

Dà Jīnsī Hútòng 1 21
大金丝胡同1号

Dali Courtyard
(Dà Lǐ) 29
大理

Dào 19
道

Huājiā Yíyuán 40
花家怡园

Hútòng Pizza 22
胡同比萨

Jaan
(Jiā Ān) 65
家安

Kèjiā Cài 23
客家菜

Kǒng Yǐjǐ Jiǔdiàn 6
孔乙己酒店

Made in China 68

My Humble House
(Dōngfāng Hánshè) 66
东方寒舍

Nuage
(Qìng Yún Lóu) 20
庆云楼

Otto's Restaurant
(Rìchāng Chácāntīng) 24, 64
日昌茶餐厅

Paper
(Jiǎn) 27
简

Source
(Dūjiāngyuán) 33
渡江源

Vineyard
(Pútáoyuán'r) 37
葡萄院儿

Xiàn'r Lǎo Mǎn 35
馅老满

Beijing South

ACCOMMODATIONS ■

City Central Youth Hostel
(Chéngshì Qīngnián Jiǔdiàn) **26**
城市青年酒店

Far East Youth Hostel
(Yuǎn Dōng Qīngnián Lǔshè) **16**
远东青年旅社

Fēiyīng Bīnguǎn **10**
飞鹰宾馆

Harmony Hotel
(Huáměilún Jiǔdiàn) **25**
华美伦酒店

Holiday Inn Central Plaza
(Zhōnghuán Jiǎrì Jiǔdiàn) **5**
中环假日酒店

The Marco Polo
(Mǎgē Bóluó Jiǔdiàn) **13**
马哥孛罗酒店

Qián Mén Chánggōng Fàndiàn **19**
前门长工饭店

Shǎnxī Xiàng Dì'èr Bīnguǎn **17**
陕西巷第二宾馆

DINING ◆

Málà Yòuhuò **6**
麻辣诱惑

Pamer
(Pàmǐ'ěr Shífǔ) **2**
帕米尔食府

Tàipó Tiānfǔ Shānzhēn **4**
太婆天府山珍

Tiānjīn Bǎi Jiǎo Yuán **12**
天津百饺园

Yúnténg Bīnguǎn **28**
云腾宾馆

Yúxiāng Rénjiā **29**
渝乡人家

Beijing West & Haidian

Metro & Station

Ⓜ
MUXIDI
112

| Bus Station |
| Ⓨ Bank |
| ⓘ Information |
| ✉ Post Office |
| 🚇 Rail Station |
| **PSB** Public-Security Visas |

0 ······· 1 Mi
0 ······· 1 Km

Yuanmingyuan Xi Lu

圆明园西路

Botanic Gardens

Summer Palace
6

Xiangshan Lu
香山路

Wuhuan Lu 五环路

Yuquan Shan Lu
玉泉山路

Yuquan Shan Lu
玉泉山路

1
2

Xiang Shan Nan Lu
青山南路

Bei Wucun Lu 北坞村路

Minzhuang Lu 闵庄路

Ba Da Chu Park
八大处公园

Badachu Lu
八大处路

Fourth Ring Road (Si Huan Lu)
四环路

Yuanda Lu
远大路

Xingshikou Lu
杏石口路

3
4

Tiancun Lu 田村路

阜成路
Fucheng Lu

PINGGUO YUAN
Ⓜ **103**

Fushi Lu 阜石路

八宝山
Ba Bao Shan

BAJIAO YULEYUAN
Ⓜ **105**

石景山路
Shijing Shan Lu

BA BAO SHAN
Ⓜ **106**

YUQUAN LU
Ⓜ **107**

WU KE SONG
Ⓜ **108**

GUCHENG LU
Ⓜ **104**

5

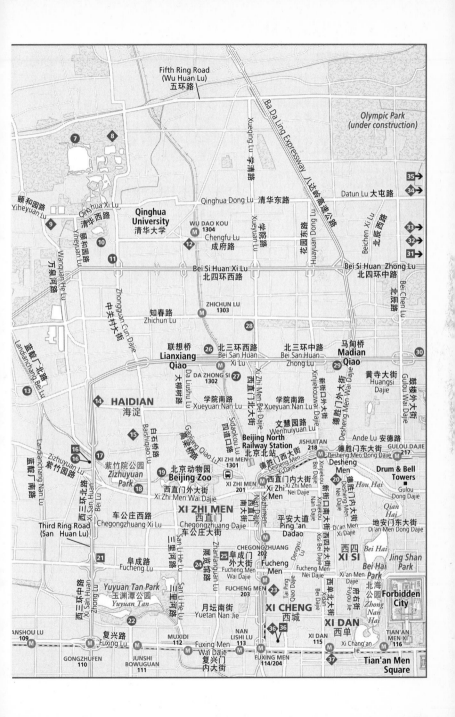

Fifth Ring Road
(Wu Huan Lu)
五环路

Olympic Park
(under construction)

Qinghua University
清华大学

Ba Da Ling Expressway 八达岭高速公路

Qinghua Xi Lu
清华西路

Qinghua Dong Lu 清华东路

Datun Lu 大屯路

Beichen Xi Lu 北辰西路

Xueqing Lu 学清路

WU DAO KOU
1304
Chengfu Lu
成府路

Xueyuan Lu 学院路

Huayuan Dong Lu 花园东路

Bei Si Huan Zhong Lu
北四环中路

Yiheyuan Lu
颐和园路

Yiheyuan Lu 颐和园路

Bei Si Huan Xi Lu
北四环西路

Wanquan He Lu 万泉河路

Landianchang Bei Lu 蓝靛厂北路

ZHICHUN LU
1303

Zhongguan Cun Dajie 中关村大街

知春路
Zhichun Lu

北三环西路
Bei San Huan
Xi Lu

北三环中路
Bei San Huan
Zhong Lu

马甸桥
Madian

Lianxiang
Qiao
联想桥

Da Liushu Lu 大柳树路

DA ZHONG SI
1302

Xi Zhi Men Bei Dajie 西直门北大街

Xinjiekouwai Dajie 新街口外大街

Desheng Men Wai Dajie 德胜门外大街

Gulou Wai Dajie 鼓楼外大街

Bei Chen Lu 北辰路

HAIDIAN
海淀

学院南路
Xueyuan Nan Lu

学院南路
Xueyuan Nan Lu

黄寺大街
Huangsi
Dajie

GULOU DAJIE
217

Baishiqiao Lu 白石桥路

Guojiang Qiao Lu 国强桥路

Sidaokou Lu 四道口路

文慧园路
Wenhuiyuan Lu

Ande Lu 安德路

Zhizhuyuan Park
紫竹院公园
Zizhuyuan
Park

Beijing North
Railway Station
北京北站
1301

JISHUITAN
218

德胜门东大街
Desheng Men Dong Dajie

Drum & Bell
Towers

Gulou
Dong Dajie

北京动物园
Beijing Zoo

德胜门内大街
Desheng Men Nei Dajie

Hou Hai

XI ZHI MEN
201

Xi Zhi Men Wai Dajie
西直门外大街

西直门内大街
Xi Zhi Men Nei Dajie

新街口南大街 Xinjiekou Nan Dajie

Desheng
Men

Qian
Hai

地安门东大街
Di'an Men Dong Dajie

XI ZHI MEN
西直门

San Li He Lu 三里河路

Xizhimen Nan Dajie 西直门南大街

平安大道
Ping'an
Dadao

Di'an Men
Xi Dajie

Third Ring Road
(San Huan Lu)

Chegongzhuang Xi Lu
车公庄西路

Chegongzhuang Dajie
车公庄大街

平安大道
Ping'an
Dadao

西四北大街 Xisi Bei Dajie

Bei Hai

西四
XI SI

Jing Shan
Park

阜成路
Fucheng Lu

CHEGONGZHUANG

Zhanlanguan Lu 展览馆路

阜成门
外大街
Fucheng Men
Wai Dajie

阜成门
Fucheng
Men

Dengshi

Fucheng Men
Nei Dajie

西安门大街 Xi'an Men Dajie

Bei Hai
Park
北海
公园

Forbidden
City

Yuyuan Tan Park
玉渊潭公园
Yuyuan Tan

FUCHENG MEN
203

月坛南街
Yuetan Nan Jie

Tai Ping

Xidan Bei Dajie 西单北大街

Xi'an Men
Dajie

Fuyou Lu 府右街

Zhong
Nan
Hai

XI CHENG
西城

XI DAN
西单

ANSHOU LU
109

复兴路
Fuxing Lu

MUXIDI
112

NAN LISHI LU
113

Fuxing Men
Wai Dajie
复兴门
外大街

FUXING MEN
114/204

复兴门
内大街
Fuxing Men
Nei Dajie

XI DAN
115

Xi Chang'an Jie 西长安街

TIAN'AN
MEN XI
116

Tian'an Men
Square

GONGZHUFEN
110

JUNSHI
BOWUGUAN
111

Xi San Huan Zhong Lu 西三环中路

Junshi He Lu 军事河路

Key for Beijing West & Haidian

Chaoyang

Key for Chaoyang

ACCOMMODATIONS ■

China World Hotel
(Zhōngguó Dàfàndiàn) **47**
中国大饭店

Gōngtǐ Youth Hostel
(Gōngtǐ Qīngnián Lǚshè) **31**
工体青年旅社

Hilton Běijīng
(Běijīng Xīěrdùn Fàndiàn) **9**
北京希尔顿饭店

Holiday Inn Lido
(Lìdū Jiàrì Fàndiàn) **2**
丽都假日饭店

Jiànguó Hotel
(Jiànguó Fàndiàn) **44**
建国饭店

Kerry Centre Hotel
(Běijīng Jiālǐ Zhōngxīn Fàndiàn) **38**
北京嘉里中心饭店

St. Regis Běijīng
(Běijīng Guójì Jùlèbù Fàndiàn) **41**
北京国际俱乐部饭店

Traders Hotel Běijīng
(Guómào Fàndiàn) **45**
国贸饭店

Zhàolóng Qīngnián Lǚguǎn **25**
兆龙青年旅馆

DINING ◆

Alameda **22**

Annie's Café
(Ānnī Yìdàlì Cāntīng) **13**
安妮意大利餐厅

Assaggi
(Chángshì) **6**
尝试

Běijīng Dàdǒng Kǎoyā Diàn **26, 28**
北京大董烤鸭

Bellagio
(Lù Gǎng Xiǎozhèn) **8, 29**
鹿港小镇

Běijīng Dàdǒng Kǎoyā Diàn **26**
北京大董烤鸭店

The Bookworm
(Lǎo Shūchóng) **20**
老书虫

Dào Jiā Cháng **1**
到家尝

Dǐng Dǐng Xiāng **5**
鼎鼎香

Flo (Fú Lóu) **23**
福楼

Green T. House
(Zǐ Yún Xuān) **29**
紫云轩

Haiku by Hatsune
(Yǐn Quán Zhī Yǔ) **12**
隐泉之语

Hatsune
(Yǐn Quán) **48**
隐泉

Horizon
(Hǎitiān Gé) **39**
海天阁

Huángchéng Lǎo Mā **54**
皇城老妈

Lán **50**
兰

Le Cafe Igosso **52**

Mare
(Dá Pà Shì) **18**
大怕世

Morel's
(Mòláolóngxǐ Xīcāntīng) **15**
莫劳龙玺西餐厅

Noodle Loft
(Miàn Kù Shānxī Shíyì) **55**
面酷山西食艺

People 8
(Rénjiān Xuánsè) **49**
人间玄色

1 Tian'an Men Square (Tian'an Men Guangchang)

This is the world's largest public square, the size of 90 American football fields (40 hectares/99 acres), with standing room for 300,000 people. It is surrounded by the Forbidden City in the north, the Great Hall of the People in the west, and the museums of Chinese History and Chinese Revolution in the east. In the center of the square stands the Monument to the People's Heroes (Renmin Yingxiong Jinian Bei), a 37m (121-ft.) granite obelisk erected in 1958, engraved with scenes from famous uprisings and bearing a central inscription (in Mao's handwriting): THE PEOPLE'S HEROES ARE IMMORTAL. The twin-tiered dais is said to be an intentional contrast to the imperial preference for three-tiered platforms; the *yin* of the people's martyrs contrasted with the *yang* of the emperors (see the "Lucky Numbers" box on p. 127).

The area on which the square stands was originally occupied by the **Imperial Way**—a central road that stretched from inside the Forbidden City, through Tian'an Men, and south to Da Qing Men (known as Zhonghua Men during the Nationalist era), which was demolished to make way for Mao's corpse in 1976 (see the review for Chairman Mao's Mausoleum, below). This road, lined on either side with imperial government ministries, was the site of the pivotal May Fourth movement (1919), in which thousands of university students gathered to protest the weakness and corruption of China's then-Republican government. Mao ordered destruction of the old ministries. The vast but largely empty **Great Hall of the People** rose from the rubble to the west, and equally vast but unimpressive **museums** were erected to the east, as part of a spate of construction to celebrate 10 years of Communist rule. But the site has remained a magnet for politically charged assemblies; the most famous was the gathering of **student protesters** in late spring of 1989. That movement, and the government's violent suppression of it, still defines Tian'an Men Square in most minds. You'll search in vain for bullet holes and bloodstains. The killing took place elsewhere. Brutal scenes were witnessed near Fuxing Men and Xi Dan (west of the square), as workers and students were shot in the back as the regime showed its true colors, bringing a halt to a decade of

---

Fun Fact National Theatrics

At a crowded restaurant, a group of Beijing's Olympic planners gather for a lavish meal. "Bring me your finest, most expensive dish, and hang the cost!" bellows one. The flamboyant meal eventually arrives, overshadowing the surrounding dishes. The diners are stunned into silence. The complaints begin, "How much did we pay for that?" "It's un-Chinese." "Can we get a discount?" "Who ordered this?" The official who ordered the dish is either keeping his silence, or has slipped away quietly. In essence, such has been the drama played out over Paul Andreu's controversial **National Theatre,** due to open west of the **Great Hall of the People** within the lifetime of this book. Andreu was awarded the project in 2000, and Beijingers have nicknamed it *jidanke'r* (The Eggshell). Although the project has been downsized, it still features a dazzling titanium-and-glass dome perched on a lake and encasing three auditoriums. Patrons descend on escalators through the waters of the lake.

WEGEN BISSIGEN
EICHHÖRNCHEN GESCHLOSSEN

CERRADO

CABRAS

Κλειστό
Μετεωρίτες

POOL CLOSED

ELECTRIC EELS

Hotel
closed for
facelifting

FERMÉ POUR
RAISON
DE GRÈVE
DES BONNES

FECHADO!
POR CAUSA DE
ATAQUES DOS CROCODILOS

I don't speak sign language.

A hotel can close for all kinds of reasons.

Our Guarantee ensures that if your hotel's undergoing construction, we'll
let you know in advance. In fact, we cover your entire travel experience.
See www.travelocity.com/guarantee for details.

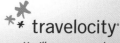

travelocity

You'll never roam alone.

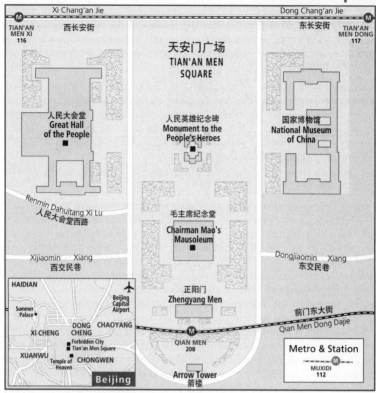

Xi Chang'an Jie — 西长安街

Dong Chang'an Jie — 东长安街

TIAN'AN MEN XI 116

TIAN'AN MEN DONG 117

天安门广场
TIAN'AN MEN SQUARE

人民大会堂
Great Hall of the People

人民英雄纪念碑
Monument to the People's Heroes

国家博物馆
National Museum of China

Renmin Dahuitang Xi Lu — 人民大会堂西路

Xijiaomin Xiang — 西交民巷

毛主席纪念堂
Chairman Mao's Mausoleum

Dongjiaomin Xiang — 东交民巷

正阳门
Zhengyang Men

前门东大街
Qian Men Dong Dajie

HAIDIAN

Beijing Capital Airport

Summer Palace

DONG CHAOYANG CHENG

XI CHENG

Forbidden City
Tian'an Men Square

XUANWU CHONGWEN

Temple of Heaven

Beijing

QIAN MEN 208

Metro & Station

MUXIDI 112

Arrow Tower — 箭楼

intermittent political reform. Today, stiff-backed soldiers, video cameras, and plain-clothed police still keep a close watch on the square.

Other than flying a kite and playing "spot the plain-clothed policeman," there isn't much to do in the square, but early risers can line up in front of Tian'an Men at dawn to watch the **flag-raising ceremony,** a unique suffocation-in-the-throng experience on National Day (Oct 1), when what seems like the entire Chinese population arrives to jostle for the best view.

Chairman Mao's Mausoleum (Mao Zhuxi Jinian Guan)   This is one of the eeriest experiences in Beijing. The decision to preserve Mao's body was made hours after his death in 1976. Panicked and inexperienced, his doctors reportedly pumped him so full of formaldehyde his face and body swelled almost beyond recognition. They drained the corpse and managed to get it back into acceptable shape, but they also created a wax model of the Great Helmsman just in case. There's no telling which version—the real or the waxen—is on display at any given time. The mausoleum itself was built in 1977, near the center of Tian'an Men Square. However much Mao may be mocked outside his tomb (earnest arguments about whether he was 70% right or 60% right are perhaps the biggest joke), he still commands a terrifying sort of respect inside it. It's not quite the kitsch experience some expect. The tour is free and fast, with no stopping, photos, or bags allowed inside. *Note:* The mausoleum was being renovated at time of writing, but should be finished by the time you read this.

South end of Tian'an Men Sq.; see map p. 121. (𝄐 010/6513-2277. Free admission. Mon–Sat 8–11:30am; sometimes also 2–4pm (usually Tues and Thurs). Bag storage in building across the street, directly west: ¥3 (40¢/20p) per piece. Metro: Qian Men (208).

Qian Men (Front Gate)   The phrase Qian Men is actually a reference to two separate towers on the south side of the square which together formed the main entrance to the Tartar (or Inner) City. The southernmost Arrow Tower (Jian Lou) is no longer open to the public. You can, however, still climb up inside the rear building, called the Zhengyang Men, where an enjoyable photo exhibition depicts life in Beijing's pre-1949 markets, temples, and *hutong*.

South end of Tian'an Men Sq.; see map p. 121. (𝄐 010/6522-9382. Admission ¥20 ($2.65/£1.35). 8:30am–4pm. Metro: Qian Men (208).

2 Forbidden City (Gu Gong)

The universally accepted symbol for the length and grandeur of Chinese civilization is undoubtedly the Great Wall, but the Forbidden City is more immediately impressive. A 720,000-sq.-m (7,750,015-sq.-ft.) complex of red-walled buildings and pavilions topped by a sea of glazed vermilion tile, it dwarfs nearby Tian'an Men Square and is by far the largest and most intricate imperial palace in China. The palace receives more visitors than any other attraction in the country (over seven million a year, the government says), and has been praised in Western travel literature ever since the first Europeans laid eyes on it in the late 1500s. Yet despite the flood of superlatives and exaggerated statistics that inevitably go into its description, it is impervious to an excess of hype, and it is large and compelling enough to draw repeat visits from even the most jaded travelers. Make more time for it than you think you'll need.

The palace, most commonly referred to in Chinese as Gu Gong (Former Palace), is on the north side of Tian'an Men Square across Chang'an Dajie (𝄐 010/6513-2255; www.dpm.org.cn). It is best approached on foot or via metro (Tian'an Men Dong, 117), as taxis are not allowed to stop in front. The palace is open daily from 8:30am to 5pm during summer and from 8:30am to 4:30pm in winter. Regular admission *(men piao)* in summer costs ¥60 ($8/£4), dropping to ¥40 ($5.35/£2.65) in winter; last tickets are sold an hour before the doors close. Various exhibition halls and gardens inside the palace charge additional fees. All-inclusive tickets *(lian piao)* had been discontinued at press time, perhaps in an effort to increase revenues (see the box "The Big Makeover" below), but it's always possible these will be reinstated. *Tip:* If you have a little more time, it is highly recommended that you approach the entrance at **Wu Men (Meridian Gate)** via **Tai Miao** (p. 136) to the east, and avoid the gauntlet of tiresome touts and tacky souvenir stalls.

Map of the Forbidden City
For a map of the palace, see the inside back cover of this book.

Ticket counters are marked on either side as you approach. **Audio tours** in several languages (¥40/$5.35/£2.65 plus ¥100/$13/£6.65 deposit; the English version is narrated by Roger Moore) are available at the gate itself, through the door to the right. Those looking to spend more money can hire **"English"-speaking tour guides** on the other side of the gate (¥200–¥350/$27–$47/£13–£23) per person, depending on tour

The Big Makeover

An immense **$75-million renovation of the Forbidden City,** the largest in 90 years, will be completed in two phases (the first by 2008, the second by 2020). Work began on halls and gardens in the closed western sections of the palace in 2002. Effort was concentrated on opening the **Wuying Dian (Hall of Valiance and Heroism)** in the southwest corner of the palace; the **Jianfu Gong Huayuan (Garden of the Palace of Building Happiness)** in the northwest; followed by **Cining Huayuan (Garden of Love and Tranquillity)** next to the Taihe Dian. Wuying Dian, formerly the site of the Imperial printing press, should be open when you arrive, displaying a collection of Buddhist sutras, palace records, and calligraphy. Also slated to reopen is Jianfu Gong Huayuan, which has undergone an ambitious restoration as the entire section was devastated by fire in 1923. Cining Huayuan is said to be opening in 2008. Plans also call for the construction of new temperature-controlled buildings to house and exhibit what is claimed to be a collection of **930,000 Ming and Qing imperial relics,** most now stored underground.

On the other side of the palace, within the northern section of the Ningshou Gong Huayuan, a remarkable building is undergoing restoration with assistance from the World Cultural Heritage Foundation. Qianlong commissioned the European Jesuit painters in his employ to create large-scale *trompe l'oeil* paintings, which were used both in the Forbidden City and in the Yuan Ming Yuan (p. 140). **Juanqin Zhai,** an elaborately constructed private opera house, houses the best remaining examples of these paintings, including a stunning image of a wisteria trellis, almost certainly painted by Italian master Castiglione.

length). The tour guide booth also rents **wheelchairs** and **strollers** at reasonable rates. *Note:* Only the central route through the palace is wheelchair-accessible, and steeply so.

BACKGROUND & LAYOUT

Sourcing of materials for the original palace buildings began in 1406, during the reign of the Yongle emperor, and construction was completed in 1420. Much of it was designed by a eunuch from Annam (now Vietnam), Nguyen An, but without improvements to the Grand Canal, construction would have been impossible—timber came from as far away as Sichuan, and logs took up to 4 years to reach the capital. The Yuan palace was demolished to make way for the Forbidden City, but the lakes created during the Jin (1122–1215) were retained and expanded. Between 1420 and 1923, the palace was home to 24 emperors of the Ming and Qing dynasties. The last of these was Aisin-Gioro Puyi, who was forced to abdicate in 1912 but remained in the palace until 1924.

The Forbidden City is arranged along a north–south meridian, aligned on the Pole Star. The Qing court was unimpressed when the barbarians designated Greenwich Royal Observatory as the source of the prime meridian in 1885; they believed the Imperial Way marked the center of the temporal world. Major halls open to the south.

Furthest south and in the center is the symmetrical **outer court,** dominated by immense ceremonial halls where the emperor conducted official business. Beyond the outer court and surrounding it on both sides is the **inner court,** a series of smaller buildings and gardens that served as living quarters. During the Ming, only eunuchs were allowed to pass between the two courts, enhancing their power.

The palace has been ransacked and parts destroyed by fire several times over the centuries, so most of the existing buildings date from the Qing rather than the Ming. The original complex was said to contain 9,999 rooms, testament to the Chinese love of the number nine (see the box "Lucky Numbers," p. 127), and also to an unusual counting method. The square space between columns is counted as a room *(jian),* so the largest building, **Taihe Dian,** counts as 55 rooms. Using the Western method of counting, there are now 980 rooms. Only half of the complex is open to visitors (expected to increase to 70% after repairs are completed in 2020; see the box, "The Big Makeover," above), but this still leaves plenty to see.

THE ENTRANCE GATES

Tian'an Men (Gate of Heavenly Peace) ✰✰   This gate is the largest in what was once known as the Imperial City and the most emblematic of Chinese government grandeur. Above the central door, once reserved for the emperor, now hangs the famous **portrait of Mao,** flanked by inscriptions that read: LONG LIVE THE PEOPLE'S REPUBLIC OF CHINA (left) and LONG LIVE THE GREAT UNITY OF THE PEOPLES OF THE WORLD (right). Mao declared the founding of the People's Republic from atop the gate on October 1, 1949. There is no charge to walk through, but tickets are required if you want to ascend to the **upper platform** for worthwhile views of Tian'an Men Square. You might imagine yourself as the Great Helmsman addressing a sea of Red Guards, all struggling to understand your thick Hunan accent while waving your little red book. Note the pair of *huabiao* (ornamental columns) topped with lions, wreathed in dragons and clouds, and facing the square. In their original form, *huabiao* were wooden posts in the shapes of a battle-axes, upon which subjects would attach petitions or scrawl their grievances to the king. Over time, their function was reversed. Turned to stone and wreathed in the ultimate symbol of the emperor's mandate—the dragon—they became a warning to the ruled to keep out.

North of Tian'an Men Sq.; ticket office to left as you enter. Admission ¥20 ($2.65/£1.35) in summer, ¥15 ($2/£1) in winter. 8am–4:30pm in summer; 8:30am–4pm in winter. Mandatory bag storage (¥2–¥6/25¢–80¢/15p–40p) behind and to left of ticket booth; cameras allowed.

Taihe Men (Gate of Great Harmony)   Immediately inside the Meridian Gate entrance is a wide courtyard with five marble bridges spanning the Jin He (Golden River), followed by Taihe Men. Ming emperors came here to consult with their ministers; this function moved further inside under the Qing.

Wu Men (Meridian Gate)   Built in 1420 and last restored in 1801, Wu Men is the actual entrance to the Forbidden City. The emperor would sit atop the gate to receive prisoners of war, flanked by a battalion of imperial guards clad in full battle armor. The prisoners, clad in chains and red cloth, kneeled in the courtyard while charges were read before the emperor confirmed they would be taken to the marketplace for execution. The order would be repeated first by two, then four, then eight officers, until the entire battalion was thundering the edict in unison. The watchtowers extending out either side of the gate *(que)* are an expression of imperial power. This style was prevalent during the Han dynasty (206 B.C.–A.D. 220); this is the only example from the Ming and Qing. The trees leading up to this gate are recent additions. Originally no trees were planted along the Imperial Way, stretching over 2km (1¼ miles) from **Da Qing Men** (now demolished) to **Qianqing Men (Gate of Heavenly Purity)** in the Inner Court, as according to the "five processes" *(wu xing)*, wood (green) subdues earth (yellow), the element associated with the emperor (hence the yellow glazed tiles).

THE OUTER COURT (QIAN CHAO)

Baohe Dian (Hall of Preserving Harmony)   This last hall, supported by only a few columns, is where the highest level of imperial examinations was held until the exams were suspended in 1901 and abolished in 1905. To the southwest, you can spy **Wenyuan Ge** (the former Imperial Archive), easily recognized by its black-tiled roof with green trim. (Black is associated with water, which, it was hoped, would protect the building from fire.) At the rear is an impressive carved marble slab weighing about 180 tons; during the reign of the Wanli emperor (1573–1620) 20,000 men spent 28 days dragging it to this position from Fangshan, roughly 50km (31 miles) to the southwest.

Taihe Dian (Hall of Great Harmony) 𝔞𝔞   Located beyond Taihe Men, and across an even grander stone courtyard, is an imposing double-roofed structure mounted atop a three-tiered marble terrace with elaborately carved balustrades. This is the largest wooden hall in China, and the most elaborate and prestigious of the palaces' throne halls; it was therefore rarely used. Emperors came here to mark the New Year and winter solstice. Note the row of ceramic figurines on the roof, led by a man on a chicken (a despotic prince) fleeing a terrible dragon that heads a group of nine animal figures. The number of figures reflects the importance of the building.

Zhonghe Dian (Hall of Middle Harmony)   The second great hall of the outer court houses a smaller imperial throne. The emperor would prepare for annual rites, such as sowing the fields at the Altar of Agriculture (Xian Nong Tan; see Gudai Jianzhu Bowuguan, p. 141) in spring, by examining the appropriate manuals here.

THE INNER COURT (NEI TING)

During the Ming, only the emperor, his family, his concubines, and the palace eunuchs (who numbered 1,500 at the end of the Qing dynasty) were allowed in this section. It begins with the **Qianqing Men (Gate of Heavenly Purity),** directly north of the Baohe Dian, fronted by a magnificent pair of **bronze lions** 𝔞 and flanked by a **Ba Zi Yingbi** (a screen wall in the shape of the character for "eight"), both warning non-royals not to stray inside. Beyond are three palaces designed to mirror the three halls of the Outer Court.

The first of these is the **Qianqing Gong (Palace of Heavenly Purity),** where the emperors lived until Yongzheng decided to move to the western side of the palace in the 1720s. Beyond is **Jiaotai Dian (Hall of Union),** containing the throne of the empress and 25 boxes that once contained the Qing imperial seals. A considerable expansion on eight seals used during the Qin dynasty, the number 25 was chosen because it is the sum of all single-digit odd numbers (see the box "Lucky Numbers," p. 127). Next is the more interesting **Kunning Gong (Palace of Earthly Tranquillity),** a Manchu-style bedchamber where a nervous Puyi was expected to spend his wedding night before he fled to more comfortable rooms elsewhere.

At the rear of the inner court is the elaborate **Yu Huayuan (Imperial Garden)** 𝔞, a marvelous scattering of ancient conifers, rockeries, and pavilions, largely unchanged since it was built in the Ming dynasty. The crags allowed court ladies, who spent their lives inside the Inner Court, a glimpse of the world outside. Puyi's British tutor, Reginald Fleming Johnston, lived in the **Yangxin Zhai,** the first building on the west side of the garden (now a tea shop).

From behind the mountain, you can exit the palace through the **Shenwu Men (Gate of Martial Spirit)** and continue on to Jing Shan and/or Bei Hai Park. Those with time to spare, however, should take the opportunity to explore less-visited sections on either side of the central path.

WESTERN AXIS

Most of this area is in a state of heavy disrepair, but a few buildings have been restored and are open to visitors. Most notable among these is the **Yangxin Dian (Hall of Mental Cultivation),** southwest of the Imperial Garden. The reviled Empress Dowager Cixi, who ruled China for much of the late Qing period, made decisions on behalf of her infant nephew, the Guangxu emperor, from behind a screen in the east room. This is also where emperors lived after Yongzheng moved out of the Qianqing Gong.

EASTERN AXIS

This side tends to be peaceful and quiet even when other sections are crowded. Entrance costs ¥10 ($1.35/65p) and requires purchase of useless over-shoe slippers, which quickly disintegrate (¥2/25¢/15p). The most convenient ticket booth is 5 minutes' walk southwest of the Qianqing Men, opposite **Jiulong Bi (Nine Dragon Screen),** a 3.5m-high (111/2-ft.) wall covered in striking glazed-tile dragons depicted frolicking above a frothing sea, built to protect the Qianlong emperor from prying eyes and malevolent spirits (that are only able to move in straight lines). The Qianlong emperor (reign 1736–1795) abdicated at the age of 85, and this section was built for his retirement, although he never really moved in, continuing to "mentor" his son while living in the Yangxin Dian, a practice later adopted by Empress Dowager Cixi, who also partially took up residence here in 1894.

Zhenbao Guan (Hall of Jewelry) ✮, just north of the ticket booth, has all 25 of the Qing imperial seals, ornate swords, and bejeweled minipagodas—evidence that the Qing emperors were devoted to Tibetan Buddhism. One of the highlights is the secluded **Ningshou Gong Huayuan** ✮✮✮, where the Qianlong emperor was meant to spend his retirement. Water was directed along a snakelike trough carved in the floor of the main pavilion. A cup of wine would be floated down the miniature stream, and the person nearest wherever it stopped would have to compose a poem, or drink the wine. The Qianlong emperor, whose personal compendium of verse ran to a modest 50,000 poems, was seldom short of words.

East of the garden is the **Changyin Ge,** sometimes called Cixi's Theater, an elaborate green-tiled three-tiered structure with trap doors and hidden passageways to allow movement between stages. Further north is sumptuous **Leshou Tang** ✮✮, built entirely from sandalwood, where the Qianlong emperor would read, surrounded by poems and paintings composed by loyal ministers set into the walls and framed by blue cloisonné tablets. Cixi slept in the room to the west. The following hall, **Yihe Xuan,** is not a good place to bring friends from Mongolia or Xinjiang. The west wall has an essay justifying the Qianlong emperor's decision to colonize the latter, while the east wall has a poem celebrating the invasion of Mongolia. In the far northeastern corner is **Zhen Fei Jing (Well of the Pearl Concubine),** a surprisingly narrow hole covered by a large circle of stone. The Pearl Concubine, one of the Guangxu emperor's favorites, was 25 when Cixi had her stuffed down the well by a eunuch as they were

> **Fun Fact** **Lucky Numbers**
>
> The layout of imperial Beijing is based on an ancient system of numerology that still resonates today. Odd numbers are seen as *yang* (male, positive, light) and are more auspicious than even numbers, which are viewed as *yin* (female, negative, dark). **Three** is a positive number, as seen in the three-tiered platforms that are reserved for Beijing's most sacred structures—Taihe Dian in the Forbidden City; Tai Miao, the Hall of Prayer for Good Harvests at Tian Tan; and Chang Ling at the Ming Tombs. It's also the number chosen for China's latest political theory, the Three Represents, which explains how a Communist party can be staffed by capitalists. **Four** *(si)*, as a *yin* number, signifies submission. When the emperor carried out sacrifices at the Temple of Heaven, he would face north and bow four times. It's also faintly similar to the word for death *(si)*, and is the most inauspicious number. Many Chinese apartment buildings lack a fourth floor. **Five** is revered as the center of the Luo Diagram (which allows single-digit numbers arranged in noughts-and-crosses formation to add up to 15). It also signifies the "five processes" *(wu xing)*—metal, wood, water, fire, and earth, which also correspond to the five points of the Chinese compass and to the five colors. Significant imperial buildings are five rooms *(jian)* deep; five openings welcome you into Tian'an Men; and until Zhonghua Men was razed to make way for Mao's corpse, the Imperial Way had five gates. Though an even number, **eight** has gained popularity because it is homophonous with "get rich" in Cantonese: The Olympic Games are scheduled to open on August 8, 2008. **Nine,** situated at the top of the Luo Diagram and the largest single-digit odd number, was reserved for the imperial house, with grand buildings measuring nine rooms across.

fleeing in the aftermath of the Boxer Rebellion. According to most accounts, Cixi was miffed at the girl's insistence that Guangxu stay and take responsibility for the imperial family's support of the Boxers.

Also worth seeing is the **Hall of Clocks (Zhongbiao Guan),** a collection of timepieces, many of them gifts to the emperors from European envoys. Entrance to the exhibit costs ¥10 ($1.35/65p).

3 Temple of Heaven (Tian Tan Gongyuan)

At the same time that the Yongle emperor built the Forbidden City, he also oversaw construction of this enormous park and altar to Heaven directly to the south. Each winter solstice, the Ming and Qing emperors would lead a procession here to perform rites and make sacrifices designed to promote the next year's crops and curry favor with Heaven for the general health of the empire. It was last used for this purpose by the president of the Republic, Yuan Shikai, on the winter solstice of December 23, 1914, updated with photographers, electric lights (the height of modernity at the time), and a bulletproof car for the entrance of the increasingly unpopular president. This effectively announced his intent to promote himself as the new emperor, but few onlookers shared his enthusiasm. Formerly known as the Temple of Heaven and Earth, the park is square (symbolizing Earth) in the south and rounded (symbolizing Heaven) in the north.

ESSENTIALS

Temple of Heaven Park (Tian Tan Gongyuan; ✆ **010/6702-8866**) is south of Tian'an Men Square, on the east side of Qian Men Dajie. It's open daily from 6am to 8pm (may close earlier in winter, depending on weather and staff decisions), but the ticket offices and major sights are only open from 8am to 5:30pm. All-inclusive tickets *(lian piao)* cost ¥35 ($4.65/£2.35) (¥30/$4/£2 in winter); simple park admission costs ¥15 ($2/£1). The east gate *(dong men)* is easily accessed by public transport; take the no. 39, 106, or 110 bus just north of the Chongwen Men metro stop (209, exit B) to Fahua Si. However, the best approach is from the south gate *(nan men),* the natural starting point for a walk that culminates in the magnificent Hall of Prayer for Good Harvests.

SEEING THE HIGHLIGHTS

During the Cultural Revolution, Tian Tan lost its perfect symmetry as large bites were taken out of the southwest and southeast corners. There's no sign that the land will be returned, with massive apartment blocks ready to sprout on both corners, but it's still a vast park that takes at least 2 hours to see in any depth. The west gate is convenient to the Altar of Agriculture (see Gudai Jianzhu Bowuguan, p. 141) and Wansheng Juchang (see section 1, "Performing Arts," in chapter 10). At the northeast corner lie the shopping delights of Yuanlong Silk Co. Ltd. (p. 183) and Hong Qiao Shichang (see section 2, "Markets & Bazaars" in chapter 9).

Circular Altar (Yuan Qiu)   This three-tiered marble terrace is the first major structure you'll see if you enter from the south gate *(nan men).* It was built in 1530 and enlarged in 1749, with all of its stones and balustrades organized in multiples of nine (see the box "Lucky Numbers," p. 127). Here, a slaughtered bull would be set ablaze, the culmination of an elaborate ceremonial entreaty to the gods.

Hall of Abstinence (Zhai Gong)   Yuan Shikai fasted for 3 days in his own residence rather than here, as tradition dictated. Perhaps this was his undoing (he died 1½ years later). Real emperors would fast and pray for 5 days, spending their final night in the **Living Hall (Qin Dian)** at the rear of this compound. Note the rare swastika emblems, a symbol of longevity in China, on the door piers. This green-tiled double-moated compound faces east, the best side at which to enter. The grounds are agreeably dilapidated, and are on a more human scale than the rest of the compound.

Hall of Prayer for Good Harvests (Qinian Dian) ★★   Undoubtedly the most stunning building in Beijing, this circular wooden hall, with its triple-eaved cylindrical blue-tiled roof, is perhaps the most recognizable emblem of Chinese imperial architecture outside of the Forbidden City. Completed in 1420, the original hall was struck by lightning and burned to the ground in 1889 (not a good omen for the dynasty), but a near-perfect replica was built the following year. Measuring 38m (125 ft.) high and 30m (98 ft.) in diameter, it was constructed without a single nail. The 28 massive pillars inside, made of fir imported from Oregon (China lacked timber of sufficient length), are arranged to symbolize divisions of time: The central four represent the seasons, the next 12 represent the months of the year, and the outer 12 represent traditional divisions of a single day. The hall's most striking feature is its ceiling, a kaleidoscope of painted brackets and gilded panels as intricate as anything in the

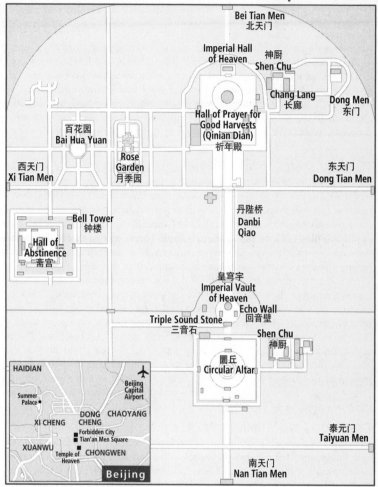

country. Don't skip the **Imperial Hall of Heaven (Huangqian Dian),** a smaller building to the north where the emperor would pray before the wooden tablets of his ancestors. Although Red Guards destroyed the tablets, the balustrades surrounding this prayer hall are elegantly carved.

Imperial Vault of Heaven (Huang Qiong Yu)   Directly north of the Circular Altar, this smaller version of the Hall of Prayer (see below) was built to store ceremonial stone tablets. The vault is surrounded by the circular **Echo Wall (Huiyin Bi).** In years past, when crowds were smaller and before the railing was installed, it was possible for two people on opposite sides of the enclosure to send whispered messages to each other along the wall with remarkable clarity. You can still experience this magical acoustic effect at the Western Qing Tombs (see section 4 in chapter 11), but there's little hope of enjoying it here.

4 Summer Palace (Yi He Yuan)

This expanse of elaborate Qing-style pavilions, bridges, walkways, and gardens, scattered along the shores of immense Kunming Lake, is the grandest imperial playground in China, constructed from 1749 to 1764. Between 1860 and 1903, it was twice leveled by foreign armies and rebuilt; hence it is often called the New Summer Palace, even though it pre-dates the ruined Old Summer Palace (Yuan Ming Yuan, p. 140). The palace is most often associated with the Empress Dowager Cixi, who resided here for much of the year and even set up a photographic studio. The grounds were declared a public park in 1924 and spruced up in 1949.

ESSENTIALS

The **Summer Palace** (✆ **010/6288-1144**) is located 12km (7½ miles) northwest of the city center in Haidian. Take **bus no. 726** from just west of Wudaokou light rail station (1304, exit A); or take a 30- to 40-minute **taxi** ride for ¥60 ($8/£4) from the center of town. A more pleasant option is to travel there by **boat** along the renovated canal system; slightly rusty "imperial yachts" leave from the Beizhan Houhu Matou (✆ **010/8836-3576**), behind the Beijing Exhibition Center just south of the Beijing Aquarium (from 10am to 5pm every hr, or every 30 minutes during student summer holidays [early July to late August]; 50-min. trip; ¥40/$5.35/£2.65 one-way; ¥70/$9.35/£4.65 round-trip; ¥100/$13/£6.65 including entrance ticket), docking at Nan Ruyi Men in the south of the park. The gates open daily at 6am; no tickets are sold after 6pm in summer and 5:30pm in winter. Admission is ¥30 ($4/£2) for entry to the grounds or ¥60 ($8/£4) for the all-inclusive *lian piao,* reduced to ¥20 ($2.65/£1.35) and ¥50 ($6.65/£3.35) respectively in winter (Nov–Mar). The most convenient entrance is Dong Gong Men (East Gate). Go early and allow at least 4 hours for touring the major sites on your own. Overpriced **imperial-style food** in a pleasant setting is available at the Tingli Guan Restaurant, at the western end of the Long Corridor. The area around the lake is perfect for a picnic, and Kunming Lake is ideal for skating in the depths of winter.

EXPLORING THE SUMMER PALACE

This park covers roughly 290 hectares (716 acres), with **Kunming Lake** in the south and **Longevity Hill (Wanshou Shan)** in the north. The lake's northern shore includes most of the buildings and other attractions and is the most popular area for strolls, although walking around the smaller lakes (Hou Hu) behind Longevity Hill is more pleasant. The hill itself has a number of temples as well as **Baoyun Ge (Precious Clouds Pavilion),** one of the few structures in the palace to escape destruction by foreign forces. There are literally dozens of pavilions and a number of bridges to be found on all sides of the lake, enough to make for a full day of exploration. Rather slow electric-powered boats may be rented; they are an appealing option on muggy summer days.

Long Corridor (Chang Lang) 🐦   Among the more memorable attractions in Beijing, this covered wooden promenade stretches 700m (nearly half a mile) along the northern shore of Kunming Lake. Each crossbeam, ceiling, and pillar is painted with a different scene (roughly 10,000 in all) taken from Chinese history, literature, myth, or geography. Politely rebuff the "students" who offer to show you their "original art" at this spot.

Summer Palace

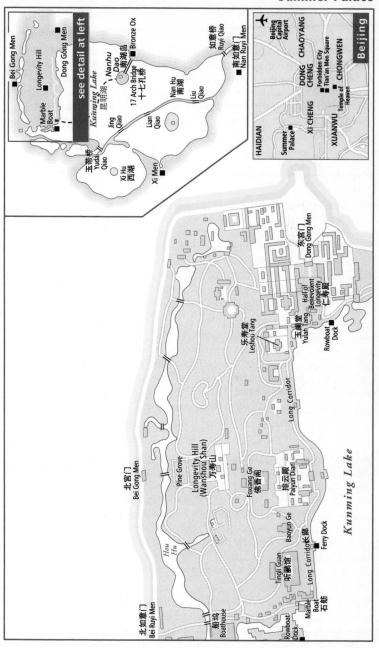

Beijing

Beijing Capital Airport

CHAOYANG

DONG CHENG

Forbidden City

Tian'an Men Square

HAIDIAN

XI CHENG

CHONGWEN

Summer Palace

XUANWU

Temple of Heaven

see detail at left

Bei Gong Men

Longevity Hill

Dong Gong Men

Marble Boat

Kunming Lake
昆明湖

Nanhu Dao
南湖岛

Bronze Ox

17 Arch Bridge
十七孔桥

如意桥
Ruyi Qiao

南如意门
Nan Ruyi Men

Nan Hu
南湖

Liu Qiao

Jing Qiao

Lian Qiao

玉带桥
Yudai Qiao

Xi Hu
西湖

Xi Men

东宫门
Dong Gong Men

Hall of Benevolent Longevity
仁寿殿

玉澜堂
Yulan Tang

Rowboat Dock

乐寿堂
Leshou Tang

Long Corridor

北宫门
Bei Gong Men

Pine Grove

Longevity Hill
(Wanshou Shan)
万寿山

Foxiang Ge
佛香阁

排云殿
Paiyun Dian

Baoyun Ge

听鹂馆
Tingli Guan

Hou Hu

Long Corridor 长廊

Ferry Dock

北如意门
Bei Ruyi Men

Rowboat Dock

船坞
Boathouse

石舫
Marble Boat

Kunming Lake

131

Impressions

"Most people hate the Old Buddha (Cixi) for diverting the naval funds. How unjust! Any navy we built in those days would have been destroyed in the first battle. Which of our enemies would have helped us build a fleet capable of destroying a single ship of theirs? They would have sent our fleet to the bottom of the sea and then charged us with the costs of the action, as they always did! As it is, the Old Buddha's palace still stands—they say there is nothing equal to it in the world! Could anyone, Chinese or foreign, of our generation duplicate it?"

—Professor Ch'eng, quoted in John Blofeld,
City of Lingering Splendour, 1961

Marble Boat (Shi Fang)   Docked at the end of the Long Corridor is an odd structure which is "neither marble nor a boat," as one novelist observed. Locals, keen to blame the Empress Dowager for China's decline during the Qing dynasty, wring their hands and cite it as the symbol of China's demise. Cixi funded a general restoration of the palace using money intended for the Chinese navy, and the (completely frivolous) boat is said to be Cixi's backhanded reference to the source of the funds. Shortly after the restoration was completed in 1888, China's paltry fleet was destroyed in a skirmish with Japan, the most glaring evidence yet of China's weakness in the modern era.

Renshou Dian (Hall of Benevolence and Longevity)   Located directly across the courtyard from the east gate entrance, Renshou Dian is the palace's main hall. This is where the Empress Dowager received members of the court, first from behind a screen and later, all pretenses dropped, from the Dragon Throne itself. North of the hall is Cixi's private theater, now a museum that contains an old Mercedes-Benz—the first car imported into China.

Seventeen-Arch Bridge (Shiqi Kong Qiao) ⚐   This marble bridge, 150m (492 ft.) long, connects South Lake Island (Nan Hu Dao) to the east shore of Kunming Lake. There is a rather striking life-size bronze ox near the eastern foot of the bridge.

5 Temples, Mosques & Churches

While signs around Beijing whip up indignation at the destruction of Chinese temples by foreign forces in 1860 and 1900, most destruction was carried out by the Chinese themselves, particularly after 1949. Medium-size houses of worship—Buddhist, Christian, Confucian, Daoist, and Muslim alike—fared badly; many were torn down straightaway, while others were converted to factories, hospitals, schools, or police stations. With the realization by the Chinese authorities that tourists are willing to pay money to inspect them, some have been converted back to a semblance of their original form, if not function.

Bai Ta Si (White Dagoba Temple)   Seemingly continuously under renovation, this Liao dynasty temple features the largest Tibetan pagoda (also called *chorten, dagoba,* or *stupa*) in China, towering over the neighborhood at 51m (167 ft.) tall. A Nepali architect built it over 700 years ago (completed 1279) by order of Kublai Khan, one of the first Mongols to convert to Tibetan Buddhism. Originally known as Miao Ying Si, the temple has undergone numerous reconstructions, usually as a result of fire. The Dajue Dian (Hall of the Great Enlightened Ones), the first building, contains thousands of little Buddhas in glass cases, set into the columns. An earthquake in 1976 turned up numerous artifacts, some of which are now on display in the museum. You'll find Buddhist statuary demonstrating ritualistic hand positions *(mudra)* and vivid *thangka* (silk hangings depicting Buddhist images).

Fucheng Men Nei Dajie 171, Xi Cheng Qu (a 10-min. walk east from the metro stop); see map p. 108. © 010/6616-0211. Admission ¥20 ($2.65/£1.35). 9am–4:30pm. Metro: Fucheng Men (203, exit B).

Baiyun Guan 🏮🏮   If the incense here somehow smells more authentic, it's because this sprawling complex, said to have been built in 739, is the most active of Beijing's Daoist temples. Chinese visitors seem intent on actual worship rather than smug tourism, and the blue-frocked monks wear their hair in the rarely seen traditional manner—long and tied in a bun at the top of the head. The temple acts as headquarters for the Chinese Daoist Association. Although the texts of Daoism (China's only native religion) decry the pursuit of wealth and honors as empty, the gods of wealth attract the most devotees. One notable structure is the Laolù Tang, a large cushion-filled hall in the third courtyard originally built in 1228, now used for teaching and ceremonies.

On Baiyun Guan Lu, east of the intersection with Baiyun Lu, Haidian Qu (1st right north of Baiyun Qiao, directly across from Baiyun Guan bus stop); see map p. 112. © 010/6346-3531. Admission ¥10 ($1.35/65p). 8:30am–4:30pm. Bus: 727 from Muxidi metro (112, exit D2) to Baiyun Guan.

Dong Tang (East Church or St. Joseph's Cathedral)   This gray Gothic structure has endured a torrid history. Built on ground donated by the Shunzhi emperor in 1655, this Jesuit church was toppled by an earthquake in 1720, then gutted by fire in 1812, after which it was leveled by an increasingly anti-foreign regime. It was rebuilt after foreigners forced their way into Beijing in 1860, and was razed again during the Boxer Rebellion of 1900. Chinese Christians were the first targets of the xenophobic Boxers, who disparagingly referred to them as "lesser hairy ones." Local converts were slaughtered in the hundreds before the Boxers (who also murdered women with unbound feet) worked up the courage to kill a real foreigner. Yet they are usually portrayed as a "patriotic" movement in China's history books. After a major renovation in 2000, Dong Tang is notable for its wide, tree-lined forecourt, a favorite spot for Beijing's skateboarders. Its counterpart in the south of town, **Nan Tang (South Church)** is just northeast of the Xuanwu Men metro stop, and has services in English. Call © **010/6603-7139** to check times. *Note:* Catholic churches in Beijing are not recognized by the Roman Catholic Church.

Wangfujing Dajie 74, Dong Cheng Qu (walk north for 10 min.); see map p. 108. © 010/6524-0634. Sunday services in Latin at 6:15 and Chinese at 7 and 8am. Metro: Wangfujing (118, exit A).

Dong Yue Miao 🏮   Reopened to the public in 1999, one of Beijing's most captivating Daoist temples stands largely disregarded. Founded in 1322 by the devotees of the Zhengyi sect, the temple is dedicated to the god Dong Yue, who resides in the sacred mountain of Tai Shan. Aside from coping with the hordes of tourists who now visit his abode, Dong Yue is charged with supervising the 18 layers of Hell and the 76 departments *(si)*.

The garishly represented emissaries of these departments may be found in the 72 halls that ring the main courtyard of the temple. Worshipers present themselves at the relevant hall, with offerings of money, incense, and red tokens inscribed with their names *(fupai)*. With 76 departments (some are forced to share a cubicle), there are emissaries for every conceivable wish, and if viewed as a straw poll of China's preoc-cupations, the results are not encouraging. The Department for Accumulating Wealth ("justifiable" is added in the translation) is busy, while the Department of Pity and Sympathy, depicting beggars, awaits its first petition, and there are an alarming num-ber of donations for the Department for Implementing 15 Kinds of Violent Death. This may or may not be related to the ongoing popularity of the Department of Offi-cial Morality, which rails against corrupt government.

A glassed-in stele at the northeast corner of the courtyard is written in the fine hand of Zhao Mengfu, recording the building of the temple and the life of its founder, Zhang Liusun, who died soon after purchasing the land. At the north of the complex stands the two-story **Minsu Bowuguan** (Folk Museum). This hosts exhibitions to remind Beijingers of their marvelous but largely forgotten traditions.

Chaoyang Men Wai Dajie 141, Chaoyang Qu (10-min. walk east on the north side); see map p. 119. ℂ 010/6551-0151. Admission ¥10 ($1.35/65p); free during festivals. Tues–Sun 8:30am–6:30pm in summer; winter until 4:30pm. Metro: Chaoyang Men (212, exit B).

Fahai Si   Located in the far west of Beijing, this early Ming temple, a must for those with an interest in Buddhist art, is easily combined with a visit to the cemetery for eunuchs, **Tian Yi Mu** (p. 146). The decoration of this temple in 1443 was funded by Li Tong, a wealthy eunuch who attracted artists from the Imperial court to produce stunning murals and statuary. The statues didn't survive the Cultural Revolution, but Red Guards failed to notice the exquisite **Buddhist murals** 𝒦𝒦 in the gloom of the main hall. These murals, miraculously preserved intact, were modeled on the art of the Tang, but show influences of Song dynasty landscape painting, and later Ming innovations in the use of perspective and depth in portraiture. The brushwork, partic-ularly in the depiction of robes, clouds, and flowers, is extraordinarily fine.

Moshi Kou Dajie, Shijing Shan Qu (from bus stop, continue up the rise and take a right after 5 min.; pass Tian Yi Mu, take a left turn, and continue uphill to a T-junction, take a right turn; the temple is a further 5 min. up the hill); see map p. 114. ℂ 010/8871-5776. Admission ¥20 ($2.65/£1.35). 8:30am–4:30pm. Bus: 959 or 746 from left of Ping-guo Yuan metro stop (103, exit D) to Shougang Xiaoqu. **Note:** This temple was being renovated at time of writing. New prices had not yet been decided. It should be open by the time you read this.

Fayuan Si (Source of Dharma Temple) *Finds*   Despite guides droning on about a long and glorious history, most of Beijing's sights are relatively new, dating from within the last 600 years. This temple, constructed in 645 in what was then the south-east corner of town, retains both an air of antiquity and the feel of a genuine Buddhist monastery. Orange-robed monks, housed in the adjacent Buddhist college, go about their business in earnest, and the visitors are asked to "respect religious ceremonies: do not interfere with religious activities." The ancient *hutong* immediately surrounding the temple are "protected" and worth a wander. Lanman Hutong, just to the east, was formerly a moat that marked the boundary of the old town during the Tang dynasty.

Fayuan Si Qian Jie 7, Xuanwu Qu; see map p. 112. Admission ¥5 (65¢/35p). Thurs–Tues 8:30–11am and 1:30–4pm. Metro: Xuanwu Men (206, exit D1).

Guo Zi Jian and Kong Miao 𝒦   Buried down a tree-shaded street west of the Lama Temple (see below), **Kong Miao**, China's second largest Confucian temple, is on the right, and **Guo Zi Jian (Directorate of Education)** is on the left; both were originally built in 1306. Two stelae at the front *(xia ma bei)* instruct you to park your horse in six different languages. The front courtyard of the temple contains 198 stelae inscribed with the names of successful candidates in the *jinshi* (highest level) imperial examinations during the Yuan, Ming, and Qing dynasties. Staff admit they see few local visitors, except during the weekend before the university entrance examinations, when students and their parents descend in droves to ask for the Great Sage's assistance. The main hall, **Dacheng Dian,** is the focus for students, who must throw their incense on the shrine rather than burn it, because of fire regulations. Ancient musical instruments, which Confucius saw as essential to self-cultivation, are the main point of interest. Behind the hall and to the left are 189 stelae, which contain the 630,000 characters that make up the Thirteen Confucian Classics—incredibly, copied by one man over a 12-year period. The attendant enhances the mood of antiquity by earnestly reciting old texts.

Success in the imperial examination was the key to social advancement, so **Guo Zi Jian** wielded immense power. It was originally joined to Kong Miao by Chijing Men, to the right as you enter. They will be reunited when the Ministry of Culture (housed in Guo Zi Jian) and the Ministry of Cultural Relics (housed in Kong Miao) can sort out their differences. A striking yellow glazed-tile *pailou* with elaborately carved stone arches leads to **Bi Yong Dadian** ☆, a square wooden hall encircled by a moat. The emperor would deliver a lecture on the classics here at the start of his reign, although the irrepressible Qianlong visited three times—after assuming the throne, after renovations were completed to mark the 50th anniversary of his reign, and when handing the throne over to his son, the Jiaqing emperor. He even wrote poems to decorate the sandalwood screen behind the throne. Ministers and the royal family were permitted inside, while three criers (to the west, south, and east) would repeat the emperor's words to students and minor officials kneeling outside.

Kong Miao at Guo Zi Jian Jie 13, Dong Cheng Qu (walk south from station along west side of Lama Temple, turn right onto street marked with arch); see map p. 108. ℭ 010/8401-1977. Admission ¥10 ($1.35/65p); Guo Zi Jian (next door) admission ¥6 (80¢/40p). 8:30am–4:30pm; Guo Zi Jian 9am–5pm. Metro: Yong He Gong/Lama Temple (215, exit C).

Lidai Diwang Miao (Temple of Past Emperors) ☆ *Finds*   Built on the grounds of

a former Buddhist temple (Bao'an Si), there's nary a Buddha in sight. Lidai Diwang Miao is where Ming and Qing emperors made sacrifices to the emperors of previous dynasties. Rulers didn't always come in person, but their representatives diligently carried out sacrifices in spring and autumn. The Yongzheng emperor, who killed his brother to usurp the throne, had more reason to pray than most, and made five appearances during his short reign. The layout is akin to Tai Miao in miniature, with an imposing spirit wall opposite the entrance, and two horse-dismounting tablets on either side of the entrance. There were originally three marble bridges and a spectacular wooden memorial arch *(pailou)* outside the entrance; these feudal elements were demolished in 1953 and 1954. Curatorial standards are improving: Patches of the original ceiling have been left in their original state, touch screen displays in the exhibition halls roughly translate the captions, and there are plush carpets and piped music, and even an admission of past vandalism. The original wooden tablets, once housed in the impressive twin-eaved main hall, were smashed during the Cultural Revolution. Their replacements look inauthentic, but the original order has been preserved. Central position goes to the legendary ruler Fuxi, and his successors are arranged outwards in order of venerability, one to the left, one to the right *(yi zuo yi you),* a seating arrangement still followed by China's rulers. The most striking feature is the intricately carved stelae (nearly 8m [26 ft.] tall) set to the east and west of the main hall.

Fucheng Men Dajie 131 (a 5 min. walk east from metro); see map p. 108. ℭ 010/6612-0186. Admission ¥20 ($2.65/£1.35). 8:30am–4:30pm. Metro: Fucheng Men (203, exit B).

Niu Jie Libai Si (Niu Jie Mosque) This is Beijing's largest mosque and the spiritual center for the city's estimated 200,000 Muslims. Built in 996, the complex looks more Eastern than Middle Eastern, with sloping tile roofs similar to those found in Buddhist temples. Halls are noticeably free of idols, however. A small courtyard on the south side contains the tombs and original gravestones of two Arab imams who lived here in the late 13th century. The main prayer hall is ghostly quiet except on Friday, the traditional day of worship.

Niu Jie 88, Xuanwu Qu (on east side of street); see map p. 112. *C* 010/6353-2564. Admission ¥10 ($1.35/65p) for non-Muslims. 8am–7pm. Bus: 10 or 66 to Libai Si from Changchun Jie metro stop (205, exit D).

Tai Miao 🕏🕏 *(finds)* Sometimes the biggest surprises are under your nose. Just east of Tian'an Men stands the only example of an imperial ancestral hall *(zu miao)* remaining in China; here are grand imperial edifices in a sleepy, atmospheric setting. Laid out in accordance with the ancient principle from the Rites of Zhou, "Ancestors to the left, land to the right" *(zuo zu you she),* the wooden tablets *(paiwei)* that represented the ancestors of the imperial house were housed to the left of the Forbidden City (the land was offered its due at the Altar of Land and Grain, housed in Zhongshan Gongyuan to the west). Beyond the Halberd Gate (Ji Men), untouched since it was constructed in 1420, the three main buildings are lined up on a central axis. Sacrifices to the ancestors took place in the southernmost building (Xiang Dian). This is one of only four buildings in Beijing to stand on a three-tiered platform, a hint that it was the most sacred site in imperial Beijing. Mao renamed it the Workers' Cultural Palace (Laodong Renmin Wenhua Gong), and the wooden tablets were pilfered during the Cultural Revolution. The workers have moved on, and the complex is largely deserted. Once you reach the moat at the northern end of the complex, turn left. Immediately opposite is **Zhongshan Gongyuan;** to the right stands **Wu Men** and the Forbidden City. Infinitely preferable to running the souvenir vendor gauntlet north from Tian'an Men, entering the Forbidden City from Tai Miao may be the best ¥2 (25¢/15p) you'll ever spend.

East of Tian'an Men, Dong Cheng Qu; see map p. 108. *C* 010/6525-2189. June–Sept 6:30am–8:30pm; Oct–May 7am–8:30pm. Admission ¥2 (25¢/15p); admission to bell exhibit ¥10 ($1.35/65p). Metro: Tian'an Men Dong (117, exit A).

Wanshou Si 🕏 The Longevity Temple, now home to the **Beijing Art Museum (Beijing Yishu Bowuguan),** was funded by a eunuch and was originally constructed in 1577. It later became a stopping point for the Qianlong emperor and his successors (particularly the Empress Dowager Cixi) on their way to the Summer Palace by boat, a route now followed by tour boats departing from just north of the zoo. The long sequence of heavily restored but low-key halls now houses an odd set of exhibitions, featuring everything from early ceramics, iron, and copperware, to late and very intricate lacquerware and carved ivory. Puzzlingly, the museum's most interesting exhibit, highly decorated and ancient seals *(zhuanzhang)* wrought from a variety of precious and semiprecious materials, are now kept in storage. At the rear of the complex is a rock garden from whose top Cixi is supposed to have admired the surrounding countryside, now long built over. Also visible are the original east and west wings of the complex, now occupied by squatters and staff, although there are plans to renovate the west wing.

Xi San Huan Bei Lu 18, Haidian Qu (on north side of Chang He, east side of the West Third Ring Rd.); see map p. 114. *C* 010/6841-3380. Admission ¥20 ($2.65/£1.35); ¥60 ($8/£4), including cup of tea. 8:30am–4:30pm. Bus: 811 from Gongzhu Fen metro stop (110) to Wanshou Si.

Wu Ta Si (Five Pagoda Temple)   More correctly known as Zhenjue Si (Temple of True Awakening), the one ancient building remaining on this site is a massive stone block with magnificently preserved Indian Buddhist motifs carved out of the bare rock. Peacocks, elephants, and dharma wheels adorn the base, which is also decorated with sutras copied out in Sanskrit (the large script) and Tibetan (the small script). The central pagoda has an image of two feet, harking back to an age when artisans could only hint at the presence of Buddha through symbols. The circular pavilion was added by the Qianlong emperor to honor his mother, an act of architectural vandalism which ruined the original simplicity and symmetry of the pagoda. The surrounding courtyard is gradually filling up with stone tombstones, spirit-way figures, and stelae commemorating the construction or renovation of temples; most are refugees from construction and road-widening projects around the capital. The wonderfully curated **Shike Yishu Bowuguan (Stone Carving Museum)** 👁👁 is at the rear of the complex. Beijing Aquarium is a 15-minute walk to the northeast.

Wu Ta Si Cun 24, Haidian Qu (from Beijing Tushuguan walk south and turn left at the Nanchang Canal; the walk takes 10 min.); see map p. 115. ℂ 010/6217-3836. Admission ¥20 ($2.65/£1.35). 9am–4:30pm. Bus: 808 from just east of Xi Zhi Men metro stop (201, exit B) to Beijing Tushuguan.

Yonghe Gong (Lama Temple) 👁👁👁   If you only visit one temple after the Temple of Heaven, this should be it. A complex of progressively larger buildings topped with ornate yellow-tiled roofs, Yonghe Gong was built in 1694 and originally belonged to the Qing prince who would become the Yongzheng emperor. As was the custom, the complex was converted to a temple after Yongzheng's move to the Forbidden City in 1744. The temple is home to several rather beautiful **incense burners,** including a particularly ornate one in the second courtyard that dates back to 1746. The Falun Dian (Hall of the Wheel of Law), second to last of the major buildings, contains a 6m (20-ft.) bronze statue of Tsongkapa (1357–1419), the founder of the reformist Yellow Hat (Geluk) sect of Tibetan Buddhism, which is now the dominant school of Tibetan Buddhism. He's easily recognized by his pointed cap with long earflaps. The last of the five central halls, the Wanfu Ge (Tower of Ten Thousand Happinesses), houses the temple's prize possession—an ominous Tibetan-style **statue of Maitreya** (the future Buddha), 18m (59 ft.) tall, carved from a single piece of white sandalwood. Once something of a circus, Yonghe Gong is slowly starting to feel like a place of worship, as there are now many Chinese devotees of Tibetan Buddhism.

Yong He Gong Dajie 12, south of the North Second Ring Rd. (entrance on the south end of the complex); see map p. 108. ℂ 010/6404-3769. 9am–4pm. Admission ¥25 ($3.35/£1.65); audio tours in English additional ¥25 ($3.35/£1.65). Metro: Yong He Gong/Lama Temple (215, exit C).

6 Parks & Gardens

Imperial parks, used either for sacrifices to the gods or for leisure activities, were once off-limits to the common folk. Now the parks are overrun with them, particularly just after dawn, when the older generation turns out in force to practice *taijiquan* and ballroom dancing, or to chat and show off their caged birds *(zou niao)*.

Bei Hai Gongyuan (Beihai Park) 👁   An imperial playground dating back to the Tartar Jin dynasty (1115–1234), Bei Hai lies to the north of Zhong Hai and Nan Hai, which were also opened to the public in 1925. In the best tradition of *Animal Farm,* the Communist leaders created a new Forbidden City and named it Zhong Nan Hai. Bei Hai was left to the masses. Although it's a convenient way to combine a morning visit to the Forbidden City with a more relaxing afternoon in the Back Lakes area, most visitors have a quick peek at the southern half and then disappear. Unfortunately, they miss the north side of the park, which is more interesting.

Entering from the south, you come to **Tuan Cheng (Round City)**, a small citadel on a raised platform whose most notable structure, **Chengguang Dian**, houses a 1.5m-tall (5-ft.) statue of a feminine-looking Buddha, crafted from Burmese white jade. Crossing the Yong'an Bridge to **Qiong Dao (Qiong Islet)**, you soon reach **Yong'an Si**, where the founder of the prominent Geluk sect, Tsongkapa, was the focus of devotion. He is now portrayed as a Chinese reformer of corrupt Tibetan Buddhism, on the grounds that he was born in Qinghai rather than "autonomous" Tibet. From here, boats run to the north side of the park for ¥5 (65¢/35p), or you can walk around the east side, passing calligraphers wielding enormous sponge-tipped brushes to compose rapidly evaporating poems on the flagstones.

Boats pull in to the east of **Wu Long Ting (Five Dragon Pavilion)**, where aspiring singers treat the public to revolutionary airs popular in the 1950s. Off to the left is an impressive green-tiled *pailou* (memorial arch; the green tiles signify a religious purpose, in contrast to the yellow imperial tiles of the Forbidden City and Guo Zi Jian). Continue on to the square-shaped **Jile Shijie Dian** ⚐, encircled by a dry moat. Built by the Qianlong emperor to honor his mother, the sandalwood structure is exquisite, topped with a priceless gold dome (apparently too high for either foreign troops or local warlords to reach). The gaudy fiberglass statuary inside brings you back to the present. To the west stands an impressive **Nine Dragon Screen,** which guarded the entrance to a now-vanished temple. Further east is **Daci Zhenru Bao Dian** ⚐⚐, an atmospheric Buddhist hall built during the late Ming from unpainted cedar; topped with a black roof (to protect the precious wood from fire), it has a cool slate floor. Continue east to the northern exit onto Ping'an Dadao, which marks the southern end of the Shicha Hai (Back Lakes) area.

Wenjin Jie 1, Xi Cheng Qu (south entrance is just west of the north gate of the Forbidden City; east entrance is opposite the west entrance of Jing Shan Park); see map p. 108. ℂ 010/6404-0610. Admission summer ¥10 ($1.35/65p); winter ¥5 (65¢/35p); ¥10 ($1.35/65p) extra for Yong'an Si; ¥1 (15¢/10p) extra for Tuancheng. 6am–9:30pm. Bus: 812 or 814 from Dong Dan metro stop (119, exit A) to Bei Hai.

Jing Shan Gongyuan (Jing Shan Park)   If you want a clear aerial view of the Forbidden City, you'll find it here. The park's central hill was created using earth left over from the digging of the imperial moat and was the highest point in the city during the Ming dynasty. It was designed to enhance the *fengshui* of the Forbidden City, by blocking the harsh northern wind and by burying a Mongol Yuan dynasty pavilion, the Yanchun Ge. In something of a riposte to the Chinese Ming dynasty, the Manchu Qianlong emperor built a tower by the same name (albeit in a very different style) in the Jianfu Gong Huayuan, within the Forbidden City. A tree on the east side of the hill marks the spot where the last Ming emperor, Chongzhen, supposedly hanged himself in 1644, just before Manchu and rebel armies overran the city. The original tree, derided as the "guilty sophora" during the Qing, was hacked down by Red Guards who failed to recognize a fellow anti-imperialist.

Jing Shan Qian Jie 1, Dong Cheng Qu (opposite Forbidden City north gate); see map p. 108. ℂ 010/6404-4071. Admission ¥5 (65¢/35p). Jan–Mar 6:30am–8pm; Apr–June 6am–9pm; July–Aug 6am–10pm; Sep–Oct 6am–9pm; Nov–Dec 6:30–8pm. Bus: 812 from Dong Dan metro stop (119, exit A) to Gu Gong.

The Olympic Green and Olympic Forest Park

Everything in Beijing is big. Tian'an Men Square is roughly the size of 90 football fields, wandering through the Forbidden City feels like a mini-marathon, and of course the Great Wall is . . . very long. It is fitting then that hosting the Olympics in Beijing means building awe-inspiring, people-dwarfing structures. And all at a sizeable price tag of $40 billion.

Beijing's **Olympic Green** will be the main Olympics attraction, both during and after the Games. It is about a 30-minute drive north of the Forbidden City and covers an area roughly six times the size of Athens' Olympic Green and three times the size of New York's Central Park. The main attractions here will be the **Beijing National Stadium** and **National Aquatics Center,** both of which were still being built at time of writing. The former has been nicknamed "the Bird's Nest" because of its oblong shape and inter-locking steel grids that closely resemble the twigs and branches of, well, a bird's nest. The original design featured an innovative retractable roof, but with only one year left to the XXIX Olympiad, roof plans were scrapped due to cost and time pressures. But even without a fancy convertible-like ceiling, the Bird's Nest will be an impressive architectural feat. It was designed by architecture darlings Jacques Herzog and Pierre de Meuron, cost roughly $400 million, and can hold 91,000 spectators. It will host the opening and closing ceremonies, as well as athletics events and football. A healthy stone's throw away is the Aquatics Center, dubbed "the Water Cube" (it's actually a rectangle, but "Water Rectangle" didn't have the same ring). From the outside, if all goes according to plan, it will look like a giant cube made up of hundreds of suspended aqua bubbles. Swimming, diving, synchronized swimming, and water polo events will be held here. Both venues are slated for cultural and entertainment events post-Olympics. North of the Water Cube is the **National Indoor Stadium,** which will host gymnastics and handball events. Its design plays on the theme of a traditional Chinese folding fan. Unlike its neighbors, it doesn't have a cutesy nickname, perhaps because "The Fan" has a slightly stalkerish sound to it.

Behind the Olympic Green will be the **Olympic Forest Park.** At 640 hectares (1,581 acres), this back garden of the Olympic Games will be Beijing's largest city park. During the Olympics, the park will host tennis, archery, and hockey events. Afterwards visitors will flock to this spacious bit of greenery to check out **Main Mountain,** a man-made pile of 3.98 million cubic meters (141 million cubic ft.) of earth, and **Main Lake,** a 110-hectare (272-acre, roughly 205 football fields) body of water shaped like the Olympic torch. The park will be open to the public on September 30, 2008. At time of writing, folks at the Olympic committee had not yet decided on admission fees.

Ming Chengqiang Gongyuan (Ming City Wall Park) ✿   The section of wall presented here, running a mile east-to-west from Dongbian Men to Chongwen Men, was originally built in the Yuan dynasty (1279–1368) and reconstructed in the mid-1500s by the Ming. Modern restoration work on the section began in 2002 and is still in progress, using bricks from the original Ming reconstruction collected from nearby residents (some of whom employed them to build toilets after the wall was demolished in the 1950s). A pleasant park runs east along the length of the wall to the dramatic Dongnan Jiaolou (Southeast Corner Tower; daily 9am–5pm; ¥10/$1.35/65p), with its dozens of arrow slots; a contemporary art gallery and interesting exhibition on the history of Chongwen can be found inside.

East of metro stop. ✆ 010/6527-0574. Open 24 hr. Metro: Chongwen Men (209, exit B).

Ri Tan Gongyuan (Ri Tan Park)   The Temple of the Sun (Ri Tan) served as an altar where the emperor conducted annual rites. Built in 1530, Ri Tan is a pleasant park with a delightful outdoor **teahouse** ✿ and a **rock-climbing wall** at its heart. Fishponds, a pedal-powered monorail, kites, and a bonsai market also keep the locals amused.

The other imperial altars are located in similar city parks, roughly marking the five points of the Chinese compass. To the north is **Di Tan Gongyuan (Temple of Earth),** just north of the Lama Temple; to the west is **Yue Tan Gongyuan (Temple of the Moon);** the much grander **Tian Tan Gongyuan (Temple of Heaven)** marks the southern point. **She Ji Tan (Altar of Land and Grain)** in Zhongshan Gongyuan southwest of the Forbidden City, pre-dates them all by several centuries, and marks that peculiarly Chinese compass point, the center.

Ri Tan Lu 6, Chaoyang Qu; see map p. 117. ✆ 010/8561-1389. Admission free. 6am–9:30pm (from 6:30am–9pm in winter). Metro: Yong'an Li (121, exit A).

Yuan Ming Yuan (Old Summer Palace) ★ (Kids)   An amalgamation of three separate imperial gardens, these ruins create a ghostly and oddly enjoyable scene, beloved for years as a picnic spot. Established by the Kangxi emperor in 1707, Yuan Ming Yuan is a more recent construction than the New Summer Palace to the west, but it is misleadingly called the Old Summer Palace because it was never rebuilt after French and British troops looted and burned it down during the Second Opium War of 1860. Ironically, some of the buildings were Western-style and filled with European furnishings and art. Two Jesuit priests, Italian painter Castiglione and French scientist Benoist, were commissioned by Qianlong to design the 75-acre **Xi Yang Lou (Western Mansions)** in the northeast section of the park. Perhaps the most remarkable structure was a zodiac water clock which spouted from 12 bronze heads, three of which (an ox, a monkey, and a tiger) are now housed in the otherwise unremarkable **Poly Art Museum,** immediately above Dong Si Shi Tiao metro stop. Inaccurate models suggest that the structures were entirely European in style, but they were curious hybrids, featuring Imperial-style vermillion walls and yellow-tiled roofs. A few restorations have begun, starting with the **Wanhua Zhen (10,000 Flowers Maze),** a nicely reconstructed labyrinth in the **Changchun Yuan (Garden of Eternal Spring).** Recently, the park has been the center of environmental controversy. Park management and the district government decided to line the lakes (an integral part of Beijing's water ecology and a magnet for bird life) with plastic sheeting to save on water bills and raise the water levels to allow for a duck-boat business.

Qinghua Xi Lu 28, Haidian Qu (north of Peking University); see map p. 115. ✆ 010/6262-8501. 7am–7pm (to 5:30pm in winter). Admission ¥10 ($1.35/65p); ¥15 ($2/£1) to enter Xi Yang Lou. Bus: 743 or 375 from east of Wudaokou metro stop (1304) to Yuan Ming Yuan.

7 Museums

In keeping with the Communist (and Confucian) passion for naming and quantification, Beijing has a museum for everything—police, bees, even the humble watermelon. If you share this passion and plan on spending a week or more in the capital, invest in a *bowuguan tong piao* (¥60/$8/£4), which grants you free (or half price) admission to over 70 sites in and around Beijing.

Beijing Guihua Bowuguan (Beijing Planning and Exhibition Hall) *Kids*   This high-tech museum gives you of a glimpse of tomorrow's Beijing. Several of the exhibitions are interactive, including the scale model of Beijing that you can actually walk on. We highly recommend the short movies, offered at half-hour intervals and in English on request. The 3D movie, complete with the funny glasses, tells the history of Beijing's development. The 4D movie—more like a ride at an amusement park—whisks you on a tour of Beijing's future subway lines, which will supposedly connect any two points in Beijing in less than an hour. Even if it is propaganda, it's still good fun.

20 Qianmen Dong Lu. (℗ 010/6702-4559. www.bjghzl.com.cn. Admission ¥30 ($4/£2); ¥10 ($1.35/65p) additional for each movie. Tues–Sun 9am–5pm. Metro: Qianmen (208).

Capital Museum (Shou Du Bo Wu Guan) *Kids*   This surprisingly well-curated museum of Beijing history and culture includes plenty of English subtitles that are often too scarce at other Beijing museums. Exhibitions on Chinese courtyard architecture and Buddhist sculpture are some of the highlights. Especially fun for the kids is the fifth floor's folk exhibition, which includes displays on Chinese traditional dress and live demonstrations of Peking Opera on Saturdays.

16 Fùxīng Mén Wài Dàjiē. (℗ 010/6337-0491. www.capitalmuseum.org.cn. Admission ¥30 ($4/£2). Tues–Sun 9am–5pm, ticket booth closes at 4pm. Metro: Muxidi (112).

Da Zhong Si (Great Bell Temple)   An attraction to bring out the hunchback in anyone, this Qing temple now houses the **Ancient Bell Museum (Gu Zhong Bowuguan),** best visited on the way to the **Summer Palace** or in conjunction with **Wanshou Si,** which lies to the southwest along the Third Ring Road. The temple was known as Juesheng Si (Awakened Life Temple). But the 47-ton bell transported here on ice sleds in 1743 clearly took center stage, hence the temple's current moniker. The third hall on the right houses clangers garnered from around Beijing. Some were donated by eunuchs wishing the relevant emperor long life, with hundreds of donors' names scrawled on their sides. But frustratingly, none of this is fleshed out. The main attraction is housed in the rear hall, carved inside and out with 230,000 Chinese and Sanskrit characters. The big bell tolls but once a year, on New Year's Eve. Visitors rub the handles of Qianlong's old washbasin, and scramble up narrow steps to make a wish while throwing coins through a hole in the top of the monster. But it is no longer the "King of Bells"—that honor now goes to the 50-ton bell housed in the **Altar to the Century (Zhonghua Shiji Tan),** constructed in 1999 to prove that China could waste money on the millennium, too.

Bei San Huan Xi Lu 31A, Haidian Qu (west of metro stop, north of Lianxiang Qiao on the northwest side of the Third Ring Rd.); see map p. 114. (℗ 010/6255-0819. Admission ¥10 ($1.35/65p); ¥2 (25¢/15p) extra to climb the Bell Tower. Tues–Sun 8:30am–4:30pm. Metro: Da Zhong Si (1302, exit A).

Gudai Jianzhu Bowuguan (Museum of Ancient Architecture) *★★*   This exhibition, a mixture of models of China's most famous architecture and fragments of buildings long disappeared, is housed in halls as dramatic as those on the central axis of the Forbidden City. These were once part of the **Xian Nong Tan,** or Altar of Agriculture, now as obscure as its neighbor, Tian Tan, the Temple (properly Altar) of Heaven, is famous. From about 1410, emperors came to this once-extensive site to perform rituals in which they started the agricultural cycle by playing farmer and plowing the first furrows. The site where they once toiled is now a basketball court.

The exhibition in the surviving halls is striking in its extensive English explanations of everything from the construction of the complicated bracket sets, which support temple roofs, to the role of geomancy in Chinese architectural thinking, and curiosities from now razed sites such as Longfu Si. Models of significant buildings around Beijing can help you select what to see in the capital during the remainder of your trip.

The rearmost **Taisui Dian (Hall of Jupiter)** of 1532, with its vast, sweeping roof, is only exceeded in magnificence by the Forbidden City's Hall of Supreme Harmony.

Dong Jing Lu 21, Xuanwu Qu (from bus stop, take 1st right into Nan Wei Lu and walk for 5 min., look out for an archway down a street on the left); see map p. 112. ℂ 010/6301-7620. Admission ¥15 ($2/£1). 9am–4pm. Bus: 803 from just south of Wangfujing (118) or Qian Men (208) metro stops to Tian Qiao Shangchang.

National Museum of China (Guojia Bowuguan) ☆   The Museum of the Chinese Revolution and the Museum of History have been united in a single building, but renovations won't be completed until 2008. Until then, a series of exhibits emphasizing the greatness of the Chinese civilization will be shown. Some effort has been made to spruce things up, and English captions have been added to a number of the displays, although they are conspicuously lacking from the hilarious wax figure hall. In the past, interest centered on who was omitted from Chinese history; now it focuses on who is included. Former unpersons such as Liu Shaoqi and Lin Biao, Mao's ill-fated heirs apparent, are displayed alongside their tormentors. The Party line is scrupulously followed: The passive and obsequious Lin, whose death went unreported for nearly a year, is still said to have plotted to seize power from Mao. *Note:* This museum is undergoing a massive facelift and will not reopen until sometime in 2009.

East side of Tian'an Men Sq., Dong Cheng Qu; see map p. 108. ℂ 010/6512-8901. www.nmch.gov.cn. Admission ¥30 ($4/£2) for *tong piao,* or ¥10–¥20 ($1.35–$2.65/65p–£1.35) for each exhibit; English audio tours ¥30 ($4/£2). 9am–3:30pm. Metro: Tian'an Men East (117, exit D).

Zhongguo Dianying Bowuguan (China National Film Museum)   If you're a Chinese movie buff, you'll love this place. The building exterior is black and white and loosely designed to look like a giant screen and a movie clipboard. Inside, you'll find a huge IMAX theater on your right; to your left is a four-story circular ramp leading to exhibits stuffed with black and white photos, old camera equipment and movie memorabilia, and even a mini-set of Old China. Wall-mounted plasma TVs show clips from various films. Hubs reminiscent of those found at hair salons hang suspended from the ceilings and play the accompanying audio. In the special effects hall on the 5th floor, fork over ¥10 ($1.35/65p) to buy yourself a ride on a motorcycle or carpet and chose from seven different blue screen backgrounds—escaping the snapping jaws of a T-rex, or floating peacefully over the Temple of Heaven. You'll get a CD of your ride afterwards, and yes, it will look very cheesy. There are English translations for introductions to exhibits, but otherwise information is in Chinese only. The biggest drawback of this museum is its location—it's halfway to the airport. Combine a visit here with a trip to nearby art district 798.

20 Nanying Lu. ℂ 010/6431-9548. www.cnfm.org.cn. Admission ¥20 ($2.65/£1.35). Tues–Sun 9am–4:30pm.

Zhongguo Gongyi Meishuguan (National Arts & Crafts Museum)   Located on the fifth floor of Parkson Department Store (Baisheng Gouwu Zhongxin), you'll find no ancient, dusty treasures here. This is a museum to prove that contemporary Chinese craftsmanship is every bit as good as it was during the Tang dynasty. Many items suggest otherwise, particularly large chunks of jade painstakingly carved into monuments to bad taste, and ceramic statues of arhats picking wax from their ears. But it's a good introduction to traditional crafts in their places of origin. Striking exhibits include clay figurines from Jiangsu, cloisonné from Beijing, lacquerware from Fujian, and ceramics from Jingde Zhen, which steal the show.

Fuxing Men Nei Dajie 101, Xi Cheng Qu; see map p. 108. (✆ 010/6605-3476. Admission ¥8 ($1.05/55p). Tues–Sun 9:30am–4pm. Metro: Fuxing Men (114/204, exit B).

8 Former Residences & Other Curiosities

Constructing memorial halls to the heroes of past and present dynasties has a long history, and the Communists have adopted this tradition with élan. As before, historical accuracy matters little; cultivating patriotic subjects is the goal.

Ancient Observatory (Gu Guanxiang Tai)   Most of the observatory's large bronze astronomical instruments—mystifying combinations of hoops, slides, and rulers stylishly embellished with dragons and clouds—were built by the Jesuits in the 17th and 18th centuries. You can play with reproductions of the Chinese-designed instruments they superseded (the originals were moved to Nanjing in 1933 and, for unexplained reasons, haven't been returned) in the grassy courtyard below. At the back of the garden, there's a "we-invented-it-first" display outlining the achievements of Song dynasty astronomer Guo Shoujing, who also has his own memorial hall on the northern tip of Xi Hai. To the right of the entrance there's a more useful exhibition, which houses a photo of a bone from 1300 B.C. on which China's first astronomers etched a record of solar eclipses, details of which are still used in present-day astronomy.

Jianguo Men Dong Biaobei 2, Dong Cheng Qu (southwest side of Jianguo Men intersection, just south of metro); see map p. 108. (✆ 010/6512-8923. Admission ¥10 ($1.35/65p). 9am–5pm. Metro: Jianguo Men (120/211, exit C).

Dixia Cheng (Underground City) ★ *Kids*   A sign near the entrance proclaims this seldom-visited attraction a "human fairyland and underground paradise." Far from it. Aside from odd recent additions, such as a silk factory, these tunnels are dark, damp, and genuinely eerie. A portrait of Mao stands amid murals of ordinary folk "volunteering" to dig tunnels, and fading but catchy slogans (DIG THE TUNNELS DEEP, ACCUMULATE GRAIN, OPPOSE HEGEMONY, and FOR THE PEOPLE: PREPARE FOR WAR, PREPARE FOR FAMINE). Unintentional humor is provided by propaganda posters from the era, which advise citizens to cover their mouths in the event of nuclear, chemical, or biological attack. Built during the 1960s, with border skirmishes with the USSR as the pretext, the tunnels could accommodate all of Beijing's six million inhabitants upon completion—or so it was boasted. Army engineers were said to have built a secret network of tunnels connecting the residences of Party leaders at Zhong Nan Hai to the Great Hall of the People and the numerous military bases near Ba Da Chu to the west of town. Suspicions were confirmed in 1976 and 1989 when large numbers of troops emerged from the Great Hall of the People to keep the people in check. The construction boom means that this is the only remaining entrance to the non-secret tunnels; it may disappear soon.

Xi Damochang Jie 64, Chongwen Qu (from metro stop, walk west; take the 1st left into Qinian Dajie, then the 2nd right; entrance is on south side, just past Qian Men Xiaoxue); see map p. 108. ⓒ 010/6702-2657. Admission ¥20 ($2.65/£1.35). 8:30am–5:30pm. Metro: Chongwen Men (209, exit D).

Factory 798 (Qijiuba Gongchang) ⭐⭐
Optimistically billed as a rival to New York's SoHo district, this Soviet-designed former weapons factory is a center for local modern art and fashion. Factory 798's long-term survival is uncertain, with Beijing's mayor musing that they would "look, regulate, and discuss" the use of the space, which the owners and the Chaoyang municipal government hope will become a technology park. Purchase a map for ¥2 (25¢/15p) on arrival. From entrance no. 2, you'll soon arrive at the **Hart Center of Arts** on the right, which holds regular screenings of alternative films (see chapter 10, p. 190) and also sells interesting hand-painted T-shirts. Further down on the right is the remarkable Bauhaus-inspired **798 Space,** still daubed with slogans offering praise to Mao. The most consistently interesting exhibitions are held by **798 Photo,** immediately opposite. Turn right and right again as you emerge from the building to find the first gallery to open in Factory 798, **Beijing Tokyo Art Projects** (www.tokyo-gallery.com), which boasts a formidable stable of local and international artists. Turn left and duck down a narrow lane, to emerge at the Gao Brothers' cuddly **Beijing New Art Projects** (ⓒ 010/8456-6660). **At Cafe (Aite Kafei;** ⓒ 010/6438-7264), just across the road, is the best of Dashanzi's middling cafes. If a visit to 798 whets your appetite for more avant-garde Chinese art, many of 798's artists, faced with spiraling rents and an increasingly commercial atmosphere, have moved to **Song Zhuang,** a village to the east of town (www.artistvillagegallery.com).

Jiuxian Qiao Lu 4, Chaoyang Qu (north of Dashanzi Huandao); see map p. 117. www.798space.com. 10:30am–7pm (some galleries closed Mon). Bus: 813 east from Chaoyang Men metro (212, exit A) to Wangye Fen.

Lao She Jinianguan (Former Residence of Lao She)
The courtyard home of one of Beijing's best-loved writers, Lao She (1899–1966), is the most charming of many converted homes scattered around Beijing's *hutong.* Despite being granted this home by Zhou Enlai in 1950, the writer refused to become a cheerleader for the regime, and his post-revolution years were remarkably quiet for such a prolific writer. He recently came in at no. 5 in an online survey of "China's leading cultural icons," ahead of pop diva Wang Faye but well behind the no. 1 choice, the iconoclastic writer Lu Xun (who has a memorial hall in the west of town; see chapter 8, p. 166). Lao She is renowned for the novel *Rickshaw (Luotuo Xiangzi),* a darkly humorous tale of a hardworking rickshaw puller, Happy Boy.

Start in Hall 3, to the right, which records his early years in London, the United States, and Shandong Province. Hall 2 is an attempt to re-create the mood of his original study and sitting room, with his personal library untouched and his desk calendar left open at the day of his disappearance—August 24, 1966. While the date of his death is certain, the details are murky. The official line has him committing a poetic suicide in nearby Taiping Hu (pictured in Hall 1) after enduring a "struggle session" at Kong Miao. It's possible that he was simply murdered by Red Guards.

Fengfu Hutong 19, Dong Cheng Qu (from Wangfujing Dajie, turn left at the Crowne Plaza along Dengshikou Xi Jie to the 2nd *hutong* on your right); see map p. 108. ⓒ 010/6514-2612. Admission ¥10 ($1.35/65p). 9am–6pm. Metro: Wangfujing (118, exit A).

Prince Gong's Mansion (Gong Wang Fu)
This splendid imperial residence belonged to several people, including the sixth son of the Guangxu emperor (Prince Gong) who, at the age of 27, was left to sign the Convention of Peking in 1860, after

> (*Fun Fact*   **Going, Going, Gong?**
>
> Beijing's most remarkable building, Heshen's opulent pleasure house (constructed entirely from precious *nanmu*) is found in the southern half of Prince Gong's Mansion. It should be a major tourist attraction, but the site is currently occupied by the China Arts Research Council and a high school. When ordinary *Beijingren* are served with an eviction notice, they often have as little as 24 hours to move out before the demolition crews arrive, but when government ministries are involved, the game is rather different. In the 1980s, offices occupying the site were allocated relocation funds and ordered to move. New headquarters were duly built, but 20 years on, the mandarins have yet to quit their imperial surroundings. They have now been instructed to "act in accordance with the Three Represents," and move out before 2008 to make way for a "Princes' Museum" (Wangfu Bowuguan).

the Qing royal family took an early summer holiday when British and French forces advanced on the capital. The convention (which ratified the ill-enforced Treaty of Tianjin) is reproduced in an exhibition hall. But other than one picture, there's little information concerning the original owner, Heshen (1750–1799), the infamously corrupt Manchu official. Thought to have been the Qianlong emperor's lover, he ruled China for his own gain when Qianlong abdicated in 1796, embezzling funds earmarked for suppressing the White Lotus rebellion. After Qianlong's death, his demise was swift. While he was mourning in the Forbidden City, officials were dispatched to this mansion. Though the extent of his graft was widely known, officials were shocked by the piles of gold and silver ingots uncovered. His remaining friends at court managed to persuade the Qianlong emperor's son to spare him from "death by a thousand cuts," but he was soon hanged. The labyrinthine combination of rockeries and pavilions here offers plenty to see, but you're only seeing half of the mansion (see below) and it's often overrun by tour groups. Short but sweet performances of opera and acrobatics are served up in the three-story "Grand Opera House."

Liuyin Jie 17 (signposted in English at top of Qian Hai Xi Dajie running north off Ping'an Dadao opposite north gate of Bei Hai Park; turn left at sign and follow alley past large parking lot; entrance marked with huge red lanterns); see map p. 108. (*C*) **010/6618-0573.** Admission ¥20 ($2.65/£1.35); ¥60 ($8/£4) including guide and opera performance. 7:30am–4:30pm. Metro: Jishui Tan (218, exit C).

Song Qingling Guju (Former Residence of Soong Ching Ling)   Song Qingling

is as close as you'll get to a modern Chinese Communist saint—wealthy, obsessed with children, and a friend of Mao to boot. She married Sun Yat-sen, 30 years her senior, a diminutive man acknowledged as the "father of modern China" on both sides of the Taiwan Strait (even though he was in Denver during the 1911 Revolution). Qingling showed some sympathy to the Communist cause only after her husband's death in 1925. Her younger sister married Chiang Kai-shek (leader of the Nationalist Party and China's public enemy no. 1 until his death in 1975), while Qingling nearly died during the "white terror" of 1927 when the Nationalist Party was purged of Communist sympathizers. Mao rewarded Qingling for her loyalty by granting her this mansion in 1963, and she lived here until her death in 1981, devoting much time to education.

Eunuchs: The Unkindest Cut

The practice that created eunuchs is said to date back 4,000 years, when it was an alternative to the death penalty, often used in the case of political crimes. By the Ming dynasty, most eunuchs submitted to this operation voluntarily, usually as a way out of poverty. The eunuch's abdomen and upper thighs were bound tightly with coarse rope or bandages; his penis was anesthetized with hot pepper water. He was then seated in a semi-reclining chair, with waist and legs held down by three assistants. At this point, he was asked if he would have any regrets. Consent given, the small curved blade flashed and "fountains of red, white, and yellow liquid spouted from the wound" as both the testes and penis were removed. A goose quill would then quickly be inserted into the urethra to prevent it from closing, and the wound plugged with cloth previously dipped in wax, sesame oil, and pepper. The surplus organs (or "treasure") were plopped in a jar and jealously guarded, as they were necessary to establish a eunuch's credentials for promotions, and to pass into the next life as complete men. After the patient (often unconscious by this point) had endured 3 days without food or drink, the plug was removed. If urine gushed out, the operation was a success, and a lifetime in service waited. If not, there would be a horrible, lingering death. A less violent alternative involved slitting the scrotum and removing the testicles. Both operations were preferable to criminal castration, where the testicles were beaten off with a club.

The grounds are well-kept, making them the most popular spot in Beijing for soon-to-be-weds to be photographed. The exhibition on her life seems to contain nearly every article of clothing she wore and every letter she wrote. It's all a little too perfect.

Hou Hai Bei Yan 46, Xi Cheng Qu (northeast shore of Hou Hai); see map p. 108. ℂ 010/6404-4205. Admission ¥20 ($2.65/£1.35). 9am–5pm (to 4:30pm in winter). Metro: Jishui Tan (218, exit B).

Tian Yi Mu ✸ *Finds*   The first Ming emperor had a dim view of eunuchs, noting "not one or two of these people out of thousands are good . . . These people can only be given sprinkling and sweeping jobs," but upon the accession of the Wanli emperor (reign 1573–1620), the Imperial City housed nearly 20,000 eunuchs (*huanguan,* later *taijian*), from powerful bureaucrats enjoying their own mansions, down to junior eunuchs scraping by through petty graft. The cemetery was built in 1605 for Wanli's favorite eunuch, Tian Yi, who served three emperors and acted as Wanli's mentor and confidant. It has a spirit way, an underground tomb complex, and memorial stelae wreathed in dragons, an unprecedented honor for a eunuch. It's a way from the city center, best combined with a visit to Tanzhe Si or Chuan Di Xia (see chapter 11 for both) and Fahai Si (p. 134), a 10-minute walk to the northeast. Unlike its occupants, the cemetery has survived almost intact, and provides insight into their fraught spirituality. Buddhist and Taoist motifs are carved onto their graves, along with images depicting morality tales.

A small exhibition hall is set to the left of the entrance, but all captions are in Chinese. China's last eunuch, Sun Yaoting (1902–1996) is pictured making a visit to the

Forbidden City in 1993, his first since Puyi was driven out in 1924. He is said to have taken issue with the accuracy of the captions there. On the right a naïve letter describes his years in service. Castrated at the age of 8, he was devastated when the emperor abdicated months later, although he continued to serve Puyi. He earned enough money to adopt a son, but lost his "treasure" during the Cultural Revolution (see the box, "Eunuchs: The Unkindest Cut" below).

Cixi is photographed with a large entourage of eunuchs at the Summer Palace, and the temples pictured were sponsored by eunuchs. Buddhism, with its emphasis on celibacy and renunciation, had more appeal for eunuchs than Confucianism. Wealthier eunuchs would adopt sons, but most relied on Buddhist monks to tend their graves. A second eunuch museum will be opening soon inside a late Qing temple, **Lima Guandi Miao.** Built for one of Cixi's most trusted eunuchs, Liu Chengyin, the keeper of the imperial seals, it stands south of the Summer Palace in an area akin to a eunuch retirement village.

Moshi Kou Dajie 80, Shijing Shan Qu (from bus stop, continue up the rise; take a right after 5 min.; cemetery is on the left); see map p. 114. ✆ 010/8872-4148. Admission ¥8 ($1.05/55p). 9am–5pm. Bus: 959 or 746 from left of Pingguo Yuan metro stop (103, exit D) to Shougang Xiaoqu.

9 Hutong & Siheyuan (Lanes & Courtyard Compounds)

As distinct as Beijing's palaces, temples, and parks may be, it is the *hutong* that ultimately set the city apart. Prior to the 20th century, when cars and the Communist love of grandeur made them impracticable, these narrow and often winding lanes were the city's dominant passageways. Old maps of Beijing show the city to be an immense and intricate maze composed almost entirely of *hutong,* most no wider than 10m (33 ft.) and some as narrow as 50cm (20 in.).

Beijing's other famous feature is the *siheyuan* **(courtyard houses)**—traditional dwellings typically composed of four single-story rectangular buildings arranged around a central courtyard with a door at one corner (ideally facing south). Originally designed to house a single family, they now house up to five or six. Mao brought the countryside to the city during the Cultural Revolution, and most of these squatters never left. Foreign visitors charmed by the quaintness of the old houses often assume migration into modern apartment buildings is forced, and it often is. But many move willingly, eager for central heating, indoor plumbing, and most importantly, security of ownership. Many locals will try to convince you that *hutong* are inherently run-down, but why would you renovate a house that could be torn down next week?

The *hutong* are being leveled so rapidly the term **"fast-disappearing"** is now a permanent part of their description. With the 2008 Olympics, destruction carries the imprimatur of modernization. Never mind that visitors prefer quiet lanes to endless blocks of identical flats. But the main driving force behind the destruction is banal: taxes. Municipal governments are desperately short of revenue (following reforms implemented by the oft-lauded Zhu Rongji), and land is the one thing they can sell. Property developers, who now rely on evictees for one-third of their sales, are happy to oblige. Drunk from these runoff influxes of capital, municipal governments expand further. New departments are created, and new jobs are found for friends and relatives. So the next time around, the hit has to be bigger. The Dong Cheng government in particular has a reputation for ordering forceful evictions and arranging unfavorable resettlement schemes.

Our Favorite Hutong Names

The names of *hutong* are a link to the history and humor of the capital. **San Bu Lao Hutong,** a couple of blocks west of Prince Gong's Mansion, is named for its famous former resident, Admiral Zheng He, whose nickname was San Bao (three treasures, possibly a reference to his eunuch status). As described in *1421: The Year China Discovered America,* this Hui Muslim led a vast armada of ships to Southeast Asia, India, Ceylon, the Persian Gulf (where he was able to visit Mecca), and West Africa over seven voyages between 1405 and 1433. Detachments of his fleet probably reached Australia, but the central contention of the book is dubious. Other names hint at long-forgotten markets. **Yandai Xie Jie (Tobacco Pipe Lane),** east of Yinding Qiao, now harbors the capital's hippest cafes, but it once provided smoking paraphernalia for the capital's numerous opium dens. The meaning of **Xian Yu Kou Jie (Fresh Fish Corner Street)** seems straightforward, but locals swear it's a corruption of *xianyu* (salty fish), a reference to a man who burned down half the street while preparing his favorite meal. **Shoushui Hutong (Gathering Water Lane),** where you'll find the Liu Ren Papercut House (see below), was originally known by the less-saleable name of **Choushui Hutong (Smelly Water Lane),** as it was a ditch which ran along the north side of the old city wall.

The most dynamic of these *hutong* can be found around the alley of Nan Luogu Xiang, a gentrifying neighborhood filled with Chinese hipsters, grungy French and Americans, and old Beijingers. Nan Luogu Xiang is the name of the north–south alley filled with a growing number of cafes, bars, restaurants, and hotels listed throughout our pages. Bar highlights include MAO Livehouse (see p. 190) and Pass-By Bar (see p. 194), one of the first establishments to open on the street in the early 2000's. Hotels in the area include Guxiang 20, Hutonger, Lǔsong Yuan Binguan, and Peking Downtown Backpackers Accommodation (see Chapter 5, Where to Stay).

Intriguing swathes of *hutong* still stand south of **Heping Men** and **Qian Men** (though parts of them are quickly being demolished), as well as northwest of **Xi Si,** surrounding **Bai Ta Si.** Here you may hear strange humming sounds, produced by pigeons wheeling overhead with small whistles attached to their feathers. For now, the destitution of these areas makes them unattractive to property developers, but their long-term survival is improbable. See them now. The *hutong* most likely to survive because of their popularity with tourists are in the **Back Lakes (Shicha Hai)** area and in nearby **Di'an Men.** Pedicab tour companies offer to bike you around this area and take you inside a couple of courtyards, but they all charge absurd rates. It's much cheaper, and far more enjoyable, to explore on your own by foot or bicycle (see chapter 8 for suggested routes). If you must, the **Beijing Hutong Tourist Agency (© 010/ 6615-9097)** offers tours in English for ¥70 ($9.35/£4.65) for the whole trip. It takes about 2.5 hours. You can also book ahead for a ¥240 ($32/£16) trip, which takes the same route and includes a meal at local resident's home. *Tip:* However you travel, *never* enter a *siheyuan* uninvited.

10 Especially for Kids

Competition for the disposable income of Beijing's one-child families is intense—advertising ruthlessly targets children. Alas, few of Beijing's just-for-kids attractions are of a standard that will appeal to Western children, and those few tend to be overcrowded. Some exceptions are noted below.

Beijing Haiyangguan (Beijing Aquarium) ✮ "The world's largest inland aquarium" attracted plenty of opposition from local environmental groups when it opened in 1999, and the logic of keeping countless marine animals so far from the sea is questionable. Efforts to compensate are obvious—an environmental message is laid on thickly in the Chinese captions. Introducing Chinese children to the concept that shrimp can exist somewhere other than in a sea of garlic sauce has to be commended, although descriptions of "horrible" sharks show there's a ways to go in its efforts. **Dolphin shows** at 11am and 3pm pack in the one-child families. **Beijing Zoo (Beijing Dongwuyuan)** lies to the south, and despite improvements to some areas—notably the **Panda House**—the zoo is more likely to traumatize your child than provide entertainment. It is possible to take a boat from the canal south of the aquarium to the Summer Palace (50-min. trip; ¥40/$5.35/£2.65 one-way, ¥70/$9.35/£4.65 round-trip).

Gaoliang Qiao Xie Jie 18B, Haidian Qu (from Beifang Jiao Da cross road and walk west; north gate of the Beijing Zoo); see map p. 108. ☏ 010/6217-6655. Admission ¥110 ($15/£7.35) includes admission to Beijing Zoo; children ¥60 ($8/£4); 2 children (under 1.2 meter/4ft) free with 1 paid adult ticket. 9am–4:30pm (to 9pm during summer holidays). Bus: 16 *(zhi xian)* from Xi Zhi Men metro stop (201) to Beifang Jiao Da.

Beijing Huanle Gu (Happy Valley Amusement Park) ✮ Beijing's answer to Disneyland, this theme park features stomach-turning roller coasters, and themed sections called Shangri-La Land, a Mayan Aztec Village, and Greek Town. Lines for rides can be 3 hours long, so arrive early and avoid the weekends. Opened by overseas Chinese investors and designed with the help of Westerners, the roller coasters are supposedly state-of-the-art.

Xiao Wu Ji Bei Lu, Dong Si Huan (East Fourth Ring Road) ☏ 010/6738-3333. Admission ¥160 ($21/£11) adults, ¥80 ($11/£5.35) kids 1.2–1.4m 4–4½ft, free for kids under 1.2m (4ft). Open daily Apr 1-Nov 14 9am-7:30 pm (last ticket at 5:30 pm), Nov 15-March 31 10am-5pm.

Gudai Qianbi Zhanlanguan (Ancient Coin Exhibition Hall) If your child is at the collecting phase, this may or may not be a wise place to visit, although the vast range of shells, coins, and notes is as likely to bewilder as to fascinate. While the tour guides' chant of "5,000 years of history" rings hollow, "5,000 years of retail" rings true. Confucius and Mao both railed in vain against the mercantile spirit. The exhibition should also impress upon you how simple it is to mint coins; the stalls of the **Ancient Coin Market (Gudai Qianbi Jiaoyi Shichang)** outside are testament to how easy they are to duplicate—*don't* make large purchases. **Desheng Men Jianlou (Desheng Men Arrow Tower),** which houses the exhibition, is akin to an imposing castle, with many dark crannies to explore.

Desheng Men Jianlou, Bei Er Huan Zhong Lu, Xi Cheng Qu (north side of North Second Ring Rd., just east of metro stop); see map p. 108. ☏ 010/6201-8073. Admission ¥10 ($1.35/65p). Tues–Sun 9am–4pm. Metro: Jishui Tan (218, exit A).

Liu Ren Papercut House (Liu Ren Jianzhi Wu) The art of paper cutting might not sound exciting, but self-taught artist Liu Ren, who works out of a charming courtyard house, works up such a good spiel you may be converted. Papercuts *(jianzhi)* were gifts in rural China, to be stuck on windows, doors, or lanterns. There's nothing subtle about the traditional papercuts—a baby with a large member marks the birth of a boy, and a baby surrounded by protective wolves is appropriate for a girl. Liu Ren knows her craft, and is happy to provide instruction (¥200/$27/£13 per hr.; ¥60/$8/£4 if taught by her students). Call ahead to book.

Shou Shui He Hutong 16, Xi Cheng Qu (walk south on Xuanwu Men Wai Dajie, take the 2nd *hutong* on the right, turn left down the 1st lane, then take the 1st right); see map p. 112. ℂ 010/6601-1946. Metro: Xi Dan (115, exit E).

Milu Yuan (Milu Park) 🐾🐾 *(Finds)*   Located on the site of the Southern Marshes (Nan Haizi) where Yuan, Ming, and Qing emperors would hunt deer, rabbit, and pheasant, and practice military exercises, this ecological research center is the most humane place to view animals in Beijing. The main attraction is Pere David's deer *(milu),* a strange deerlike creature that became extinct in China toward the end of the Qing dynasty. The *milu* you see today are the descendants of 18 animals that were collected in 1898 by the far-sighted Lord Bedford from zoos around Europe. In 1985, a group of 20 *milu* was reintroduced to China; they now number about 200, and over 400 animals have returned to the wild. The expansive marshlands attract migratory birds, and also house other endangered animals, a maze, plots of land where members can grow vegetables without pesticides, and the chillingly effective World Extinct Wildlife Cemetery, which illustrates the plight of endangered species.

Nan Haizi Milu Yuan, Daxing Qu; see map p. 200. ℂ 010/8796-2105. www.milupark.org.cn. Free admission. 8am–5:30pm. Bus: 729 from Qian Men metro stop (208) to Jiu Gong. Change for minibus no. 4, which will drop you at the signposted turnoff.

Sony ExploraScience (Suoni Tan Meng) *(Kids)*   This museum has live science shows (in Chinese) and plenty of interactive exhibits. We love the swipe cards, which act as keys that unlock the secrets of each science station (English text provided). This is an excellent place to spend a few hours if it's raining or too hot and humid outside.

Inside Chaoyang Gongyuan (Chaoyang Park), Chaoyang Qu. ℂ 010/6501-8800. Admission ¥30 ($4/£2) adults, ¥20 ($2.65/£1.35) students, and free for kids under 1.2m (4ft). Buy your tickets at the park's south or east gates and you won't have to buy park entry tickets. Mon–Fri 9:30am–6pm; Sat–Sun until 7:30pm.

11 Organized Tours

During a visit to Bei Hai, writer John Blofeld chanced upon an elderly eunuch, and inquired as to how he was making a living. He touchily replied, "I manage well. I am a guide—not one of those so-called guides who live by inventing history for foreigners and by making commissions on things they purchase. I have not fallen that far yet . . ." Little has changed. In a country where children are taught that South Korea and their American allies started the Korean War when they invaded innocent North Korea, many modern historical accounts are inventions. Many visitors assume locals have a unique insight into their own culture. In China, and Beijing in particular, all-pervasive censorship and a general lack of curiosity ensures this is rarely the case. You *do not* need the services of a local guide.

Several companies offer guided group tours of Beijing for English speakers, but these are almost always overpriced, often incomplete, and best thought of as an emergency measure when time is short. The most popular operators are **BTG Travel** (ℂ 010/8563-9959; www.btgtravel.com) and **Panda Tours** (ℂ 010/6522-2991), both with offices scattered through the four- and five-star hotels. City highlight tours by air-conditioned bus typically cost around ¥300 ($40/£20) per person for a half-day and around ¥500 ($67/£33) for a full day with a mediocre lunch. **China International Travel Service (CITS)** (© 010/6515-8566; www.cits.net), offers tours that are more customizable, but at a much higher fee. The options listed below are infinitely preferable.

The **Chinese Culture Club** (© 010/8462-2081; www.chinesecultureclub.org) organizes outings, lectures, and film screenings for expatriates with an interest in Chinese culture. There's usually a weekend half-day or full-day tour. Events are often led by prominent lecturers, and discussions go well beyond the palaver you're subjected to at CITS. They are constantly on the lookout for new attractions, and multi-day tours to sites far afield are now offered. A smaller operation with a similar philosophy is **Cycle China** (© 010/6424-5913; www.cyclechina.com). Many sights around Beijing, such as the Ming tombs, are more appealing on two wheels than on two feet. *Hutong* cycle tours are a specialty.

Surrounded by mountains on three sides, the environs of Beijing provide tremendous scope for 1- or 2-day walks taking in scenery, ancient villages, and, of course, the Great Wall. **Beijing Hikers** (contact Huijie at © 1391/002-5516 or Vicky at © 1381/016-5056; www.beijinghikers.com) organize day hikes for ¥200 ($27/£13) for adults, ¥150 ($20/£10) for children under 12 departing from the Lido Hotel. Though popular with North American expatriates, groups are often too large. A cheaper and more interesting alternative is to join a hike organized by **Sanfo Outdoors** (© 010/6201-5550; www.sanfo.com.cn). Originally a small club at Peking University, they now have at least four hikes every weekend advertised (in Chinese) on their website. Visit one of their shops (p. 182) to obtain information on the weekend's activities, but take the grading system seriously—difficult hikes are really tough, while outings with all luxuries provided are humorously referred to as "corrupt" *(fubai)*.

12 Staying Active

Foreign-run five-star hotels offer the cleanest and best-equipped fitness centers and swimming pools for those desperate to work out. Most locals can't afford this, and head for the parks early in the morning to practice *taijiquan,* practice ballroom dancing, or walk the bird (walking the dog is prohibited during daylight hours). At night, Beijing's undersize canines emerge, along with seniors dancing (waddling, really) and beating drums to the rhythm of rice-planting songs *(yang ge)*. However, if you know where to look, you can find other leisure experiences with a local flavor.

ACTIVITIES A TO Z

BOWLING (BAOLINGQIU) With bottles of Johnnie Walker Red Label and French perfume readily traced, and visits to "karaoke" clubs easily photographed, the favorite way to curry favor with a Chinese official is . . . bowling. During the 1990s, more than 15,000 alleys were built, many in Beijing. The biggest and most fun place to bowl is 24-hour **Gongti Yibai** at Gongti Xi Lu 6 (just south of the west gate of the Worker's Stadium), with 100 lanes, thumping music, and flashing video games to bring in the kids (© 010/6552-2688 ¥30/$4/£2 per game).

GOLF (GAO'ERFUQIU) If playing golf in a region desperately short of land and water doesn't bother you, then try negotiating the water hazards of **Beijing International Golf Club** (Beijing Guoji Gao'erfu Julebu; © 010/6076-2288), northwest of town near the Ming Tombs. Eighteen holes including caddie fees cost ¥800 ($107/£53) during the week, rising to ¥1,400 ($187/£93) on weekends.

Winding Down

While Beijing is fascinating, it is *not* relaxing. A slew of hotel spas have opened recently, including the **Ritz-Carlton, Financial Street** spa (✆ 010/6601-6666). The signature Treasure Island treatment (¥980/$131/£65) is 90 minutes of bliss. The **Chi Spa** at the Shangri-La Beijing (✆ 010/6841-2211) offers Tibetan-style treatments in a dimmed, meditative environment. Another choice for unwinding is the **St. Regis Spa** (✆ 010/6460-6688, ext. 2745). One of the best values in town and a favorite with expats is **Bodhi** (✆ 010/6417-9595; www.bodhi.com.cn) at Gongti Bei Lu 17 (opposite the north gate of the Workers' Stadium). A full-body massage before 5pm costs as little as ¥78 ($10/£5.20) per hour from Monday to Thursday and includes complimentary food and beverages. Open 11am till midnight. Traditionally, massage was a profession reserved for the blind. Experience mangren anmo (blind massage) at the friendly **Lesheng Mangren Baojian Anmo Zhongxin,** Dengshikou Xi Jie 32 (✆ 010/6525-7532, ext. 3201), on the second floor of Donghua Fandian, a long block west of the Crowne Plaza in Wangfujing. A 1-hour massage costs ¥88 ($12/£5.85). It's open 11am to midnight.

ICE-SKATING (LIUBING)   Beijing has superb outdoor ice-skating in the winter at **Bei Hai Gongyuan, Qian Hai,** and the **Summer Palace.** Skate rental outfits charge about ¥20 ($2.65/£1.35), but you might not find boots that fit. Even more popular in winter are "ice cars" *(bing che),* box sleds propelled by ski poles. Warnings about the thickness of ice sheets apply—global warming makes for a shorter skating season each year. Beijing's largest skate rink is **Le Cool,** Guomao Liubing Chang (✆ 010/6505-5776), in the underground shopping center that connects Traders Hotel to China World Hotel. Open Monday through Friday from 10am to 9pm, Saturday from 10am to 10pm, and Sunday from 10am to 7:30pm. The rink charges ¥30 ($4/£2) for 90 minutes from 10am to 9pm, ¥40 ($5.35/£2.65) from 6 to 10pm, and ¥50 ($6.65/£3.35) on Saturday and Sunday.

KITE-FLYING (FANG FENGZHENG)   Flying kites in China began at least 2,000 years before they were seen in Europe. The humble kite has been used in the sport of kitefighting, and even as a device to frighten enemy troops. But most locals fly kites peacefully, particularly at **Tian'an Men Square** (where you can rent kites) or in parks such as **Ri Tan Gongyuan.** You can purchase kites at several markets; good selections are available at Guanyuan Shichang and on the fourth floor of Yaxiu Fuzhuang Shichang (see section 2, "Markets & Bazaars," in chapter 9).

TABLE TENNIS (PING PANG QIU)   Every community center in Beijing has a ping pong table with willing opponents. It's an excellent way to meet locals, but humiliating when your conqueror is a generation or two older than you. Beijing now has a table tennis bar, **W Restaurant and Bar** (✆ 010/6595-8039) at Nan San Li Tun Lu 120. It was opened by Swedish table-tennis ace Jan-Ove Waldner, whose cardboard effigy stands outside. There's also a Ping Pong Club (mostly Chinese-speaking, but who needs to talk during ping pong?) at Peking University (✆ 010/6261-1188).

TAIJIQUAN   Tai Chi practitioners can visit any park at daybreak, and enjoy the thrill of practicing with hundreds of others. The **Chinese Culture Club** (see above) has a regular course in English.

YOGA (YUJIA)   If you need to stretch out, the Yoga Yard, Gongti Lu 17 (6/F, above Bodhi) (✆ **010/6413-0774;** www.yogayard.com) offers Hatha Yoga classes for all levels.

SPECTATOR SPORTS

Gongren Tiyuchang (Workers' Stadium) is the home of the capital's football (soccer) team, formerly known as Beijing Guo An, now called **Beijing Xiandai** (named for the Hyundai car company). A fanatical green-and-white army of fans follows the team, which perennially wallows in mid-table mediocrity. Referees are usually corrupt, and fans shower them with invective you won't find in any language textbook. Tickets can be purchased at the Workers' Stadium north gate, **Lisheng Tiyu Shangsha,** Wangfu-jing Dajie 201 (✆ **010/6525-0581;** Sun–Thurs 9am–9pm; Fri–Sat 9am–10pm). The season runs from April through November.

8

Beijing Strolls

Taking a stroll in Beijing can be hard work. The main boulevard, Chang'an Dajie, is a soulless and windswept thoroughfare, and the rest of town seems to be a huge construction site choking on dust and car fumes. These strolls will show you a gentler Beijing, where older Beijingers push cane shopping carts through even more ancient tree-lined *hutong*, where young lovers clasp hands nervously as they gaze across the Back Lakes, and where pot-bellied cab drivers quaff beer while enjoying boisterous games of poker or chess in the middle of the sidewalk.

You'll need to keep your wits about you. No one in Beijing seems capable of walking in a straight line. Pedestrian crossings are decorative, and newly installed crossings with traffic lights are often ignored by motorists. The car, particularly the four-wheel-drive, dominates both the road and the sidewalk. Cars are the main source of the air pollution that

blankets the capital. Beijing already boasts the highest rate of car ownership in China, and more than a thousand new cars hit the road every day; a suicidal path, akin to turning New York into Los Angeles.

Renting or purchasing a bike moves you one rung up the traffic food chain and is a less tiring way to get around. Youth hostels rent out bikes for around ¥30 ($4/£2) per day, while bike parking stations next to metro stops are cheaper yet at ¥10 ($1.35/65p) per day, but you'll need a native speaker to assist you. You can purchase a second-hand bike from a street-side repair stall for less than ¥100 ($13/£6.65); new bikes start from ¥140 ($19/£9.35). Bike traffic is orderly, and unlike Guangzhou and Shanghai, the capital has yet to block off large numbers of streets to cyclists. Whether you walk or ride a bike, avoid sudden changes of direction, and go with the substantial flow around you.

WALKING TOUR 1	LIULICHANG & DA ZHALAN

Start:	Zhengyi Ci Xilou, just south of the metro on Qian Men Xi Heyan Jie (metro: Heping Men, 207).
Finish:	Qian Men, south end of Tian'an Men Guangchang (metro: Qian Men, 208).
Time:	3 hours.
Best times:	Any weekday starting at about 9am or 2pm.
Worst times:	Weekends are crowded. Most shops close about 8:30pm.

This pleasant stroll takes in many of Beijing's most famous shops. Even if you're not interested in buying anything, it makes an agreeable break from the fumes of the capital's constantly gridlocked streets. **Liulichang,** named for a factory that once turned out the glazed roof tiles that clearly delineated the rank of Beijing's buildings, was renovated in the 1980s to capture the look and atmosphere of the late Qing dynasty.

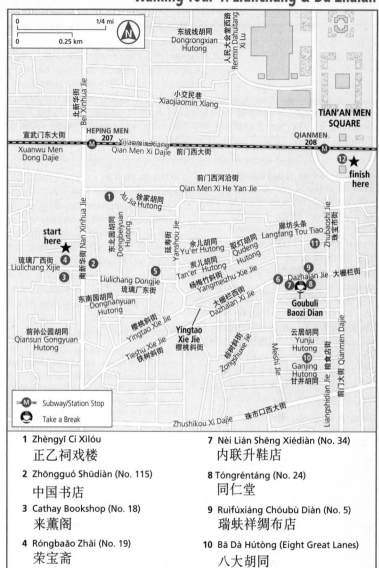

1 **Zhèngyǐ Cí Xìlóu**
正乙祠戏楼

2 **Zhōngguó Shūdiàn (No. 115)**
中国书店

3 **Cathay Bookshop (No. 18)**
来薰阁

4 **Róngbaǒo Zhāi (No. 19)**
荣宝斋

5 **Curio Shops**

6 **Dà Zhàlán**
大栅栏

7 **Nèi Lián Shēng Xiédiàn (No. 34)**
内联升鞋店

8 **Tóngréntáng (No. 24)**
同仁堂

9 **Ruìfúxiáng Chóubù Diàn (No. 5)**
瑞蚨祥绸布店

10 **Bā Dà Hútòng (Eight Great Lanes)**
八大胡同

11 **Lángfáng Èr Tiáo**
廊房二条

12 **Qián Mén (Front Gate)**
前门

Scholars and art connoisseurs once frequented Liulichang, and it is still home to the most famous art-supplies store in China, **Rongbao Zhai.** There is a cluster (at times it feels like a gauntlet) of shops selling art books, scrolls, rubbings, handmade paper, paintbrushes, ink sticks, "jade," and antiques (which are nearly all fakes). Liulichang runs about 6 blocks east–west. Southeast of it is **Da Zhalan,** an ancient, but more plebeian, shopping street that has been converted into a cobblestoned pedestrian-only mall. There are many ancient shops on Da Zhalan, including tailors, shoe stores, and apothecaries selling traditional medicines. North of Da Zhalan, the market streets of **Langfang Er Tiao** and **Langfang Tou Tiao** wind their ways towards **Qian Men (Front Gate)** overlooking **Tian'an Men Square.**

Walk south from the Heping Men metro station down Nan Xinhua Jie, and take the first left onto Qian Men Xi Heyan Jie, where you'll find:

❶ Zhengyi Ci Xilou

This soon-to-be demolished theater (hopefully it's still there when you arrive) will be replaced by a new theater next door, marked with an opera mask. The original theater dated back more than 340 years, and began as a Buddhist temple during the Ming dynasty. The new theater will hold occasional evening performances (call ✆ 010/8315-1649 to check). During the day, opera fans gather to practice their art, and for a fee of ¥5 (65¢/35p), you will be allowed to view the magnificently restored interior.

Backtrack to the main road and go south for a few minutes. On the left, extending to the corner of Liulichang Dong Jie, you will see:

❷ Zhongguo Shudian (No. 115)

Although it's sprawling and state-run, the largest branch of China Books offers a wide range of new and used books on Chinese art, architecture, and literature without the markups that plague arty bookstores.

Cross the main road to Liulichang Xi Jie. On the left-hand side of the road is:

❸ Cathay Bookshop (No. 18)

One of several branches of China Books, this bookshop (south side of street; ✆ 010/6301-7678) has an interesting paper-cut exhibit upstairs and a great range of art materials—paper, ink stones, chops, brushes, and frames—at reasonable prices.

Across the street is:

❹ Rongbao Zhai (No. 19)

The most renowned art shop in China (north side of street) greets you with what may be the world's largest ink stone. Rongbao Zhai sells woodblock prints, copies of famous calligraphy, historic paintings (reproductions), and art supplies. The handful of workers who are more interested in doing their jobs than in reading the paper are goldmines of information on Beijing's art scene.

Further west, the street has more shops and traditional-style facades for another 100 meters, until you get to the wall explaining the history of glazed tile. When you are finished, backtrack to Nan Xinhua Jie and cross over to Liulichang Dong Jie. Continue east to browse:

❺ Curio Shops

Liulichang Dong Jie eventually peters out into a series of touristy shops that sell Buddhist statues, ceramics, and reproductions of Tang Dynasty horses and emperors. No. 71 sells good chrysanthemum and green tea. Most of the street contains shops that sell the same knickknacks, but No. 58 carries some quality antiques and reproductions like grandfather clocks and jewelry. Just before No. 65, turn right down an alley marked with a gate bafflingly labeled "Pradiprion Sculpture," and follow the signs that say "Antique Carpets" to 54 Dong Bei Yun Hutong. A couple sells Mongolian and Tibetan carpets in their small courtyard living room. No. 28 Liulichang Dong Lu sells elegant grey-green celadon teapots and vases.

Liulichang Dong Jie ends at Yanshou Jie. Checking with the map carefully, head south before turning onto the second street on your left (Yingtao Xie Jie), which leads to:

6 Da Zhalan (Dashilanr in Beijing Dialect)

Known as Langfang Si Tiao during the Ming dynasty, its name was changed to Da Zhalan after a large stockade was built, presumably to give peace of mind to the wealthy retailers who set up shop here. Now the proletarian answer to Wangfujing, it's a bustling pedestrian-only street with some of Beijing's oldest retailers.

Cross Meishi Jie, and then in the first block on the right side, you'll find:

7 Nei Lian Sheng Xiedian (No. 34)

Established in 1853, this famous shoe store (*C* **010/6301-4863**) still crafts cloth "happy shoes" *(qianceng buxie)* and delicately embroidered women's shoes by hand. Using a little bit of charm, you may get a peek at the workshop out back.

Continue east, and on the right is a well-known restaurant selling traditional steamed buns as well as other Chinese dishes:

TAKE A BREAK
Locals certainly love the steamed buns sold at **Goubuli Baozi Dian** (29 Da Shilan; *C* **010/6315-2389**), a recently renovated and attractive restaurant by the steamer basket. We prefer the ¥22 (3¢/1p) buns stuffed with wild vegetables and pork (ask for the *yeshu bao*) to the original pork flavored buns. On the west side of Meishi Jie, there are a number of cafes if you prefer coffee and Western food.

8 Tongren Tang (No. 24)

Beijing's most celebrated Chinese-medicine pharmacy was established in 1669. In the western wing, you can make an appointment to see a Chinese-medicine doctor while in the main hall people of all ages—from youthful twenty-somethings

to senior citizens pushing ancient-looking wooden carts—browse the medicine counters. On the second floor, a precious ginseng root that was harvested 80 years ago in Manchuria sells for a staggering ¥680,000 ($90,667/£45,333).

You're nearly at the east end of Da Zhalan. Don't miss its most famous store, on the left (north) side:

9 Ruifuxiang Choubu Dian (No. 5)

Established in 1893 on the north side of Da Zhalan is the steel baroque facade of a fabric store that once supplied silk to the Qing Dynasty royalty. The company brochure claims that one of the first Chinese flags raised by Chairman Mao was also made from Ruifuxiang fabric.

When you reach the end of the street you should be at the newly renovated Qianmen Dajie. (If renovations are not complete, you may have to turn at an earlier alleyway.) Turn right and explore the quiet lanes of the area once known as:

10 Ba Da Hutong (Eight Great Lanes)

A 1906 survey found that the capital was home to 308 brothels (more than the number of hotels or restaurants), most of them in this district. While there are assuredly now many multiples of that number in Beijing, the government is embarrassed by this area, and forbids local tour agents from visiting or even mentioning Ba Da Hutong. Lanes were once graded into three levels, from "lower area" *(xia chu)* streets such as Wangpi Hutong, where prostitutes satisfied the needs of the masses, up to lanes such as Baishun Hutong, where "flower girls" versed in classical poetry and music awaited. Money was no guarantee of success; there were various manuals on the etiquette of wooing courtesans. The Tongzhi emperor (reign 1862–1874) was notorious for creeping out at night to sample the delights of "clouds and rain." He died of syphilis. These days, hair salons in nearby alleys are unlikely to house courtesans skilled in the arts of conversation and playing the lute, but the basic requirements of the masses are provided for.

North of the east end of Da Zhalan the *hutong* **becomes Zhubaoshi Jie, a jumble of stands, shops, and carts peddling cheap clothing and bric-a-brac. Take the first left into:**

⓫ Langfang Er Tiao

During the Qing dynasty, this *hutong* was renowned for its jade and antiques vendors, but by the time you get here, it may all be bulldozed. Two- and three-story houses with beautifully carved wooden balconies hint at past wealth. To the south is Langfang San Tiao, the heart of the former banking district.

Head right (north) along Meishi Jie up to Langfang Tou Tiao, known as Lantern Street (Deng Jie) during the Qing dynasty. Turn right (east), then left (north) when the street ends. Ahead looms:

⓬ Qian Men (Front Gate)

North of Zhubaoshi Jie is the south end of Tian'an Men Square. To the northeast you'll see the old Front Gate (Qian Men or more correctly Zhengyang Men), a towering remnant of the city wall through which the emperors passed on their annual procession from the Forbidden City to the Temple of Heaven. Find the underground crossover and ascend the tower for excellent views of Tian'an Men Square to the north and Da Zhalan to the southwest. There's also a photographic exhibition of the streets and walls of old Beijing.

WALKING TOUR 2	BACK LAKES RAMBLE

Start:	Huitong Ci (metro: Jishui Tan, 218, exit B).
Finish:	Mei Lanfang Guju, west side of Qian Hai (metro: Jishui Tan, 218, exit C).
Time:	4 hours.
Best times:	Any time between 9am and noon.
Worst times:	Mondays, when some sites are closed. Weekends can also be crowded.

There is, quite simply, no finer place to walk in Beijing. The Back Lakes area (Shicha Hai) is composed of three idyllic lakes—Qian Hai (Front Lake), Hou Hai (Back Lake), and Xi Hai (West Lake)—and the tree-shaded neighborhoods that surround them. Combined with other man-made pools to the south, these lakes were once part of a system used to transport grain by barge from the Grand Canal to the Forbidden City. Prior to 1911, this was an exclusive area, and only people with connections to the imperial family were permitted to maintain houses here (a situation that seems destined to return). A profusion of bars and cafes has sprung up around the lakes in recent years (see chapter 10, "Beijing After Dark"), providing ample opportunities to take breaks from your walk.

Beyond the lakes, stretching out to the east and west is the city's best-maintained network of *hutong*. Many families have lived in these lanes for generations, their insular communities a last link to Old Beijing. The energetic (or those with bikes) may wish to combine this stroll with stroll no. 4, "Lidai Diwang Miao and Huguo Si."

Begin at Mei Lanfang Guju, corner of Deshengmen Nei Dajie.:

❶ Mei Lanfang Guju

Look for the red lanterns outside this superbly preserved courtyard residence that belonged to Peking Opera star Mei

Lanfang, who rose to the height of his fame in 1935. The pictures of the opera singer displayed inside the home demonstrate the wide-ranging number of expressions used in the art form.

Walking Tour 2: Back Lakes Ramble

1 Mei Lanfang Guju
梅兰芳故居

2 Former Campus of Fǔrén Dàxué
(Furen University)
辅仁大学旧址

3 Prince Gōng's Mansion
(Gōng Wáng Fǔ)
恭王府

4 Wild Duck Island
野生鸭岛

5 Former Residence of Soong Ching-ling
(Sòng Qìnglíng Gùjū)
宋庆龄故居

6 Dàzàng Lónghuá Sì
大藏隆化寺

7 Guǎnghuà Sì
广化寺

8 Yíndìng Qiáo (Silver Ingot Bridge)
银锭桥

9 Yāndài Xiéjiē (Tobacco Alley)
烟袋斜街道

10 Drum Tower (Gǔ Lóu)
鼓楼

Turn left out of Mei Lanfang Guju and cross Deshengmen Nei Dajie. On the left, you'll walk past:

❷ Former Campus of Furen Daxue (Furen University)

The original campus of Furen University (1 Dingfu Jie), a Catholic institution set up by Chinese priests, was built in 1925. The university was shuttered after the Communists came to power and was moved to Taiwan. Note the ornate facade featuring an arched doorway and the traditional sloping Chinese roof.

At the T-intersection, turn left on Liuyin Jie, and walk north. On your right is:

❸ Prince Gong's Mansion (Gong Wang Fu)

This is the most lavish courtyard residence (Liuyin Jie 14; ✆ **010/6616-8149;** admission ¥20/$2.65/£1.35; open daily 8:30am–4:30pm), in the Back Lakes. The 1777 mansion was occupied by Heshen, a corrupt official who was rumored to be the Emperor Qianlong's lover. Later, it became the home of Prince Gong, who negotiated on behalf of China at the end of the Second Opium War. See p. 144 for a more detailed description of Prince Gong's Mansion.

Turn right when leaving the mansion, and make a left at the T onto Yangfang Hutong. Take a right at the park and walk through it to:

TAKE A BREAK
At **Family Fu's Teahouse** (✆ **010/6616-0725**), you can relax lakeside on Ming Dynasty furniture while sipping longjing, a green tea from Hangzhou, one of China's famed tea-producing areas. The English-speaking owner is particularly friendly.

Right outside the teahouse, stop and have a gawk at:

❹ Wild Duck Island

Beijing is full of loopy attractions, including this man-made island built of steel in Hou Hai Lake for the ducks in the area.

March is a particularly busy time on the island as it's mating season.

Make a left out of the teahouse, and you'll pass Kong Yi Ji, one of Beijing's most famous restaurants on the left. Turn right at the footbridge and continue around the lake. On the left is:

❺ Former Residence of Soong Ching-ling (Song Qingling Guju)

This former imperial palace (✆ **010/ 6404-4205;** admission ¥20/$2.65/£1.35; open daily 9am–5pm, 9am–4:30pm in winter), once famously housed the wife of Sun Yat-sen, modern China's founder. This feminist hero later became a friend of Mao's and a Communist sympathizer. China's last emperor, Henry Puyi, is said to have been born on this site. On weekends, there's a risk of being trampled by soon-to-be-wed brides in their finery.

Turn left from the residence and continue along the lake. After passing the outdoor exercise equipment, look for the gate of:

❻ Dazang Longhua Si

This temple dates back to 1719. Though it's now the grounds of a kindergarten, the facade—with intricate animal-shaped stone gargoyles—has been nicely preserved.

Continue along the lake and turn left at the next alley, then take a quick right on Ya'er Hutong to:

❼ Guanghua Si

Though this temple is not officially open to the public, monks have snuck us in more than once. China's last known eunuch was a caretaker of this temple for two decades and died here in 1996.

Retrace your steps back the lake, then turn left and continue to:

❽ Yinding Qiao (Silver Ingot Bridge)

This bridge separates Hou Hai from Qianhai (Front Lake). It's usually a mess of tourists, aggressive rickshaws, and cars.

Walk away from the bridge and turn right at the sign that reads MASTER OF FOLK ARTS AND CRAFTS FINE WORK SALE.

⑨ Yandai Xiejie (Tobacco Alley)

This touristy pedestrian street houses a few gems. No. 63 on the left, a folk art store, features stylish Chinese pillow covers, framed paper cuts, and cloth coasters. No. 20 on the right sells cute totes and lipstick cases made with Chinese patterns. No. 12 is the Tibetan Jewelry & Tea Bar where you can stop for a drink in the airy back room and browse their collection of Tibetan bracelets, rings, and clothing.

The end of Yandai Xiejie brings you to Dianmen Wai Dajie. Turning left, you will see a number of kitchen supply shops on your left, and in front of you, the looming:

⑩ Drum Tower (Gu Lou)

Drumming performances are held daily every half hour (from 9–11:30am and 1:30–5pm), underneath the bright yellow tile roof of the looming Drum Tower. Highly recommended.

WINDING DOWN
Retrace your steps back to the Silver Ingot Bridge. Don't cross it, but head left down the small street. Set back from the road is **Nuage**, which delivers pricey but heavenly Vietnamese cuisine amid delightful colonial ambience (p. 88). If the weather is fine, aim for a seat on the rooftop.

WALKING TOUR 3 · WANGFUJING

Start: Wangfujing Paleolithic Museum (metro: Wangfujing, 118, exit A).
Finish: Dong Si Mosque (metro: Dong Dan, 119, exit A).
Time: 3 to 4 hours.
Best times: Weekday mornings or late afternoons.
Worst times: Weekends when window shoppers run rampant. Lunchtime can also be crowded.

Wangfujing (Well of the Prince's Palace) is the commercial heart of Beijing, the modern face that China's leaders desperately want the world to see. However, as you'll find on this tour, simply duck down alleyways in any direction and the facade melts away. Situated east of the Forbidden City, Wangfujing was the favorite residential neighborhood of royalty during the Ming and Qing dynasties. At the end of the Qing, when the princes fell on hard times, there was plenty of family silver to be sold. Pawnshops sprang up, and the street got its start as a commercial area. It also began catering to foreign tastes, not only for Chinese antiques but for imported luxuries. Unsurprisingly, it was one of the first targets of the Boxer Rebellion in 1900.

You wonder what the xenophobic Boxers would make of it now. There are only a handful of traditional Chinese stores left—most of them have been razed to make way for huge mega-malls. The cathedral leveled by the Boxers was soon rebuilt and was fully refurbished in 1999; its forecourt is a magnet for local skaters, talking a talk that owes nothing to the Confucian Classics. But continuing on, the Boxers might find solace in the small remnants of *hutong* and the distinctly Chinese (and more affordable) fashions and street food on offer in the stalls of **Longfu Si Jie** and **Dong Si.**

Taking exit A from the metro, you'll find:

① Wangfujing Paleolithic Museum

The owners of Oriental Plaza were unimpressed when they struck 24,000-year-old bone in the basement of the largest mall in Asia. However, the powers-that-be couldn't resist the urge to build yet another monument to the longevity of Chinese civilization, and forced the Hong Kong developers to build this museum to house their ancestors (☏ **010/8518-6306;** admission ¥10/$1.35/65p; open weekdays 10am–4:30pm, weekends 10am–6pm).

Descend the escalator to find yourself in the basement of:

❷ Oriental Plaza (Dongfang Xin Tiandi)

Critics wrongly predicted that this high-end mall would fail when it opened. Although the critics were right that former residents—evicted so that developers could build Oriental Plaza—can't afford to shop here, plenty of nouveau riche Chinese can. We tend to skip the familiar American and European brand-name stores, and hit the more unusual Chinese shops. The mall also includes a good basement-level cinema and food court. Shop AA10 **[2a] Shanghaixu** has a large selection of *qipaos*, traditional tight-fitting, high-collared Chinese dresses. If they don't have anything you like, you can get one made to order. Next door, **[2b] Emperor** has a nice assortment of embroidered napkins and housewares. A few shops down at AA20, **[2c] Art of Shirts** boasts a nice collection of button-down and casual shirts for men and women. **[2d] The Herborist** at EE05 carries a line of traditional Chinese medicine toiletries.

Emerging from the west side of the mall, stick to the right (east) side and head north up Wangfujing Dajie, passing the huge but chaotic Wangfujing Bookstore. Cross the road to:

❸ Gongmei Dasha (No. 200)

You're guaranteed to get the real thing at this large jade store, rather than the colored glass you might find elsewhere. Bargain down to a third of the marked price (☏ **010/6528-8866;** open daily 9am–9:30pm).

Continue along the right-hand side of Wangfujing Dajie to:

❹ Shengxifu (No. 196)

Established in 1912, this famed hat shop is the place to get your proletarian Mao cap or a furry hat with earflaps decorated with Communist red stars. Return to Wangfujing Dajie, and continue north along the left (west) side to the next attraction.

Return to the main street, and continue north. On the right (east) side is:

❺ Wuyutai Tea Shop (No. 186)

The second floor of this quality tea shop has an interesting exhibition of tea culture, including a collection of teapots, and a lively teahouse.

Return to the main street and head north for a few steps. On the left (west) side is a place to:

TAKE A BREAK
Our favorite stalls in town for street food are at **Wangfujing Xiaochi Jie (Small Eats Street).** Don't be afraid to try to lamb skewers or the squid on the stick—though they may look suspect, we assure you, they are clean and scrumptious!

Return to the main street and continue north to:

❻ Foreign Language Bookstore (No. 235)

The Waiwen Shudian (☏ **010/6512-6911;** open daily 9am–9pm) houses Beijing's largest selection of English-language materials on the first and third floors. The second floor has a surprisingly wide range of CDs featuring local alternative bands, as well as Beijing opera and soothing instrumental music.

Continue north. It's hard to miss:

❼ Dong Tang (East Church)

Also known as St. Joseph's Cathedral, this gray Gothic structure has endured a torrid history. Built on ground donated by the Shunzhi emperor in 1655, this Jesuit church was toppled by an earthquake in 1720, gutted by a fire in 1807, and completely razed during the Boxer Rebellion of 1900. After a major renovation from 1999 to 2000, the church became notable

1 Wángfǔjǐng Palaeolithic Museum
   王府井古人类文化遗址博物馆
2 Oriental Plaza
   (Dōngfāng Xīn Tiāndì)
   东方新天地
3 Gōngměi Dàshà (No. 200)
   工美大厦
4 Shèngxīfú (No. 196)
   盛锡福
5 Wuyutai Tea Shop (no. 186)
   吴裕泰茶庄
6 Foreign Language
   Bookstore (No. 235)
   外文书店

7 Dōng Táng (East Church)
   东堂
8 Lǎo Shě
   Jiniànguǎn (No. 19)
   老舍纪念馆
9 Fùqiáng Hútòng
   富强胡同
10 Zhōngguó Měishùguǎn
   (National Art Museum of China)
   中国美术馆
11 Lóngfú Sì Jiē
   隆福寺街
12 Dōng Sì Qīngzhēn Sì
   东四清真寺

for its wide, tree-lined forecourt, the favorite spot of Beijing's skaters. Sunday services are held at 6:15, 7, and 8am.

Across the street are two narrow lanes. Take the lane on the left to reach this memorial hall:

⑧ Lao She Jinianguan

Lao She was one of China's most famous writers. When Lao She returned to a newly Communist China in 1950, then-premier Zhou Enlai gave him this courtyard residence with the hopes that he would write propaganda novels for the new government. But he never turned out another famous novel, and he drowned himself during the Cultural Revolution.

Retrace your steps back to the street, and take the right alley into:

⑨ Fuqiang Hutong

This alley is immodestly named "Rich and Powerful Alley." Note the finely carved roof lintels with Buddhist swastikas and the lotus-emblazoned door piers at No. 18. While the rectangular

Loving Life Massage Center

Chinese believe that the blind make superior masseuses because, with the loss of one sense, they are supposed to have a heightened sense of touch. **The Lesheng Mangren Baojian Anmo Zhongxin (Loving Life Massage Center),** 32 Dengshikou Xi Jie (① 010/6525-7531, ext. 3201;) offers one-hour full-body and foot massages for ¥88 ($12/£5.85) each. You can also try cupping, in which hot glass jars are used to suck out bad energy from your back, leaving funny-looking red welts. The massage center is on the second floor of the Donghua Hotel. Hours are daily 11am to midnight.

door pier indicates that the residents weren't officials (whose houses were marked by circular door piers) they must have been well-off to be able to afford skilled stonemasons. Party General Secretary Zhao Ziyang, who was ousted during the Tian'an Men Massacre, lived at no. 3 under house arrest until his death in January 2005.

Following the *hutong* to the end, turn right to get back on Wangfujing. Then turn left, heading north until you reach the intersection with Wusi Dajie. Across the street on the left is:

⑩ Zhongguo Meishuguan (National Art Museum of China)

This museum has a good permanent collection of Chinese oil paintings and hosts international exhibitions curated by the likes of New York's Guggenheim.

Turn left out of the museum, and make a left at the next intersection. On the right side of the street is:

⑪ Longfu Si Jie

In this small alley you'll find bargain clothes, music, and street food that make an interesting contrast to the bustle and commercial flair of Wangfujing.

At the archway at the end of the alley, turn right and head south to Dongsi Nan Dajie. On the right side of the street is:

⑫ Dong Si Qingzhen Si (Dong Si Mosque)

One of Beijing's oldest mosques, Dong Si Qingzhen Si has been around since the 14th century. The second courtyard is especially serene—a nice place to unwind and rest your feet.

WALKING TOUR 4   LIDAI DIWANG MIAO & HUGUO SI

Start:	Lu Xun Bowuguan (metro: Fucheng Men, 203, exit B).
Finish:	Desheng Men Jianlou (metro: Jishui Tan, 218, exit A).
Time:	4 to 5 hours.
Best times:	Any time between 9am and noon.
Worst times:	Mondays, when some of the museums and sites are closed.

With the Shicha Hai area increasingly overrun with bar touts, "To the Hutong" tours, and Beijing's nouveau riche blocking the way with their Audis, this walking tour will let you rub shoulders with real *Beijingren.* You'll ramble along tree-lined quiescent lanes too narrow for automobiles, uncovering recently re-opened and long-forgotten temples; you'll explore the tranquil former residences of two of China's most influential

Walking Tour 4: Lidai Diwang Miao & Huguo Si

1 Lǔ Xùn Bówùguǎn
鲁迅博物馆

2 Bái Tǎ Sì
白塔寺

3 Lìdài Dìwáng Miào
历代帝王庙

4 Guǎngjǐ Sì
广济寺

5 Xīsì Běi Sān Tiáo
西四北三条

6 Shèngzuò Lóngcháng Sì
圣祚隆长寺

7 Rénmín Jùchǎng
人民剧场

8 Hùguó Sì Xiǎochī
护国寺小吃

9 Tiānmíng Pénjǐng Qíshíguǎn
天明盆景奇石馆

10 Rùndélì Zōnghé Shìchǎng
润得立综合市场

11 Xú Bēihóng Jìniànguǎn
徐悲鸿纪念馆

165

artists and a lively local wet market; you'll meet bonsai and Peking opera aficionados and drink tea in a former concubine's residence. *Tip:* **Take this tour soon.** Much of the area is threatening to disappear by way of the wrecking ball . . .

Taking exit B from the metro, turn left (east) along Fucheng Men Nei Dajie, taking the first left (north) into Fucheng Men Nei Bei Jie. Ahead is:

❶ Lu Xun Bowuguan

An online poll saw Lu Xun (1881–1936), an acerbic essayist, outpoll pop divas and basketball stars as the most popular figure in China. Young visitors display something approaching reverence when they photograph the desk where the young Lu carved the character for early *(zao)* to remind him not to be late for school. Seek out a gruesome photo of a Japanese soldier beheading a Chinese national during the Russo-Japanese war of 1905. His Chinese compatriots look on with blank countenances. Lu, then a medical student in Japan, saw this as symptomatic of a national sickness, and credited the picture with changing the direction of his life towards literature. His charming residence (one of three in Beijing), is set to the west side (Tues–Sun 9am–3:30pm; admission ¥5 (65¢/35p).

Turning left as you emerge, your next destination is immediately visible. Pick your way southeast through unmarked lanes.

❷ Bai Ta Si

This massive Nepali-designed stupa (p. 132) has been under renovation. On our last visit, only a small sliver of the stupa was covered by scaffolding and workers assured us it would be open to visitors in time for the games. The surrounding temple is still worth a gander, with one hall showing thousands of carved Buddha behind glass encasements. A new exhibit in the western hall shows a chilling vision for "modernizing" the surrounding area. Open daily from 9am till 4:30pm; admission ¥20 ($2.65/£1.35).

Turn left as you exit, and you'll soon reach:

❸ Lidai Diwang Miao

This icon-free temple (p. 135), whose grounds were occupied by a school until recently, is where Ming and Qing emperors would come to pay tribute to their predecessors. It boasts impressive stone carvings, and there are signs of improvements in local curatorial standards—some of the original roof murals have been left untouched; there are touchscreen displays; and there's even admission of past vandalism. Open daily 8:30am till 4:30pm; admission ¥20 ($2.65/£1.35).

Turn left, and after a few minutes you'll find:

❹ Guangji Si

This is the closest thing Beijing has to a real Buddhist temple. If you can arrange a visit on the first or 15th day of the lunar calendar, the impressive grounds are open to the public; otherwise, the monks will usually politely refuse you entry. If you'd like to meet the monks, visit **Lily Vegetarian Restaurant** (p. 104) where they often dine.

Backtrack west in the direction of Lidai Diwang Miao, taking the third right turn into a narrow lane that changes its name frequently as it jinks north to:

❺ Xisi Bei San Tiao

Formerly known as Bozi Hutong, this is where bamboo screens for writing were produced. From this lane northwards, the original Yuan street grid remains intact, with east–west *hutong* spaced exactly 79m (260 ft.) apart. Many of the original entrances and door piers *(men dun'r)* are in excellent condition, and this lane may be spared from development.

At no. 3, to the east of the *hutong*, is a striking monastery gate, embellished with faded murals, which formerly marked the entrance to:

❻ Shengzuo Longchang Si

A Buddhist temple dating from the Ming, this was the site of scripture reproduction, transcribed on the bamboo strips the street was famed for. It is possible to (discreetly) wander among the former halls; the original outlay of the temple is readily discerned. There are no plans for restoring these ancient halls.

Continue east to the busy Xi Si Bei Dajie, turn left, and continue north past electronics shops until you reach a Bank of China. At this point, carefully cross the road and duck into Zhong Mao Jia Wan. The south side of this street was the residence of Mao's ill-fated deputy, Marshal Lin Biao. Appropriately, the residence is now occupied by the army. After 60m (197 ft.) turn left and a few steps in on your right is a place to:

TAKE A BREAK
Jin Long Ge Chaguan occupies the two-story residence of a former imperial concubine. She sold the house in 2004, and lives nearby in a retirement home. Tea, served in traditional style on elaborate wood and bamboo sets, is affordable at ¥50–¥180 ($6.65–$24/£3.35–£12) per pot, and homemade *jiaozi* and *huntun* (ravioli soup) are also on offer.

From the teahouse, turn right and continue up this winding *hutong*. At the main road, turn left to continue north, crossing Di'an Men Xi Dajie into Hucang Hutong. This area was formerly a prince's mansion, Zhuang Qin Wang Fu. Turn left at a busy Huguo Si Jie and look for number 74, which is:

❼ Renmin Juchang

Built in honor of Mei Lanfang (see stroll no. 2, p. 158) during the 1950s, this impressive wooden structure has been deemed too much of a fire hazard to host performances, although at the time of writing renovations were underway. It may eventually reopen as a Peking Opera museum. Next door is **Beijing**

Yangguang Yunzhi Shudian (p. 181), which stocks Peking Opera DVDs, CDs, and instruments.

Immediately opposite is:

❽ Huguo Si Xiaochi

From the late Yuan onwards, Huguo Si was the site of a huge temple fair (second only to Longfu Si, see stroll no. 3, p. 161), held on the seventh and eighth days of Chinese New Year. Beijing's most renowned snack shop claims to be faithful to temple fairs of the past, and at lunchtime, it's as chaotic as one. Tasty dishes include *xingren doufu* (chilled almond pudding), and *shaobing jia rou* (miniburgers inside sesame buns), *wandou huang* (green pea pudding), and *saqima* (candied rice fritter). Open daily 5:30am till 9pm.

Turn left to head north along Huguo Si Xi Jie, right next to the snack shop. You'll pass a neighborhood notice board on the right, and shortly on the left, at number 33, you'll find:

❾ Tianming Penjing Qishiguan

While bonsai is normally associated with Japan, quite a number of elderly *Beijingren* are passionate about its antecedent, *penjing*. The owner of this exhibit is a quietly fanatical collector and creator of stunted trees and bizarrely shaped rocks.

Bear right and make your way back to Mianhua Hutong (which is just Hucang Hutong under a different name) and continue north, passing old men playing chess and selling grasshoppers. Shortly, you'll arrive at a more densely forested section, and you'll notice people emerging from the lanes to your right with bags of fruit and vegetables. Follow them to the source to find:

❿ Rundeli Zonghe Shichang

Still widely known as Si Huan Shichang, this is one of the few large open food markets (known as a wet market) still located within the city. There are vast stalls hawking clothing and fabric, animals (not intended as pets), and colorful spices.

Duck back out to Luo'r Hutong (again, just Hucang Hutong under another name) and continue north until you reach a major intersection, just before a hospital gate. Turn left into bustling Xinjiekou Dong Jie. This soon runs into still livelier Xinjiekou Bei Dajie, crammed with clothing and music shops. Continue north. On the left (west) side you'll soon find:

⓫ Xu Beihong Jinianguan

The work on display in this memorial hall at Xinjiekou Bei Dajie 53 (admission ¥5/65¢/35p; open Tues–Sun 9am–4pm) is instantly familiar—copies of the watercolors of Xu Beihong are on display at most tourist sites. Xu did much to revive a moribund art, combining traditional Chinese brushwork with Western techniques he assimilated while studying and traveling in Europe and Japan.

Head north along this bustling thoroughfare, pass a KFC, and turn right (east) onto Ban Qiao Tou Tiao. At this point, you can join up with the "Walking Tour 2: Back Lakes Ramble," or when you spy the waters of Hou Hai, keep to the right side and you'll reach:

WINDING DOWN
The restaurant **Kong Yiji Jiudian** (p. 91), named for the drunken hero of one of Lu Xun's best-known short stories, serves delicate Huaiyang cuisine in a scholarly setting. Slightly farther south is the tranquil **Teahouse of Family Fu** (p. 196).

9

Shopping

Writer Wang Shuo once observed that there were still devout Communists to be found in China, all of them safely under lock and key in a mental asylum. Consumerism is the official ideology of China, and shopping is the national sport. Spend, spend, and spend some more is the message drummed into China's bewildered citizens at every turn.

Dusty, empty, and useless state-run department stores are thankfully a thing of the past, though the **Friendship Store** still stands as an amusing reminder of the old days. Mega-malls, shopping streets, and the few remaining open-air markets fight for a share of the spoils. Avoid shopping forays on weekends and evenings, when it can feel as if all of Beijing's 15 million residents line up at the cash registers to do their bit for the economic miracle.

1 The Shopping Scene

Western-style shopping malls are flexing their muscles in Beijing, replacing the traditional storefronts, Chinese department stores, and alley markets. Even the new, privately run stores on major shopping streets tend to be versions of the boutiques and specialty outlets familiar to shoppers in the West. But there are still plenty of open-air markets and street-side vendors offering more traditional arts and crafts, collectibles, and clothing, usually at prices far below those in the big plazas and modern stores.

BEIJING'S BEST BUYS

Stores and markets in Beijing sell everything from cashmere and silk to knockoff designer-label clothing and athletic wear, antiques, traditional art, cloisonné, lacquerware, Ming furniture, Mao memorabilia, and enough miscellaneous Chinesey doo-dads to stuff Christmas stockings from now until eternity. Prices are reasonable (certainly lower than in the Asian goods boutiques back home), though increasingly less so. Cheap one-time-use luggage is widely available for hauling your booty if you get carried away.

Before you rush to the ATM, however, it is important to remember that not all that is green and gleams in Beijing is jade. Indeed, the majority of it is colored glass. The same principle holds for pearls, famous-brand clothing, antiques, and just about everything else. If you plan to make big purchases, you should educate yourself about quality and price well beforehand.

BEIJING'S TOP SHOPPING AREAS

The grandest shopping area in Beijing is **Wangfujing Dajie,** east of the Forbidden City. The street was overhauled in 1999, and the south section was turned into a pedestrian-only commercial avenue lined with clothing outlets, souvenir shops, fast-food restaurants, and the city's top two malls—the Sun (Xin) Dong An Plaza and Oriental

---

⌐Warning⌐ "Hello, I'm an Art Student"

Be leery of any English-speaking youngsters who claim to be **art students** and offer to take you to a special exhibit of their work. This is a **scam.** The art, which you will be compelled to buy, almost always consists of assembly-line reproductions of famous (or not so famous) paintings offered at prices several dozen times higher than their actual value. You are almost sure to encounter this nonsense in the **Wangfujing** and **Liulichang** areas.

Plaza (Dongfang Guangchang). **Dong Dan Bei Dajie,** a long block east, is a strip of clothing boutiques and CD shops popular among fashionable Beijing youth. On the western side of town is the mirror image of Dong Dan, bustling **Xi Dan,** and further north, **Xinjiekou Dajie.**

Other major Westernized shopping areas include the section of **Jianguo Men Wai Dajie** between the Friendship Store and the China World Trade Center, and the neighborhood outside the **Northeast Third Ring Road North,** southeast of San Yuan Qiao around the new embassy district.

Beijing's liveliest shopping zone, beloved for its atmosphere and Chinese-style goods, is the centuries-old commercial district southwest of Qian Men. **Liulichang** is an almost too-quaint collection of art, book, tea, and antiques shops. The stores are lined up side by side in a polished-for-tourists Old Beijing–style *hutong,* running east–west 2 blocks south of the Heping Men metro stop. The street is good for window-shopping strolls and small purchases—like the unavoidable **chop** (*tuzhang;* stone or jade stamp), carved with your name. But beware of large purchases: Almost everything here is fake and overpriced. In a similar setting but more raucous, Da Zhalan (pronounced Dashilanr in the Beijing dialect) is the prole alternative. Located in a pedestrian-only *hutong* 2 blocks south of Qian Men, it is jammed on either side with cheap clothing outlets, restaurants, and luggage shops (see "Walking Tour 1: Liulichang & Da Zhalan" in chapter 8).

2 Markets & Bazaars

Although malls and shopping centers are becoming more popular, the majority of Beijing residents still shop in markets. Whether indoors or out, these markets are inexpensive, chaotic and, for the visitor, tremendously interesting. Payment is in cash, bargaining is essential, and pickpockets are plentiful. Perhaps the most common item you'll find in the markets these days is not silk, souvenirs, or crafts, but designer-label clothing, much of it knockoffs with the upscale labels sewn in, although some items are factory seconds or overruns (sometimes smuggled out of legitimate brand-name factories). Before you stock up on too many fake items, however, check the U.S. Customs website, www.customs.ustreas.gov, to see what you are allowed to bring home.

The most popular market is **Yaxiu Fuzhuang Shichang;** the best for jewelry is **Hong Qiao Shichang;** the most interesting is **Panjiayuan Jiuhuo Shichang;** but there are others worth browsing.

SILK ALLEY (XIUSHUI JIE)   Herded indoors in 2005, Beijing's most famous market among foreign visitors is a crowded maze of stalls with a large selection of shoes and clothing (and very little silk). Vendors formerly enjoyed so much trade they could afford to be rude, but the knockoff boot is now firmly on the shopper's foot, as Silk Alley now sees only a fraction of the business of Yaxiu (see below). Most of the original vendors are gone, unwilling (or unable) to pay the new steep rental fees. Good riddance. Under no circumstances should you pay more than ¥150 ($20/£10) for a North Face (or "North Fake," as the expats call it) jacket, ¥50 ($6.65/£3.35) for a business shirt, or ¥100 ($13/£6.65) for a pair of jeans. Stores which sport a red flag are purported to "subscribe to higher ethics." Spot the ethical pirates. Corner of Jianguo Men Wai Dajie and Xiushui Dong Jie, above the Yong'an Li metro stop (121, exit A). It's open daily from 9am to 9pm.

HONG QIAO SHICHANG ✿   Also called the **Pearl Market,** Hong Qiao Shichang is located at Hong Qiao Lu 16 (© **010/6713-3354**), just northeast of Tian Tan Gongyuan (Temple of Heaven Park) and north of Tiyuguan Lu. Hong Qiao began life as a fascinating curio market outside Tian Tan Gongyuan, but like most outdoor markets it was forced indoors and now sits above a malodorous wet market. Popular purchases include reproductions of 1920s Shanghai advertisements for "cow soap." Also popular is Cultural Revolution kitsch: Look out for flamethrower-like cigarette lighters that play "The East is Red" *("Dongfang Hong")* when you light up. Elsewhere in the store, you'll need to bargain hard for brand-name clothing, footwear, luggage, watches, and **pearls** (see below), which attract swarms of bottle-blonde Russian women. The **toy market** *(wanju shichang),* housed in a separate building at the back, is overlooked by visitors, so starting prices are more reasonable; there are candles, incense, and stationery. There's a post office on the fourth floor. From Chongwen Men metro (209, exit A) take bus no. 807 to Hong Qiao, and cross the footbridge. Open daily from 8:30am to 7pm.

PANJIAYUAN JIUHUO SHICHANG ✿✿✿   Eureka! This is the Chinese shopping experience of dreams: row upon crowded row of calligraphy, jewelry, ceramics, teapots, ethnic clothing, Buddha statues, paper lanterns, Cultural Revolution memorabilia, PLA belts, little wooden boxes, Ming- and Qing-style furniture, old pipes, opium scales, and painted human skulls. The market is also known as the Dirt or Ghost Market. There are some real antiques scattered among the junk, but you'd have to be an expert to pick them out. Locals arrive Saturday and Sunday mornings at dawn

---

Tips **Buying Pearls**

Most of the pearls on sale at **Hong Qiao Shichang** are genuine, although of too low quality to be sold in Western jewelry shops. However, some fakes are floating around. To test if the pearls you want to buy are real, try any one of the following:

- Nick the surface with a sharp blade (the color should be uniform within and without)
- Rub the pearl across your teeth (this should make a grating sound)
- Scrape the pearl on a piece of glass (real pearls leave a mark)
- Pass it through a flame (fake pearls turn black, real ones don't)

Oddly, vendors are generally willing to let you carry out these tests, and may even help, albeit with bemused faces. If you'd rather not bother (most don't), assume the worst, shop for fun, and spend modestly.

or shortly after (hence the "ghost" label) to find the best stuff; vendors start to leave around 4pm. Initial prices given to foreigners are always absurdly high—Mao clocks, for instance, should cost less than ¥40 ($5.35/£2.65) rather than the ¥400 ($53/£27) you'll likely be asked to pay. Handily located just south of Panjiayuan on the west side of Huawei Qiao, **Curio City** (**Guwan Cheng;** ✆ 010/6774-7711) boasts four floors of jewelry (including diamonds and jade), old clocks, cloisonné, furniture, and porcelain, as well as curios and the odd genuine antique. International shipping is provided. Curio City is open daily from 9:30am to 6:30pm. Panjiayuan market is located on the south side of Panjiayuan Lu, just inside the southeast corner of the Third Ring Road. It's open Saturday and Sunday from noon until about 4pm.

YAXIU FUZHUANG SHICHANG 🎄   Whatever you may think of their business practices, Beijing's clothing vendors are nimble: Here you'll find refugees from two now-extinct outdoor markets, Yabao Lu and San Li Tun. Opened in 2002, the market occupies the old Kylin Plaza building (Qilin Dasha) and retains at least one feature of the old Kylin—excellent tailors can be found on the third floor. The fourth floor is a fine hunting ground for souvenirs and gifts—there are kites from Weifang in Shandong, calligraphy materials, army surplus gear, tea sets, and farmer's paintings from Xi'an (laughably claiming to be originals by Pan Xiaoling, the most frequently copied artist). You can even treat yourself to a ¥20 ($2.65/£1.35) manicure. The basement and the first two floors house a predictable but comprehensive collection of imitation and pilfered brand-name clothing, shoes, and luggage. The market has been "discovered" by fashion-conscious locals, and starting prices are often ridiculous. *Note:* Be especially aware of pickpockets in this market; we know of friends who have had their cellphones stolen while shopping. The market is just west of San Li Tun Jiuba Jie, at Gongti Bei Lu 58 (✆ **010/6415-1726**), and is open daily from 9:30am to 9pm. Metro: Gongti Bei Lu.

SHOPPING WITH THE LOCALS

These markets are unknown to visitors and most expatriates. Asking prices are more reasonable than the markets listed above, and the quality of goods is often superior. **Tianyi Xiaoshangpin Pifa Shichang** is the ultimate "Made in China" shopping experience. You'll find it 4 blocks west of the Fucheng Men metro stop (203, exit A) at Fucheng Men Wai Dajie 259 (✆ **010/6832-7529**), on the north side of the road. Everything is here, crammed into hundreds of stalls in a spanking-new five-story building tucked behind the old market. The range of toys, sporting equipment, electronic appliances, and luggage is eye-popping. Open daily from 7:30am to 5pm.

Jin Wuxing Baihuo Pifa Cheng (✆ **010/6222-6827**), a single-story wholesale market just south of Da Zhong Si metro (1302), is even more comprehensive and more chaotic. They have every item imaginable. Open 8:30am to 7pm. **Baoguo Si Wenhua Gongyipin Shichang** (✆ **010/6303-0976**), Panjiayuan in miniature, is more relaxing. This delightful market has been a site of commerce since the Qing dynasty, and is set in the leafy grounds of a Liao dynasty (930–1122) temple. It offers mostly bric-a-brac, but vendors aren't pushy, and asking prices are reasonable. Coins, antiquarian books, and Cultural Revolution memorabilia abound. The market is liveliest on Thursday and Saturday mornings. From Changchun Jie metro (205, exit D1), walk south along Changchun Jie and take the third right onto a tree-lined avenue that ends at the east gate of Xuanwu Yiyuan. Turn left and follow your nose southwest through the *hutong* to Baoguo Si. It's open daily from 8am to 4pm.

3 Shopping A to Z

ANTIQUES & CURIOS

The **Panjiayuan Jiuhuo Shichang** market (see above) was once *the* place to look for antiques, and it still is for bric-a-brac and oddities. If you're not in town on the weekend, visit **Baoguo Si Wenhua Gongyipin Shichang** market (see above), which has similar curiosities in a more pleasant setting. Any cracked and dusty treasure you find is almost certainly fake, but you won't have trouble taking it home. Genuine antiques are not allowed out of the country without bearing an official **red wax seal,** and pieces made prior to 1795 cannot be exported at all. "Certified" antiques are available at astronomical prices in the **Friendship Store** (p. 176), at a few hotel gift shops, and in some of the nicer malls. But determined antiques lovers should look elsewhere.

Guang Han Tang ⭑   Set in a delightful courtyard house constructed from the ruins of a derelict factory, all of Guang Han Tang's pieces could be described as partially restored, as they maintain a feeling of antiquity. Furniture made from fir *(shanmu)* and elm *(yumu)* is disparagingly referred to as "firewood" *(chaimu)* by the locals, though the sturdiness of the latter wood is recognized in the expression for a die-hard traditionalist, *yumu naodai,* literally "elm brain." Furniture made from rosewood *(zitan* or *hongmu)* commands a higher price. Prices are serious, but so is the owner, Mr. Liang. No fakes here. Open daily 9am to 6pm. Caochangdi. ℂ 010/8456-7943. www.guanghantang. com. Bus: 418 from Dong Zhi Men metro stop (214/1316, exit B) to Caochangdi. Take the Da Shanzi exit off the airport expwy., follow Jichang Fu Lu northeast, and take the 2nd right onto Nan Gao Lu. After passing under the railway line, take the left fork in the road and follow the signs.

Lu Ban Gudian Jiaju Cheng *(Finds*   Just east of town, Gaobeidian—one of the largest antique furniture markets in China—is one of Beijing's best-kept secrets. Lu Ban was the first shop to open at the location in 1991, but it's remarkable that over a decade later so few locals know of its existence. This outlet is the most reliable of the many furniture stores in Gaobeidian. But if you know what you're looking for, the real bargains can be found in small workshops opened by enterprising peasants from Shandong, Shanxi, and Anhui. At least half of the merchandise is bogus, and any furniture marked with a tag that says TIBETAN should be regarded as counterfeit until proven otherwise. Open daily 8am to 6pm. Gaobeidian 4 Dui (from Gaobeidian bus stop continue south for around 90m/295 ft.; turn left just before the railway tracks). ℂ 010/8575-6516. Bus: 363 from Sihui Dong metro stop (125, exit B, cross road) to Gaobeidian.

ART SUPPLIES

Liulichang (see "Walking Tour 1: Liulichang & Da Zhalan" in chapter 8) has many small shops and stalls selling calligraphy brushes, brush racks, chops, fans, ink stones, paper, and other art supplies. The best bargains are found in the stalls toward the far west end. The most famous outlet is **Rongbao Zhai,** Liulichang Xi Jie 19 (ℂ 010/ 6303-6090; Metro: Heping Men), although its prices are pushed ever higher by tour groups. Even if you can't afford the prices, take a peek at the gallery on the second floor. It's open daily 9am to 5:30pm. Many art-supply shops cluster around the **National Gallery. Baihua Meishu Yongpin,** located diagonally across from the gallery at Wusi Dajie 10–12 (ℂ 010/6525-9701), stocks a wide range of modern art supplies and also has a reliable framing service. It's open daily 9am to 6:30pm. The largest art store in Beijing is **Gongmei Dasha** at Wangfujing Dajie 200 (ℂ 010/ 6528-8866), although its prices are high. Open daily from 9am to 9pm. Metro: Wangfujing (118, exit A).

BIKES

Qian Men Zixingche Shangdian One of Beijing's largest bike stores is handily located a short walk south of Qian Men. It's dominated by new brands, such as Giant and Strong. However, you can still find some old-style Forever *(Yongjiu)* bicycles. Sadly, there's not a Flying Pigeon in sight. Open daily 8:30am to 6:30pm. Qian Men Dajie 97, Xuanwu Qu. ℂ **010/6303-1014.** Metro: Qian Men (208, exit C).

BOARD GAMES

Xing Qiyi Yuan Shangmao Zhongxin Better known in the West by the Japanese name of *go,* the complex game of strategy, *weiqi,* is undergoing a welcome resurgence in its native land, if the number of TV programs dedicated to its exposition are any guide (although it doesn't make for great television). This friendly shop outside the south gate of the National Sports Training Center, where many of China's *weiqi* masters work, sells boards and the 361 black-and-white pieces that fill in the spaces. These start at ¥40 ($5.35/£2.65) for metal pieces in a wicker basket, and rise to ¥3,600 ($480/£240) for agate stones in a jade bowl. "Traditional" Chinese chess, or *xiangqi,* is more commonly seen on the street. Elaborate *xiangqi* sets are also sold. Open weekdays 9am to 5pm; weekends 9am to 4pm. Tian Tan Dong Lu 80. ℂ **010/6711-4691.** Metro: Chongwen Men (209), then bus 807 to Dong Ce Lu; cross bridge and head south, then turn left onto Chang Qing Lu.

BOOKSTORES

Maps of anyplace in China can be found on the first floor of **Wangfujing Shudian,** Wangfujing Dajie 218 (ℂ **010/6513-2842;** open daily 9am–9:30pm). The finest library of English language books and magazines can be found at **The Bookworm** (p. 195).

Foreign Language Bookstore (Waiwen Shudian) A few years ago, China's strict censorship laws restricted the stock in this bookstore to boring Western classics. Nowadays, we're happy to find the latest bestsellers, novels by Haruki Murakami, and good biographies alongside classics by the likes of Jane Austen. Open daily 9am to 9pm. Wangfujing Dajie 235, Dongcheng Qu. ℂ **010/6512-6903.** Metro: Wangfujing (118, exit A).

Sanlian Taofen Tushu Zhongxin Come here for the most interesting selection of Chinese-language books in Beijing, although **Wansheng Shudian,** south of Qinghua University in Haidian, runs a close second. There's a quiet cafe on the second floor, but most patrons prefer the stairwell. Open daily 9am to 9pm. Meishuguan Dong Jie 22, Dongcheng Qu. ℂ **010/6400-1122.** Bus: 803 from north of Wangfujing metro stop (118, exit A) to Meishuguan.

Sanwei Shuwu Public outrage spared Beijing's original "dissident bookstore" from being converted into a patch of lawn in 2002. Downstairs is a small bookstore with a few English-language titles. Upstairs is a tranquil, traditional teahouse (p. 190), ideal for a quiet read during the day. Open daily 10am to 10pm. Fuxing Men Nei Dajie 60, Xicheng Qu (west of the metro stop, opposite Minzu Wenhua Gong, on the corner of Tonglinge Lu). ℂ **010/6601-3204.** Metro: Xidan (115, exit E).

Timezone 8 Art Books Xiandai Shudian Beijing Yishu Shuwu) ⭐ This store has the best selection of art books in town. The decor is converted factory chic, with bookshelves nestled against exposed brick and cement walls. They are located in Factory 798 (see p. 144), so if you're a little rusty on your contemporary Chinese art, pop in here to refresh your memory before hitting the nearby galleries. Open daily 10am to 8pm. Jiuxianqiao Lu 4, Chaoyang Qu. ℂ 010/8459-9332.

CAMERAS & FILM

Color film and processing are readily arranged, but you're probably better off waiting until you return home or pass through Hong Kong. For black-and-white processing (the only choice for depicting Beijing in winter), try **Aitumei Caise Kuoyin Zhongxin,** Xinjiekou Nan Dajie 87 (ℂ 010/6616-0718), open daily 9am to 9pm. Beijing is not the place to buy new cameras and accessories, but those looking for secondhand parts for their ancient SLR camera, or wanting to experiment with ancient Russian swing lens cameras, have the two excellent markets listed in this section.

Beijing Sheying Qicai Cheng *(Finds)*   Beijing's largest camera market has a bewildering array of equipment—one shop only sells lens filters! If you're looking for the old, obscure parts they just don't make any more, you'll find them here. Competition between vendors is fierce. Open daily 9am to 4:30pm. Xi Si Huan Lu 40, Xicheng Qu (a mile south of the metro stop on the west side). ℂ 010/8811-9797. Bus: 748 from south of Wukesong metro stop (108, exit D) to Zhengchang Zhuang.

Malian Dao Sheying Qicai Cheng   Located on the top floor of Malian Dao Tea City is a cluster of secondhand camera shops. **Hongsheng Sheying Fuwu Zhongxin,** on the north side, has the widest range of gear and the best repair service. Open daily 9am to 7pm. Malian Dao 11 (cross road and walk south for 5 min.). ℂ 010/6339-5250. Bus: 719 from Fucheng Men metro stop (203, exit A) to Wanzi.

CARPETS

Qian Men Carpet Factory   Most modern Chinese carpets are testaments to what azo compounds are capable of if they fall into the wrong hands. Fortunately, the carpets in this dusty basement emporium (which was once a bomb shelter) are largely antiques. Rugs from Gansu and Ningxia in northwest China feature swastikas, dragons, phoenixes, and auspicious symbols, and are free of alarming pinks and oranges. Antiques include Tibetan prayer rugs, Xinjiang yurt rugs, and Mongolian saddle rugs, all handmade using natural dyes. The factory also makes antique "reproductions" and Henan silk carpets. Cleaning and repair services are available. The factory is located at the back of the Chongwen Worker's Cultural Palace; follow the ANTIQUE CARPETS signs. Open daily 9:30am to 5:30pm. Xingfu Dajie 59, Chongwen Qu (opposite the east side of Tian Tan Fandian). ℂ 010/6715-1687. Bus: 807 from Chongwen Men metro stop (209, exit A) to Beijing Tiyuguan.

Torana Gallery (Tu Lan NaYouyi Shangdian)   Run by Englishman Chris Buckley, a guidebook writer turned entrepreneur, Torana sources its exquisite Tibetan and Chinese wool rugs from Gangchen Carpets and Michaelian and Kohlberg. Chris has a passion for Tibet, and often hosts photographic exhibitions. No bargains, but if you're looking for a genuine hand-woven rug, and lack the time or expertise to hunt one down, Torana should be your first choice. Open daily 10am to 10pm. Shop 8, in the lobby of the Kempinski Hotel. ℂ 010/6465-3388, ext. 5542. Metro: Liangmahe.

COINS & STAMPS

Coin collectors and philatelists rub shoulders in Beijing. The largest market is **Malian Dao You Bi Ka Shichang** at Malian Dao 15 (open daily 8:30am–5pm), tucked away behind the tea shops, just south of yet another Carrefour supermarket. Housed in a half-empty building that resembles an aircraft hangar, you'll find stamps and envelopes commemorating great moments in Chinese diplomacy (more than you'd expect), coins and notes of all imaginable vintages, phone cards (popular with locals—there's even a Phone Card Museum), and a large range of Cultural Revolution memorabilia. To get here, take bus no. 719 from the Fucheng Men metro stop (203, exit A) to Wanzi, cross the road, and walk south for 5 minutes. Larger post offices also have special sections offering limited-issue stamps. Coin collectors should make the trip to the **Ancient Coin Market (Gudai Qianbi Jiaoyi Shichang; ✆ 010/6201-8073; open 9am–4pm)** at Desheng Men (p. 149).

COMPUTERS

In a recent local soap opera, **Zhongguan Cun** (touted as China's Silicon Valley), to the northwest of Beijing, was depicted as innovative, dynamic, and even sexy. Alas, with an education system that stifles creativity and a legal system incapable of enforcing intellectual property laws, copying software remains China's forte. (And software engineers are seldom sexy.) Don't rely on pirated software, but computer games usually work and computer whizzes have been known to build a computer from scratch here. Take bus no. 808 from Xi Zhi Men.

Bai Nao Hui   Less dodgy and easier to reach than Zhongguan Cun, this four-story amalgam of stores sells computers, digital cameras, and accessories. Software is not sold inside, but a gaggle of gentlemen from Anhui loitering outside greet you with a chorus of "Hello. CD-ROM!" Open daily 9am to 8pm. Chaowai Dajie 10 (10-min. walk east, on the south side of the street). ✆ 010/6599-5947. Metro: Chaoyang Men (212, exit B).

DEPARTMENT STORES

Friendship Store (Youyi Shangdian)   Friendship Stores were once the only places where locals and foreigners alike could purchase imported goodies. You even needed "foreign exchange currency" to obtain the viciously overpriced merchandise. This is the largest store, and it was recently spared demolition when plans for a high-rise complex caused a stir among nearby embassies, but its days are numbered. You can bargain for their overpriced wares, but it's really not worth your while. Starbucks, Baskin-Robbins, Délifrance, and Pizza Hut are all here, and the first-floor bookshop stocks a decent range of English-language magazines. Open daily 9am to 8:30pm. Jianguo Men Wai Dajie 17, Chaoyang Qu. ✆ 010/6500-3311. Metro: Jianguo Men (120/211, exit B).

Pacific Century Place   This department store is packed with familiar brand names like Nine West, Hush Puppies, Esprit, and Columbia. Expat and local mommies swear by the toy selection on the 6th floor. It is located a short block east of Yashow, and is a great place to shop for authentic labels in a sterile, hassle-free environment. Open daily 10am to 10pm. A2 Gongti Bei Lu. ✆ 010/6539-3888. Metro: Gongti Bei Lu.

DRUGSTORES

International SOS   Sure they charge high prices, but they are probably the safest place in town to purchase medicine. They have a good selection of familiar Western names. Open Monday through Friday from 8am to 8pm and Saturday and Sunday from 8:30am to 5:30pm. Sanlitun Xi Wu Jie 5. ✆ 010/6410-5794. Metro: Nong Zhan Guan.

Wangfujing Drugstore   This emporium has a small selection of Western cosmetics and health aids, along with a large selection of traditional Chinese medicines. Open daily 8:30am to 10pm. Wangfujing Dajie 267, Dongcheng Qu. ✆ 010/6524-0199. Metro: Wangfujing (118, exit A).

Watson's   Another pawn in the Li Ka-Hsing empire, Watson's has been quick to expand in the nation's capital. At the time of writing, there were 41 stores occupying prime Beijing real estate. This should be your first choice for Western cosmetics and toiletries, though the range of over-the-counter medicines is limited. Open daily 10:30am to 9:30pm (Holiday Inn Lido branch 9am–9pm; Oriental Plaza branch 9:30am–10pm). Full Link Plaza (see below). ✆ 010/6588-2145. Another branch at Holiday Inn Lido, ✆ 010/6436-7653. Metro: Chaoyang Men (212, exit B); and at Oriental Plaza (see below), ✆ 010/8518-6426.

FASHION

Fashion is a baby industry in Beijing. For the most part, the city is not known for being fashion-forward. However, there are interesting couture outlets emerging at Factory 798 (p. 144), and you can find funky stores with original designs.

Botao Haute Couture (Botao Gaojishi Zhuang Zhan) ✦   Head to Botao if you want to order high-quality, original Chinese designs. The store employs a team of young Chinese designers, several of whom studied abroad in fashion hotspots like Paris, and most clothing is made-to-order. You get to chose from the store's fantastic fabric collection. Allow yourself several weeks for fittings. Dongzhimenwai Dajie 18, Chaoyang Qu. ✆ 010/6417-2472. Metro: Nongzhan Guan.

Cana Cloth and Clothes   This store adds a bit of sophistication to Nan Luogu Xiang. The interior is all open spaces and minimalist chic. About two dozen shirts and pants are sparsely hung on a couple racks that line one corner. The pieces are original and produced by a team of Beijing designers. Mostly it's solid color linen basics like white shirts or tunics. They've also got colorful pants that clearly draw on the fisherman pant style loved by backpackers the world over. Open Monday through Friday from 4 to 10pm and Saturday and Sunday from 4 to 10:30pm. Nan Luogu Xiang 29, Dongcheng Qu. ✆ 010/6406-0699. Metro: Bei Xin Qiao.

Exception de Mixmind   Exceptional indeed. This Guangzhou-based store offers an original selection of women's clothing using high-quality knitwear, funky linens, and soft cottons. The designs all play off basic, conventional designs. A floor length loose-knit sweater is topped with a gigantic hood, or simple tank tops come with a skewed neckline. Definitely a place to check out if you're looking to support innovative Chinese design. Open daily 9:30am to 9:30pm. Store BB104 China World Shopping Center, Jianguo Men Wai Dajie 1, Chaoyang Qu. ✆ 010/6505-2268. Metro: Guomao (122).

Plastered T-Shirts ✦   Simply the best place to get a quirky, original souvenir T-shirt. A British-Canadian couple opened the store over a year ago, and it is going strong. Shirts bear cute designs like "I heart Beijing," as well as some nods to Beijing life like the blown-up label of *Ergoutou*, a 56 proof rice wine that sells for less than $2. Their newest collection features designs inspired by the Olympic games and the artistry of Cultural Revolution posters. Open daily 10am till 10pm. Nan Luogu Xiang 61, Dongcheng Qu. ✆ 139/1020-5721. Metro: Bei Xin Qiao.

Ri Tan Shangwu Lou ✦✦   Not as cheap as Yaxiu, but a far more pleasant experience. If you lack the patience to wade through cheap copies of designer clothing in search of the genuine (or near-genuine) item at the markets listed above, or simply wouldn't be seen dead wearing such clothes, then swan on down to Ritan Office Building. From outside, it looks like an uninspiring office building, but inside is shopping nirvana: more than 70 shops stocking high-quality women's clothing, footwear, and accessories. There is a smattering of shops for the chaps, too. Open daily 10am till 8pm. Guanghua Lu 15A, Chaoyang Qu (just east of the south gate of Ritan Park, next to Schindlers). ⓒ 010/8561-9556. Metro: Yong'an Li metro stop (121, exit A).

Shine   A funky new store that lies just around the corner from, unfortunately, Beijing's Hooters restaurant, this is one of Beijing's most interesting multi-brand stores. They carry a small collection of the latest designs from high-end, cult labels like Rick Owens, Comme des Garçons, DSquared, and even Alaïa. But be forewarned: Everything is real, there's no bargaining, and prices are steep. Open daily noon to 9:30pm. China View, Gongti Dong Lu 108, Shop 3, Chaoyang Qu. ⓒ 010/6500-1101. Metro: Gongti.

Su Ren ⓐⓐ   This place carries fantastic leather goods. It is our favorite place to buy quality bags and shoes that aren't knockoffs or cheap fakes. Styles are original and quirky, like leather gladiator-style sandals embellished with horse hair, or slender leather wallets tied together with silk string looped through a jade stone. Open daily 9:30am to 10pm. Jinyü Hutong 3, Chaoyang Qu. ⓒ 010/6513-5580. Metro: Wangfujing (118, exit A). Other stores at Yaxiu Market, store 18 right beside the main entrance, on the east side, ⓒ 010/8700-0099; and Huaqing Jia Yuan 2, Chengfu Lu, ⓒ 010/8286-5563.

FOOD
Carrefours dot the city, but the most convenient supermarkets for travelers to stock up on snacks are found above the metro stops, including: **CRC** (Guomao [122, exit A] and Wangfujing [118, exit A]), **Parksons** (Fuxing Men [114/204, exit A]), **Oriental Kenzo** (Dong Zhi Men [214, exit C]), and **Sogo** (Xuanwu Men [206, exit C2]).

April Gourmet   This place carries excellent fresh fruits and vegetables, with decent cheese, bread, and wine selections. They will deliver within 2.5km (1½ miles) for purchases over ¥50 ($6.65/£3.35). Their best-stocked branch is opposite On/Off. Open daily 8am to midnight. Xingfu2 Ercu1n, Jiezuo Dasha, Chaoyang Qu. ⓒ 010/6417-7970. Another convenient location is at Sanlitun Bei Xiao Jie 1. ⓒ 010/8455-1245. Metro: Nong Zhan Guan.

Jenny Lou's (Tianshun Chaoshi)   Similar to April Gourmet, though with a less impressive cheese and bread selection, Jenny's empire continues to expand, with six outlets in total. The best branches are at Sanlitun Bei Xiao Jie and Chaoyang Park. Open daily 7am to 10pm. Sanlitun Bei Xiao Jie 6. ⓒ 010/6461-6928. Metro: Nong Zhan Guan. Other location at Chaoyang Park West Gate; ⓒ 010/6507-5207.

JEWELRY
Beijing Gongmei Dasha   The third-floor stalls stock all varieties of jade, from green Khotanese nephrite to Burmese jadeite. They're terribly popular with Hong Kong visitors. Count on paying no more than a third of the marked price. Open daily 9am to 9pm. Wangfujing Dajie 200, Dongcheng Qu. ⓒ 010/6528-8866. Metro: Wangfujing (118, exit A).

Hong Qiao Shichang (see section 2 of this chapter), also known as the Pearl Market, has dozens of jewelry stalls (mostly pearls and jade) on its third and fourth floors. Unless you're an expert, this is not a place to make large purchases.

Shard Box Store (Shendege Gongyipin)   The wall of JCB, Amex, and Visa credit-card stickers on the front door are fair warning—you aren't the first to discover this charming jewelry shop. The shard boxes—supposedly made from fragments of porcelain vessels smashed during the Cultural Revolution—are gorgeous. The rather more ordinary jewelry is a mixture of colorful curiosities gathered from Mongolian and Tibetan regions, and pieces crafted in nearby workshops. Jewelry can also be made to order. Open daily 9am to 7pm. Ritan Bei Lu 1, Chaoyang Qu (continue east from northeast corner of Ritan Gongyuan). ℰ 010/8561-3712. Metro: Yong'an Li (121, exit A).

Things of the Jing   Local designer Gabrielle Harris creates original jewelry that merges eastern designs with Western functionality. Find abacus earrings (with tiny beads that actually move), gorgeous streamlined silverware, and beautiful rings and pendants with inlaid turquoise, amber, and jade. The main store at Shunyi is a bit of a hike, so head to the more centrally located Bookworm (see p. 195) to view a small sample collection. Since this store is out in the suburbs, the best way to get there is by cab. Open daily 10am to 6pm. Houshayu, Xi Baixinzhuang, Kaifa Jie. ℰ 013/6915-13985.

Xincang Zhubao   Jewelry Street (Zhubao Yi Tiao Jie) is another traditional market cleaned up and forced indoors. This is the largest of more than 20 shops. The first floor stocks a full range of gemstones, wedding rings, and necklaces. Have a peek at the second floor, which stocks Western antiques—Swiss gramophones, American bibles, old telephones, and a suit of plate armor. There's even some fine French chinoiserie, which has come full circle. Open daily 9am to 7pm. Yangrou Hutong 2, Xicheng Qu (cross over and continue north; Jewelry St. is marked by an archway). ℰ 010/6618-2888. Bus: 808 from north of Xidan metro stop (115, exit A) to Xisi.

MALLS & SHOPPING PLAZAS
China's new generation of leaders would love nothing better than to wake up and find a more populous version of Singapore outside the gates of Zhong Nan Hai. With the increasingly growing middle class and the arrival of swanky malls like The Place (p. 180) and Shin Kong Place (p. 180), this may be a reality sooner than any of us had ever imagined.

China World Trade Center Shopping Center (Zhongguo Guoji Maoyi Zhongxin)   Usually simply called "Guomao," this three-level mall caters to foreign business travelers and expatriate families. The ground level of China World contains airline offices, American Express, a food court, and Beijing's first (but now far from only) Starbucks. There are stores such as Louis Vuitton and Jack and Jones, as well as a CRC Supermarket and a specialty wine shop. Open daily 9:30am to 9:30pm. Jianguo Men Wai Dajie 1, Chaoyang Qu. ℰ 010/6505-2288. Metro: Guomao (122).

Full Link Plaza (Fenglian Guangchang)   This spacious mall is a collection of chic foreign and local chain stores. The first floor has a Watson's Drug Store, there's a Kenny Roger's Roasters Restaurant on the fourth floor, and Air France is on the fifth floor. On the first floor is Beijing's most lavish Starbucks. Park 'N' Shop in the basement has been replaced by a lively market, where you'll find last season's clothes at affordable prices. Open daily 10:30am to 9:30pm. Chaoyang Men Wai Dajie 18, Chaoyang Qu. ℰ 010/6588-1483. Metro: Chaoyang Men (212, exit B).

Oriental Plaza (Dongfang Xin Tiandi)   Asia's second-largest shopping complex stretches from Wangfujing to Dong Dan (the largest is Golden Resources Mall, an empty shopping complex in the west of town). Supplanting the world's biggest McDonald's, the project was backed by Hong Kong billionaire Li Ka-Hsing. The two-story arcade houses hip clothing stores such as π Art of Shirts and Kookai; the Wangfujing Paleolithic Museum; and another Ole supermarket. The Grand Hyatt (p. 64) stands above all the consumption. In summer, it is open daily 9:30am to 10:30pm; winter daily 9:30am to 10pm. Dong Chang'an Dajie 1, Dongcheng Qu. ℰ 010/8518-6363. www.orientalplaza.com. Metro: Wangfujing (118, exit A).

The Place (Shimao Tianjie)   This new behemoth, marked by a huge outdoor screen playing clips of random fashion shows, sees plenty of fashionista traffic. Spanish retailer Zara chose to set up shop here; their arrival in Beijing was highly anticipated by locals and expats alike. Make-up gurus MAC also chose The Place for their flagship store. Other retailers like French Connection, Mango, and Adidas ensure this place is virtually bargain hunter-free. Open daily 10am to 10pm. Guanghua Lu Jia 9. ℂ 010/8595-1755. Metro: Yong'an Li metro stop (121, exit A).

Shin Kong Place (Xin Guang Tiandi)   Shin Kong Place sets the gold standard in Beijing luxury shopping. Newly opened in spring 2007, this indoor mall has all the labels that break the bank: Coach, Gucci, Salvatore Ferragamo, Marc Jacobs, as well as high-end but more affordable retailers like Anya Hindmarch, Juicy Couture, Diesel, and Club Monaco. Open daily 10am to 10pm. Jianguo Lu 87, Chaoyang Qu. ℂ 010/6530-5888. Metro: Dawang Lu (123).

Sun Dong An Plaza (Xin Dong'an Shichang)   This huge mall surrounds twin atriums and is filled with designer clothing shops. Aside from the usual Western food chains—Baskin-Robbins, Pizza Hut, McDonald's, KFC, Starbucks, and Délifrance—there's an excellent hot pot restaurant, Dong Lai Shun, on the fifth floor. Chinese medicine outlets, tea shops, and tacky "Old Beijing Street" await in the basement, which also holds a children's jungle gym. Bank of China has a branch on the first floor. Open daily 9:30am to 10pm. Wangfujing Dajie 138, Dongcheng Qu. ℂ 010/6527-6688. Metro: Wangfujing (118, exit A).

MODERN ART
Many branches of traditional Chinese art have been on the wane since the Tang dynasty (A.D. 618–907). So rather than encourage the 5,000-year-old tradition of regurgitation, look for something different. It's a much better investment.

East Gallery (Yisen Hualang)   Although quality varies, the East Gallery is the best of the locally run modern art galleries. The backdrop is magnificent, as you clamber up the narrow stairwells of the Desheng Men arrow tower (p. 149). You can visit the Ancient Coin Exhibition Hall downstairs. Open daily 9am to 5:30pm. Bei Er Huan Lu, Desheng Men Jianlou, Xicheng Qu (just east of the metro stop). ℂ 010/8201-4962. Metro: Jishuitan (218, exit A).

Red Gate Gallery (Hong Men Hualang) ✦   Opened by the delightfully camp Brian Wallace in the early 1990s, Red Gate has regular exhibitions featuring the work of its dozen or so artists. The Dongbian Men watchtower (admission ¥5/65¢/35p) provides an airy and atmospheric viewing space. Open daily 10am to 5pm. Chongwen Men Dong Dajie, Dongbian Men Jiaolou, Dongcheng Qu (10-min. walk south). ℂ 010/6525-1005. www.redgategallery.com. Metro: Jianguo Men (120/211, exit C).

MUSIC
Despite numerous well-publicized and photogenic police crackdowns, pirated *(daoban)* CDs and DVDs are readily available in Beijing, and with the proliferation of illegal music download sites, even the pirates are having it rough. If you want to support local music, it's best to go to a concert and buy the music directly from the band. The second floor of the **Foreign Language Bookstore** (p. 174) boasts a wide range of Chinese music. There's maddening cross-talk *(xiangsheng),* bland mandopop, and even a small alternative *(fei zhuliu)* music section featuring local bands such as Thin Man and Second Hand Rose. The alternative philosophy doesn't extend to the

Western music section, which relies heavily on Richard Clayderman, Kenny G, and Boyzone.

Beijing Yangguang Yunzhi Shūdian   An essential stop for those looking to develop an appreciation (or at least an understanding) of Peking Opera. Located next to the People's Theater, this tiny shop is crammed with DVDs and CDs featuring Peking opera's leading man, Mei Lanfang. Traditionally, only three instruments were essential—the ubiquitous two-stringed *erhu;* its smaller cousin, the *jinghuu;* and the banjolike *yueqiin.* Elegant handmade versions of all three are found here. Lessons can be arranged. Open daily 8am to 6:30pm. Huguo Si 4 Dajie 74, Xicheng Qu 1 (next to Renmin Juchang). ℂ 010/6617-2931. Metro: Jishuitan (218, exit C).

Beijing Yinyue Shudian   At this store, located just to the east of the north end of the Wangfujing pedestrian mall, the top floor has a large range of sheet music at prices far cheaper than in the West. Composers' names are in Chinese, of course, but names are transliterated (Beethoven becomes Beiduofen, Liszt is rendered as Lisite), so you may be able to make yourself understood. If not, names are often written in English above the scores. 1/F open daily 9am to 10:30pm, 2/F–4/F open to 9pm only. Dong'an Men Dajie 16. ℂ 010/6525-4458. Metro: Wangfujing (118, exit A).

ODDITIES

Gong'anbu Diyi Yanjiusuo *(Finds*   More *Get Smart* than James Bond, the commercial outlet of the "No. 1 Police Research Unit" is a bizarre example of socialist marketization. Aside from a range of authentic Chinese police gear—bulletproof vests, sturdy boots—there's a full range of dated surveillance equipment, including nifty spy pens. Suspicious (often with good reason) wives are said to be their main clients. Open daily 9am to 5:30pm. Zhengyi 4 Lu, Dongcheng Qu (walk east to 1st intersection and turn right, walk for a few minutes; opposite Beijing City Government Headquarters). ℂ 010/6522-9312. Metro: Tian'an Men Dong (117, exit C).

Pyongyang Art Studio   More disturbing than odd, this tiny shop, opened by a Brit who has been traveling to the DPRK since 1993, is crammed with North Korean goods and socialist realist art. Cultural Revolution kitsch, while in questionable taste, has some distance to it. This is more confronting: There are anti-U.S. tracts, and paeans to the Dear Leader, Kim Il-Sung, the only man to card a perfect 18 in a round of golf. His love of cinema is described in "Great Man and Cinema," while "A Great Mind" celebrates his father, Kim Jong-Il. There are propaganda posters (many hand-painted), magazines, flags, T-shirts, cigarettes, and even North Korean hooch. Compelling. Open daily 9am to 9:30pm. Chunxiu Lu 10, Chaoyang Qu (inside the Red House). ℂ 010/6416-7810. www.pyongyangartstudio.com.

3501 PLA Surplus Store (3501 Gongchang) *(★*   The official disposal store of the world's largest army is a delightful mix of fur-lined boots, army greatcoats, and kitsch Communist memorabilia. Where else will you find Lei Feng hats, sturdy compasses and binoculars, and waist watches commemorating the 50th anniversary of liberation? Open daily 9am to 5:30pm. Dong San Huan 23, Dongcheng Qu (just south of Jing Guang Zhongxin). ℂ 010/6585-9312. Metro: Guomao (122, exit A).

OUTDOOR EQUIPMENT

Decathlon *(Value*   A place to get the real stuff—we think. This is basically an outlet of the sporty French retailer. It has everything for the outdoors, from tents to hiking boots, at significantly lower prices than what you would find back home. And for the ladies, this is the only place in Beijing where we have found non-padded sports bras. Open Monday through Thursday from 9am to 9pm, and weekends until 10pm. 195 Dongsihuan Zhonglu (corner of Nanmofang Lu and East 4th Ring Road). ✆ 010/8777-8788.

Sanfu Huwai Yongpin (Sanfo Outdoors) _√Value_   This shop began life as an outdoor club at Peking University, and has a dedicated following among students and young professionals. Unlike the knockoffs for sale at Hong Qiao and elsewhere, Sanfo only stocks the genuine article, and most products come with a warranty. They have their own line of sleeping bags, and still organize weekend trips to the wilderness around Beijing (p. 151). There are branches in Jin Zhi Qiao Dasha west of Guomao, and northwest of Peking University. Open daily 9am to 8pm. Madian Nan Cun 4 Lou 5. ✆ 010/8202-1113, ext. 12. www.sanfo.com.cn. Metro: Jishuitan (218, exit A), then bus no. 919 to Beijiao Shichang.

SHOES

Lao Fan Jie Fuzhuang Shichang (Alien's Street)   It's hard to imagine anything more chaotic than the original Yabao Lu Market, but this brushed-down version comes close. It is impossible not to get lost. The first floor houses shoes, shoes, and more shoes, which mercifully come in sizes suitable for Western feet. Cheap, expansive, and often nasty, this market is popular with Russian traders. Open daily 9:30am to 6pm. Yabao Lu, Chaoyang Qu1 (head east and take the 2nd right; continue south, and the market is on the left side). ✆ 010/8561-4641. Metro: Chaoyang Men (212, exit A).

Nei Lian Sheng Xiedian   Cloth-soled "thousand layer happy shoes" _(qianceng buxie)_, loved by martial arts stars and aging Communist leaders alike, are hard to find. Cheaper plastic-soled shoes are taking their place. A workshop behind this shop, founded in 1853, still turns them out; these shoes are well stitched and very comfortable. There are also some gorgeous women's shoes, modeled on Qing fashions. Fortunately, they are now available in larger sizes. Bargaining is fruitless. Open daily from 9am to 9pm. Dazhalan Jie 34. ✆ 010/6301-4863. Metro: Qian Men (208, exit C).

SILK, FABRIC & TAILORS

The third floor of **Yaxiu Fuzhuang Shichang** is a fine place to look for a tailor (see section 2 of this chapter).

Beijing Sichou Dian (Beijing Silk Store)   Tucked away in a narrow _hutong_ just west of and running parallel with Qian Men Dajie, this bustling store is said to date from 1840. Prices for tailoring and raw materials are affordable. Open daily 9am to 7:30pm. Zhubao Shi 5, Chongwen Qu (just south of metro stop). ✆ 010/6301-6658. Metro: Qian Men (208, exit C).

Daxin Fangzhi Gongsi _√Value_   It might not be as prestigious as other tailors, but with hand-tailored _qipao_ typically costing less than ¥200 ($27/£13), it's impossible to argue with the price. Right next door to Yoshinoya Dairy Queen. Open daily 8:30am to 8pm. Xinjiekou Nan Dajie 22, Xicheng Qu (walk south for 10 min.; the shop is on the left side, just beyond the main intersection). ✆ 010/6618-7843. Metro: Jishuitan (218, exit C).

Ruifuxiang Choubu Dian ✿   You'll find piles of gorgeous silk brocade at this store, in the trade for 110 years. They specialize in _qipao_, a body-hugging one-piece dress for ¥500 ($67/£33) and up. It takes 1 week to tailor, with a couple of fittings. If you're pushed for time, they can complete it in 2 days for an additional charge. They also have an outlet at Wangfujing Dajie 190 (✆ 010/6525-0764), just north of Gongmei

Dasha. Aim to bargain 30% to 50% off the marked prices. Open daily 9am to 10pm in summer; 9am to 9pm in winter. Dazhalan Jie 5, west off Qian Men Dajie, Chongwen Qu. ✆ 010/6303-5313. Metro: Qian Men (208, exit C).

Yuanlong Sichou Gufen Youxian Gongsi (Yuanlong Silk Co. Ltd.)   A huge range of silk fabric occupies the third floor; prices are clearly marked and surprisingly competitive. A *qipao* or suit can be made in a couple of days, but it's best to allow at least a week. Exquisite (and expensive!) silk carpets from Henan are sold on the first floor. Try not to visit at midday, when the third floor is overrun by tour groups. Open daily 9am to 6:30pm. Tian Tan Lu 55, Chongwen Qu (northeast side of Tian Tan Gongyuan). ✆ 010/6702-2288. Bus: 807 from Chongwen Men metro stop (209, exit B) to Hong Qiao.

SKATEWEAR

Yan Cheng Yu (Over Workshop) *Kids*   With acres of empty concrete, the capital is a skateboarder's paradise. The skating park in Tian'an Men Square is a distant memory, but the owners of this shop can steer you in the right direction. Decks and wheels are imported, but local skate fashions feature striking designs. Danny Way, who skated over the Juyong Guan section of the Great Wall in 2005, figures prominently. Some designs can be viewed online at www.skatechina.com and www.shehuisk8.com. Open daily 10am to 6pm. Xinjiekou Xi Li Yi Qu1 6-002, Xicheng Qu (cross road, take 1st right after Xu2 Beihong Memorial Hall, inside a block of yellow apartments on left side). ✆ 010/8201-1266. Metro: Jishuitan (218, exit C).

TEA

Geng Xiang   With a survey finding that more than half of Beijing's teas have traces of pesticides or heavy metals, organic teas are a sensible choice. The largest retailer of organic tea in Beijing, Geng Xiang, survived the scandal with its reputation enhanced. Their green tea *(lu cha)* is among the best in China. Open daily 8:30am to 9pm. Di'an Men Wai Dajie 116, Xicheng Qu (south of Drum Tower on east side of street). ✆ 010/6404-0846. Metro: Gu Lou Dajie (217).

Malian Dao ✰✰   This might not be all the tea in China, but with over a mile of shops hawking tea leaves and tea paraphernalia, it feels like it. Shops are run by the families of tea growers from Fujian and Zhejiang, and many rate this friendly street as the highlight of their visit. The four-story Tea City *(Cha Cheng),* halfway down the street, is a pleasant spot to start. Black tea *(hong cha)* and Pu'er tea (sold in round briquettes, a tea that improves with age) are usually sold by the same vendors. The Beijing outlet of **Menghai Chachang** (ext. 8165), at the south end of the first floor, stocks exquisite black tea. Oolong tea *(wulong cha)* is usually encountered in the West in substandard form: Here is the genuine article. There is such a wide range of flavors—from flowery *gaoshan* to caffeine-laden *tie guanyin,* from milky *jinxuan* to the sweet aftertaste of *renshen* (ginseng)—that most shoppers find a brew to suit. Try **Taiwan Tianbaoyang Mingcha** (ext. 8177), on the west side of Tea City's first floor. Ceramic and cloisonné tea sets are the other big draw. **Ziyu Taofang** (✆ 010/6327-5268), on the east side of the second floor, sells fine pots and cups molded from Yixing clay. Bargain hunters should visit **Jingmin Chacheng,** an older wholesale market, further south on the same side of the street. Open daily 8:30am to 7pm. Malian Dao Cha Cheng, Fengtai Qu1. ✆ 010/6328-1177.

Tian Fu Jituan (Ten Fu Tea)   While not quite the McDonald's of tea, at last count there were 26 branches in Beijing. This store is the largest. Their jasmine tea *(hua cha)*

is excellent. Open daily 8:30am to 7:30pm. Wangfujing Dajie 176, Dongcheng Qu. ✆ 010/
6525-4722. Metro: Wangfujing (118, exit A).

TOYS

Mass-produced toys can be found at the **toy market** *(wanju shichang)* behind Hong
Qiao Shichang, or at **Alien's Street Market.** Check carefully before you purchase:
There are no warranties or safety guarantees. We infinitely prefer:

Bannerman Tang's Toys and Crafts (Shengtang Xuan) ⍟   A world away from
the baubles produced in the sweatshops of Shenzhen, this tiny shop offers delightful
handcrafted toys. It's run by fifth-generation toymaker Tang Yujie and stocked with a
delightful collection of figurines, paper lanterns, and other childish delights made
from wood, clay, paper, and cloth. Toys depict scenes from old Beijing—the street barber, the fortune teller, and old men playing chess. Beijing opera figurines betray influences from Japanese *manga.* Open daily 9am to 7pm. Guo Zi Jian Jie, Dongcheng Qu (just
west of Kong Miao, on the south side of the street). ✆ 010/8404-7179. Metro: Yonghe Gong/Lama Temple (215, exit C).

10

Beijing After Dark

If you measure a city's nightlife by the number of chances for debauchery it offers, then Beijing has never held (and probably will never hold) a candle to such neon-lit Babylons as Shanghai and Hong Kong. If, instead, you measure nightlife by its diversity, the Chinese capital rivals any major city in Asia.

Such was not always the case. As recently as a decade ago, Beijing's populace routinely tucked itself into bed under a blanket of Mao-inspired Puritanism shortly after nightfall, leaving visitors with one of two tourist-approved options: Attend Beijing opera and acrobatic performances in a sterile theater, or wander listlessly around the hotel in search of a drink to make sleep come faster.

Since then, the government has realized there is money to be made on both sides of the Earth's rotation. The resulting relaxation in nocturnal regulations, set against the backdrop of Beijing residents' historical affinity for cultural diversions, has helped remake the city's nightlife. Opera and acrobatics are still available,

but now in more interesting venues, and to them have been added an impressive range of other worthwhile cultural events: teahouse theater, puppet shows, intimate traditional music concerts, live jazz, even the occasional subtitled film.

This diversity continues with Beijing's drinking and dance establishments, of which there are scores. Although they don't quite match Shanghai's for style, they are generally cheaper and offer something for just about every mood. With the opening of a few modern dance clubs, the city's cheesy old discos are thankfully no longer the only dance option, although the latter can still be tremendously entertaining for kitsch value. The same goes for karaoke, a favorite in China as it is in Japan. Foreign-Chinese interaction in bars hasn't progressed much beyond the sexual exploitation rampant in the 1920s and 1930s, but this is by no means a necessary dynamic. The traveler not afraid to bumble through language barriers can often connect with local people over a bottle or two of beer.

1 Performing Arts

BEIJING OPERA

Beijing opera *(jingju)* is described by some as the apogee of traditional Chinese culture and, at least according to one modest Chinese connoisseur, is "perhaps the most refined form of opera in the world." Many who have actually seen a performance might beg to differ with these claims, but few other Chinese artistic traditions can match it for sophistication and pure stylized spectacle.

The Beijing tradition is young as Chinese opera styles go. Its origins are most commonly traced to 1790, when four opera troupes from Anhui Province arrived in Beijing to perform for the Qing court and decided to stay, eventually absorbing elements of a popular opera tradition from Hubei Province. Initially performed exclusively for the royal family, the new blended style eventually trickled out to the public and was well received as a more accessible alternative to the elegant but stuffy operas dominant at the time.

How it could have ever been considered accessible is mystifying to most foreign audiences. The typical performance is loud and long, with archaic dialogue sung on a screeching pentatonic scale, accompanied by a cacophony of gongs, cymbals, drums, clappers, and strings. This leaves most first-timers exhausted, but the exquisite costumes and martial arts–inspired movements ultimately make it worthwhile. Probably the opera's most distinctive feature is its elaborate system of face paints, with each color representing a character's disposition: red for loyalty, blue for bravery, black for honesty, and white for cruelty.

Communist authorities outlawed the "feudalistic" classics after 1949 and replaced them with the Eight Model Plays—a series of propaganda-style operas based on 20th-century events that focus heavily on class struggle. Many of these are still performed and are worth viewing if only to watch reactions from audience members, some of whom have seen these plays dozens of times and loudly express their disgust when a mistake is made. But the older stories, allowed again after Mao's death, are more visually stunning. Among the most popular are *Farewell My Concubine,* made famous through Chen Kaige's film of the same name, and *Havoc in Heaven,* which follows the mischievous Monkey King character from the Chinese literary classic *Journey to the West.*

Several theaters now offer shortened programs more amenable to the foreign attention span, usually with English subtitles or plot summaries. Most people on tours are taken to the cinema-style **Liyuan Theater (Liyuan Juchang)** inside the Qian Men Hotel (nightly performances at 7:30pm; © **010/6301-6688;** ¥80–¥480/$11–$64/ £5.35–£32) or to one of several other modern venues. These are affordable but supremely boring. Your time and money are much better spent at one of the traditional theaters below.

Huguang Guild Hall (Huguang Huiguan Xilou)   This combination museum-theater, housed in a complex of traditional buildings with gray tile roofs and bright red gables, has a connection with Beijing Opera dating back to 1830. To the right of the main entrance is a small museum filled with old opera robes and photos of famous performers (including the legendary Mei Lanfang), probably interesting only to aficionados. On the left is the expertly restored theater, a riot of color with a beautifully adorned traditional stage, paper lanterns hung from the high ceilings, and gallery seating on all three sides. Subtitles are in Chinese only, but brochures contain brief plot explanations in English. Performances take place nightly at 7:30pm. Hufang Lu 3 (at intersection with Luomashi Dajie; plaza out front contains colorful opera mask sculpture). © **010/6351-8284.** Tickets ¥150–¥580 ($20–$77/£10–£39). Metro: Heping Men (207, exit D1); walk south 10 min.

Teahouse of Prince Gong's Mansion (Gong Wang Fu Chaguan)   Not a traditional opera venue, Prince Gong's teahouse is nevertheless picturesque, with a rare bamboo motif on the exterior beams and columns and an intimate interior outfitted with polished wood tables and pleasing tea paraphernalia. This is opera for tourists, kept short and sweet, with a guided tour of the surrounding gardens included in the price (see Prince Gong's Mansion, p. 144). There are several performances daily until 4:30pm. Liuyin Jie 17. (Signposted in English at top of Qian Hai Xi Dajie [running north off Ping'an Dadao opposite north gate of Bei Hai Park]; turn left at sign and follow alley past large parking lot. Entrance marked with huge red lanterns.) © **010/6616-8149.** Tickets ¥60 ($8/£4).

Zhengyi Ci Xilou (Zhengyi Ci Theater) The 340-year-old Zhengyi Ci is under constant threat of extinction but is the first choice for authentic Beijing opera when it's open. A Ming dynasty temple converted into an opera theater in 1712, it fell to other uses after 1949 and was in danger of being torn down until a local businessman reopened it in 1995. Since then, funding problems and its position at the center of an urban reconstruction project have limited the number of performances. The theater itself is similar to the Huguang Guild Hall, with the same high ceilings and gallery seating, but it has a decidedly more local feel. The staff themselves are connoisseurs, more interested in opera than collecting tourist dollars. Pray it survives. Performances are held most nights at 7:30pm (call to check). Qian Men Xi Heyan Jie 220 (walk south of the Heping Men Quanjude, take 1st left). ℂ 010/8315-1649. Tickets ¥150–¥280 ($20–$37/£10–£19). Metro: Heping Men (207, exit C2).

ACROBATICS

China's acrobats are justifiably famous, and probably just a little bit insane. This was the only traditional Chinese art form to receive Mao's explicit approval (back flips, apparently, don't count as counterrevolution). While not culturally stimulating, the combination of plate spinning, hoop jumping, bodily contortion, and seemingly suicidal balancing acts make for slack-jawed entertainment of the highest order. Shanghai is the traditional home of acrobatics and boasts its best troupes, but the capital has done a fair job of transplanting the tradition.

The city's best acrobatics *(zaji)* venue is the **Wansheng Juchang** on the north side of Bei Wei Lu just off Qian Men Dajie (west side of the Temple of Heaven); performances are by the famous Beijing Acrobatics Troupe (ℂ 010/6303-7449; nightly shows at 5:30pm and 7:15pm; ¥100–¥380/$13–$51/£6.65–£25). The acrobats at the **Chaoyang Juchang** (ℂ 010/6507-2421; Dong San Huan Bei Lu 36, south of Tuanjie Hu Park; nightly shows at 7:15pm; ¥120–¥300/$16–$40/£8–£20) are clumsier but the theater is more conveniently located, a short taxi ride from the main bar district. Metro: Guanghua Lu.

PUPPETS

Puppet shows *(mu'ou xi)* have been performed in China since the Han dynasty (206 B.C.–A.D. 220). The art form has diversified somewhat over the past two millennia, coming to include everything from the traditional hand puppets to string and shadow varieties. Plot lines are simple, but the manipulations are deft and the craftsmanship is exquisite. Most performances, including weekend matinees, are held at the **China Puppet Art Theater (Zhongguo Mu'ou Juyuan),** in Anhua Xi Li near the North Third Ring Road (ℂ 010/6425-4798); tickets cost ¥100 to ¥220 ($13–$29/£6.65–£15).

OTHER VENUES

Beijing hosts a growing number of international music and theater events every year, and its own increasingly respectable outfits—including the Beijing Symphony Orchestra—give frequent performances. Among the most popular venues for this sort of thing is the **Beijing Concert Hall (Beijing Yinyue Ting;** ℂ 010/6605-5812), at Bei Xinhua Jie in Liubukou (Xuanwu). The **Poly Theater (Baoli Dasha Guoji Juyuan;** ℂ 010/6506-5343), in the Poly Plaza complex on the East Third Ring Road (northeast exit of Dong Si Shi Tiao metro station), also hosts many large-scale performances, including the occasional revolutionary ballet. For information on additional venues and the shows they're hosting, check one of the expatriate magazines.

2 Teahouse Theater

Traditional teahouse entertainment disappeared from Beijing after 1949, but some semblance survives in a number of modern teahouses that have grown up with the tourism industry. Snippets of Beijing opera, cross-talk (stand-up) comedy, acrobatics, traditional music, singing, and dancing flow across the stage as you sip tea and nibble on snacks. If you don't have time to see these kinds of performances individually, the teahouse is an adequate solution. If you're looking for a quiet place to enjoy a cup of jasmine and maybe do some reading, look to one of the real teahouses listed later in this chapter.

Lao She's Teahouse (Lao She Chaguan)   This somewhat garishly decorated teahouse is named for one of the most famous plays by celebrated Chinese writer Lao She (see Lao She Jinianguan [Former Residence of Lao She], p. 144). Performances change nightly but always include opera and acrobatics. It pays to buy the more expensive tickets, as views from the rear seats are frequently obscured. Nightly shows at 7:50pm. Qianmen Xi Dajie 3 (west of Qian Men on south side of the street). ✆ 010/6303-6830. Tickets ¥40–¥130 ($5.35–$17/£2.65–£8.65).

Tianqiao Happy Tea House (Tianqiao Le Chaguan)   The Tianqiao puts on essentially the same show as Lao She's Teahouse, but in a gallery seating framed in dark lacquered wood and a less eye-straining color scheme. The quality of the performances has declined markedly, however: Many performers are well past their prime. There's a roast duck dinner option (reservations required). Performances take place nightly at 8pm (arrive at 6:30pm for dinner). Bei Wei Lu (just west of intersection with Qian Men Dajie, west side of Temple of Heaven). ✆ 010/6304-0617. Tickets ¥150 ($20/£10), or ¥330 ($44/£22) with dinner.

3 Cinemas

State limitations on freedom of expression, the profusion of black market DVDs, and ready access to illegal download sites have taken their toll on China's film industry, but Beijing has enough film fanatics to support a handful of theaters. **Cherry Lane Movies** (✆ 0/13901134745; ¥50/$6.65/£3.35), run by a long-tenured and long-winded American expatriate, shows older and some new Chinese films with English subtitles on the weekends; films are listed at www.cherrylanemovies.com.cn and are screened inside the Kent Centre, at Liangma Qiao Lu 29. They also have summer screenings at the Sino-Swiss Hotel (see chapter 5, p. 78). **Box Cafe** (**Hezi Kafeiguan;** Xi Wang Zhuang Xiaoqu 5; ✆ 010/6279-1280), a smallish cafe near the east gate of Tsinghua University (Qinghua Daxue), offers free screenings on Tuesday and Saturday (screenings usually start at 7:30pm) of Chinese independent and experimental films and a few foreign films of the same nature. The **UME International Cineplex** (**Huaxing Guoji Yingcheng;** Shuangyushu Xueyuan Nan Lu 44; ✆ 010/8211-5566; ¥50–¥80/$6.65–$11/£3.35–5.35), a full-scale theater just north of the Third Ring Road and southeast of Renmin University, occasionally shows undubbed Hollywood films and Chinese blockbusters with English subtitles, as does the more conveniently located **Star City** (**Xinshi Ji Ying Cheng;** inside Oriental Plaza on the east side of the mall; ✆ 010/8518-6778. Metro: Wangfujing). The newest, and, for now, biggest cinema is **Wanda International Cinema** (**Wanda Guoji Dianying Cheng;** 3/F, Building B, Wanda Plaza Jianguo Lu 93; ✆ 010/5960-3399; Metro: Da Wang

Rainbow Sexuality under the Red Flag

Same-sex relationships between men have a history of acceptance in China dating as far back as the Zhou period (1100–256 B.C.). In official records of the Han dynasty (206 B.C.–A.D. 220), 10 emperors are described as openly bisexual and are listed with the names of their lovers. In the centuries following the Han, homosexuality was generally accepted among men, so long as it didn't interfere with their Confucian duty to marry and perpetuate the family name. Partly due to the influence of Western missionaries, homosexuality was outlawed by official decree in 1740, but Judeo-Christian notions of shame never fully took root in China and the practice persisted. Under the Communists, however, homosexuality came to be seen as disruptive of the social order, and persecution of gays was sanctioned during the Cultural Revolution.

The situation has improved markedly over the past decade. In 2002, the government rescinded its 1989 edict describing homosexuality as a psychological disorder, but laws still prohibit expat magazines from talking about gay bars (described instead as bars "for the alternative set"). *Time Out,* a popular expat periodical, runs a monthly column that gets around the censors with a subtle header: G&L. The general populace tends to ignore the existence of gay relationships, made easier by the fact that it's considered normal for men to be physically affectionate regardless of sexual orientation. As in ancient times, many gay men still marry and have children to satisfy their parents.

The best gay club in Beijing is **Destination (Mudidi; ✆ 010/6551-5138)** at Gongti Xi Lu 7, south of the Worker's Stadium west gate, where the crowd revels and the beats are right. **On/Off (Shang Xia Xian; ✆ 010/6415-8083)** at Xingfu Yi Cun Xi Li 5, is one of Beijing's longest standing "alternative" venues. Things have turned a tad seedy in recent times, but the crowds still flock to this venue, which now includes a bar, a restaurant, and even an Internet cafe.

For lesbians, the scene is slightly grimmer. Women perceived as homosexual are often subject to harassment. In the context of Chinese patriarchy, lesbianism has never received much attention. Outside a brief appearance in the Chinese classic *Dream of the Red Mansion,* it is invisible in literature, and the pressures of China's skewed gender ratio—an excess of boys brought on by age-old prejudices in response to the one-child policy—has made many single Chinese men resentful of any reduction in the pool of potential wives.

Aside from Thursday nights at Destination, try the Feng Bar, just east of the south gate of the Worker's Stadium, on Saturday nights. As the scene is still developing, try connecting online, through the newly established Beijing's Other Attractions (boa_productions@yahoo.com), or more general websites for lesbians in Asia, such as www.fridae.com or www.utopia.asia.com.

Lu). Have your hotel concierge double-check that the movie you want to see has English subtitles.

When international film festival directors go looking for new, edgy films, they visit **Hart Center of Arts (Hate Shalong;** ℂ **010/6435-3570;** www.hart.com.cn) in the Factory 798 complex (see chapter 7, p. 144) which hosts festivals with themes no one else is game to touch, and regularly screens movies at 8pm on Saturday (call to check). Most of the work shown here has not passed the censors.

4 Live Music

Most of the bars on San Li Tun North Bar Street offer nightly live "music" perform-ances by cover bands, usually of scant talent and almost invariably Filipino in origin. But there are several small venues, most of them in Chaoyang, which host an increas-ingly varied lineup of musical acts. Performers range from traditional folk instrumen-talists to jazz ensembles and rock outfits, and are usually interesting, if not always good. (See Appendix A: "Beijing in Depth" for more on the city's better bands.) Most venues are bars open nightly from around 5pm to 1 or 2am, although few offer live acts every night. There is usually a small cover charge of about ¥5–¥50 (65¢–$6.65/ 35p–£3.35) on performance nights, depending on the number of acts and their pres-tige. *Time Out* and *that's Beijing* maintain somewhat accurate listings of what is play-ing where and when.

CD Jazz Cafe (Sendi Jueshi)   After much upheaval, this amalgamation of CD Cafe and the short-lived Treelounge is the best place to see local jazz and blues acts in Beijing. If it's a special act, get there early. Dong San Huan, south of the Agricultural Exhibition Center (Nongzhan Guan) main gate (down small path behind trees that line sidewalk). ℂ 010/6506-8288. Cover ¥30 ($4/£2). Metro: Nong Zhan Guan.

D-22   It's a long way from the center of town, but this tight two-floor venue is the best place for experimental music acts. On certain weekdays, the club hosts art-house movie nights. 13 Chengfu Lu. ℂ 010/6265-3177. www.d22beijing.com. Cover ¥30 ($4/£2). Metro: Wu Dao Kou.

MAO Livehouse   This newly opened live music venue is backed by Japanese label Bad News, home of local punk band *Brain Failure*. Plenty of aspiring punk rocksters have already become loyal fans, to both the band and the bar. The exterior looks like a rusty, unfinished steel warehouse. Inside, the decor is an eclectic mix of chairs and tables sandwiched between black walls. 111 Guloudajie. ℂ 010/6402-5080. Cover ¥30 ($4/£2). Metro: Bei Xin Qiao.

Salud   This cozy bar often hosts local live music acts, usually upbeat South Ameri-can music or jazz. They've got fabulous loft seating, and an understated decor of blond wood with a couple artsy paintings on the wall. Glass jars filled with the bar's home-made rum line one wall. Service is horrible when things get busy, but the French own-ers proudly shrug it all off, "We're not 'ere to make money!" A refreshing sentiment. Nan Luogu Xiang 66. ℂ 010/6402-5086. Metro: Bei Xin Qiao.

Sanwei Bookstore (Sanwei Shuwu)   The tiny Sanwei has a well-worn teahouse upstairs that hosts intimate concerts on the weekends. Fridays it's jazz and Saturdays it's classical Chinese, usually with a minority twist. This is the city's finest venue for Chinese traditional music, if only because you sit close enough to really experience it. Tea and snacks are included in the price. Friday and Saturday performances take place at 8:30pm. Fuxing Men Nei Dajie 60 (opposite the Minorities Palace [Minzu Gong]). *© 010/6601-3204.* Cover ¥30 ($4/£2).

The Star Live   The cool music acts (Ziggy Marley, The Roots, Sonic Youth) are finally coming to Beijing, and they seem to like playing at Star Live. This place is nothing like their thumping, downstairs neighbor Tango; it is small and intimate and has excellent acoustics. Ticket prices depend on the artist, but expect to pay between ¥100 and ¥300 ($13–$40/£6.65–£20). 3/F, Tango, 70 Heping Xijie (50m/164 ft. north of subway station). *© 010/6425-5166.* www.thestarlive.com. Metro: Yongheegong.

Yu Gong Yi Shan   This wonderful performance space is the best live music venue in Beijing, period. The owners have a knack for turning up the best local acts. Run by the owners of the now defunct Loup Chante, the diverse lineup—from punk to Mongolian mouth music, and everything in-between—means you can visit night after night. Having enjoyed a successful two-year run in the parking lot across from the Worker's Stadium, the bar was moving to their new space near Lotus Lane in Hou Hai at time of writing. Daily 2pm to 2am. Zhangzizhong Lu 3, east of Lotus Lane. *© 010/6415-0687.* Cover varies for performances. Metro: Zhangzizhong Lu.

5 Clubs & Discos

The average Chinese will lump all dancing establishments into a single category—*tiaowudian* (dancing place), or, if they try it in English, "dee-si-ko." But while the distinction between a Beijing disco and a Beijing dance club is lost on most locals, it is readily apparent to any foreigner. Discos are typically old and cavernous, with exaggerated decor, horrible music, and a wholly Chinese clientele whose attempts to imitate Western modes of style and dance will send shivers down your spine. Clubs, by contrast, are newer, smaller, and more stylish, with a DJ-dominated atmosphere closer in feel to what you'd find in the United States or Europe. The club clientele is wealthier, more diverse (with both Chinese and foreigners), and not quite as clueless.

Both discos and dance clubs charge high covers, at anywhere from ¥50–¥150 ($6.65–$20/£3.35–£10). Both tend to get crowded on weekends around 10pm and empty around 3am, although a few clubs will host special parties that last until dawn. There is some activity on Thursday nights, but the rest of the week is slow. Discos predate the days of the drinking district and hence are scattered randomly around the city. Clubs tend to be situated next to bars, in foreigner-heavy areas like San Li Tun and Chaoyang Park.

Alfa   This Southeast Asian bar recently transformed their patio into a covered, harem dream world. It's as spacious as ever, with two glowing floor pools and cozy bed nooks covered in drapes and pillows. Inside, private booths on the second floor are where crowds gather to people-watch while shooting back green tea and whiskey. The small, claustrophobic dance floor is fun on Fridays, when the DJ spins '80s music. Xingfu Yicun 5 (in the alley opposite the Workers' Stadium west gate). *© 010/6413-0086.* No cover.

Babyface   Definitely not a place to come for a quiet chat, Babyface serves it up for the wealthy young elite of the capital. If you think shows like *Laguna Beach* only apply to the West Coast, Babyface will make you think again. The Valley Girl is on the march. Dance floors are small and much of the clientele has an air of studied boredom, but it's near impossible to fault the music (often supplied by Ministry of Sound DJs) and the stylish metal-and-glass decor. Try not to scratch the paint on anyone's

Mercedes when you stumble back outside, disoriented by the thumping bass and the potent shooters. Gongti Xi Lu 6 (just south of the Workers' Stadium west gate). ℂ 010/6551-9081. When there's a cover charge (depends on the night and the DJ), it's usually ¥50 ($6.65/£3.35).

Banana   Banana is one of Beijing's oldest and most popular discos. This new, larger location is a classic bit of 1990s Miami Beach postmodernism with fake palm trees and white Doric columns. The crowd is mostly black-clad men and skinny women who wear sunglasses at night. The sound system produces enough bass to loosen tooth fillings. Jianguo Men Wai Dajie 22 (in front of Scitech Hotel). ℂ 010/6528-3636. Cover ¥30 ($4/£2).

China Doll (Zhongguo Wawa) ✦   The photos here of semi-naked, nubile figures suspended in water make us a little uneasy. But the cool funk/drum and bass tunes and the hip crowd turn China Doll into a great place to dance away a Saturday night. The bar's main floor is a chill place to escape from the poorly ventilated dance floor. 2/F Tongli Studios, Sanlitun Beijie (off the main drag, behind 3.3). ℂ 010/6417-4699. No cover. Metro: Gongti Bei Lu.

The Den (Dunhuang)   The Den is Beijing's longest-standing meat market and an institution among youthful travelers. There's a vague opium den theme downstairs, with low light and lots of quasi-ornate wood embellishments, but the main draw is the sweaty, no-frills dance floor upstairs, crowded until the wee hours. Music is mostly 1990s pop dance hits and half-hearted R&B. There's an authentic Western brunch here, with eggs Benedict and bagels, daily from 9am to 1pm. The half-price happy hour, which runs for 5 hours (5–10pm), is unbeatable. Intersection of Gongti Dong Lu 4A, next to the City Hotel (Chengshi Binguan). ℂ 010/6592-6290. Cover ¥30 ($4/£2), includes one free drink.

Destination (Mudidi)   Jokingly renamed "Desperation" by locals, Beijing's most successful (almost openly) gay club is indeed a fine spot to meet locals of the same sex, without the rent boy seediness that now afflicts On/Off. Bare grey concrete walls, dark lounges, and odd subtitled video footage that never quite seems to match the tunes doesn't sound like a successful formula, but somehow it works. Beautiful hunky men crowd the sweaty nightclub featuring a bouncing dance floor. The music isn't so loud that you can't duck into a corner for a chat, and is slightly camp without being cliché. Insanely crowded on weekends. Gongti Xi Lu 7 (south of the west gate of the Workers' Stadium, opposite Bellagio's). ℂ 010/6551-5138. Cover ¥30 ($4/£2), includes one free drink.

Mix (Mi Ke Si)   If you want thumping hip hop beats, young gyrating bodies, and a sweaty dance floor, then Mix is the place for you. They've also got some of the tallest, beefiest bouncers in town—no small feat considering we're in China! The relaxation zone, featuring trance music, is a great place to unwind from the main dance floor. Otherwise, music is hip-hop and R&B. Gongti Bei Men Xi Ce (inside Workers' Stadium north gate, on the west side). ℂ 010/6551-5138.

Propaganda   The place to see (and hope that you're not seen), Propaganda is the bass-pumping club of the student district. Its dance floor has witnessed many a hot and heavy make-out session. Huaqing Jiayuan Don Men Wang Bei (100m/328 ft. north of the east gate of Huaqing Jiayuan). ℂ 010/8286-3679. Metro: Wudaokou. Cover ¥20 ($2.65/£1.35).

Vic's (Wei Ke Si)   Vic's is located directly opposite Mix (see above) and patrons who come here are often flipping a coin, deciding between Vic's 'n' Mix. They recently renovated, adding flashier lights and a multi-colored psychedelic decor. Girls in heels: watch out for the unexpected steps on the long, floor-lit catwalk entrance. Music formula follows that of Mix (see above). Gongti Bei Men Dong Ce (inside Worker's stadium north gate, on the east side). ℂ 010/5293-0333.

Moments **Karaoke: Down that Drink, It's Time to Sing**

No one knows why Asian cultures have embraced karaoke (pronounced "*kala* okay" in Mandarin) with such red-faced gusto, or why so many foreigners become just as enthusiastic once they're on Eastern soil. Maybe the food lacks some amino acid crucial to the brain's shame function. Or maybe it's just fun to get soused and pretend you have talent, thousands of miles away from home. Spend enough time in Beijing and sooner or later you'll find yourself standing before a TV screen, beer and microphone in hand, with a crowd of drunkards insisting you sing to the Muzak version of a Beatles hit. Refuse and your Chinese host loses face; comply and you receive applause. Resistance is futile. Most karaoke venues in Beijing are seedy and given over to less-than-legal side entertainment, so if you have any choice in the matter head to **Party World,** also known as the Cash Box (Qian Gui; 🕾 **010/6588-3333;** open 24 hr.), the city's classiest and best-equipped do-it-yourself concert venue. It's located southeast of the Full Link Plaza, at the corner of Chaowai Shichang Jie and Chaowai Nan Jie, and there's another location at Teng Da Da Sha, Xi Zhi Men Wai DaJie (🕾 **010/8857-6566** is the reservation service line for either branch). Cash Box has a hotel-like lobby, pleasantly decorated private rooms, and a wide selection of Western songs, with some even released in the last decade. Prices range from ¥39 to ¥365 ($5.20–$49/£2.60–£24) per hour, depending on the size of the room and night of the week. There's usually a line, so you'll have to give them your name early. You wouldn't want to embarrass yourself anywhere else.

6 Bars

Although most average Chinese still prefer to get drunk at dinner, the Western pub tradition has gained ground among younger locals, and the city boasts a large, ever-growing population of establishments devoted exclusively to alcohol.

Drinking in Beijing occurs in one of several districts, each with its own atmosphere and social connotations. The city's oldest and still most popular drinking district is **San Li Tun,** located between the east second and third ring roads around the Workers' Stadium (Gongren Tiyuchang). The area's name comes from San Li Tun Lu, a north–south strip of drinking establishments a long block east of the Workers' Stadium that at one time contained practically all of the city's bars. Now known as North Bar Street (San Li Tun Jiuba Jie), it has been overshadowed by other clusters of bars in the Xingfu Cun area north of the stadium and scattered around the stadium itself. Bars here are rowdy and raunchy, and packed to overflowing on weekends. Similar watering holes surround the south and west gates of **Chaoyang Gongyuan** (park) to the east, an area the government has tried to promote as the new drinking district because it has fewer residential buildings. The development of **Nuren Jie,** northeast of the Kempinski Hotel, followed a similar logic. Bars and clubs in **Haidian,** the city's university district to the northwest, are clustered around the gates of several universities and cater to a crowd of local English majors and foreign students.

The fastest-growing spot for late-night drinking is the **Back Lakes (Shicha Hai** or **Hou Hai**), a previously serene spot with a few discreetly fashionable bars north of Bei Hai Park. It has exploded into a riot of neon, capped by Lotus Lane. **Nan Luogu Xiang,** to the east of the Back Lakes area, was previously home to only one cafe; now they are wall-to-wall. Perhaps the most notable trend is the resurgence of hotel bars. These are the most appealing and stylish spots in Beijing, most notably **Centro** (Kerry Centre), **Red Moon** (Grand Hyatt), and **Cloud Nine** (Shangri-La).

Beijing bars generally open around 5 or 6pm and stay open until the last patrons leave or the staff decides it wants to go home, usually by 2am on Friday and Saturday nights. Several of the Back Lakes bars double as cafes and open as early as 11am.

Bed Tapas & Bar (Chuang Ba)   The risqué decor of this courtyard bar is the work of a New York designer. All bare concrete, gauze, four-poster beds, and antique furnishings, Bed pushes the boundaries of what constitutes an acceptable leisure space for wholesome Socialist citizens. The olive tapenade is ideal finger food; the sangria and mojito are suitably refreshing. Bed is a block north of its sister establishment, Cafe Sambal, and attracts a similar crowd of design professionals. The rear courtyard is sublime on a warm summer evening. Open 3pm to 2am. Zhangwang Hutong 17 (from Gulou Dajie metro station, head south along Jiu Gulou Dajie, take the 4th lane on your left). ✆ 010/8400-1554.

Face Bar (Fei Si) ☆   Penny-pinching Beijing expats complain about the exorbitant prices for drinks here, but it's still an upscale bar that's far cheaper than Hong Kong or New York. Plus, you get a classy, Southeast Asian–inspired decor that incorporates Buddhist statues. The first bar has an annoying pool table smack in the center of everything, but just bypass that room and head for the outdoor terrace or one of the cozy opium beds. Open 6pm until late. 25 Dongcaoyuan, Gongti Nanlu (just south of Workers' Stadium south gate). ✆ 010/6551-6738.

Lush   Students on a budget love the affordable drinks at this bar, located in Wu Dao Kou, the heart of the student district. By day, the young ones come and pretend to study while they check out who else is there. By night, they come for drinks, dancing, and debauchery. Sunday open-mic nights are a big hit. Open 24 hours. 2/F, Building 1, Huaqing Jia Yuan. ✆ 010/8286-3566. Metro: Wu Dao Kou.

Palace View Bar (Guan Jing Jiuba)   The best panorama in Beijing. If you can bear Celine Dion on continuous rotation, do not miss this largely undiscovered rooftop bar. With nothing but air between yourself and the Imperial City, you probably won't be perturbed by banal music or by drink portions that put the teeny back in martini. Open May through September, daily 5:30 to 9:30pm. Rooftop of Grand Hotel. ✆ **010/6513-7788,** ext. 458. Metro: Wangfujing (118, exit A).

Pass-By Bar (Guoke Jiuba)   Relocated in a restored courtyard house down a *hutong* east of Qian Hai in 2002, Tibetan-themed Pass-By is more gathering place than nightspot, with an extensive English-language library, a useful message board, and rotating photo exhibits on the walls. There's great Italian food by a chef stolen from Annie's (p. 95), free Wi-Fi, and a separate nonsmoking section—almost unheard-of in a Beijing bar. The courtyard is idyllic in the summertime. Open 9:30am to 2am. Nan Luogu Xiang 108 (Back Lakes; alley is to left/west of a Muslim restaurant on the north side of Ping'an Dadao; walk north 150m/492 ft.). ✆ **010/8403-8004.**

Press Club Bar (Jizhe Julebu)   The nearby Beijing International Club, renowned in a previous bygone era as the meeting spot for foreign correspondents, inspired this upscale bar inside the St. Regis Hotel. The elegant space, with leather-bound tomes, marble fireplace, leather armchairs, and brocade sofas, seats just 55. Old prints and vintage photos of Beijing pundits and reporters from days past line the long bar. Open 4:30pm to 1am. Jianguomen Wai Dajie 21 (at rear of St. Regis's main building). © 010/6460-6688. Metro: Jianguomen.

Q Bar 🐈🐈 Don't be put off by the drab interior of the hotel that houses Q Bar. The bar, located on the top floor, is an oasis of style, with dim lighting, lounge music, and a long bar nestled against a window with panoramic views. Here you will find the best martinis in town. Unfortunately, the love and devotion owners George and Echo pour into those drinks often translate into slow service. The expansive rooftop seating is fantastic and DJs spin lounge and house music on weekends. Open 6pm to 2am. Nan Sanlitun Lu (on top floor of Eastern Inn Hotel). © 010/6595-9239. Metro: Nong Zhan Guan.

Stone Boat Bar 🐈🐈 This is our favorite place for a Sunday afternoon coffee and a game of Scrabble . . . but also our favorite evening spot for live music, ranging from local drumming groups to experimental ambient music. This little gem by the lake in Ritan Park also features a tiny upstairs alcove great for romantic dates. Southwest corner of Ritan Park (south end of the lake). © 010/6501-9986.

The Tree (Yinbi de Shu) Uprooted from South Bar street, the former Hidden Tree sports a new tree but is slightly more tranquil than its former incarnation. It still offers an unmatched selection of Belgian beer: Trappist and abbey ales, lighter wild-fermented lambics, and several wheat (white) beers. The stock changes, but there's always bottled Chimay and draft Hoegaarden. Passable single-malts, cigars, thin-crust pizzas, and a pleasant but unpretentious brick and wood interior complete the picture. West of San Li Tun North Bar St. (behind Poachers Inn). © 010/6415-1954. Metro: Gongti Bei Lu.

World of Suzie Wong (Suxi Huang) Named for the fictional Hong Kong hooker who falls for a much older William Holden (ironic given the current dynamic of the bar), this is the see-and-be-seen venue for nouveau-riche Chinese and newly arrived expatriates. DJs so cool it hurts play music for head-bobbers in the main room, and there's a Ming-style canopy bed next to the bar where the exhibitionists sit. Get there early to stake out one of the row of semi-private alcoves to the side, luridly lit and luxuriously outfitted with plush couches covered in brocaded pillows. The rooftop seating makes for a cool getaway during summer months. West gate of Chaoyang Park. © 010/6593-6049.

7 Cafes & Other Drink Spots

Just like the Manchurian hordes did 3½ centuries earlier, **Starbucks** swept into Beijing in the 1990s and quickly conquered it. Branches are everywhere, including the China World complex, the Oriental Plaza, the Pacific Century Plaza near San Li Tun, and a myriad of other places. They were, however, recently driven out of the inner court of the Forbidden City. By far the city's most popular coffee chain, it is particularly beloved of young local women in search of eligible expatriates. But there are other options (see below), many of which offer a better brew.

Despite the coffee invasion, Beijing is still ultimately tea territory, and the most pleasant sipping experiences can be found in small teahouses scattered about the city.

The Bookworm (Lao Shu Chong) Come here for a quiet read—better yet, there's no need to bring your own book. This San Li Tun fixture, recently forced to move by developers, boasts a library of 6,000 English-language titles, including most of the works recommended in chapter 2. The new venue, which was undergoing the finishing touches at press time, will have three separate sections: a European restaurant which will house the library, a cafe, and a kids' corner which should also house a new bookshop. Open 9am to 2am. Nan San Li Tun Lu Si Lou (behind Pacific Century shopping center, near The Loft). *C* 010/6586-9507. Metro: Gongti Bei Lu.

Comptoirs de France (Fa Pai)   The best place to stock up on chocolate and calories. Apart from perfect chocolate truffles, this cafe also makes the best opera slices and strawberry tarts in town. And they serve excellent coffee to boot! The location at China Central Place is more charming than the Dongzhi Men cafe, but go to whichever one is closest to you—you won't be disappointed. Open 7am to 9pm. 102 China Central Place, 89 Jianguo Lu (on the left side of the main walkway heading into the apartment complex). *C* 010/6530-5480. Other location at East Lake Club, 35 Dongzhi Men Wai Dajie; *C* 010/6461-1525. Metro: Dongzhi Men.

Gustamenta   This is the best place in town to get gelato. They're on the northern end of Sanlitun Bar Street, perfectly placed to satisfy those midnight sweet tooth cravings. They also serve a mean espresso. Open daily 9am to 2am. 24 Sanlitun Lu. *C* 010/6417-8890. Other location at 1301 SOHO New Town (daily 7am–midnight); *C* 010/8580-5111. Metro: Nong Zhan Guan.

Sculpting in Time (Diaoke Shiguang)   This was once Beijing's most famous film cafe, but it's since lost that title to Box Cafe (see section 3 of this chapter) when it moved from its location in a charming (now demolished) *hutong* east of Peking University. Now at the Beijing Institute of Technology, it seldom shows films but is still popular with students, foreign and Chinese both. A second branch south of the main entrance to Fragrant Hills Park (*C* 010/8259-0040), has a pleasant remoteness and a large outdoor deck with views of the park, while the largest branch, just west of Wudaokou metro stop (*C* 010/8286-7025), has less charm but is handy to the university district. This coffee shop is on the rise, and they have a total of seven branches throughout the city. All serve adequate coffee and Western snacks, and have wireless Internet. Open daily from 9am to 12:30am. Weigongcun Xi Kou 7 (Ligong Da Nan Men), just to left of the university's south gate. *C* 010/6894-6825.

Tasty Taste (Taidi Daisi)   Don't be deterred by the corny name, or the half-hearted decor, for here is some of the best coffee in Beijing. In a town where innumerable crimes are committed against the bean, it's a relief to find Italian espresso without any bitter aftertaste from poorly cleaned machines, milk frothed just so rather than tortured to produce enormous bubbles, and even cocoa powder and cinnamon served on the side with your cappuccino. Open 9am to midnight. Gongti Bei Men (on the southwest corner of Gongti Bei Lu and Gongti Xi Lu). *C* 010/6551-1822.

The Teahouse of Family Fu (Cha Jia Fu)   Located in a unique octagonal building on the south bank of Hou Hai, the Fu family's teahouse is among the city's most charming, furnished throughout with a pleasantly haphazard assortment of Ming reproduction furniture. Owned by a former mechanics professor and run with help from his friendly English-speaking mother, it sometimes plays host to poetry readings, lectures, and classical Chinese music performances. Teas are reasonably priced at ¥50 to ¥152 ($6.65–$20/£3.35–£10) for a pot with unlimited refills, presented on a fan. There are also free snacks. Semi-private rooms branch off to all sides. Open from 10:30am to midnight. Hou Hai Xibei An (northwest side of Hou Hai, next to Kong Yiji). *C* 010/6616-0725.

Zuo You Jian (Mima Cafe)   The coffee and cuisine are just passable, but if you need a touch of serenity, visit Mima on a weekday afternoon or a summer evening. Located just north of the east gate of Yuan Ming Yuan (p. 140), outdoor courtyard seating is covered over by rice paper domes, set around clusters of bamboo. The washroom is the most stunning we have ever encountered, and worth the trek in itself. Open daily from 10am to midnight. Yuan Ming Yuan Dong Men Nei Bei Liu Jian Yuan. © 010/ 8268-8003.

11

The Great Wall & Other Side Trips

The hills around Beijing are dotted with fascinating sights, the foremost, of course, being the **Great Wall.** Many of the sights listed in this chapter can be seen in a single excursion, which can include other sights just on the outskirts of the city. Nearly all organized tours include a stop at the **Ming Tombs** on the way to the Great Wall at **Ba Da Ling** and **Juyong Guan. Tanzhe Si** and **Jietai Si** are readily combined as an agreeable day trip, and the intriguing **Tian Yi Mu** (p. 146), a cemetery for eunuchs on the western outskirts of town, is on the road to the quiet courtyard houses of **Chuan Di Xia.**

Surprisingly, the most enjoyable way to reach many of these sights is by public transportation. Although slower than an organized tour, public bus or train travel is flexible, doesn't drag you to dubious attractions, and costs a fraction of the overpriced tours offered by hotels. If you're short on time, an option is to hire a taxi for the day (see section 2, "Getting Around," in chapter 4). An entertaining (if slightly rushed) choice is to join a Chinese bus tour. Air-conditioned buses for these tours leave when full early in the morning from various metro stations, and make stops at two or three sites. Your last resort should be hiring a car through your hotel or a tour agency for a ludicrous fee.

When heading out of town, avoid weekend mornings when traffic can be gridlocked. Attempting to return on Sunday afternoon is also frustrating. Even on weekdays, allow at least half a day, and usually a full day, to explore the sights listed in this chapter. Have a picnic and take your time.

1 The Great Wall (Wanli Changcheng) ★★★

Even after you dispense with the myths that it is a single continuous structure and that it can be seen from space (it can't, any more than a fishing line can be seen from the other side of a river), China's best-known attraction is still mind-boggling. The world's largest historical site is referred to in Mandarin as **Wanli Changcheng** ("10,000-Li Long Wall" or simply "Very Long Wall"). The Great Wall begins at Shanhai Guan on the Bo Hai Sea and snakes west to a fort at Jiayu Guan in the Gobi Desert. Its origins date back to the Warring States Period (453–221 B.C.), when rival kingdoms began building defensive walls to thwart each other's armies. The king of Qin, who eventually conquered the other states to become the first emperor of a unified China, engaged in large-scale wall building toward the end of his reign, although tales of 300,000 conscripted laborers are embellishments of subsequent dynasties. During the Han dynasty (206 B.C.–A.D. 220), the Wall was extended west, and additions were made in completely different locations, according to the military needs of the day.

Tips **On the Wild Wall**

Travelers with time and the inclination to explore beyond the typical tourist haunts are strongly encouraged to join a trip to the crumbling **"unofficial" sections of the Wall** that snake through more remote areas north of Beijing. William Lindesay, a Briton who has been walking along and writing about the Great Wall since the mid-1980s, organizes excursions for the company **Wild Wall.** Joining one of his tours is the best way to learn about the Wall's construction and destruction, both by human and natural forces, from a knowledgeable source.

Wild Wall is based out of two modernized farmhouses, the first and more fully outfitted just north of Beijing, and the second somewhat more primitive (but still comfortable) in Hebei. Wild Wall's most common weekend trips run 3 days (Fri–Sun) and cost $450 (prices are quoted in U.S. dollars), including guided hikes, two nights' accommodations in a farmhouse, six meals, drinks and snacks, research and conservation contribution and book. Although pricey, these weekend trips are highly recommended and typically take place two or three times a month. Day hikes and strenuous "Extreme Treks" are also available. For details see **www.wildwall.com.**

Although many tour guides will try to persuade you otherwise, the Ming Wall you see today is unrelated to the Qin Wall, which lies far to the north. The Ming even went to the trouble of calling their wall Bian Qiang (Frontier Wall) to avoid comparisons with the tyrannical first emperor of China, Qin Shi Huangdi. The original Wall was built almost entirely from tamped earth, and often crumbled away within decades of being constructed. Talk of satellite mapping the current Wall is fanciful—for most of its length, the structure is barely visible from the ground. This, and the fact that there is no single "Great Wall," makes it impossible to pin down the Wall's precise length.

Those with an interest in exaggerating Chinese xenophobia portray Wall building as an essential part of the national psyche, but after the Han, few dynasties bothered with Wall construction, and relied mostly on trade, diplomacy, and the odd punitive expedition to keep the peace. Even during the inward-looking Ming dynasty, the Wall was viewed by many at court as an ancient version of the Star Wars missile-defense idea—ineffective, absurdly expensive, and successful only in antagonizing China's neighbors. With the Ming wracked by internal rebellion, the Qing armies simply bribed the demoralized sentries. The Qing left the Wall as a monument to folly, and while early Western visitors were awed, it became a source of national pride only recently. Sun Yat-sen was among the first to view it as a symbol of national strength, an idea the Communists adopted, including it in the National Anthem.

The Wall's most easily visited sections are **Ba Da Ling** and **Juyong Guan,** while **Mutianyu, Jin Shan Ling,** and the vertiginous **Simatai** require a full day's outing. Appealing options for overnight stays are **The Red Capital Ranch** at Mutianyu and the more basic **Simatai YHA.**

Side Trips from Beijing

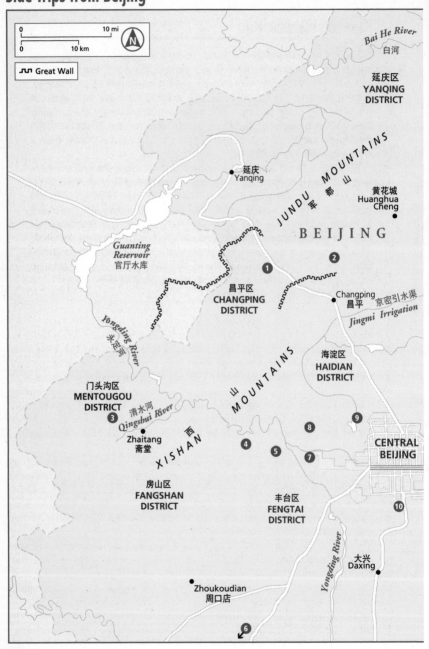

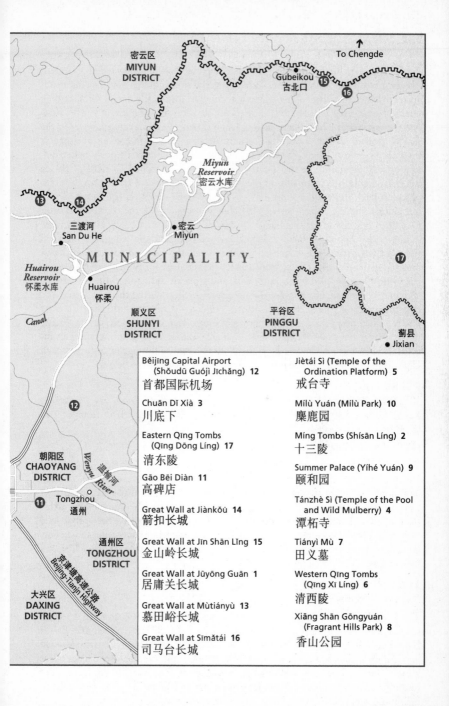

密云区
MIYUN
DISTRICT

To Chengde ↑

Gubeikou
古北口 **15**

16

*Miyun
Reservoir*
密云水库

13   **14**

三渡河
San Du He

密云
Miyun

17

M U N I C I P A L I T Y

*Huairou
Reservoir*
怀柔水库

Huairou
怀柔

Canal

顺义区
SHUNYI
DISTRICT

平谷区
PINGGU
DISTRICT

蓟县
● Jixian

12

朝阳区
CHAOYANG
DISTRICT

Wenyu River
温榆河

11 Tongzhou
通州

通州区
TONGZHOU
DISTRICT

京津塘高速公路
Beijing-Tianjin Highway

大兴区
DAXING
DISTRICT

Běijīng Capital Airport
(Shǒudū Guójì Jīchǎng) **12**
首都国际机场

Chuān Dǐ Xià **3**
川底下

Eastern Qīng Tombs
(Qīng Dōng Líng) **17**
清东陵

Gāo Bēi Diàn **11**
高碑店

Great Wall at Jiànkǒu **14**
箭扣长城

Great Wall at Jīn Shān Lǐng **15**
金山岭长城

Great Wall at Jūyōng Guān **1**
居庸关长城

Great Wall at Mùtiányù **13**
慕田峪长城

Great Wall at Sīmǎtái **16**
司马台长城

Jiètái Sì (Temple of the
Ordination Platform) **5**
戒台寺

Mílù Yuán (Mílù Park) **10**
麋鹿园

Míng Tombs (Shísān Líng) **2**
十三陵

Summer Palace (Yíhé Yuán) **9**
颐和园

Tánzhè Sì (Temple of the Pool
and Wild Mulberry) **4**
潭柘寺

Tiányì Mù **7**
田义墓

Western Qīng Tombs
(Qīng Xī Líng) **6**
清西陵

Xiāng Shān Gōngyuán
(Fragrant Hills Park) **8**
香山公园

THE GREAT WALL AT JUYONG GUAN
59km (37 miles) NW of Beijing

Just before you get to the madness of Ba Da Ling, the most touristed and tacky section (we don't recommend it), lies this relatively peaceful stretch of the Wall. The most conveniently accessed section of the Wall is also the most historically significant. Guarding one of the two crucial passes to Beijing (the other is to the northeast, at Gu Bei Kou) and the vast North China Plain, **Juyong Guan (Dwelling in Harmony Pass)** was the site of pitched battles, involving Jurchen, Mongol, and, more recently, Japanese invaders. There may have been fortifications here as early as the 6th century, before Beijing existed. Climbing the steep section to the left offers marvelous views of Ba Da Ling, snaking up the mountains to the north, and south toward Beijing (in the event of a clear day). Restorations from 1993 to 1997 created over 4km (2½ miles) of wall, but railings mar the effect; there's little feeling of antiquity. All the construction must have eaten into the advertising budget, as crowds are thinner here than at Ba Da Ling.

It's worth stopping at Juyong Guan to view the ancient and remarkable **Yun Tai (Cloud Platform)** ✺✺✺, which once stood astride the old road running northwest into Mongol territories. Dating from 1342, it was the base for three Tibetan-style stupas, which were toppled by an earthquake and replaced during the Ming dynasty by a Chinese-style Buddhist temple, also destroyed (by fire) during the early Qing. The central tunnel is carved with elephants, Buddha figures demonstrating different *mudra* (hand positions), the four heavenly kings, and six different scripts. Facing north, the languages on the right-hand wall are Chinese, Xi Xia (the script of a vanished Tibetan race, decimated by Genghis Khan's armies during the 14th century), Uighur, and Mongolian. The top script is Sanskrit, with Tibetan below.

ESSENTIALS
VISITOR INFORMATION   The ticket office at Juyong Guan (✆ **010/6977-1665**) is open daily from 8am to 5pm. Admission is ¥45 ($6/£3) in summer, ¥40 ($5.35/£2.65) in winter.

GETTING THERE   A round-trip **taxi** should cost less than ¥200 ($27/£13).

WHERE TO STAY   Giving the Red Capital Ranch (see below) a run for its money is the newly opened **The Commune** (✆ **010/8118-1888;** www.commune.com.cn). This hotel's stunning architecture and location near the Great Wall make it a perfect place to retreat from the city. The 12 original villas designed by international architects are often rented for lavish parties while copies of the homes have been subdivided into more affordable hotel rooms. A large kids' club offers free babysitting and an outdoor wading pool. Doubles run for ¥1,650 to ¥2,600 ($220–$347/£110–£173) and include breakfast. Exit at Shuiguan, Ba Da Ling Highway.

THE GREAT WALL AT MUTIANYU ✺
90km (56 miles) NE of Beijing

The Great Wall at Ba Da Ling proved so popular that authorities restored a second section of the Wall to the east in 1986. **Mutianyu** is slightly less crowded than Ba Da Ling, but it does have its own traffic jams in summer. Located in a heavily forested area, it's especially photogenic in rainy, misty weather. You can hop over a fence to see more tempting, unrestored sections, but those planning to survey the entire length of restored wall will find themselves with little energy remaining. There is a cable car to help those who need it.

> ## ⌜Tips Travelers with Disabilities
>
> Exploring the Great Wall is tough enough for people in good shape. For those with disabilities, the Wall is a nightmare. At Mutianyu a cable car provides access, but there are still steps to negotiate up to the cable car, and steep steps up to the Wall. There are no elevators or wheelchair assists at any of the sections.

ESSENTIALS

VISITOR INFORMATION   The ticket office (© **010/6162-6505**) is open from 7:30am to 6:30pm. Admission is ¥40 ($5.35/£2.65); the cable car costs ¥50 ($6.65/£3.35) round-trip.

GETTING THERE   Mutianyu is not as easy to reach as Ba Da Ling. Most hotels can arrange **guided group tours** for around ¥250 ($33/£17). The *you* **no. 6** combines a trip to Mutianyu with visits to a temple and a lake; it leaves from the northeast side of the Xuanwu Men (206) metro stop (Sat–Sun 6:30–8am, every 30 min.; ¥50/$6.65/£3.35). The bus stops at Mutianyu for about 3 hours. A **taxi** will cost between ¥200 and ¥400 ($27–$53/£13–£27).

WHERE TO STAY   A popular Great Wall resort lies in a quiet river valley close to Mutianyu at the **Red Capital Ranch** ⌖⌖ (© **010/8401-8886;** $190–$200 including breakfast, plus 15% service charge; Apr–Nov). Similar to the Red Capital Residence (p. 68), all 10 rooms are thoughtfully decorated with antique furnishings. The oddly shaped Yan'an room has considerable charm and a *very* firm bed. The Ranch sits next to a dramatic section of the wall that is good for a challenge; there's a steep drop towards the end to the last tower that should only be attempted by advanced hikers. (*Tip:* You may also choose to hike this section of the wall without staying at the Ranch—arrange your own driver (see Jiankou below) and grab a post-hike tea in the Ranch's lodge.) Fishing, bike riding, and even a Tibetan essential oil massage are offered. A twice-daily shuttle bus connects with the Red Capital Residence.

THE GREAT WALL AT JIN SHAN LING
130km (81 miles) NE of Beijing, 90km (56 miles) SW of Chengde

Located in Hebei Province, this is the least visited and least spoiled of the Wall sections listed in this chapter. **Jin Shan Ling** is 10km (6¼ miles) east of Gu Bei Kou (Old Northern Pass), through which Qing royalty passed on the way to their summer retreat at Chengde (Jehol). The Wall here is in good condition, as it was a recent (after 1570) rebuild of an existing Ming wall, and construction was overseen by the outstanding general, Qi Jiguang. The defensible pass, whose heart lies to the west at Gu Bei Kou, was 27km (17 miles), stretching all the way to Simatai in the east. Bricks are smaller, reflecting advances in wall-building technique. The Wall features unusual circular towers and elaborate defensive walls leading up to towers. Management dreams of tourist hordes—a cable car has been built, along with gradually rusting amusements—but the remoteness of the site makes large-scale tourism unlikely. The walk to **Simatai** (see below) is reason enough to visit.

ESSENTIALS
VISITOR INFORMATION   The ticket office (© **010/8402-4628**) is open 24 hours. Admission is ¥50 ($6.65/£3.35).

GETTING THERE   Appealingly, Jin Shan Ling can be reached by **train** from the Beijing Bei Zhan (North Railway Station), just north of the Xi Zhi Men metro stop (201, exit A). A special tourist train for Gu Bei Kou, the L671 departs daily from mid-April to October at 7:25am (2½-hr. trip; ¥20/$2.65/£1.35). The rest of the year, the slower L815, departing at 8am, will take you there (4-hr. trip; ¥10/$1.35/65p). Returning trains depart at 3:05pm and 4:15pm, respectively. Walking down from the station, you can either find lodgings in the village of Gu Bei Kou Hexi Cun, or take a minivan directly to the Wall (25-min. trip, ¥20/$2.65/£1.35). From Xi Zhi Men bus station, some **buses** to Chengde (daily 6am–5:30pm, about every 20 min.; 2½-hr. trip; ¥46/$6.15/£3.05 for an Iveco or similar) also pass the turnoff, where you face either a 6km (3¼-mile) hike or haggling for a minivan (¥10/$1.35/65p).

WHERE TO STAY   Standard rooms start at ¥140 ($19/£9.35) in the dull but clean **Jin Shan Ling Binguan,** to the right just inside the entrance of the wall. Staying at one of the simple courtyard houses in **Gu Bei Kou Hexi Cun,** just below the railway station, is a cheaper and more appealing option; accommodations are usually ¥10 ($1.35/65p) per person, and home-cooked meals are similarly priced.

THE GREAT WALL AT SIMATAI ✿✿
124km (77 miles) NE of Beijing

Somewhat tamed after a series of deaths led to the closing of its most dangerous stretch, Simatai nevertheless remains one of the best options for those who want more of a challenge from the Great Wall. The most harrowing portion, steep and unrestored, is on the east (right) side of the Miyun Reservoir. Several gravel-strewn spots require all four limbs to navigate. The endpoint is the **Wangjing Ta,** the 12th watchtower. Beyond this is the appropriately named **Tian Qiao (Heavenly Bridge),** a thin, tilted ridge where the Wall narrows to only a few feet—the section that is now off-limits. Despite the danger, Simatai can get rather crowded on weekends, especially since a cable car was installed, and souvenir vendors can be a nuisance. Those who speak Chinese would do well to pretend otherwise, or risk listening to hard-luck stories ("I've walked all the way from Mongolia."). The round-trip hike to Tian Qiao takes 3 hours at a moderate pace. The section of Simatai west of the reservoir is initially better restored and connects to another section of the Great Wall, Jin Shan Ling, in Hebei Province.

ESSENTIALS
VISITOR INFORMATION   The ticket office (© **010/6903-1051**), a 10-minute walk away in a village south of the reservoir, is open 8am to 7:30pm in summer and 8am to dusk in winter. Admission is ¥40 ($5.35/£2.65). The cable car runs from 8am to 5pm, April to November; a round-trip ride to the no. 8 Tower costs ¥50 ($6.65/£3.35), or ¥30 ($4/£2) one-way. Those walking west to Jin Shan Ling will be charged ¥5 (65¢/35p) to cross a bridge.

GETTING THERE   The best no-hassle option is to visit with one of the **Youth Hostelling International tours** (© **010/8188-9323**); these leave the YHAs daily between 7 and 8am and cost ¥150 ($20/£10) for simple transportation. The *you* no. **12** travels to Simatai from northeast of the Xuanwu Men (206) metro stop (Apr to mid-Oct Sat–Sun 6:30–8:30am, every 30 min; ¥70/$9.35/£4.65); you get about 3 hours at the site. A round-trip **taxi** ride should cost less than ¥400 ($53/£27).

WHERE TO STAY   Responding to the popularity of the Jin Shan Ling to Simatai hike, Simatai YHA (✆ **010/8188-9323;** standard room ¥288/$38/£19) opened in 2004. Courtyard-style rooms are basic, but the coffee is world-class, and the view of the Wall from the patio is wonderful.

THE GREAT WALL AT JIANKOU 𝒜𝒜𝒜
70km (44 miles) NE of Beijing

This is our favorite part of the Wall. Few tourist buses make the journey here, and there is no cable car shuttling out-of-shape tourists to the top. Even more amazing, there are no touts selling knickknacks and there is no admission fee (though it's possible that unscrupulous villagers may try to collect one). We've spent plenty of time near here, since we rent a house in the nearby countryside. This section is for serious hikers only. Start at Xin Zhai Zi Cun where the road dead-ends into a parking lot, following the trail up to the Wall. Turn left once you reach the wall, and prepare yourself for an intense five-hour hike. The tallest watchtower in the distance is Jiankou, and just before you reach it, there is a turn-off point that is marked by a flat, paved section of the Wall that leads you back down to the road. From the road, it's a 20-minute walk back to the parking lot.

ESSENTIALS
VISITOR INFORMATION   This is pure, unadulterated Wall, so there is no ticket office. Villagers charge ¥5 (65¢/35p) for parking, and may tack on ¥10 to ¥20 ($1.35–$2.65/65p–£1.35) per person, but you can decline to pay all but the parking fee. Open 24 hours. Bring your own lunch. Bottled water is usually available at the parking lot—bring plenty of water for the hike.

GETTING THERE   Since it's a remote location, you'll have to arrange a private car. Have your hotel concierge arrange a driver, or have them call one of two drivers: Mr. Liu (✆ **0/13661162308**) or Mr. Zhang (✆ **0/13501189730**) (neither speaks English, so you may need your concierge to help ring them up). The return trip takes 4 hours (plus figure in 5 hours of wait time for your hike) and will cost ¥500 ($67/£33), more if arranged by your hotel.

WHERE TO STAY   Many small peasant homes at the base of the mountain (near the parking lot) offer accommodations, but we don't recommend any in particular as the area is rather rustic. If you'd like to overnight, your best bet is to head to Mountain Bar Lodge (✆ **010/8989-7738;** Hong Zun Yu Yi Tiao Gou; www.ourshanba.com), 30 minutes away from Jiankou, on the return trip to Beijing. The Chinese resort offers small chalets perched on a hill and excellent fare at its massive, meandering restaurant that serves up to 1,000 people per night. Try the excellent barbecued pork ribs *(kao zhupai)* and the mixed eggplant, potato, and green peppers *(disanxian)*.

2 Ming Tombs (Shisan Ling)
48km (30 miles) NW of Beijing

Of the 16 emperors who ruled China during the Ming dynasty (1368–1644), 13 are buried in a box canyon at the southern foot of Tianshou Shan (hence the Chinese name Shisan Ling, the 13 Tombs). The first emperor of the Ming, Hongwu, is entombed in Xiao Ling, near Nanjing. The location of the second emperor's tomb is uncertain, while the unfilial seventh emperor, who usurped the throne after his brother was taken by the Mongols, was buried near the Summer Palace among the graves of concubines. Despite these omissions, this is the most extensive burial complex of any Chinese dynasty. A red gate sealed off the valley, guards were posted, and no one, not even the emperor, could ride a horse on these grounds. The site was chosen by the Yongle emperor, who also oversaw the construction of the Forbidden City. Protected from the bitter northern winds by a mountain range, the tombs are constructed in conventional fashion, with memorial halls at the front and burial chambers to the rear.

The entrance to the **Ming Tombs,** a long and celebrated **shen dao (spirit way)** is lined with statues of guardian animals and officials. Only three of the Ming Tombs—**Ding Ling, Chang Ling,** and **Zhao Ling**—have been restored, and only one (Ding Ling) has been fully excavated. Many of the buildings mirror Ming palaces found in the city. Because of this, the sight can be boring to people who've had their fill of imperial architecture. The Ming Tombs are at their most charming along the **shen dao** and on the grounds of **unrestored tombs** (free admission). In contrast, the restored tombs are dank, overcrowded, and uninspiring. The Ming Tombs are so unpopular with foreign tourists that they are often excluded from tour-group itineraries.

ESSENTIALS
GETTING THERE   The valley is just off the freeway that goes to Ba Da Ling. Many **Chinese bus tours** to Ba Da Ling also come here, visiting the spirit way and one of the tombs at blinding speed, but if you want time to explore some unrestored tombs (highly recommended), you'll have to make a separate trip. The most comfortable means of public transport is air-conditioned **bus no. 845** from the Chegong Zhuang (202) metro stop (a 5-min. walk north of exit B) to Zhengfa Daxue in Changping (daily, about every 15 min.; 1½-hr. trip; ¥9/$1.20/60p), then cross the street and take **bus no. 314** to the Nan Xin Cun stop (daily, about every 20 min.; 15-min. trip; ¥1/15¢/10p), which is adjacent to the entrance to the spirit way. From there, you can continue north to either Ding Ling Daokou to visit Ding Ling, a further 2km (1¼-mile) walk to the west, or on to the terminus at Chang Ling. It is also possible to take the green-and-white *zhi* (express) version of **bus no. 919** to Zhengfa Daxue from Desheng Men (daily, about every 30 min.; 1-hr. trip; ¥9/$1.20/60p). A **taxi** hired in Beijing should cost less than ¥400 ($53/£27).

EXPLORING THE AREA
The **spirit way (shen dao)** ⚑ (admission Apr–Nov ¥30/$4/£2, Dec–Mar ¥20/$2.65/£1.35; daily 8am till dusk) is not to be missed. The main entrance to the valley is the **Da Hong Men (Great Red Gate),** beyond which is a pavilion housing China's largest memorial stele, and beyond that the spirit way. The path, slightly curved to fool malevolent spirits, is lined on either side with willows and remarkable **carved stone animals** and human figures, considered among the best in China. The statuary includes pairs of camels, lions, elephants, and mythical beasts, such as the *qilin,* a creature of immense virtue referred to as the "Chinese unicorn" even though it has two horns.

The largest and best preserved of the 13 tombs is 4km (2½ miles) ahead: **Chang Ling** (admission ¥45/$6/£3 summer, ¥30/$4/£2 winter; daily 7am–4:30pm), the tomb of the Yongle emperor (reign 1403–1424). The layout is identical to the tomb of the first Ming emperor in Nanjing. It feels like the Forbidden City in miniature, and is perhaps disappointing if you've seen the palace already. Most striking is **Ling'en Dian** ⟨★⟩, an immense hall in which the interior columns and brackets have been left unpainted, creating an eye-catching contrast with the green ceiling panels. Slightly wider than the Hall of Supreme Harmony, Ling'en Dian contains a three-tiered platform and building materials that are superior to those of the Forbidden City.

The 1,195-sq.-m (12863-sq.-ft.) **Underground Palace** at **Ding Ling** (admission ¥65/$8.65/£4.35 summer, ¥45/$6/£3 winter; 8:30am–5pm), rediscovered in 1956, was the burial place of the Wanli emperor (reign 1572–1620), his wife, and his favorite concubine. Construction of the burial chamber commenced before the emperor was 20 years old, making him "the living ancestor" in the words of Ray Huang, author of *1587, A Year of No Significance.* The "palace" is a vast marble vault, buried 27m (89 ft.) underground and divided into five large chambers. It's all a bit disappointing. The corpses have been removed, their red coffins replaced with cheap replicas, and burial objects moved to aboveground display rooms. The original marble thrones are still there, now covered in a small fortune of *renminbi* notes tossed by Chinese visitors hoping to bribe the emperor's ghost. Outside, behind the ticket office, is the respectable **Shisan Ling Bowuguan (Ming Tombs Museum),** with short biographies of all the entombed emperors; several reproduced artifacts; a detailed, wood reproduction of the Ling'en Dian; and a 1954 photo of Mao reclining and reading a newspaper on a half-buried marble incense burner at Chang Ling.

3 Eastern Qing Tombs (Qing Dong Ling) ⟨★⟩⟨★⟩

125km (77 miles) E of Beijing

The **Qing Dong Ling** have been open for more than 20 years but are still little visited despite offering considerably more to visitors than tombs of the Ming. Altogether 5 emperors, 15 empresses, 136 concubines, 3 princes, and 2 princesses are buried in 15 tombs here. The first to be buried was Shunzhi—the first Qing emperor to reign from Beijing—in 1663, and the last was an imperial concubine in 1935. The tomb chambers of four imperial tombs, the **Xiao Ling** (the Shunzhi emperor), **Jing Ling** (Kangxi), **Yu Ling** (Qianlong), and **Ding Ling** (Xianfeng), are open as well as the twin **Ding Dong Ling** tombs (Dowager Empress Cixi and Empress Ci'an). Others of interest include a group site for the Qianlong emperor's concubines.

ESSENTIALS
VISITOR INFORMATION   The tombs are in Zunhua County, Hebei Province (daily 8am–5:30pm summer, 9am–4:30pm winter). The *tong piao,* which offers access to all the tombs, costs ¥120 ($16/£8).

GETTING THERE   A special Qing Dong Ling *you* bus departs from northeast of the Xuanwu Men (206) metro stop (summer only, daily 7:30am; 3-hr. trip; ¥80/$11/£5.35); this gives you about 3 hours at the site. If you want to explore at your own pace, you'll have to hire a cab or take a rickety local bus (daily 6:30am–4:30pm; 3½-hr. trip; ¥24/$3.20/£1.60) to Zunhua from just east of the Dawang Lu metro stop (123, exit C). Alight just before Zunhua at Shi Men Zhen then hire a *miandi* (minivan) to take you the rest of the way (about ¥20/$2.65/£1.35). An assortment of three-wheelers will offer to take you around the site with a first asking price of ¥10 ($1.35/65p).

WHERE TO STAY AND DINE   The **Yuyuan Shanzhuang (Imperial Gardens Mountain Villa; ☎ 0315/694-5348)** is a battered three-star set to the east of the tombs where the asking price for a twin room is ¥288 ($38/£19), about twice what it's worth. Its best feature is the attached Manchurian restaurant, **Qing Yan Lou** (daily 11am–noon and 5–9pm), which offers inexpensive game meats, and delicious green bean flour noodles *(culiu laozha)*.

EXPLORING THE AREA

Although few others are as elaborate, the **Xiao Ling** was the first tomb on the site, and a model for others both here and at the Western Qing Tombs. As here, usually an approach road or **spirit way** may have guardian figures, and the entrance to the tomb itself is usually preceded by a large stele pavilion and marble bridges over a stream. To the right, the buildings used for preparation of sacrifices are now usually the residences of the staff, and hung with washing. Inside the gate, halls to the left and right were for enrobing and other preparations, and now house exhibitions, as usually does each **Hall of Eminent Favor,** at the rear, where ceremonies in honor of the deceased took place. Behind, if open, a doorway allows access past a stone altar to a steep ramp leading to the base of the **Soul Tower.** Through a passageway beneath, stairs to either side lead to a walkway encircling the mound, giving views across the countryside. If the tomb chamber is open, a ramp from beneath the Soul Tower leads down to a series of chambers.

The twin **Ding Dong Ling** ✿✿ tombs have nearly identical exteriors, but Cixi had hers rebuilt in 1895, 14 years after Ci'an's death (in which she is suspected of having had a hand), using far more expensive materials. The main hall contains reproductions of pictures produced in 1903 by Cixi's photo studio within the Summer Palace. Everywhere there are reminders of the Forbidden City, such as the terrace-corner spouts carved as water-loving dragons *(che)*. The interior has motifs strikingly painted in gold on dark wood, recalling the buildings where she spent her last years. There are walls of carved and gilded brick, and superbly fearsome wooden dragons writhe down the columns. After this, the other tombs seem gaudy.

The enclosure of the **Yu Fei Yuan Qin (Garden of Rest)** contains moss-covered tumuli for 35 of the Qianlong emperor's concubines. Another is buried in a proper tomb chamber, along with an empress whom Qianlong had grown to dislike.

The **Jing Ling** is the tomb of Qianlong's grandfather, the Kangxi emperor, and is surprisingly modest given that he was possibly the greatest emperor the Chinese ever had, but that's in keeping with what is known of his character. The spirit way leading to the tomb has an elegant five-arch bridge; the guardian figures are placed on an unusual curve quite close to the tomb itself, and are more decorated than those at earlier tombs. The **Yu Ling** ✿✿✿ has the finest tomb chamber, a series of rooms separated by solid marble doors, with its walls and arched ceilings engraved with Buddha figures and more than 30,000 words of Tibetan scripture. The 3-ton doors themselves have reliefs of bodhisattvas (beings on the road to enlightenment) and the four protective kings usually found at temple entrances. This tomb is worth the trip in its own right.

4 Western Qing Tombs (Qing Xi Ling) ✿

140km (87 miles) SW of Beijing

The Yongzheng emperor broke with tradition and ordered his tomb to be constructed here, away from his father (the Kangxi emperor). His son, the Qianlong emperor, decided to be buried near his grandfather and that thereafter burials should alternate between the eastern (see above) and western sites, although this was not followed consistently. The first tomb, the **Tai Ling,** was completed in 1737, 2 years after the Yongzheng reign. The last imperial interment was in 1998, when the ashes of Aisin Gioro Henry Puyi, the last emperor, were moved to a commercial cemetery here. He and 2 consorts were added to 4 emperors, 4 empresses, 4 princes, 2 princesses, and 57 concubines. The site is rural, more densely forested than the Qing Dong Ling, overlapped by orchards and agriculture, and with chickens, goats, and the odd rabbit to be encountered.

The **Chang Ling** (tomb of the Jiaqing emperor) and **Chong Ling** (tomb of the Guangxu emperor) are also open, as well as the **Chang Xi Ling** with the extraordinary sonic effects of its **Huiyin Bi**—an echo wall where, as the only visitor, you can try out the special effects available only in theory at the Temple of Heaven (p. 127).

ESSENTIALS

VISITOR INFORMATION   The ticket office is open from 8am to 5pm; a *tong piao* (for access to all the tombs) costs ¥90 ($12/£6) and is good for 2 days. There's no access by tourist bus—part of the appeal for most visitors.

GETTING THERE   Take a **bus** to Yixian from the Lize Qiao long-distance bus station (daily 6:50am–5pm, every 15 min.; 3-hr. trip; ¥20/$2.65/£1.35; last bus returns at 4pm), then switch to a minivan *(miandi)* for the 15km (9⅓-mile) ride to the tombs (around ¥20/$2.65/£1.35; ¥100/$13/£6.65 to visit all the tombs), or turn right as you exit the bus station to find bus no. 9 waiting on the first corner (every hour; ¥3/40¢/20p). By **taxi** it's a reasonable day-trip down the Jingshi Freeway from the Southwest Third Ring Road to the turnoff for Gao Bei Dian to the west, and beyond to Yi Xian. It's possible to visit **Marco Polo Bridge (Lu Gou Qiao)** on the way.

WHERE TO STAY   The modest, Manchu-themed **Ba Jiao Lou Manzu Zhuangyuan** lies just east of Tai Ling (© **0312/826-0828;** ¥120/$16/£8 standard room). **Xing Gong Binguan,** near Yongfu Si on the eastern side of the tomb complex (© **0312/471-0038;** standard room ¥150/$20/£10 after discount), was where Manchu rulers stayed when they came to pay their respects. The room constructed in 1748 to house the Qianlong emperor is now rented as two suites for ¥660 ($88/£44 after discount)—though the 1980s decor there now is criminal.

EXPLORING THE AREA

The **Da Bei Lou,** a pavilion containing two vast stelae, is on the curved route to the **Tai Ling.** The general plan of the major tombs follows that of the eastern tombs and, in fact, the **Chang Ling,** slightly to the west, is almost identical, brick for brick, to the Tai Ling, with the addition of a purple-tinged marble floor. The Jiaqing empress is buried just to the west on a far smaller scale in the **Chang Xi Ling,** the tomb mound a brick drum. But the perfectly semicircular rear wall offers the whispering gallery effects found at some domed European cathedrals, and clapping while standing on various marked stones in the center of the site produces a variety of multiple echoes, while speech is amazingly amplified. The empress can't get much peace.

Jiaqing's son, the Daoguang emperor, was meant to be buried at Qing Dong Ling, but his tomb there was flooded. The relocated **Mu Ling** appears much more modest than those of his predecessors. No stele pavilion or spirit way, largely unpainted, and the tomb mound is a modest brick-wall drum, but this is the most expensive tomb: Wood used to construct the exquisite main hall is fragrant *nanmu,* sourced from as far away as Myanmar. The Guangxu emperor was the last to complete his reign (although

Cixi, who died the next day, is again suspected of shortening it), and his **Chong Ling,** which has the only tomb chamber that is open, uses more modern materials than other tombs. It wasn't completed until 1915, well after the last emperor's abdication.

Several other rather battered tombs are open, and more are being opened, including the **Tai Ling Fei Yuan Qin,** a group of concubine tumuli, individually labeled with the years in which the concubines entered the Yongzheng emperor's service and their grades in the complex harem hierarchy.

The ashes of **Puyi** (properly known as the Xuantong emperor) lie buried on the eastern end of the site, up a slope behind a brand-new Qing-style memorial arch *(pailou),* and behind a shoddy, modern carved balustrade.

5 Tanzhe Si & Jietai Si ⟨★

Tanzhe Si 48km (30 miles) W of Beijing; Jietai Si 35km (22 miles) W of Beijing

Buried in the hills west of Beijing, **Tanzhe Si (Temple of the Pool and Wild Mulberry)** and **Jietai Si (Temple of the Ordination Platform)** are the tranquil kinds of Chinese temples visitors imagine before they actually come to China. These temples were unusual because they received imperial support (Qing rulers preferred Tibetan Buddhism), and both have long been popular with local pilgrims. They were also loved by early Western residents, who rented out halls inside the temples.

ESSENTIALS
VISITOR INFORMATION   Admission to Tanzhe Si (✆ **010/6086-2505**) is ¥35 ($4.65/£2.35), and the ticket office is open from 8am to 5pm in summer (8:30am–4:30pm in winter). Admission to Jietai Si (✆ **010/6980-6611**) is ¥35 ($4.65/£2.35), and the ticket office is open Monday through Friday from 8am to 5pm; weekends until 5:30pm.

GETTING THERE   Both temples are easily accessible by taking **bus no. 931** from the Pingguo Yuan (103) metro stop to **Tanzhe Si** (daily 7am–5:30pm, about every 30 min.; 1-hr. trip; ¥2.50/35¢/15p). At the far western end of Line 1 at the Pingguo Yuan metro stop (exit D), take a right and continue straight a few minutes to the bus station (be sure to take the plain red-and-beige, rather than the red-and-yellow *zhi* version of the bus). At Tanzhe Si, the last stop on this line, hike up the stone path at the end of the parking lot. From there, take **bus no. 931** east 13km (8 miles) to **Jietai Si,** where you reach the site by walking uphill from the bus stop. On weekends, the *you* **no. 7** tourist bus runs from the northeast corner of Qian Men (Sat–Sun 7–8:30am, every 30 min.; ¥60/$8/£4), but it regrettably includes a stop at the garish Shihua Caves. Round-trip by **taxi** costs less than ¥300 ($40/£20).

WHERE TO STAY   At both temples, basic but acceptable accommodations are available for those who want (or need) to spend more time in quietude.

EXPLORING THE AREA
Tanzhe Si ★★, set in peaceful forested grounds, dates back to the Western Jin dynasty (265–316), well before Beijing was founded. In the main courtyard on the central axis is a pair of 30m (100-ft.) ginkgo trees, supposedly planted in the Tang dynasty (618–907), as well as several apricot trees, cypresses, peonies, and purple jade orchids. The complex is extensive, and is said to have provided a model for the layout of the Forbidden City. Above and to the right of the main courtyard lies a rare **stupa yard** *(ta yuan),* stone monuments built in different styles over a period of several centuries

and housing the remains of eminent monks. The **Guanyin Dian,** at the top of the western axis, was favored by Princess Miao Yan, a daughter of Kublai Khan; she is said to have prayed so fervently here that she left footprints in one of the floor stones (now stored in a box to the left). The main object of interest to local visitors is the **stone fish** *(shi yu)* to the left and behind this hall. Rubbing the relevant part of the fish is said to cure the corresponding malady. Everyone seems to rub its stomach.

The **ordination platform** *(jietai)* at **Jietai Si** ✿, China's largest, is a three-tiered structure with 113 statues of the God of Ordination placed in niches around the base; it's located in the **Jie Tan Dian (Hall of the Altar of Ordination)** in the far right (northwest) corner of the temple. It looks, as novelist Ann Bridge put it, "like a very high four-poster bed." Ceremonies conducted on this platform to commemorate the ascension of a devotee to full monkhood required permission from the emperor. Often referred to as the "Beida [Peking University, nominally the best university in China] of Buddhism" for its ability to attract the most promising monastic scholars, along with temples in Quanzhou and Hangzhou, it has been the most significant site for the ordination of Buddhist monks for 900 years. Surrounding courtyards have ancient, twisted pines (as venerable as the temple itself) and fragrant peony gardens.

6 Chuan Di Xia

100km (62 miles) W of Beijing

Originally called **Cuan Di Xia (Under the Stove),** this tiny village of around 100 is an ideal 2-day trip for those with a passion for Chinese vernacular architecture or keen to experience life in rural China. Set in a narrow valley off the old trade route to Shanxi, Chuan Di Xia has the best-preserved *siheyuan* **(courtyard houses)** in the Beijing region. Opened to tourism in 1997, more than 70 dwellings are said to be here.

The impressive dwellings were designed by scholar-officials from the Ming who fled to this remote village toward the end of the dynasty. There they lived out one of the most pervasive legends in Chinese literature, that of the Peach Sanctuary (Taohua Yuan). Inhabitants live peacefully in a hidden rural Arcadia, preserving the traditions of an earlier era. Corn dangles from the eaves of the ancient dwellings, donkeys plow the fields, and the hills are alive with wildflowers.

ESSENTIALS
VISITOR INFORMATION The ticket office (📞 **010/6981-9090**) is open 24 hours. Admission to the village costs ¥20 ($2.65/£1.35).

GETTING THERE From the Pingguo Yuan (103) metro stop, turn right out of the southeast (D) exit and continue for a few minutes to the **bus no. 929** *zhixian* **stop** (the last sign) for the bus to Zhaitang (daily 7am–5pm, every hour; 2½-hr. trip; ¥6/ 80¢/40p). While traveling from the city, you'll leave behind the smokestacks of Shou Gang (Capital Iron and Steel Works, Beijing's number-one polluter). From Zhaitang, **minivans** *(miandi)* (¥10/$1.35/65p) travel to Chuan Di Xia. The last bus returns from Zhaitang at 4:10pm. A *miandi* from Pingguo Yuan costs ¥130 ($17/£8.65) one-way. A **taxi** from Beijing costs ¥400 ($53/£27) round-trip.

WHERE TO STAY For those staying overnight, most lodgings offer basic accommodations (no shower) for ¥50 ($6.65/£3.35), or one bed for ¥15 ($2/£1). We recommend the friendly and freshly renovated **Lao Meng Kezhan,** no. 23 in the lower part of the village (📞 **010/6981-9788**). Their restaurant, which adjoins the rather quiet main road, is an agreeable spot for alfresco dining.

EXPLORING THE AREA

The area is a magnet for artists, poets, and period-drama camera crews; many local tourists are mystified by the lack of karaoke bars and duck boats. One Beijinger asked in frustration, "Is there anything at all to do here?" A local, not much caring for his tone, deadpanned, "Absolutely nothing. You'd better go home."

Wander through the narrow lanes, their walls still showing faded slogans from the 1966–76 Cultural Revolution, including LONG LIVE CHAIRMAN MAO, WORKERS OF THE WORLD UNITE, and USE MAO ZEDONG THOUGHT TO ARM YOUR MINDS. Beyond the village, the path continues to rise, passing an intriguing open-air grain mill before entering groves of peach trees. The next village, **Baiyu Cun,** is around 6km (3¾ miles) northwest. The dwellings of this larger settlement are arranged in the more plebeian *pingfang* (bungalow) style.

Appendix A:
Beijing in Depth

by Jen Lin-Liu

1 Beijing Today

The first time I arrived in Beijing, in 1997, a crush of locals pushed and shoved at the arrivals gate in a crumbling little terminal with a spittle-covered floor. I had flown via Hong Kong because there were no direct flights to Beijing from the United States. A decade later, numerous nonstop, direct flights make the journey from America and nearly every developed country in the world, and passengers' first glimpse of Beijing is through a sleek airport terminal designed by British architect Norman Foster.

The changes Beijing has gone through in the past decade are staggering. The city buzzes with a dynamism that few cities in the world have. Visitors to Beijing undoubtedly come to see the 5,000 years of history and culture, but they are also lured by the lightening-fast changes that have taken place. Beijing, once abundant with factories and farms, has became a landscape of glass-and-steel skyscrapers, cosmopolitan restaurants and cafes, and elevated highways, inevitably choked with traffic.

A city that is going from the status of "developing" to "developed" certainly has had its improvements. People are starting to line up, rather than push and shove, their way onto buses and in ticket lines. More exposure to the western world means that Beijing is becoming a cosmopolitan city, with vibrant and international arts, culinary, and nightlife scenes. And with the Cultural Revolution and Mao's legacy growing ever dimmer in their memories, Beijingers are less paranoid and less swayed by government propaganda than they were in the past.

As you walk through the old neighborhoods you'll see painted on certain ramshackle buildings a character: chai. It means "to tear down" and anything marked with this word will be bulldozed imminently. Much of Beijing's change could only have occurred with the displacement of families from old neighborhoods and the loss of historic architecture. The winners here are government officials and developers, who work hand-in-hand to bump people from their homes and profit from skyrocketing real estate prices. (Though prices, at the moment, still remain relatively cheaper than in most international capitals.)

While much about Beijing has changed on the surface, many things remain the same. In the old neighborhood that I live in, not far from the Back Lakes, vendors on bicycle—selling everything from vegetables to toilet paper to knife-sharpening services—still make the rounds every morning and afternoon. Many Beijingers—and particularly migrants who come to the capital to earn a decent living—still live in substandard conditions. The default mode of transportation for the average city dweller is still the bicycle, families still shop at open markets for their produce and meat, and the average salary hovers around ¥2,000 ($267/£133) per month.

THE POLITICAL LIFE OF BEIJING Sitting at the heart of power, Beijingers are supposedly the nation's most sensitive to subtle changes in the political winds, but these days there is ever-decreasing interest. Officials are almost universally deemed corrupt, and the leadership's gyrations in trying to demonstrate that the capitalism red in tooth and claw to which it now subjects its citizens is actually socialism "with Chinese characteristics" make the supposedly heroic leaders increasingly ridiculous. This is a pensionless "socialism," with no job security, no free medicine or free schooling, massive and growing unemployment (at least double the official figures), and bribes necessary at every turn to get things done. To most young people who missed the vast political movements of the second half of the 20th century, the Communist Party is irrelevant—something that merely gets in the way on the road to a better life.

You'll find no free discussion of such issues in the government-controlled press, of which it is sometimes joked that the only true piece of information is the date. Constant announcements that production is up, that the minorities are happy, and that standards of one kind or another have been improved are usually fair indications that the opposite is true.

Television and print media, largely under government control, are stuck in a time warp. Instructions to study the latest political "theory," such as ex-president Jiang Zemin's "Three Represents," an attempt to pass off the Party's U-turn to capitalism as a development of Marxism, is headline news. China's president Hu Jintao's latest buzzwords are about building a "harmonious society," a phrase often repeated in newspaper articles.

Even five-star-hotel access to the BBC or other foreign news channels (forbidden to ordinary domestic viewers) may suddenly "break down" around important political anniversaries, June 4 in particular. Once the anniversary is safely past, access is mysteriously restored. No view other than that sanctioned by the Party may be broadcast.

Even so, there has been some relaxation of strict media regulations in the leadup to the Olympics. Previously, foreign journalists based in China were required to receive permission from the government to make any reporting trips outside of Beijing. The government now allows foreign journalists to report outside of the capital without prior government approval, and journalists need only the approval of the person or institution they are interviewing. But there are still some caveats. The autonomous regions of Tibet and Xinjiang are still restricted, the loosening of the rules only applies to foreign journalists rather than the domestic press, and nobody knows if the relaxation of the rules will continue after the Olympics.

Some foreign bodies have been chillingly compliant with Communist Party restrictions. International Olympic Committee Vice President Kevan Gosper, in a interview on China Central Sports, told his shocked interviewer that the Australian press would just "make up stories." China, by contrast, was praised for its skill in "the management of information." Also, the Internet company Yahoo has handed over confidential information about its users at the request of the Communist government.

A CONSUMER SOCIETY Until the 1980s it seemed that everyone was in uniform. The very rare young man wearing a pair of jeans might as well have been carrying a big banner saying "counter-revolutionary." Blue or green "Mao" suits (*Zhongshan fu*) or uniforms provided by work units (employers) were the norm for both sexes.

But as soon as she was permitted to do so, Miss Beijing gradually removed her peaked cap, shook down her tresses, and went wild. From the sighting of the first pair of high heels and the return of the skirt, hemlines crept up from calf to nearly waist level and stayed there. Colors went from khaki to clashing neons, simply because they could. Bus conductresses, now able to own more than just their uniforms, could be found selling tickets in spangled Lycra more suitable for the primitive discos that were sprouting up.

Things have now settled down, but anything goes, including dresses diaphanous enough to reveal more than a glimpse of stocking. The male, on the other hand, has remained dowdy, and seems to have swapped one uniform for another.

As late as the early 1990s, foreign residents would coo with delight at the sight of milk and butter in the Friendship Stores, which only accepted hard-currency vouchers and which Chinese were not permitted to enter. Now most Western fashion labels have Beijing outlets, as do supermarkets, fast-food chains, and luxury-car suppliers. Numerous foreign companies sucked in by the promise of fast growth are making a loss or a far from respectable return on their investment. But they comfort each other in their far-sightedness, and wait for the economic miracle repeatedly promised in the press.

EVERY MAN FOR HIMSELF Beijingers expect to be cheated both by their rulers and by each other. They complain bitterly, but they have no hesitation in cheating others when they can wangle a university place for an academically unsuccessful child because of a favor owed, when they can get access to rail tickets at peak periods because an uncle works at the station, or when they barter their own access to some privilege for something else they want. When they need something, their first question is not "Where do I line up?" but "Who do I know?" The Chinese expression *xian lai, xian chi,* means "first to come, first to eat." This suggests not the idea of forming a fair lineup, but the necessity of barging to the front.

Complaints about government corruption and the privileges reserved for cadres are not usually based on a general moral principle, but on not getting a slice of the pie. Sympathy for others tends to extend no further than immediate family members, close friends, and those with whom the Chinese have *guanxi*—people who owe them or to whom they owe favors. Everyone else is just in the way and is often simply pushed out of it, as you will discover when you try to board a bus, line up to buy a ticket, or stand at any junction and observe the driving.

2 Religion

Freedom to practice religion is enshrined in the Chinese constitution. In reality, of course, this right is subject to frequent and occasionally violent suspension—during times of political upheaval like the Cultural Revolution (1966–76) or, as

Dateline

- **930–1122** A provincial town roughly on the site of modern Beijing becomes the southern capital of the Khitan Mongol Liao dynasty, thousands of kilometers from the ancient centers of early Han Chinese empires.
- **1122–1215** The city is taken over by the Jurchen Tartar Jin dynasty, first as Southern Capital, then Central Capital, as its empire expands.

- **1267–1367** The Mongol Yuan dynasty, having conquered most of Asia and eastern Europe, rebuilds the city on the modern site as the capital Khanbalik; Da Du (Great Capital) in Mandarin; Cambulac in Marco Polo's account of the city.
- **1273–1292** Marco Polo, his father, and his uncle are in China, much of the time in Khanbalik. Polo's ghostwrit-

ten account of the capital captures the imagination of European readers for several centuries afterward.

- **1368** The Ming dynasty, having driven out the Mongols, establishes its capital at Nanjing. Da Du becomes Beiping (The Pacified North).
- **1420** The Yongle emperor, third of the Ming, returns the city to capital status, the

continues

in the case of Tibetan Buddhism and the banned spiritual movement Falun Gong, when specific groups are thought to pose a threat to Communist rule. Despite this, China has maintained what must rank among the world's most eclectic collection of religious traditions, encompassing not only native belief systems—Confucianism and Daoism—but Buddhism, Islam, and several strains of Christianity as well.

Those on tours of Chinese temples, churches, and mosques in the 1980s and early 1990s were wise to exercise a robust skepticism. The monks and nuns you encountered were invariably a specially selected bunch, likely to bombard foreigners with tales of how wonderfully supportive the government was. And the prettiest and best-restored temples were often barely more than showpieces, where it seemed incense was burned only to cover the sour smell of an Epcot-style cultural commodification.

But as faith in Communism wanes (to the point where some Chinese use the greeting *tongzhi,* or comrade, with thinly veiled sarcasm), religious buildings are slowly recovering their vitality as places of genuine worship, sources of guidance in the moral vacuum of a new market-driven society.

Maps of pre-Communist Beijing show an astoundingly large number of religious structures, from the grandest of glazed-tile complexes in the city's imperial quarter to hundreds of tiny shrines nestled in the maze of *hutong.* Most were destroyed or converted to other uses immediately following the Communist victory in 1949 and during the Cultural Revolution. Several dozen more have been bulldozed as part of modern reconstruction efforts, and all but the most prestigious will probably disappear in the future.

China has always been a secular state, but as in European capitals prior to the 20th century, the line between religion and government in Ming- and Qing-era Beijing was usually blurred. The most direct example is the **Lama Temple (Yonghe Gong),** an immense imperial residence-turned-temple that houses a ritual urn used during the reign of the Qing Qianlong emperor to determine reincarnations of the Dalai Lama, leader of the dominant Buddhist sect in distant Tibet.

The tradition continues today, with Communist leaders playing a controversial role in selecting the most recent Panchen Lama (second from the top in the Tibetan Buddhist hierarchy) and threatening to do the same after the death of the current Dalai Lama, the exiled Tenzin Gyatso.

CONFUCIANISM

The moral philosophy said to have originated with Kongzi—a 5th-century-B.C.

better to repel attacks by the Mongols from the north. He becomes the first Chinese emperor to reign from Beijing, and the first to give it that name: "Northern Capital." Ming dynasty Beijing is overlaid on the Yuan foundations, and the Forbidden City and Temple of Heaven are constructed.

- 1549 Mongol horsemen fire a message-bearing arrow

into a Chinese general's camp saying that they will attack Beijing the following year. Despite this advance announcement, they duly make their way up to the city walls as promised. So much for the Great Wall.

- 1550 In response to Mongol attacks, a lower southern extension to the city wall is begun, eventually enclosing the commercial district, the

important ceremonial sites of the Temple (Altar) of Heaven and Altar of Agriculture, and a broad swath of country-side (which remains free of buildings well into the 20th century). The whole system of walls is clad in brick. Beijing remains largely the same for the next 400 years, when casual and organized destruction begins with the Republic

figure also known as Kong Fuzi (Latinized to "Confucius" by Jesuit supporters enthusiastic about his "family values")—is not really a religion or even a well-defined thought system. Indeed, there is no word in Chinese for Confucianism but only *ru*, a rather vague term that connotes scholarship and refinement. The ideas about proper conduct and government as remembered by Kongzi's disciples in works like the *Lunyu (Analects)* have nevertheless exerted more influence on China than either Buddhism or Daoism and have proven more resilient than anything written by Marx or Mao.

The *Analects* offer pithy observations on dozens of topics ("Those who make virtue their profession are the ruin of virtue," "The noble person is not a pot," and so on), but the three most important concepts are filial piety, proper execution of ritual, and humanity toward others. Confucius has little trust in Heaven or nature. The ultimate concern is with tangible human relationships: those of the son with the father, the subject with the emperor, and friends with each other. These relationships are rigidly defined, and acknowledgement of them is the highest virtue. Chinese rulers recognized early on that this philosophy was perfectly suited to governing their vast empire. Mastery of Confucian classics, proven through a series of increasingly difficult Imperial Examinations, was a prerequisite for all government officials up until the very end of the 19th century.

Confucian ideas were denounced as "feudal thought" after the Communists took over, but visitors to Beijing need only go as far as a restaurant to realize how little this has meant. At any large table, diners will take seats according to their relationship with the host, toasts will be carried out with ritual precision, and forms of address will vary depending on who is speaking to whom. The Imperial Examinations, too, have been resurrected in the nationwide College Entrance Exam, success in which is considered vital to any young person's future. Some students even study for the exam at **Guo Zi Jian** (the old Imperial College) in northeast Beijing while their parents burn incense for them next door at the **Kong Miao,** the second largest Confucian temple after the one in Confucius's hometown of Qufu in Shandong Province.

Although even the most modern Chinese display an attachment to family and ritual, cynical observers note that the emphasis on humanity seems to have disappeared. It is debatable, however, whether this was ever as forceful an idea in China as Confucius wanted it to be.

DAOISM

China's only native-born religion, Daoism (Taoism) began, like Confucianism, as a

and is hastened under the People's Republic.

- **1601–1610** After years of campaigning, Italian Jesuit Matteo Ricci finally receives permission to reside in Beijing and stays until his death, founding an influential Jesuit presence that survives well into the Qing dynasty.
- **1644–1911** As peasant rebels overrun the capital, the last Ming emperor is driven to suicide by hanging himself from a tree in what is now Jing Shan Park, behind the Forbidden City. Shortly afterward, the rebels are driven out by invading Manchu forces, whose Qing dynasty transfers its capital from Manchuria to Beijing, absorbing China into its own empire. Chinese are expelled from the northern section of the city, which becomes the home of Manchu military and courtiers. The southern section becomes the Chinese quarter of Beijing.
- **1793–1794** George III's emissary to the Qianlong emperor visits China and passes through Beijing, staying outside the city at a vast area of parks and palaces. His requests for increased trade and for a permanent trade

continues

philosophical response to the chaos and bloodshed prevalent in China during the Warring States period (403–221 B.C.). It later split into several schools, certain of which absorbed elements of folk religion and concentrated on alchemy and other practices it was hoped would lead to immortality. With its emphasis on change and general distrust of authority, Daoism was the antithesis of Confucianism and remained largely on the fringes of Chinese civil society, more at home in the mountains than in the cities.

The oldest Daoist texts are the esoteric *Dao De Jing* (or *Tao Te Ching,* "Classic of the Way and Virtue") and the *Zhuangzi,* a prose book sometimes compared in its sly playfulness with the work of Nietzsche. Both deal with the Way *(Dao),* a broad philosophical concept also mentioned by Confucius but described in a wholly different manner. In the *Dao De Jing,* ostensibly written by a quasi-mythical figure named Laozi, the Way is more gestured at than defined, as in the famous opening line: "The way that can be spoken of/Is not the constant way."

The Daoists' dismissal of language, their habit of asking absurd questions, and their frequent self-contradictions are attempts to shake readers free of reason, which is said to obscure an understanding of the Way because it seeks to impose a rigid framework on a universe that is constantly changing.

Despite the *Dao De Jing*'s remarkable global popularity as a deep source of mystical truths, one scholar, D. C. Lau, makes a convincing case that the book is best understood as a simple survival manual, its support for strength-in-supplication designed to help powerless Chinese avoid having their heads cut off at a time when such brutality was not at all uncommon.

There has been a revival of interest in both folk Daoism (particularly in the countryside) and the philosophical side of Daoism in recent years, but this is largely invisible, and visitors who've read the *Tao of Pooh* and *Te of Piglet* are often disappointed by what they find at the few remaining active temples. Daoist complexes like Beijing's immense **Baiyun Guan** are garish and loud, reflecting the religious branch's fondness for magic potions and spells, with little of the contemplative feel most Westerners expect.

BUDDHISM

Buddhism traveled from India through Central Asia and along the Silk Routes to China sometime in the 1st century and began to flourish after a crisis of confidence in Confucianism caused by the fall of the Later Han dynasty (A.D. 25–220). But it would never achieve

---

representative in Beijing are turned down in a patronizing edict written even before he arrives. China has no inkling that Great Britain, and not itself, will soon be the superpower of the day. When the Qianlong emperor dies in 1799, the government is terminally corrupt and in decline.

■ **1858** The Second Opium War sees the Qing and their Chinese subjects capitulating in the face of the superior military technology of "barbarians" (principally the British) for the second time in 16 years. Under the terms of the Treaty of Nanjing, China is forced to permit the permanent residence of foreign diplomats and trade representatives in the capital.

■ **1860** The Qing imprison and murder foreign representatives sent for the treaty's ratification. British and French rescue forces occupy Beijing and destroy a vast area of parks and palaces to the northwest, some of the remnants of which form the modern Summer Palace. The Chinese loot what little the foreigners leave and put most of the area back under the plow. Foreign powers begin to construct diplomatic legation buildings just inside

the same dominance as Confucianism, in large part because of the Buddhists' insistence that they exist beyond the power of the state, the monks' rejection of traditional family relationships, and the populace's xenophobic wariness of a foreign philosophy. Buddhism did become sufficiently pervasive during the Tang dynasty (618–907) to merit its own department in the government, but a neo-Confucian backlash under the succeeding Song dynasty (960–1279) saw it lose influence again. Although it never fully recovered the power it held under the Tang, Buddhism continued to have wide popular appeal and is still China's most prevalent organized religion.

All Buddhists believe human suffering can be stopped by eliminating attachment. But where the older Buddhism of India was a sparse atheistic tradition concerned with little more than the individual's achievement of Nirvana (enlightened detachment and extinction), Buddhism in China gradually absorbed elements of Daoism and local folk religion to become an incredibly complex belief system with various gods and demons, an intricately conceived heaven, several hells, and dozens of bodhisattvas (beings who have attained enlightenment but delay entry into Nirvana out of a desire to help others overcome suffering).

Among the various schools that eventually developed, the most popular was the Pure Land School, a faith-based tradition not unlike Christianity whose followers believe the simple evocation of the name of Amitabha Buddha will result in the devotee's being reborn in the western paradise (the Pure Land), from which it will be easier to attain enlightenment. This tradition is still so popular in China that visitors will hear chants of Amituofo (the Mandarin transliteration of Amitabha) at several temples throughout Beijing. A more revolutionary development was achieved by the Chan school (better known by its Japanese name, Zen), which held that even laypeople could achieve instantaneous enlightenment through a simplified but intense form of meditation.

Buddhist temples in Beijing often contain large images of Milefo (Maitreya, the Future Buddha) depicted in both Chinese (fat and jolly) and Tibetan (thinner and more somber) guises, and of Guanyin (Avalokitesvara, the Bodhisattva of Compassion), a lithe woman in the Chinese style and a multi-armed, multi-headed man in the Tibetan pantheon, now incarnated as the Dalai Lama. The Manchu rulers of China's final dynasty, the Qing (1644–1911), tried to maintain cultural ties with several ethnic groups on

the Tartar City's wall east of the Qian Men.

■ **1900** The Harmonious Fists, nicknamed the Boxers, a superstitious anti-foreign peasant movement, besieges the foreign residents of the Legation Quarter, with the initially covert and finally open assistance of imperial troops. The siege begins on June 19 and is only lifted, after extensive destruction

and many deaths, by the forces of Eight Allied Powers (several European nations, Japanese, and Americans) on August 14. Boxers, imperial troops, Chinese, foreign survivors, and allied soldiers take to looting the city. Payments on a vast indemnity take the Qing a further 39 years to pay in full, although the British and Americans use much of the income to help found

Yan-ching (now Peking) University and other institutions, and to pay for young Chinese to study overseas.

■ **1911** The Qing dynasty's downfall is brought about by an almost accidental revolution, and betrayal by Yuan Shikai, the man the Qing trusted to crush it. He negotiates with both sides and extracts an abdication

continues

the fringes of the Chinese empire, which explains the unusual prevalence of Tibetan Buddhist architecture in Beijing. Most noticeable are the two *dagobas* (Tibetan-style stupas), towering white structures like upside-down ice cream cones, at **Bei Hai Gongyuan** and **Bai Ta Si.**

ISLAM & CHRISTIANITY

Islam entered China through Central Asia in the 7th century, staying mostly in the northwestern corner of the empire, in what is now the Xinjiang Autonomous Region. It was introduced to more central regions through the occasional eastward migration of Xinjiang's Uighur people, and through the arrival of Arab trading vessels in southeastern ports like Quanzhou during the Song dynasty (960–1270), but it failed to catch on with Han Chinese the way Buddhism did. Those Han who did convert are now lumped into a separate ethnic group, the Hui. Beijing's Hui and Uighur populations don't mix as much as their shared religious beliefs might lead you to expect, the former dominating southeastern Beijing around the **Niu Jie Mosque** and the latter kept mostly in a series of constantly shifting ghettos. A visit to the mosque on Niu Jie reveals Chinese Islam to be pretty much the same as Islam anywhere else; the glazed-tile roofs and basic layout resemble those of Buddhist or Daoist temples, but the main hall faces west (toward Mecca) rather than south, women and men pray separately, and there are absolutely no idols anywhere.

The first Christian missionary push to make much headway in China came in the 17th century, when Jesuits, led by Italian Matteo Ricci, sought to convert the country by first converting the imperial court. Ricci and his cohorts wowed the Qing rulers with their knowledge of science, art, and architecture (see Jonathan Spence's *The Memory Palace of Matteo Ricci* for more about this) but ultimately failed to make Catholics of the Manchus. Subsequent missionaries, both Catholic and Protestant, continued the war on Chinese superstition and met with some success, but they were also seen as a nuisance. Christianity was linked with both major popular uprisings in the Qing period—the Taiping Rebellion, led by a man named Hong Xiuquan, who claimed to be Jesus's younger brother; and the Boxer Rebellion, a violent reaction to the aggressive tactics of missionaries in northern China which led to the siege of Beijing's Legation Quarter.

Beijing is particularly leery of Catholics, many of whom refused to join Protestants in pledging first allegiance to the state after 1949 and instead remained loyal to the Pope. Missionaries, it goes without saying, are not allowed in China

---

agreement from the infant emperor's regent and an agreement from the rebels that he will become the first president of the new republic.

- **1915** Yuan Shikai revives annual ceremonies at the Temple of Heaven, and prepares to install himself as first emperor of a new dynasty, but widespread demonstrations and the fomenting of a new rebellion in the south lead him

to cancel his plans. He dies the following year.

- **1917** In July a pro-monarchist warlord puts Puyi back on the throne, but he is driven out by another who drops three bombs on the Forbidden City, only one of which actually explodes on target. The imperial restoration lasts exactly 12 days.
- **1919** Students and citizens gather on May 4 in Tian'an

Men Square to protest the government's agreement that Chinese territory formerly under German control be handed to the Japanese.

- **1924** The "Articles Providing for the Favourable Treatment of the Great Ch'ing [Qing] Emperor after his Abdication" provide for the emperor to continue to live in the Forbidden City pending an eventual move to the Summer Palace.

anymore, but many sneak in as English teachers (a favorite tactic of the Mormons in particular). There are separate churches in Beijing for foreigners, off-limits to Chinese, although foreigners are allowed to attend Chinese services. The Gothic-style church built in 1904 on the site of Ricci's house still stands near the Xuanwu Men metro stop, and replicas of the Jesuits' bronze astronomical devices can be seen at the Ancient Observatory northeast of the main railway station.

Outside of monks and nuns, few Chinese people limit their devotion to a single tradition, instead choosing elements from each as they suit their particular circumstances. "Every Chinese," a popular saying goes, "is a Confucian when things are going well, a Daoist when things are going badly, and a Buddhist just before they die." But even this is a relatively rigid formulation—a Chinese person will often cross religious boundaries in the space of a single day if he thinks his problems merit the effort.

3 Film & Music

FILM

It is a source of frustration to some Chinese filmmakers that foreign audiences are easily duped. The most internationally successful films about China—Ang Lee's *Crouching Tiger, Hidden Dragon,* Zhang Yimou's *Raise the Red Lantern,* Bernardo Bertolucci's *The Last Emperor*—wallow in marketable clichés. The China presented by these films exists almost solely in the simplified past tense, a mélange of incense, bound feet, and silk brocade designed to appeal to foreign notions of the country as unfathomably brutal and beautiful with an interminably long history.

Up until the late 1990s, much of the blame for this belonged to the government, which allowed the export of only those movies unlikely to provoke criti-

cism of the present state of things, regardless of what they said about the past. Recently, however, films that deal with modern China, complex and often comic stories about everything from politics to relationships to harebrained attempts at money-making, have found their way to foreign viewers.

Beijing sits at the center of the Chinese film world and serves as the setting for most of the best films now being produced in China. Many of these cannot be seen even in Beijing itself except at small screenings unlikely to attract the attention of state censors. But those with access to a decent video rental shop will find a few.

Even Blockbuster carries copies of *Shower (Xizao,* 1999), Zhang Yang's at

But in November he is removed by a hostile warlord and put under house arrest, later escaping to the Legation Quarter with the help of his Scottish former tutor.
- **1928** Despite fighting among warlords, many of whom are only nominally loyal to the Republic, the Nationalist Party forces in the south declare Nanjing the capital, and Beijing reverts to

the name of Beiping. In the following years many ancient buildings are vandalized or covered in political slogans.
- **1933** With Japanese armies seemingly poised to occupy Beiping, the most important pieces of the imperial collection of antiquities in the Forbidden City are packed into 19,557 crates and moved to Shanghai. They move again when the Japanese take

Shanghai in 1937, and after an incredible journey around the country in the thick of civil war, 13,484 crates end up with the Nationalist government in Taiwan in 1949.
- **1937** Japanese forces, long in occupation of Manchuria and patrolling far beyond what the treaty permits them, pretend to have come under attack near the Marco Polo

continues

times sappy but ultimately enjoyable story of a Beijing bathhouse owner and his two sons (one of them retarded) struggling to maintain a sense of family despite pressures of modernization. The film's depiction of a doomed *hutong* neighborhood and the comic old characters who inhabit it won smatterings of praise in limited U.S. release and criticism from the Chinese authorities, who claimed it was anti-progress. Director Feng Xiaogang tried and failed to make it big in the U.S. with *Big Shot's Funeral* (*Da Wan,* 2001) featuring a (figuratively and literally) catatonic Donald Sutherland. But in a previous film set in and around Beijing, *Sorry Baby* (*Mei Wan Mei Liao,* 1999), Feng displays a defter touch in a romantic comedy featuring bald-headed comic Ge You at his brilliant best.

Among the earlier generation of films, two that deal specifically with Beijing were big hits at Cannes, and you should have no trouble finding them. *Farewell My Concubine* (*Ba Wang Bie Ji,* 1993), directed by Chen Kaige and starring the talented Gong Li, is a long bit of lushness about a pair of Beijing opera stars more dramatic in their alleged rivalry over a woman than they are on stage. Zhang Yimou's unrelenting primer on modern Chinese history, *To Live* (*Huozhe,* 1994), also with Gong Li, traces the unbelievable tragedies of a single Beijing family

as it bumbles through the upheavals of 20th-century China, from the civil war through the Great Leap Forward and Cultural Revolution and into the post-Mao reform period. More difficult to find (particularly with English subtitles), but very much worth the effort, are 1980s productions of Lao She's darkly satirical works, *The Teahouse* (*Cha Guan,* 1982) and *Rickshaw Boy* (*Luotuo Xiangzi,* 1982).

Only specialty shops will carry *In the Heat of the Sun* (*Yangguang Canlan de Rizi,* 1995), a smart and deceptively nostalgic coming-of-age film about a pack of mischievous boys left to their own devices in Cultural Revolution–era Beijing. Penned with help from celebrity rebel writer Wang Shuo, it was one of the first pictures to break free of the ponderous melodrama that dominated Chinese cinema through most of the 1990s. Life for migrant workers on the margins of Beijing is captured in the bleak but dryly witty *The World* (*Shijie,* 2004), set in The World Park in the southwestern suburbs of Beijing. At times it borders on melodrama, and much of the subtlety is lost in translation, but Jia Zhangke's film craft delivers a satisfying reverie on alienation, fantasy, and trust. If the film inspires you to "see the world without leaving Beijing," take bus 744 from opposite Beijing Railway Station to the terminus.

Bridge, occupy Beiping, and stay until the end of World War II ("The War Against Japanese Aggression" to the Chinese).

■ 1949 Mao Zedong proclaims the creation of the People's Republic of China from atop the Tian'an Men on October 1. A vast flood of refugees from the countryside takes over the courtyard houses commandeered from their

owners, and those houses which once held a single family now house a dozen. Temples are turned into army barracks, storehouses, and light industrial units.

■ 1958–59 In a series of major projects to mark 10 years of Communist rule, the old ministries lining what will be Tian'an Men Square and its surrounding walls are all flattened for the

construction of the Great Hall of the People and the vast museums opposite. These and Beijing Railway Station are built with Soviet help, which shows in the design. The city walls, which have survived for 400 years, are pulled down by "volunteers," to be replaced with a metro line and a ring road for an almost completely carless society. The stone from the walls

The documentary *Gate of Heavenly Peace* (1996) is obligatory viewing for anyone hoping to understand what transpired in 1989. If all you recall is a statue of liberty and talk of democracy, you're in for a shock.

MUSIC

The vapid, factory-produced syrup of **Mandopop** (think Celine Dion by way of Britney Spears sung in Mandarin) blares out of barber shops and retail stores throughout Beijing, as elsewhere in China. But like Washington, D.C., and London, China's capital is ultimately a rock 'n' roll town.

Godfather of Chinese rock **Cui Jian,** somewhat of a joke now as he clings to fading fame, got his start here in the early 1980s. A decade later, Chinese-American Kaiser Kuo, front man for the no-longer-existent headbanger outfit **Tang Dynasty (Tang Chao),** helped kick off a pretentious and fairly derivative heavy metal scene. But it wasn't until a shipment of Nirvana CDs found its way into local record shops in the late 1990s that Beijing finally developed a genuine musical voice.

Like the Velvet Underground did in the U.S. 20 years earlier, Nirvana's *Nevermind* inspired nearly every Chinese kid who heard it to pick up a guitar and start a band. Investigations into Kurt Cobain's roots led to punk, which made its first major appearance in Beijing in late 1997 at the Scream Club, a sweaty dive in the battered Wudaokou neighborhood. It was a natural response to Beijing's swaths of urban decay and post–Tian'an Men political disillusionment, and American pop culture magazines as big as *Details* quickly tapped the snarling, mohawked youth—most better at posing with their instruments than playing them—as easy symbols of China's new lost generation.

Beijing's punks were probably never as concerned with political protest as they were made out to be, and are even less so now as they enjoy the fruits of small-scale fame (punks are among the few Chinese men able to attract Western women). But they continue to draw relatively large foreign audiences, and a handful have actually begun to produce music worthy of all the attention. The vulgar but talented **Brain Failure (Nao Zhuo)** and ska-influenced **Reflector (Fanguang Jing)**—both born at the now-defunct Scream Club—have each recorded listenable songs and evolved beyond just spitting beer in their live shows (though you can still expect the occasional shower). Also on Scream Records, the all-girl pop punk group **Hang on the Box (Gua Zai Hezi Shang)** sings in charmingly accented English.

---

goes to line a system of tunnels into which the entire city population can supposedly be evacuated in case of attack.

■ **1966–76** The destruction of old things reaches its peak as bands of Red Guards, fanatically loyal to Mao, roam around fighting each other, ransacking ancient buildings, burning books, and smashing art. Even the tree from which the last Ming emperor

supposedly hanged himself is cut down. Intellectuals are bullied, imprisoned, tortured, and murdered, as is anyone with a history of links to foreigners. Scores are settled, and millions die. The education system largely comes to a halt. Many antiquities impounded from their owners are sold to foreign dealers by weight to provide funds for the government, which

later decries foreign theft of Chinese antiquities.

■ **1976** The death of Zhou Enlai, who is credited with mitigating some of the worst excesses of the Cultural Revolution, leads to over 100,000 demonstrating against the government in Tian'an Men Square. The demonstrations are labeled counterrevolutionary, and

continues

Chinese musicians wanting to produce significant popular music suffer from the same dreadful self-consciousness of working in a foreign idiom as do artists in other imported media. Some try desperately (and without much success) to create "rock with Chinese characteristics," while others opt to simply lay Chinese lyrics over melodies lifted, sometimes note for note, from Western CDs. Even the most creative of efforts will sound suspiciously derivative, and those that don't usually appeal only to Mandarin-speaking foreigners who delight primarily in their ability to understand the lyrics. The other major barrier to the local music industry is piracy; particularly the ready availability of music downloads. Most band members still have day jobs.

For information on when and where bands might be playing, check music listings in either *that's Beijing* or *City Weekend,* both available free in hotels, bars, and cafes where foreigners gather. Currently, Yu Gong Yi Shan (p. ###) is the best live music venue in Beijing, hands down.

4 The Beijing Menu

One of the best things about any visit to China is the food, at least for the independent traveler. Tour groups are often treated to a relentless series of cheap, bland dishes designed to cause no complaints and to keep the costs down for the Chinese operator, so do everything you can to escape and order some of the specialties we've described for you in chapter 6. Here they are again, in alphabetical order and with characters you can show to the waitress.

Widely available dishes and snacks are grouped in the first list; you can order most of them in any mainstream or *jiachang cai* ("home-style") restaurant. Some dishes recommended in this guidebook's reviews of individual restaurants are commonly available enough to be on this first list. Note that some of the specialty dishes in the second list are only available in the restaurants reviewed, or in restaurants offering a particular region's cuisine.

Dishes often arrive in haphazard order, but menus generally open with *liang cai* (cold dishes). Except in top-class Sino-foreign joint-venture restaurants, you are strongly advised to avoid these for hygiene reasons. The restaurant's specialties also come early in the menu: They have significantly higher prices and if you dither, the waitress will recommend them, saying, "I hear this one's good." Waitresses always recommend ¥180 ($24/£ 12)

hundreds are arrested. The death of Mao Zedong, himself thought to be responsible for an estimated 38 million deaths, effectively brings the Cultural Revolution to an end. Blame for the Cultural Revolution is put on the "Gang of Four"—Mao's wife and three other hard-line officials, who are arrested. The 450-year-old Da Ming Men in the center of Tian'an Men Square is pulled down to make way for Mao's mausoleum. Leaders put their backing behind Deng Xiaoping, who returns from disgrace to take power and launch a program of openness and economic reform. His own toleration for public criticism also turns out to be zero, however.

- 1989 The death of the moderate but disgraced official Hu Yaobang causes public displays of mourning in Tian'an Men Square, which turn into a mass occupation of the square protesting government corruption. Its hands initially tied by the presence on a state visit of the Soviet Union's Mikhail Gorbachev, the Party sends in the tanks live on TV on the night of June 3. Estimates of the number of deaths vary wildly, but

dishes, never ¥8 ($1.05/55p) ones. Some of these dishes may occasionally be made from creatures you would regard as pets or zoo creatures (or best in the wild), and parts of them you may consider inedible or odd, like swallow saliva (the main ingredient of bird's nest soup, a rather bland Cantonese delicacy).

Main dishes come next; various meats and fish are followed by vegetables and *doufu* (tofu). Drinks come at the end. You'll rarely find desserts outside of restaurants that largely cater to foreigners. A few watermelon slices may appear, but it's best to forgo them.

Soup is usually eaten last. Rice also usually arrives at the end; if you want it with your meal, you must ask (point to the characters for rice, below, when the first dish arrives).

There is no tipping. Tea, chopsticks, and napkins should be free (although if a wrapped packet of tissues arrives you may pay a small fee); service charges do not exist outside of major hotels; and there are no cover charges or taxes. If asked what tea you would like, know that you are going to receive something above average and will be charged for it. Exercise caution—some varieties cost more than the meal!

Most Chinese food is not designed to be eaten solo, but if you do find yourself on your own, ask for small portions *(xiao pan, 小盘)*, usually about 70% of the size of a full dish and about 70% of the price. This allows you to sample the menu properly without too much waste.

WIDELY AVAILABLE DISHES & SNACKS

PINYIN	ENGLISH	CHINESE
bābǎo zhōu	rice porridge with nuts and berries	八宝粥
bǎnlì shāo chìzhōng	soy chicken wings with chestnuts	板栗烧翅中
bāozi	stuffed steamed buns	包子
bīngqílín	ice cream	冰淇淋
chǎo fàn	fried rice	炒饭
chǎo miàn	fried noodles	炒面
cōng bào niúròu	quick-fried beef and onions	葱爆牛肉
dāndān miàn	noodles in spicy broth	担担面
diǎnxin	dim sum (snacks)	点心

the number is thought to run to several hundred unarmed students and their supporters.
- 2001 Beijing is awarded the 2008 Summer Olympics, and as a result the destruction and complete redevelopment of the city accelerates, to the immense personal profit of the developers. That some are related to the top members of the administration is common knowledge.
- 2003 Severe Acute Respiratory Syndrome strikes Beijing, with more than 1,000 infected and around 100 dead. Millions of Beijingers stay indoors, while thousands of others are involuntarily quarantined in hospitals and dorm rooms. The epidemic subsides in July, and the government and the tourism industry complain of overblown media attention to the disease.
- 2007 Beijing gets ready to host the Olympic Games, with the opening ceremony to be orchestrated by Zhang Yimou. Rumors are that Steven Spielberg, who signed on earlier, plans to back out, swayed by protests over China's role in the conflict in Darfur, Sudan.

PINYIN	ENGLISH	CHINESE
dì sān xiān	braised eggplant with potatoes and spicy green peppers	地三鲜
gānbiān sìjìdòu	sautéed string beans	干煸四季豆
gōngbào jīdīng	spicy diced chicken with cashews	1辣汁腰果鸡丁
guōtiē	fried dumplings/potstickers	煎饺/锅贴
hóngshāo fǔzhú	braised tofu	红烧豆腐
hóngshāo huángyú	braised yellow croaker	红烧黄鱼
huíguō ròu	twice-cooked pork	回锅肉
huǒguō	hot pot	火锅
jiānbing	large crepe folded around fried dough with plum and hot sauces	煎饼
jiǎozi	dumplings/Chinese ravioli	饺子
jīngjiàng ròu sī	shredded pork in soya sauce	京酱肉丝
mápó dòufu	spicy tofu with chopped meat	麻婆豆腐
miàntiáo	noodles	面条
mǐfàn	rice	米饭
mù xū ròu	sliced pork with fungus (mu shu pork)	木须肉
niúròu miàn	beef noodles	牛肉面
ròu chuàn	kebabs/kabobs	肉串
sānxiān	"three flavors" (usually prawn, mushroom, pork)	三鲜
shuǐjiǎo	boiled dumplings	水饺
suānlà báicài	hot and sour cabbage	酸辣白菜
suānlà tāng	hot and sour soup	酸辣汤
sù miàn	vegetarian noodles	素面
sù shíjǐn	mixed vegetables	素什锦
tángcù lǐji	sweet-and-sour pork tenderloin	糖醋里脊
tǔdòu dùn niúròu	stewed beef and potato	土豆炖牛肉
xiàn bǐng	pork- or vegetable-stuffed fried pancake	(肉或素)馅饼
xīhóngshì chǎo jīdàn	tomatoes with eggs	西红柿炒鸡蛋
yángròu chuàn	barbecued lamb skewers with ground cumin and chili powder	羊肉串
yóutiáo	fried salty donut	油条
yúxiāng qiézi	eggplant in garlic sauce	鱼香茄子
yúxiāng ròu sī	shredded pork in garlic sauce	鱼香肉丝
zhēngjiǎo	steamed dumplings	蒸饺
zhōu	rice porridge	粥

SPECIALTY DISHES (FROM BĚIJĪNG & ELSEWHERE) RECOMMENDED IN RESTAURANT REVIEWS

PINYIN	ENGLISH	CHINESE
bābǎo làjiàng	gingko, nuts, and pork in sweet chili sauce	八宝辣酱
bōluó fàn	pineapple rice	菠萝饭
cháshùgū bāo lǎojī	chicken with tea-mushroom soup	茶树菇煲老鸡
chénpí lǎoyā shānzhēn bāo	duck, dried tangerine peel, and mushroom potage	陈皮老鸭山珍煲
cuìpí qiézi	sweet and sour battered eggplant	脆皮茄子
cùngū shāo	deep-fried pork with medicinal herbs	寸骨烧
Dǎizú xiāngmáocǎo kǎo yú	Dǎi grilled lemon grass fish	傣族香茅草烤鱼
dà lāpí	cold noodles in sesame and vinegar sauce	大拉皮
dà pán jī	diced chicken and noodles in tomato sauce	大盘鸡
Dōngběi fēngwèi dàpái	northeast-style braised ribs	东北风味大排
Dōngpō ròu	braised fatty pork in small clay pot	东坡肉
é'gān juǎn	goose liver rolls with hoisin sauce	鹅肝卷
gǒubùlǐ bāozi	pork-stuffed bread dumplings	狗不理包子
guōbā ròu piān	pork with crispy fried rice	锅巴肉片
guòqiáo mǐxiàn	crossing-the-bridge rice noodles	过桥米线
huángdì sǔn shāo wánzi	Imperial bamboo shoots and vegetarian meatballs	皇帝笋烧素丸子
huángqiáo ròu sūbǐng	shredded-pork rolls	黄桥肉酥饼
huíxiāng dòu	aniseed-flavored beans	茴香豆
jiāoliū wánzi	crisp-fried pork balls	焦熘丸子
jīngjiàng ròusī	shredded pork with green onion rolled in tofu skin	腐皮肉丝卷
jīnpái tiáoliào	"gold label" sesame sauce (for Mongolian hot pot)	金牌调料
jīròu sèlā	deep-fried chicken pieces with herb dipping sauce	炸鸡肉色拉
jiǔxiāng yúgān	dried fish in wine sauce	酒香鱼干
juébā chǎo làròu	bacon stir-fried with brake leaves	蕨粑炒腊肉
kǎo yángròu	roast mutton	烤羊肉
làbā cù	garlic-infused vinegar	腊八醋
láncài sìjìdòu láncài sìj	green beans stir-fried with salty vegetables	榄菜四季豆
lǎogānmā shāojī	spicy diced chicken with bamboo and ginger	老干妈烧鸡

PINYIN	ENGLISH	CHINESE
làròu dòuyá juǎnbǐng	spicy bacon and bean sprouts in pancakes	腊肉豆芽卷饼
làwèi huájī bāozǎi fàn	chicken and sweet sausage on rice in clay pot	腊味滑鸡煲仔饭
liángbàn zǐ lúsǔn	purple asparagus salad	凉拌紫芦笋
luóbo sī sūbǐng	shredded-daikon shortcake	萝卜丝酥饼
málà lóngxiā	spicy crayfish	麻辣小龙虾
málà tiánluó	field snails stewed in chili and Sìchuān pepper	麻辣田螺
mǎtí niúliǔ	stir-fried beef with broccoli, water chestnuts, and tofu rolls	马蹄牛柳
mìzhì zhǐbāo lúyú	paper-wrapped perch and onions on sizzling iron plate	秘制纸包鲈鱼
náng bāo ròu	lamb and vegetable stew served on flat wheat bread	馕包羊肉
nánrǔ kòuròu	braised pork in red fermented bean curd gravy	南乳扣肉
niúròu wán shuǐjiǎo	beef ball dumplings	牛肉丸水饺
nóngjiā shāo jiān jī	farmhouse spicy sautéed chicken fillet	农家烧煎鸡
nóngjiā xiǎochǎo	farmhouse soybeans, green onion, Chinese chives, and green pepper in a clay pot	农家素小炒
qiáo miàn māo ěrduo	"cat's ear shaped" buckwheat pasta with chopped meat	荞面猫耳朵
ròudīng báicài xiànbǐng	meat cabbage pie	肉丁白菜馅饼
rúyì hǎitái juǎn	"as one wishes" seaweed rolls	如意海苔卷
sān bēi jī	chicken reduced in rice wine, sesame oil, and soy sauce	三杯鸡
sānxiān làohé	seafood and garlic chive buns	三鲜烙合
sè shāo niúròu	foil-wrapped beef marinated in mountain herbs	色烧牛肉
shāchá niúròu	beef sautéed with Taiwanese BBQ sauce	沙茶牛肉
shānyao gēng	yam broth with mushrooms	山药羹
shānyao húlu	red bean rolls with mountain herbs	山药豆沙卷
shēngjiān bāozi	pork-stuffed fried bread dumplings	生煎包子
shǒuzhuā fàn	Uighur-style rice with carrot and mutton	手抓羊肉饭
shǒuzhuā yáng pái	lamb chops roasted with cumin and chili	手抓羊排
shuǐzhǔ yú	boiled fish in spicy broth with numbing peppercorns	水煮鱼

PINYIN	ENGLISH	CHINESE
suànxiāng jīchì	garlic paper-wrapped chicken wings	蒜香鸡翅
sǔngān lǎoyā bāo	stewed duck with dried bamboo shoots	笋干老鸭煲
Táiwān dòfu bāo	Taiwanese tofu and vegetables clay pot	台湾豆腐煲
tiānfú shāokǎo yángtuǐ	roasted leg of mutton with cumin and chili powder	天福烧烤羊腿
tiēbǐngzi	corn pancakes cooked on a griddle	贴玉米饼子
tǔdòu qiú	deep-fried potato balls with chili sauce	土豆球
tǔtāng shícài	clear soup with seasonal leafy greens	土汤时菜
xiāngcǎo cuìlà yú	whole fried fish with hot peppers and lemon grass	香草脆辣鱼
xiǎolóng bāozi	pork-stuffed steamed bread dumplings	小笼包子
Xībèi dà bàncài	Xībèi salad	西贝大拌菜
xièfěn dòufu	crab meat tofu	蟹粉豆腐
xièsānxiān shuǐjiǎo	boiled crab dumplings with shrimp and mushrooms	蟹三鲜水饺
yángròu chuàn	spicy mutton skewers with cumin	羊肉串
yángyóu má dòufu	mashed soybeans with lamb oil	羊油麻豆腐
yán jú xiā	shrimp skewers in rock salt	盐局虾
yè niúròu juǎn	grilled la lop leaf beef	叶牛肉卷
yì bǎ zhuā	fried wheat cakes	一把抓
yóumiàn wōwo	steamed oatmeal noodles	莜面窝窝
yóutiáo niúròu	sliced beef with fried dough in savory sauce	油条牛肉
zhá guàncháng	taro chips with garlic sauce	炸灌肠
zhāngchá yā	crispy smoked duck with plum sauce	樟茶鸭
zhá qiéhé	pork-stuffed deep-fried eggplant	炸茄合
zhēnzhū nǎichá	pearl milk tea	珍珠奶茶
zhǐbāo lúyú	paper-wrapped perch in sweet sauce	纸包鲈鱼
zhījīcǎo kǎo niúpái	lotus leaf–wrapped roast beef with mountain herbs	枳机草烤牛排
zhūròu báicài bāozi	steamed bun stuffed with pork and cabbage	猪肉白菜包子
zhúsūn qìguō jī	mushroom and mountain herbs chicken soup	竹荪气锅鸡
zhútǒng jī	chicken soup in bamboo vessel	竹筒鸡
zhútǒng páigǔ	spicy stewed pork in bamboo vessel with mint	竹筒排骨
zhútǒng zhūròu	steamed pork in bamboo vessel with coriander	竹筒猪肉
zuì jī	chicken marinated in rice wine	醉鸡
zuì xiā	live shrimp in wine	醉虾

Appendix B:
The Chinese Language

Chinese is not as difficult a language to learn as it may first appear to be—at least not once you've decided what kind of Chinese to learn. There are six major languages called Chinese. Speakers of each are unintelligible to each other, and there are, in addition, a host of dialects. The Chinese you are likely to hear spoken in your local Chinatown or Chinese restaurant, or used by your friends of Chinese descent when they speak to their parents, is more than likely to be Cantonese, which is the version of Chinese used in Hong Kong and in much of southern China. But the official national language of China is **Mandarin** (**Pǔtōnghuà**—"common speech"), sometimes called Modern Standard Chinese, and viewed in mainland China as the language of administration, of the classics, and of the educated. While throughout much of mainland China people speak their own local flavor of Chinese for everyday communication, they've all been educated in Mandarin, which, in general terms, is the language of Běijīng and the north. Mandarin is less well known in Hong Kong and Macau, but it is also spoken in Táiwān and Singapore, and among growing communities of recent immigrants to North America and Europe.

Chinese grammar is considerably more straightforward than those of English or other European languages, even Spanish or Italian. There are no genders, so there is no need to remember long lists of endings for adjectives and to make them agree, with variations according to case. There are no equivalents for the definite and indefinite articles ("the," "a," "an"), so there is no need to make those agree either. Singular and plural nouns are the same. Best of all, verbs cannot be declined. The verb "to be" is *shì*. The same sound also covers "am," "are," "is," "was," "will be," and so on, since there are also no tenses. Instead of past, present, and future, Chinese is more concerned with whether an action is continuing or has been completed, and with the order in which events take place. To make matters of time clear, Chinese depends on simple expressions such as "yesterday," "before," "originally," "next year," and the like. "Tomorrow I go New York," is clear enough, as is "Yesterday I go New York." It's a little more complicated than these brief notes can suggest, but not much.

There are a few sounds in Mandarin that are not used in English (see the rough pronunciation guide below), but the main difficulty for foreigners lies in tones. Most sounds in Mandarin begin with a consonant and end in a vowel (or -n, or -ng), which leaves the language with very few distinct noises compared to English. Originally, one sound equaled one idea and one word. Even now, each of these monosyllables is represented by a single character, but often words have been made by putting two characters together, sometimes both with the same meaning, thus reinforcing one another. The solution to this phonetic poverty is to multiply the available sounds by making them tonal—speaking them at different pitches, thereby giving them different meanings. *Mā* spoken on a high level tone (first tone) offers a set of possible meanings different from those of *má* spoken with a rising tone (second tone), *mǎ* with a dipping then rising tone (third tone), or *mà* with an abruptly falling tone (fourth tone).

There's also a different meaning for the neutral, toneless *ma*.

In the average sentence, context is your friend (there are not many occasions in which the third-tone *mǎ* or "horse" might be mistaken for the fourth-tone *mà* or "grasshopper," for instance), but without tone, there is essentially no meaning. The novice best sing his or her Mandarin very clearly, as Chinese children do—a chanted sing-song can be heard emerging from the windows of primary schools across China. With experience, the student learns to give particular emphasis to the tones on words essential to a sentence's meaning, and to treat the others more lightly. Sadly, most books using modern Romanized Chinese, called *Hànyǔ pīnyīn* ("Hàn language spell-the-sounds"), do not mark the tones, nor do these appear on **pīnyīn** signs in China. But in this book, the author has added tones to every Mandarin expression, so you can have a go at saying them for yourself. Where tones do not appear, that's usually because the name of a person or place is already familiar to many readers in an older form of Romanized Chinese such as Wade-Giles or Post Office (in which Běijīng was written misleadingly as Peking); or because it is better known in Cantonese: Sun Yat-sen, or Canton, for instance.

Cantonese has *eight* tones plus the neutral, but its grammatical structure is largely the same, as is that of all versions of Chinese. Even Chinese people who can barely understand each other's speech can at least write to each other, since written forms are similar. Mainland China, with the aim of increasing literacy (or perhaps of distancing the supposedly now thoroughly modern and socialist population from its Confucian heritage), instituted a ham-fisted simplification program in the 1950s, which reduced some characters originally taking 14 strokes of the brush, for instance, to as few as three strokes. Hong Kong, separated from the mainland and under British control until 1997, went its own way, kept the original full-form characters, and invented lots of new ones, too. Nevertheless, many characters remain the same, and some of the simplified forms are merely familiar shorthands for the full-form ones. But however many different meanings for each tone of *ma* there may be, for each meaning there's a different character. This makes the written form a far more successful communication medium than the spoken one, which leads to misunderstandings even between native speakers, who can often be seen sketching characters on their palms during conversation to confirm which one is meant.

The thought of learning 3,000 to 5,000 individual characters (at least 2,500 are needed to read a newspaper) also daunts many beginners. But look carefully at the ones below, and you'll notice many common elements. In fact, a rather limited number of smaller shapes are combined in different ways, much as we combine letters to make words. Admittedly, the characters only offer general hints as to their pronunciation, and that's often misleading—the system is not a phonetic one, so each new Mandarin word has to be learned as both a sound and a shape (or a group of them). But soon it's the similarities among the characters, not their differences, which begin to bother the student. English, a far more subtle language with a far larger vocabulary, and with so many pointless inconsistencies and exceptions to what are laughingly called its rules, is much more of a struggle for the Chinese than Mandarin should be for us.

But no knowledge of the language is needed to get around China, and it's almost of assistance that Chinese take it for granted that outlandish foreigners (that's you and me unless of Chinese descent) can speak not a word (poor things) and must use whatever other limited means we have to communicate—this book and a phrase book, for instance. For help with navigation to sights, simply point to the characters in this book's map keys. When leaving your hotel, take one of its cards with you, and show it to the taxi driver when you want to return. In section 2, below, is a limited list of useful words and phrases that is best supplemented with a proper phrase book. If you have a Mandarin-speaking friend from the north (Cantonese speakers who know Mandarin as a second language tend to have fairly heavy accents), ask him or her to pronounce the greetings and words of thanks from the list below, so you can repeat after him and practice. While you are as likely to be laughed *at* as *with* in China, such efforts are always appreciated.

1 A Guide to Pīnyīn Pronunciation

Letters in pīnyīn mostly have the values any English speaker would expect, with the following exceptions:

c *ts* as in bi*ts*

q *ch* as in *ch*in, but much harder and more forward, made with tongue and teeth

r has no true equivalent in English, but the *r* of *r*eed is close, although the tip of the tongue should be near the top of the mouth, and the teeth together

x also has no true equivalent, but is nearest to the *sh* of *sh*eep, although the tongue should be parallel to the roof of the mouth and the teeth together

zh is a soft j, like the *dge* in ju*dge*

The vowels are pronounced roughly as follows:

a as in f*a*ther

e as in *e*rr (*leng* is pronounced as English "lung")

i is pronounced *ee* after most consonants, but after c, ch, r, s, sh, z, and zh is a buzz at the front of the mouth behind closed teeth

o as in s*o*ng

u as in t*oo*

ü is the purer, lips-pursed u of French t*u* and German *ü*. Confusingly, **u** after j, x, q, and y is always ü, but in these cases the accent over "ü" does not appear.

ai sounds like *eye*

ao as in *ou*ch

ei as in h*ay*

ia as in *ya*k

ian sounds like *yen*

iang sounds like *yang*

iu sounds like *you*

ou as in t*oe*

ua as in g*ua*va

ui sounds like *way*

uo sounds like *or,* but is more abrupt

Note that when two or more third-tone "ˇ" sounds follow one another, they should all, except the last, be pronounced as second-tone "ˊ."

2 Mandarin Bare Essentials

ENGLISH	PĪNYĪN	CHINESE
Greetings & Introductions		
Hello	Nǐ hǎo	你好
How are you?	Nǐ hǎo ma?	你好吗?
Fine. And you?	Wǒ hěn hǎo. Nǐ ne?	我很好。你呢?
I'm not too well/Things aren't going well	Bù hǎo	不好
What is your name? (very polite)	Nín guì xìng?	您贵姓?
My (family) name is	Wǒ xìng	我姓……
I'm known as (family, then given name)	Wǒ jiào	我叫……
I'm from [America]	Wǒ shì cóng [Měiguó] lái de	我是从美国来的
I'm [American]	Wǒ shì [Měiguó] rén	我是美国人
[Australian]	[Àodàlìyà]	澳大利亚人
[British]	[Yīngguó]	英国人
[Canadian]	[Jiānádà]	加拿大人
[Irish]	[Àiěrlán]	爱尔兰人
[a New Zealander]	[Xīnxīlán]	新西兰人
Excuse me/I'm sorry	Duìbùqǐ	对不起
I don't understand	Wǒ tīng bù dǒng	我听不懂
Thank you	Xièxie nǐ	谢谢你
Correct (yes)	Duì	对
Not correct	Bú duì	不对
No, I don't want	Wǒ bú yào	我不要
Not acceptable	Bù xíng	不行
Basic Questions & Problems		
Excuse me/I'd like to ask	Qǐng wènyíxià	请问一下
Where is . . . ?	. . . zài nǎr?	……在哪儿?
How much is . . . ?	. . . duōshǎo qián?	……多少钱?
. . . this one?	Zhèi/Zhè ge . . .	这个……
. . . that one?	Nèi/Nà ge . . .	那个……
Do you have . . . ?	Nǐ yǒu méi yǒu . . .	你有没有……?
What time does/is . . . ?	. . . jǐ diǎn?	……几点?
What time is it now?	Xiànzài jǐ diǎn?	现在几点?
When is . . . ?	. . . shénme shíhou?	……什么时候?
Why?	Wèishénme?	为什么?
Who?	Shéi?	谁?
Is that okay?	Xíng bù xíng?	行不行?
I'm feeling ill	Wǒ shēng bìng le	我生病了

ENGLISH	PĪNYĪN	CHINESE
Travel		
luxury (bus, hotel rooms)	háohuá	豪华
high speed (buses, expressways)	gāosù	高速
air-conditioned	kōngtiáo	空调
When's the last bus?	mòbānchē jídiǎn kāi?	末班车几点开?

NUMBERS

Note that more complicated forms of numbers are often used on official documents and receipts to prevent fraud—see how easily one can be changed to two, three, or even ten. Familiar Arabic numerals appear on bank notes, most signs, taxi meters, and other places. Be particularly careful with *four* and *ten,* which sound very alike in many regions—hold up fingers to make sure. Note, too, that *yī,* meaning "one," tends to change its tone all the time depending on what it precedes. Don't worry about this— once you've started talking about money, almost any kind of squeak for "one" will do. Finally note that "two" alters when being used with expressions of quantity.

zero	líng	零
one	yī	一
two	èr	二
two (of them)	liǎng ge	两个
three	sān	三
four	sì	四
five	wǔ	五
six	liù	六
seven	qī	七
eight	bā	八
nine	jiǔ	九
10	shí	十
11	shí yī	十一
12	shí èr	十二
21	èr shí yī	二十一
22	èr shí èr	二十二
51	wǔ shí yī	五十一
100	yì bǎi	一百
101	yì bǎi líng yī	一百零一
110	yì bǎi yī (shí)	一百一（十）
111	yì bǎi yī shí yī	一百一十一
1,000	yì qiān	一千
1,500	yì qiān wǔ (bǎi)	一千五百
5,678	wǔ qiān liù bǎi qī shí bāi	五千六百七十八
10,000	yí wàn	一万

MONEY

The word *yuán* (¥) is rarely spoken, nor is *jiǎo,* the written form for one-tenth of a *yuán,* equivalent to 10 *fēn* (there are 100 *fēn* in a *yuán*). Instead, the Chinese speak of "pieces of money," *kuài qián,* usually abbreviated just to *kuài,* and they speak of *máo* for one-tenth of a *kuài. Fēn* have been overtaken by inflation and are almost useless.

Often all zeros after the last whole number are simply omitted, along with *kuài qián*, which is taken as read, especially in direct reply to the question *duōshǎo qián*—"How much?"

¥1	yí kuài qián	一块钱
¥2	liǎng kuài qián	两块钱
¥.30	sān máo qián	三毛钱
¥5.05	wǔ kuài líng wǔ fēn	五块零五分
¥5.50	wǔ kuài wǔ	五块五
¥550	wǔ bǎi wǔ shí kuài	五百五十块
¥5,500	wǔ qiān wǔ bǎi kuài	五千五百块
small change	língqián	零钱

BANKING & SHOPPING

I want to change money (foreign exchange)	Wǒ xiǎng huàn qián	我想换钱
credit card	xìnyòng kǎ	信用卡
traveler's check	lǚxíng zhīpiào	旅行支票
department store	bǎihuò shāngdiàn	百货商店
or	gòuwù zhōngxīn	购物中心
convenience store	xiǎomàibù	小卖部
market	shìchǎng	市场
May I have a look?	Wǒ kànyíxia, hǎo ma?	我看一下,好吗?
I want to buy	Wǒ xiǎng mǎi	我想买……
How many do you want?	Nǐ yào jǐ ge?	你要几个?
two of them	liǎng ge	两个
three of them	sān ge	三个
1 kilo (2¼ lb.)	yì gōngjīn	一公斤
half a kilo	yì jīn	一斤
or	bàn gōngjīn	半公斤
1 meter (3¼ ft.)	yì mǐ	一米
Too expensive!	Tài guì le!	太贵了!
Do you have change?	Yǒu língqián ma?	有零钱吗?

TIME

morning	shàngwǔ	上午
afternoon	xiàwǔ	下午
evening	wǎnshang	晚上
8:20am	shàngwǔ bā diǎn èr shí fēn	上午八点二十分
9:30am	shàngwǔ jiǔ diǎn bàn	上午九点半
noon	zhōngwǔ	中午
4:15pm	xiàwǔ sì diǎn yí kè	下午四点一刻
midnight	wǔ yè	午夜

1 hour	yí ge xiǎoshí	一个小时
8 hours	bā ge xiǎoshí	八个小时
today	jīntiān	今天
yesterday	zuótiān	昨天
tomorrow	míngtiān	明天
Monday	Xīngqī yī	星期一
Tuesday	Xīngqī èr	星期二
Wednesday	Xīngqī sān	星期三
Thursday	Xīngqī sì	星期四
Friday	Xīngqī wǔ	星期五
Saturday	Xīngqī liù	星期六
Sunday	Xīngqī tiān	星期天

TRANSPORT

I want to go to . . .	Wǒ xiǎng qù . . .	我想去……
plane	fēijī	飞机
train	huǒchē	火车
bus	gōnggòng qìchē	公共汽车
long-distance bus	chángtú qìchē	长途汽车
taxi	chūzū chē	出租车
airport	fēijīchǎng	飞机场
stop or station (bus or train)	zhàn	站
(plane/train/bus) ticket	piào	票

NAVIGATION

North	Běi	北
South	Nán	南
East	Dōng	东
West	Xī	西
Turn left	zuǒ guǎi	左拐
Turn right	yòu guǎi	右拐
Go straight on	yìzhí zǒu	一直走
Crossroads	shízì lùkǒu	十字路口
10 kilometers	shí gōnglǐ	十公里
I'm lost	Wǒ diū le	我迷路了

HOTEL

| How many days? | Zhù jǐ tiān? | 住几天? |
| standard room (twin or double with private bathroom) | biāozhǔn jiān | 标准间 |

passport	hùzhào	护照
deposit	yājīn	押金
I want to check out	Wǒ tuì fáng	我退房

RESTAURANT

How many people?	Jǐ wèi?	几位
waiter/waitress	fúwùyuán	服务员
menu	càidān	菜单
I'm vegetarian	Wǒ shì chī sù de	我是吃素的
Don't add MSG	qǐng bù fàng wèijīng	请不放味精
Do you have . . . ?	Yǒu méi yǒu . . . ?	有没有......?
Please bring a portion of . . .	Qǐng lái yí fènr . . .	请来一份儿......
I'm full	wǒ chībǎo le	我吃饱了
beer	píjiǔ	啤酒
coffee	kāfēi	咖啡
mineral water	kuàngquán shuǐ	矿泉水
tea	cháshuǐ	茶水
Bill, please	jiézhàng	结帐

SIGNS

Here's a list of common signs and notices to help you identify what you are looking for, from restaurants to condiments, and to help you choose the right door at the public toilets. These are the simplified characters in everyday use in China, but note that it's increasingly fashionable for larger businesses and for those with a long history to use more complicated traditional characters, so not all may match what's below. Also, very old restaurants and temples across China tend to write their signs from right to left.

hotel	bīnguǎn	宾馆
	dàjiǔdiàn	大酒店
	jiǔdiàn	酒店
	fàndiàn	饭店
restaurant	fànguǎn	饭馆
	jiǔdiàn	酒店
	jiǔjiā	酒家
vinegar	cù	醋
soya sauce	Jiàngyóu	酱油
bar	jiǔbā	酒吧
Internet bar	wǎngbā	网吧
cafe	kāfēiguǎn	咖啡馆
teahouse	cháguǎn	茶馆
department store	bǎihuò shāngdiàn	百货商店
shopping mall	gòuwù zhōngxīn	购物中心

market	shìchǎng	市场
bookstore	shūdiàn	书店
police (Public Security Bureau)	gōng'ānjú	公安局
Bank of China	Zhōngguó Yínháng	中国银行
public telephone	gōngyòng diànhuà	公用电话
public toilet	gōngyòng cèsuǒ	公用厕所
male	nán	男
female	nǚ	女
entrance	rùkǒu	入口
exit	chūkǒu	出口
bus stop/station	qìchē zhàn	汽车站
long-distance bus station	chángtú qìchē zhàn	长途汽车站
luxury	háohuá	豪华
using highway	gāosù	高速公路
railway station	huǒchē zhàn	火车站
hard seat	yìng zuò	硬座
soft seat	ruǎn zuò	软座
hard sleeper	yìng wò	硬卧
soft sleeper	ruǎn wò	软卧
direct (through) train	zhídá	直达
express train	tèkuài	特快
metro/subway station	dìtiě zhàn	地铁站
airport	fēijīchǎng	飞机场
dock/wharf	mǎtóu	码头
passenger terminal (bus, boat, and so on)	kèyùn zhàn	客运站
up/get on	shàng	上
down/get off	xià	下
ticket hall	shòupiào tīng	售票厅
ticket office	shòupiào chù	售票处
left-luggage office	xíngli jìcún chù	行李寄存处
temple	sì	寺
	miào	庙
museum	bówùguǎn	博物馆
memorial hall	jìniànguǎn	纪念馆
park	gōngyuán	公园
hospital	yīyuàn	医院
clinic	zhěnsuǒ	诊所
pharmacy	yàofáng/yàodiàn	药房/药店
travel agency	lǚxíngshè	旅行社

Index

See also Accommodations and Restaurant indexes, below.

CLOSED
due to
accidental demolition

WEGEN BISSIGEN
EICHHÖRNCHEN GESCHLOSSEN

CERRADO
CABRAS

Κλειστό
Μετεωρίτες

プールも

POOL CLOSED
ELECTRIC EELS

閉鎖中

Hotel
closed for
facelifting

FERMÉ POUR
RAISON
DE GRÈVE
DES BONNES

FECHADO!
POR CAUSA DE
ATAQUES DOS CROCODILOS

— I don't speak
sign language.

A hotel can close for all kinds of reasons.
Our Guarantee ensures that if your hotel's undergoing construction, we'll
let you know in advance. In fact, we cover your entire travel experience.
See www.travelocity.com/guarantee for details.

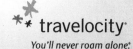

* travelocity
You'll never roam alone.

There's a parking lot where my ocean view should be.

 À la place de la vue sur l'océan, me voilà avec une vue sur un parking.

 Anstatt Meerblick habe ich Sicht auf einen Parkplatz.

 Al posto della vista sull'oceano c'è un parcheggio.

 No tengo vista al mar porque hay un parque de estacionamiento.

 Há um parque de estacionamento onde deveria estar a minha vista do oceano.

 Ett parkeringsområde har byggts på den plats där min utsikt över oceanen borde vara.

 Er ligt een parkeerterrein waar mijn zee-uitzicht zou moeten zijn.

 هنالك موقف للسيارات مكان ما وجب ان يكون المنظر الخلاب المطل على المحيط.

 眼前に広がる紺碧の海・・・じゃない。窓の外は駐車場！

 停车场的位置应该是我的海景所在。

— I'm fluent in pig latin.

Hotel mishaps aren't bound by geography.
Neither is our Guarantee. It covers your entire travel experience, including the price. So if you don't get the ocean view you booked, we'll work with our travel partners to make it right, right away. See www.travelocity.com/guarantee for details.

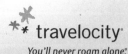
You'll never roam alone.